T0270521

Raiders, Rulers, and Traders

ALSO BY DAVID CHAFFETZ

A Journey Through Afghanistan: A Memorial

Three Asian Divas:
Women, Art and Culture in Shiraz, Delhi and Yangzhou

Raiders, Rulers, and Traders

THE HORSE AND THE RISE OF EMPIRES

David Chaffetz

W. W. NORTON & COMPANY
Independent Publishers Since 1923

For information about permission to reproduce selections from this book, write to
Permissions, W. W. Norton & Company, Inc., 500 Fifth Avenue, New York, NY 10110

For information about special discounts for bulk purchases, please contact
W. W. Norton Special Sales at specialsales@wwnorton.com or 800-233-4830

Manufacturing by Lakeside Book Company, Inc.
Book design by Chris Welch
Production manager: Louise Mattarelliano

ISBN 978-1-324-05146-6

W. W. Norton & Company, Inc.
500 Fifth Avenue, New York, N.Y. 10110
www.wwnorton.com

W. W. Norton & Company Ltd.
15 Carlisle Street, London W1D 3BS

1 2 3 4 5 6 7 8 9 0

To Marguerite Tabor Yates

وَتَقتُلُنا المَنونُ بِلا قِتالِ   نُعِدُّ المَشرَفِيَّةَ وَالعَوالي

وَما يُنجينَ مِن خَبَبِ اللَيالي   وَنَربِطُ السَوابِقَ مُقرَباتٍ

وَلَكِن لا سَبيلَ إلى الوِصالِ   وَمَن لَم يَعشَقِ الدُنيا قَديماً

نَصيبُكَ في مَنامِكَ مِن خَيالِ   نَصيبُكَ في حَياتِكَ مِن حَبيبٍ

We ready our swords and our lances;   death slays us without any battle.

We picket swift coursers besides us,   no rescue from night's steady ambling.

And who has not loved life of old;   there's no path to union for lovers.

Your portion in life of the loved one?   Your portion in dreams of a phantom

—Mutanabbi (915–965)

CONTENTS

PROLOGUE

A long journey brought us to the first Mongol encampment, after a week in a cramped compartment on the Trans-Siberian Express from Moscow to Ulan Bator, followed by hours of motoring over rugged, roadless terrain in a Toyota Land Cruiser that had known many owners. Now our guides paired us up with thick-necked, shaggy Mongolian ponies. After all that bumpy driving, I was so tired I could hardly stay in the saddle. As our guides hurried us away, I realized I could have nestled myself against the pony's mane and taken a nap, so steadily did it amble along with my 150 pounds on its back. But our guides urged us to pick up the pace because we still had a long way to go to the evening's encampment. They prodded their mounts forward with gentle flicks of their stout leather whips, but my pony, sensing my almost powerless purchase around its flanks, kept plodding along at its leisurely pace, forcing our impatient but good-humored guides to pause at intervals, waiting for me to catch up. I was the slowest of the group.

Shadows were stretching out long when we reached the encampment, a kind of Airbnb on the steppe, composed of several yurts—circular white felt tents. On the threshold of the yurts, I spilled gracelessly out of the saddle like an overturned feed sack, prompting one of the guides to remind me that I had assured him I had ridden before. "Before, yes," I pleaded, "but not every day like you." My adductor muscles were on fire. I had not ridden in years.

To celebrate our arrival at the yurts, the hosts offered us, or rather subjected us to, copious toasts of ayraq, fermented mare's milk. This is the essential drink of the steppe, known as kumis to the Russians and Central Asian Turks. It's the drink the raw, young heroes of Tolstoy's novellas discover when they embark on their steppe adventures. It attacks the palate with a fresh, grassy smell but leaves a disagreeable aftertaste of mare's sweat. Because of its low alcohol content, like small beer, we had to drink a lot of it in order to share the high spirits of our Mongol hosts, but we did, recollecting the epic drinking parties of the old Mongol princes as twilight fell. We accepted as graciously as we could a frequently refreshed cup, poured from a repurposed twenty-four-ounce plastic Coca-Cola bottle. We could no more drink all of the milky liquor on offer than we could take in all of the Milky Way above our heads. Like a single star in the night sky, our white yurt was just a speck in the vast and uniform expanse of the steppe. Empty of monuments and scarcely inhabited, the landscape seemed an unlikely locus for destiny, where history could have been made. But the steppe is precisely where humans and horses grew so fatefully entangled with one another.

No animal has had as profound an impact on human history as the horse. The journey begins in prehistory, with a small, shy animal that humans hunted for food. Hunters domesticated the horse in order to ensure a supply of meat and, later, mare's milk, which is more nutritious than cow's milk. This was a watershed event for both species, transforming the horse from an animal fleeing at a gallop from the mere smell of humans into the most valuable of their livestock. The horse's need to roam far and wide for pasture prompted the horse herders to spread out across the Eurasian steppe. Then herders learned to ride horses in order to keep up with their far-flung herds; this changed the course of history.

Riding made the horse a strategic asset, as consequential in its day as petroleum was to the twentieth century, while breeding turned the horse into the swift, powerful animal we know today. Horses and riders swarmed the steppe, forming the first steppe empires—the Huns, the Kushans, and the Celestial Turks, to name just a few. Though largely forgotten today, these empires once loomed large, dominating huge expanses of our planet. Although the steppe-based empires contained a fraction of the human population of the agricultural centers of civilization, including China,

India, and Iran, they controlled half of the world's horses. This gave horse-breeding peoples an outsized role in history. They brought the old, agricultural civilizations into contact with one another for the first time. Arts, religious beliefs, sports, and fashion spread from one end of the old world to the other in the saddlebags of the steppe horsemen. The horse itself became both a vehicle and a symbol: gods manifested themselves upon them, kings were buried with them, princesses rode them in polo matches, and poets praised them in verses that local schoolchildren still recite.

The horse is the key to understanding the history of the vast territory stretching from the Danube to the Yellow River. Huge herds of horses flourished on the cool, dry, and grassy steppe of today's Mongolia, Kazakhstan, Kyrgyzstan, Uzbekistan, Turkmenistan, Ukraine, and Hungary. The very names of these countries recall nations born out of steppe horse power.* The menace presented by steppe raiders forced settled, agriculture-based civilizations to breed their own horses, trade and fight for them, and adopt their own version of horse culture. Horses became almost as central to their economies, diplomacy, and military strategies as they were to the steppe peoples'. The steppe, with its vast pasturelands, always had an upper hand in breeding numerous horses. The settled peoples, less adept at breeding, and with less grazing land, had to expend huge efforts to maintain their own herds. They hired steppe horse breeders as grooms and mercenaries, sometimes establishing whole steppe nations on their frontiers. As steppe people thus grew more and more enmeshed with the settled peoples, the ground was laid for a steppe-based empire to take over the whole world.

This is what Genghis Khan and the Mongols achieved. Adroitly uniting far-flung steppe horsemen, Genghis Khan exploited the power of the horse more systematically than anyone had managed before. The Mongol Empire, which flourished from 1206 to 1368, represents the apogee of horse-breeding rule, with its decisive triumph over sedentary peoples.

Traditional histories explain that after the Mongol era, the increasing use of gunpowder on the battlefield made horses obsolete as a strategic asset.

---

* Ukraine, for example, means "the frontier"—i.e., the frontier with the steppe. Its horsemen were the Cossacks. The Kazakhs, Kyrghyz, Uzbeks, Turkmen, and Hungarians will appear in this text as powerful, horse-breeding nations.

Yet horses continued to power the last three great land empires of Eurasia. In the sixteenth century, a Mongol war band we know as the Mughals, mustering the biggest cavalry force India had ever seen, unified Asia's subcontinent for the first time in a millennium. By the end of the eighteenth century, Manchu China, allied with the Mongols' still-formidable horse power, had extended China's steppe frontier farther than any previous dynasty—defining the borders of today's People's Republic of China. By the end of the nineteenth century, Russia, which originated as a Mongol vassal state, had used the horse power of the Ukrainian Cossacks to conquer the largest part of Eurasia. Though Russia and China would put an end to the outsized role of the steppe horse breeders in this period, horses remained a decisive source of political power at the dawn of the twentieth century.

MUCH OF THE NARRATIVE of *Raiders, Rulers, and Traders* takes place on the Eurasian steppe, whose westernmost grassy plains give way to dense forest and rugged mountains in the Carpathians, Bohemia, and the Alps. Western Europe had a very different experience with horses. The horse-breeding peoples of the steppe never succeeded in conquering this part of the world, west of the old Iron Curtain frontier between the Soviet bloc and NATO, though they tried several times. Attila and the Huns, Bayan Khan of the Avars, the Bulghar Asparukh Khan, and Arpad Gyula of the Magyars all took advantage of the grass-rich middle Danube as a base for conquest, but their campaigns farther west ended in failure. Nevertheless, in eastern Europe, they left their traces. The steppe conquerors—Bulgarians, Serbs, Croats, and Magyars (Hungarians) durably imprinted their names across eastern Europe.* The Polish nobility claimed descent from ancient steppe invaders, whose tombs, full of treasure and sacrificial horses, are found all over that country.

Western Europe could simply not feed the number of horses the steppe peoples mustered. On the steppe, everyone rode, and all men fought. Women often rode to battle as well. Steppe armies of fifty thousand or one

---

* The Bulghars were Turkish-speaking horsemen who adopted the South Slavic language of their subjects, who, in turn, took the name Bulgarian. "Serb" and "Croat" were originally Scythian ethnonyms. Uniquely, the Hungarians preserved their name (Magyar) and their steppe language in the heart of Europe.

hundred thousand were therefore not infrequent, as they represented the whole nation in arms. In medieval western Europe, an army of ten thousand cavalry would have offered a rare and imposing sight. To be a horseman in western Europe meant to be a knight, a *chevalier*, a *ritter*, wearing golden spurs—at best 1 to 2 percent of the population. Many famous battles in western Europe were fought and won on foot, and in the mud. Decisive cavalry battles were few and far between. As a French general commented about the charge of the Light Brigade in 1854, during the Crimean War, *"C'est magnifique, mais ce n'est pas la guerre"*: "It's magnificent, but this isn't war."

In western Europe, the horse primarily provided transportation for the gentry and, with the invention of the horse collar, helped to plow the fields. Often the plow horse and the warhorse were one and the same, as Cervantes humorously reminds us with Don Quixote and his spindly steed, Rocinante. Paradoxically, the industrial revolution encouraged a huge and very late explosion of the equine population of western Europe, as horses came into high demand to haul canal barges, deliver beer kegs, and pull hackney cabs. There were 280,000 of these horses in London alone in the 1870s. Overall, the horse populations of England and Wales trebled in the nineteenth century, to three million. For most of western European history, however, the horse had a relatively minor role. Navigable rivers and seas enabled bulk transportation and trade. Europe's great empires arose to control trade by sea: Athens, Rome, Venice, Spain, Portugal, the Netherlands, France, and Britain.

Likewise, the horse plays a small if exciting role in the history of the New World. The First Nations came over from Asia with only a single domesticated species, the dog. When the Spanish appeared on the North American continent in the sixteenth century, they quickly settled the steppe-like prairies of Mexico and the southwest United States with horses and other livestock, which thrived in the wide-open spaces of ranchos and estancias. The Indigenous inhabitants of the southwest quickly saw the attraction of horseback riding and, indeed, became intrepid riders in just a few generations. Unlike Old World horse peoples, though, nations like the Apache, the Lakota, and the Comanche did not take up livestock herding. Hunting buffalo and raiding farming communities (both Indigenous and

European) became their sole occupations. Their way of life ended when the new settlers decimated the buffalo herds. Cowboys and the vaqueros carried on the ranchers' way of life. The horse flourished on America's Great Plains—an environmental twin to the Eurasian steppe—but it never played the decisive role, as in the Old World. It entered the scene too late, and was instrumental for only two centuries, versus the four millennia of horse-human entanglement in Eurasia.

It may seem a strange concept today, but the essential role of the horse was well understood over those millennia. The Chinese Han dynasty general Ma Yuan argued in the first century CE that "horses are the foundation of military power, the great resources of the state." Further, he warned the emperor, "If the power of the horse is allowed to falter, the state will totter to a fall." "The principal thing that kings, heroes, great warriors, and men of renown are in want of," wrote the seventeenth-century Mughal general Firuz Jang, "and on which the glory and majesty of the empire, and the conquest of kingdoms and regions depends, is the horse. Without him, no sovereignty could be erected, no countries subdued, nor no mighty monarch reign."

But horses were much more than the weapons of empire builders. The horse transformed more basic, everyday aspects of human life. Living on horseback entailed epic hunts, marathon steeplechases, and mounted contact sports that attracted enthusiastic spectators. What we now call the Silk Road should more accurately be called the Horse Road, for it was the horse, and not silk, that drew buyers and sellers together from all over Europe and Asia to form the first large-scale international trading routes. Equestrian beauty reverberated in poetry and the visual arts. The distinctive lifestyle centered on horse breeding appears surprisingly homogeneous and persistent throughout Eurasia. Horse culture came to be admired and imitated by all the settled civilizations around the steppe, as we see in the majestic terra-cotta horses of Tang China, the exquisite niello-silver horse tack in the Moscow Kremlin treasury, and the jewel-like equestrian portraits of Indian Mughal painters.

Only when they were displaced by cars and planes did horses cease to be a strategic asset. That spelled the end for the horse-breeding culture that had thrived for four millennia. The disappearance of the horse as a centerpiece of human civilization was so sudden and complete, in fact, that the animal's role in shaping civilization has been largely forgotten. *Raiders, Rulers, and Traders* recounts the horse's remarkable journey, and in so doing offers a new perspective about how the modern world came to be.

Indeed, given the horse's importance across so many centuries, it is surprising that, outside of specialized literature, our history books have little to say about where horses originated, how they were domesticated, how riding come about, and, more important, why these things matter. The horse should be at the center of our inquiries into ancient state formation, the relationships between settled and steppe civilizations, and the political dynamics of horse-breeding peoples.

In addition to studies from fields including anthropology, archaeology, genetics, and comparative linguistics, this book benefits from the explosion of research that occurred after the collapse of the Soviet Union. Russians, Ukrainians, Kazakhs, Mongols, and even Chinese were suddenly liberated from ideological constraints and empowered to rediscover steppe history. At the same time, great advances were made in technology, including more accurate carbon dating. Paleogenomic analysis—extracting DNA from skeletons—shows how domestication and selective breeding began to affect the horse's genetic diversity in Kazakhstan and Siberia during the Bronze Age, approximately five thousand to three thousand years ago. People learned to fight on horseback around 1000 BCE, as we now know from recent examinations of horse and human skeletons in Kazakhstan, which show old bone and ligament injuries on both the rider and the ridden. Excavations in Siberia and China show how widely that same group of horsemen originally spread, and how they connected East and West. Just as the persistent horse uncovers with its hooves the grass lying beneath a layer of snow, so, too, the role of the horse in history can be found just beneath a layer of obscurity—and we now only have to kick and scrape to find it.

That so much of historical importance took place in this flat, featureless, mostly empty setting seems improbable, and yet it did. The same thought must have occurred to every traveler who camped out here. Captain Bouillane de Lacoste, an engineer on the Trans-Siberian Railroad, recorded in his 1911 book, *In the Sacred Lands of the Ancient Turks and Mongols*, "I turned in for the night in our drafty yurt, trying vainly to stay warm at temperatures close to freezing. Sleepless, my thoughts seemed to wander around the steppe of bygone centuries, when it was so filled with horses that people likened them to the stars in the sky."

Centuries before Bouillane de Lacoste's Central Asian mission, Genghis Khan mustered more than a million horses to carry his warriors across the vast expanse of his conquests. These numbers were no chronicler's poetic license: they are confirmed by the historical record. But now, as I gazed out of my yurt, every bit as drafty as that of the French railroad engineer, the spectacle of the starry night indeed seemed the only means of imagining what such a cavalry must have resembled.

When we got up the next morning, the sun peeking early into the vents of the yurt, our hosts had already prepared breakfast, including more ayraq. A day when one was not slightly inebriated was rare among these Mongol herders. The story of human entanglement with horses begins with mare's milk. Without it there would be no horse culture—no riding, racing, hunting; no raising of prestigious breeds; no equine sports or arts. No horse-based conquest; no Genghis Khan, no Mughal or Tang Empires. Domestication of the horse took humans on a long journey in the company of an animal quite unlike any other member of our flocks. Yet all this might never have happened. Before humans developed a liking for mare's milk, before we domesticated horses, we nearly hunted them to extinction.

Raiders, Rulers, and Traders

Domesticated for Milk

The entanglement begins, 40,000–2000 BCE

The genus *Equus*, before entering human history with a bang, almost disappeared from prehistory with a whimper. The animal's original habitat was North America, where a 3.5-million-year-old fossil, discovered on an Idaho ranch in 1928, is still the oldest known evidence of its existence. Yet when Hernán Cortés's cavalry made landfall at Veracruz, Mexico, in 1519, North Americans had not seen a horse in twelve thousand years. Paleontologists hypothesize that humans, newly arrived over the land bridge between Asia and Alaska, slaughtered the horses that had roamed North America for millions of years. It is also possible that climate change transformed the original grass-rich environment of North America to a less horse-friendly forest. That would have been the end of the road for the horse, which we would have known, like the woolly mammoth and the saber-toothed tiger, only from parietal art and fossils. At about the same time as the Idaho fossil was living, however, *Equus* began to travel over the Asia-Alaskan land bridge in the opposite direction. Spreading out into the new pastures of the Old World, *Equus* then split into the three species that survive today: the horse, the zebra, and the ass, or donkey. The modern horse remained in the colder zones of Eurasia, while the zebra and the ass evolved farther south, in the hotter, drier climates of North Africa and peninsular Arabia.

Early Eurasian humans, like their Amerindian cousins, hunted horses for meat, along with other swift-running, four-legged prey like deer and antelopes. Evidence of horse hunts abounds in paintings and petroglyphs,

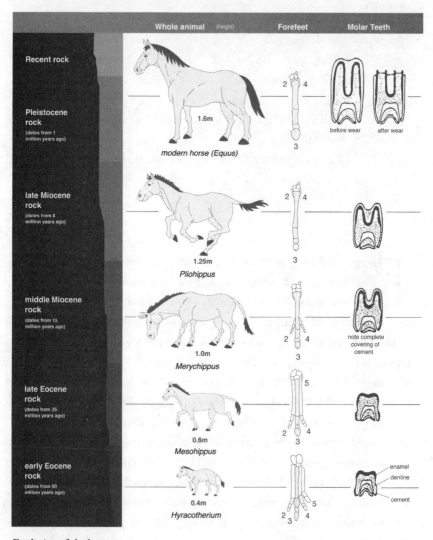

Evolution of the horse.

the most well-known site being in France's Lascaux Caves, dating back seventeen thousand years. In fact, horses are the most commonly depicted animals in ancient cave art, suggesting early human fascination with their beauty and speed. In sympathetic medicine, to obtain a desired attribute, you eat the plant or animal that exhibits that attribute. Rhino horn is a popular aliment in some cultures for people seeking the imagined potency of that beast. Ancient humans might well have prized horse meat because horses could run so fast, and hunters dreamed of keeping up with them.

Prehistoric hunters' enthusiasm for horse meat had a solid basis in nutrition, too. In the cold, harsh environment of the last Ice Age, horse meat proved to be high in protein, and rich in fatty acids essential for health and growth. Compared to other meat, it contains less saturated fat. Humans can digest horse meat more easily. Partly for this reason, today's Mongols favor horse meat to wean toddlers off mother's milk. The rarity of horse meat in European and American cuisine reflects an eighth-century ban by the Catholic Church, in an era in which the newly evangelized Germans consumed horse meat as part of their old pagan rituals. How else to explain the disappearance of this delicious and nutritious food from Western diets?

Whether for horse meat's magical properties or its high nutrition, prehistoric Europeans ate a lot of it. At the site of Solutré, not far from Lascaux, researchers identified, in 1866, the skeletons of ten thousand slaughtered horses. These belonged to the subspecies *Equus caballus gallicus*, a smaller and lighter-limbed creature than today's horses. Southern France teemed with *gallicus* horses, as those skeletons testify. During the Ice Age, Solutré enjoyed a climate similar to that of modern Mongolia, with cold and dry winters.

As happened in the New World, a combination of human hunting and the onset of a wetter, less favorable climate for horses resulted in the *Equus caballus gallicus*'s extinction at the end of the Ice Age, twelve thousand years ago. Western Europe turned into a territory where horses could not live in large numbers in a wild state. Southern Iberia and perhaps Anatolia provided smaller refuges for the shrinking *Equus* population, but paleogeneticists doubt that the modern horse emerged from either location. It looks like the ancestors of modern horses retreated to the drier, colder Eurasian steppe, as the permafrost line there moved north. That vast stretch of territory with extensive grassland provided a more secure habitat for the horse. There were very few humans, initially, and the herds multiplied in their new, natural sanctuary.

Early human penetration into the trackless steppe took place along the river valleys that flowed along its outer edges, like the Dnipro in modern-day

Ukraine and the Oxus, now called the Amu Darya, in Uzbekistan. When bands of wild horses came down to slake their thirst on the banks of these rivers, humans waiting in ambush sprang to the attack.

Scholars speculate that captured foals used as decoys to lure mares into the humans' ambushes may have been the precursor to domesticated horses. Later, humans hit on the idea of corralling captured wild horses to ensure a steady supply of meat, avoiding the hardships and unpredictability of the hunt. Starting in 1980, archaeologists excavating the steppe in Kazakhstan have found animal remains dating from approximately 3700 BCE that provide evidence of corrals and of systematic butchering that can be distinguished from hunting. There is significant room for interpretation of these weathered remains, and specialists heatedly debate which sites reflect hunting and which corralling. In any case, starting around 3000 BCE, horses and humans began to learn how to live together: horses overcoming their natural instincts of fear and flight, and humans acquiring the new technology of horse herding.

For horses, the transition from wild to domesticated life was initially superficial and easily reversible.[*] They couldn't be enclosed for long in corrals, which in these early days were essentially slaughtering pens. They had to be allowed to roam freely on the steppe, where they would mingle with still wild animals and, perhaps, again follow their natural inclination to run away from approaching humans. But humans learned to tether foals near their dwellings, so that the mares would return faithfully to suckle them. Meanwhile, the offspring of mares that grew up among humans began to look on their herders as part of the band to which they belonged, especially in the absence of wild adults. Foals learned fear of predators from their mares; wild mares taught their foals to flee humans, but mares raised among humans taught their foals to trust them. Mares and foals therefore became a familiar part of human settlements, even as stallions, invisible somewhere on the steppe, remained wild. Sometimes a wild stallion

---

[*] The *Washington Post* reported in October 2022 that a riding horse in Utah joined a herd of mustangs (feral horses), only to return to its owners after eight years in the wild; see María Luisa Paúl, "A Horse Ran Away with Wild Mustangs," October 10, 2022.

induced a mare raised in captivity to join his herd, and such a mare easily slipped back into the wild.

With the passage of time, the human-managed herds reached a critical mass of mature, fertile mares, and stallions overcame their intrinsic fear of humans and joined the captives. Even then, wild horses remained numerous, so stallions from outside the human settlements sometimes covered—that is, mated with—the domesticated mares, bringing new genetic lines into the herd. Steppe legends of wild stallions are echoes of this early phase of domestication when stallions had not yet accepted human society. In many stories, half-horse, half-dragon creatures emerged from the water, perhaps recalling the rivers where ancient hunters waited in ambush. Magical stallions were also said to have flown down from the sky, reflecting early humans' conviction that horses' speed equaled that of birds. All these legends underscored how little tamed the horse, and especially the stallion, appeared to humans. Until modern times, when the last wild horses were hunted to extinction, the permeability between the domesticated population and the wild population never ceased. Modern horses, all of which are descendants of these steppe horses, appear to have more than seventy-seven maternal DNA lineages, suggesting a long and porous process of recruitment of wild mares into the domesticated herds.

In 2008, in an effort to reverse the process initiated five millennia ago, conservationists reintroduced 325 Przewalski horses into their original habitat in Mongolia. The Przewalski, a wild or feral cousin of the modern horse, had become extinct outside of zoos by the turn of the twentieth century. Newly released Przewalski foals that had been raised in captivity were taught to cope with life on the steppe by previously rewilded mares. When the rewilded herd increased to two thousand members, foals quickly lost their willingness to socialize with humans. This conservationist campaign serves to demonstrate the uniquely superficial character of the taming of *Equus*. The domestication of the horse is only skin-deep, compared with that of other tamed animals. It is also much more recent, the dog having been domesticated as much as twenty thousand years earlier, and the sheep seven thousand years earlier, than the horse.

In the next step in the process of domestication, toward the end of the third millennium BCE, besides slaughtering horses for meat, humans began to exploit mares for their milk. This marked a major ratcheting up of human dependence on and entanglement with the horse. Millennia of prior experience with cows, ewes, and nanny goats had taught humans how to milk a tamed female quadruped. They simply dragged a nursing foal away from its feeding, held the dam steady with a nose rope, and squirted her already flowing milk into a leather bag positioned underneath her teats. The mare allowed herself to be milked only in the presence of her foal. In Mongolia today, you can observe foals with wide, envious eyes as they watch their dams being milked. Even after weaning the three- to four-month-old foals, mares continued to give milk for a year before foaling again. Mare's milk became an essential component of the herders' diet, as it remains today for the Mongols, Kazakhs, and Kyrgyz. These modern-day horse-herding people consume both fermented mare's milk and raw mare's milk, which tastes sweet and has a coconut-like perfume. These dairy products do not just supplement the herders' diet; they act as a staple food, like bread or rice for farming peoples, except that the horse herders drink mare's milk to satisfy both hunger and thirst. The milk of one mare can sustain three humans, and it has a higher protein content and more vitamins than cow's milk or, for that matter, mother's milk. It provides many of the same nutritional benefits of horse meat. It is not very fatty, and so cannot be as easily stored as cheese. That is why, in order to preserve the milk without refrigeration, the steppe horse herders ferment it into ayraq or kumis, which they so liberally share with their unwary guests from abroad. Another advantage of fermentation is to break down the milk's lactose, making it easier to digest for the lactose intolerant, including 95 percent of today's Mongols. This taste for mare's milk further deepened the dependence of humans on horses, and yet the process of our mutual entanglement had only just begun.

Horse herding resembled today's cattle ranching, where the herder's life was determined by the seasons and the horse's life cycle. Mares foaled in the spring, after which herders weaned the foals so the mares could be milked. As winter neared, two- or three-year-old colts were slaughtered for meat, as is done today for veal and lamb. Infertile mares or those who gave little milk also went to slaughter. A few colts were raised to maturity to become the herd's stallions, in the same sex ratio as in the wild, one stallion for six to ten mares. Ancient herders made no attempt to breed or improve horses, except by culling milk-poor mares, which raised the milk productivity of their herds. These more productive milk mares coincidentally produced more oxytocin. This "love hormone" caused horses to develop emotional bonds with humans, the beginning of the much richer relationship that exists between our two species compared to the bonds we experience with other domesticated animals. (Dogs, our oldest domesticated animal, alone compare with horses in this respect. That bond may have arisen from our sharing the hunt with them.)

The complexity of human and horse interaction reflects the fact that every horse, like every human, has a distinctive personality. Horses have strong likes and dislikes—particularly of some other horses and of certain people, as any pair of riders who have tried to ride two horses holding a grudge against each other will know. Horses are social animals in a way that other herd animals are not. They cooperate, compete, and play with one another, much like us. They live comparatively long lives, twenty or thirty years, and their life phases correspond to some extent to our own. They form enduring bonds with other horses, and are capable of forming such attachments with humans. This social aspect of horses is closely studied today, since many urban owners leave their horses alone in stables, ride them rarely, and discover later that the horse suffers from isolation, not only from their owners but also from other horses. They lose their social skills, and can be quite difficult or even dangerous to ride. Similar concerns are rarely expressed about the social skills of sheep or goats. Put another way, as the relationship between horses and humans evolved over the prehistoric centuries, the bond between the two became essential for the well-being of both.

Though for a long time the major role of the horse was to provide food for humans, the horse had many other distinctive characteristics that led the animal to fulfill additional roles, and that ultimately turned the horse into a strategic asset in world history.

To begin with, the horse achieved a special rank within the hierarchy of herded animals. Of course, every herded animal had features that humans could take advantage of. Sheep are hardy, adept at pasturing on poor lands and, thus, require little care. They also carry much more meat, proportionally, on their bones than horses, which make them an efficient source of protein. In addition, people can clothe themselves in sheepskins and beat sheep wool into felt for tents and hats. Goats require even less maintenance than sheep. They also have an excellent sense of direction and sometimes can be seen leading a herd of sheep, which follow and trust their caprine cousins to show them the best route to pastures. Cows provide milk, calves meat, and oxen pull heavy carts. In ancient times, cows weren't the highly efficient milk machines that modern cows have become. The hardy, steppe-grazed cattle of long ago produced hardly more milk than a mare and about a tenth as much milk as a modern dairy cow. But oxen, which are gelded males, were always preferred as beasts of burden. The first horses were too small to be of much use for traction. So, in the early herds, the roles of the horse and of cattle were reversed compared to today: the horse as a source of dairy products, cattle for mobility.

Yet herders came to see horses as the natural leaders of the flock. This leadership behavior partly originates in the horse's digestive system. They are not ruminants; that is, they do not chew their cud. They cannot vomit out food that disagrees with them. This makes them pickier eaters than the ruminants, so that horses will graze any particular piece of steppe first, picking out the best grasses, and sheep and goats will follow them. Horses will move on more rapidly in search of grass, leading the smaller ruminants in their train. If the herd is like an army, moving across the steppe, then the horses are like the vanguard.

The horse is also a fighter, unlike many other herd animals and antelopes and deer, their wild distant relations. These animals rely on their numbers for protection, but individual horses defend themselves vigorously against attacks by predators: wolves, mountain lions, and even cheetahs. This is especially true of stallions and mares with foals. For a prey animal, the horse packs quite a kick and delivers a dangerous bite. Another distinctive characteristic of the horse is that it can pasture far away from the camp without getting lost, unlike the less geospatially aware sheep. Because they are taller than sheep, they can see over the high grass of the steppe. This makes them useful not only for protecting the herd but also as companions for hunting. Horses are capable of grazing on pastures with snow up to a

Horse grazing in the snow in Kyrgyzstan.

foot deep; they use their hard hooves to break through the crust of snow in order to get to the grass beneath. Herders in Mongolia still graze horses and sheep together in wintertime to take advantage of the horse's unique ability to uncover grass for other animals, which otherwise would starve, keeping as many as one horse for every six sheep. This ability to cope with snow opens up territories to the herders that would have been previously inhospitable to livestock raising. The horse is indeed designed to be the leader of the flocks. On a more mundane level, horse manure is dry and produces too much smoke when lit, but is useful to start a fire for the longer-burning, less smoky manure of the ruminants.

Taken all together, these unique characteristics make the horse an extremely welcome addition to the herder's livestock. So began the tradition of herding "four heads," referring to horses, sheep, goats, and cattle, which persists into modern times. Other domesticated animals, like yaks in the mountains of Qinghai and Tibet or camels in the Gobi Desert, graze apart from the four heads because their preferred environment is so different. The combination of the four heads has proven to be efficient and sustainable. Modern experiments with single-species herding have failed. While Kazakhstan was part of the Soviet Union, its Communist government undertook an initiative to abolish horses altogether, considering sheep more productive and easier to manage. Many sheep then succumbed to predators, because there were no horses to defend them. On the other hand, in the 1990s, when capitalism was restored to Mongolia, replacing horses with intensive goat breeding—goats being prized for their cashmere wool—resulted in desertification of much grassland. The horse and its three ruminant companions are collectively well adapted to the steppe.

The horse not only led the flocks forward but also drew the horse herders into an increasingly distinctive, exclusive lifestyle. With their single-toed feet and their grasping front teeth, horses do more damage to cropland than the other animals in the herd. Early herders grazed their animals in pastures alongside fields planted with crops. Archaeological evidence suggests that they either practiced agriculture or coexisted with farming communities. Biblical stories remind us that herders and farmers often agreed to allow sheep and goats to clear the fields of stalks and stubble, while their droppings nourished the soil for the next year's planting. But as domesticated horse herds grew larger, competition for land arose between the horses and the crops. To find sufficient grass for the horses and to avoid conflict with neighboring farmers, herders began to drive their animals onto land that was marginally useful for farming, deeper into the steppe. This turned out to be a process full of historical portent, because it increased the dependence of the herders on their pastoral way of life and isolated the herder from the farmer. The Mongols boast about not eating vegetables ("our animals eat them and we eat *them*"), even though it isn't clear if an all-meat-and-dairy diet is desirable or even feasible. For most of history, agricultural products did form a part, however limited, of the herders' diet, even as herding became increasingly distinctive from farming. But the emergence of specialized herding, and the decrease in proximity between the herding and farming communities, increased the potential for future misunderstanding and conflict.

Meanwhile, as horses drew their herders ever farther from agricultural settlements, the fleet, four-legged animals imposed their own mobile rhythms on the two-legged animals. This mobility resulted in yet another entanglement between the two species, far more significant than corralling or milking: riding.

On Horseback

We do not know when the herders first began to ride; we only know that herding horses without riding them is extremely difficult. Horses, even without breaking into a gallop, can outrun humans. Tethering foals in the camp keeps only the lactating mares nearby. Colts, fillies, and stallions would roam far and wide. When it came time to move the camp, which included dozens of sheep, goats, and cattle, a way had to be found to round up the horses. The first riders were needed to rally the wandering herd.

They were probably children. Unworried about the inevitable tumbles and spills, Mongol toddlers still clamber on the bare back of many four-legged animals and ride them: sheep, goats, calves, and foals. Children as young as seven help herd their family's flocks. Astride a horse, they can manage two hundred head of smaller livestock, while an adult on foot will struggle to mind more than fifty. Herding on the steppe, with tall grasses growing to five feet, a youth on horseback would have been just able to see across to the horizon. Though their mounts were much smaller than today's horses, measuring no more than twelve hands, or four feet, at the withers (the top of the shoulders), they still provided the best available vantage point for herding. These early horses had strength neither in their limbs nor in their backs to carry an adult for a whole day of herding, however; the young riders changed horses frequently to reduce spine injuries to the animals, as Mongol herders still do today. Riding must have dramatically improved herding and herd mobility, as pastoralists could move their flocks farther into the steppe in search of grass and water.

Horses did not accept being ridden graciously. This human intrusion must always have been perceived as an even greater aggression than a mare being milked. After all, the mare needs to be milked, and as we saw earlier, this act of milking binds the mare and the humans together emotionally. The foal that pastured freely in the long grass, exposed only infrequently to humans, reacted with panic when mounted, as though an ancestral predator, a lion or a leopard, had leapt on its back to devour it. We see this reaction when cowboys break a bronco: the bronco bucks, rears, rolls, and does everything it can to throw off the rider. Eventually, if the animal exhausts itself before it tires out or rids itself of the human, it reluctantly settles into a passive state and ceases to struggle. An uneasy truce results, with the animal acknowledging the inevitability of the rider's weight on its back. As this struggle is played out in paddocks and pastures today, one imagines it must have been even more violent with the superficially domesticated horses of 3000 to 2500 BCE.

The process of horses accepting riders on their backs may have been helped along by the love hormone. The development of riding just happened to coincide with intensive milking of horses in the period 3000 to 2500 BCE. As people became more dependent on mare's milk as their staple diet, they bred more horses, managed bigger herds, and relied more on riders to follow the herds to fresh grass and water. This evolution appears to have begun just north of the Black Sea and the Caspian.

The beginning of horse riding, as momentous a development as it proved to be, passed unrecorded by history. The already literate societies south of the steppe, like the Sumerians and the Akkadians, did not pay much attention to this new phenomenon. After all, the peoples of the third-millennium BCE Middle East were familiar with riding donkeys, that cousin of the horse native to Africa, so there was nothing striking about the act of riding a different equid. In the most ancient depictions of animal riding from the Middle East, small statuettes and graffiti on rocks, it is hard to tell if the subject is a horse or a donkey. A distinct word for "horse," as opposed to "equid," did not exist in the different written languages of the time. Nor did it matter—the animal was not yet the tall, powerful, threatening warhorse of later centuries; nor had the herders turned into feared warriors. Horse riding was neither socially nor politically important for the urban peoples living on the fringes of the steppe. The absence of a historical record leaves modern scholars to argue about how best to date the emergence of riding.

Almost every stage of the development of riding, in fact, is the subject of controversy. We are not sure if fossil remains of horses' teeth from the third millennium BCE indisputably show signs of wearing bits. Ancient remains of bits and bridles are missing in the earlier periods, but that absence is not a decisive argument. One can ride bareback, working the knees to direct the horse and grasping the horse's mane as a handhold. Early riders may have used nose ropes, fastened around the horse's face and behind the ears, which have not survived in the archaeological record but which, by analogy with the practices of American Plains Indians, must have been a reasonably effective way to ride.

The best evidence for the emergence of riding is osteopathic: over time, surviving skeletal remains show increasing trauma to the animals and the riders. Ridden animals suffer from arthritis or fusing of the lumbar vertebrae. We begin to see these pathologies around 2000 BCE. As for the riders, their thighs and knees get a lot of work, as anyone feels after even a short time in the saddle. Remains of riders from this period show the thigh bones elongated by the continual tug of the supporting muscles. These ancient injuries demonstrate that we are dealing with the remains of a horse-riding people.

In this period (2000 BCE), indirect evidence of horse riding appears in the much wider distribution of horse herding across the steppe, the start of a thousand-year process that would take the herders into the Middle East, Europe, India, and China. The horse's wanderlust, not the human's, drove both species onward. Riding simply allowed the human to keep up. For the horse, more than any other domesticated animal, needs fresh pastures. Unlike sheep, most horses also need to drink water every day, and they tolerate salty water no better than humans. Horses will travel far to reach distant sources of water because, rare among animals but in common with humans, they perspire profusely to cool down. Because grass actually has relatively low nutritional value compared to other plants, horses have to spend their entire day eating. Horses even graze at night, sleeping just a couple of hours at a time. If the grass has lower than normal nutritional value, there are simply not enough hours in the day for the animals to feed themselves. They will starve. Finding adequate pastures is therefore vital. Modern agronomists and hydrologists are impressed by the detailed knowledge of local grass and water conditions that traditional herders exhibit, but for the herders, finding good pasture is a matter of life and death. Horses, moreover, are what herders call a "clean animal"; they won't graze in the presence of manure, which means that once a band has grazed in a pasture, the odor of its own waste drives the band elsewhere, even if there's still grass to be eaten or water to be drunk.

Raising horses, in other words, requires wide and free horizons, and the more horses are owned by a herding camp, the more the herders have to spread out over ever greater distances. Depending on local conditions, a tent of five or six family members needs to keep ten to twenty horses, several cattle, and two hundred sheep and goats to sustain itself. Encampments of five or six tents therefore need pasturage for over a thousand animals. A herding encampment of five or six tents and a thousand animals requires 23 square miles of grassy steppe land, or 70 to 140 square miles in a desert such as the Gobi or the Taklamakan. That is equivalent in size to a city like Philadelphia or Glasgow, but with a population of only a few dozen people. Historians estimate that Mongolia in Genghis Khan's time numbered one million people spread over some 600,000 square miles, an area more than twice that of Texas, or more than six times the size of Great Britain. Mongolia's livestock population may have numbered fifteen to twenty million head, including one million horses.

Even with this extensive space, herds exhausted local grasses by the end of the wet spring season, so the herders drove their flocks to higher or more northerly pastures for the summer. This annual migration marked traditional life on the steppe, and continues in parts of Mongolia today as herders migrate between summer and winter camps. The distances covered varied with the environment. In grassy Inner Mongolia, ninety miles would be a typical range, while in arid southern Kazakhstan, through the mid-nineteenth century, herders might have traveled nine hundred miles.

When they set off on these migrations, the ancient herders had to carry all their household goods with them, as well as children too small or parents too old to walk. This led them to adopt the four-wheeled cart, drawn by oxen, a technology that first appeared in the Fertile Crescent in the fourth millennium BCE. The carts allowed the steppe herders to move across large distances to suitable pastures with ever larger herds of animals, though they needed oxen to pull the carts, which were too heavy, with their solid-disk wheels, for horses. Later these carts gave way to camels.

Even seasonal migration in search of fresh grass, however, could not accommodate the growing herds. When the number of animals grew too large to be managed, they would be divided between siblings or between parents and children, and a new encampment would set off to find new pastures. In this way the herding population spread out farther and farther from its original homeland north of the Black Sea and the Caspian.

The Central Asian steppe contains harsher environments than the western steppe. As the horse breeders moved east, they had to cross the Kyzylkum, or "Red Sand" Desert, the Tian Shan, or "Heavenly Mountains," and the Altai, the "Golden Mountains." The Mongolian steppe, on the eastern side of these mountains, offered good grazing grounds but with colder winters and snow for many months of the year. Previous to the domestication of the horse, humans could not settle in the eastern steppe in any great numbers. Horses, though, could manage in the desert, and cope with the snow and ice of the Altai Mountains and Mongolia. The adaptability of the horses to harsh climates and the mobility they provided to their breeders enabled this enormous geographic expansion.

An echo of these migrations for pastureland can be heard in the earliest oral literature of these horse-herding peoples. The Avesta, the holy scripture of both the ancient Iranians and modern Zoroastrians, which broadly dates to the first millennium BCE, recalls the steppe expansion that occurred a thousand years earlier. It tells the myth of Jamshid, one of the world's first rulers, who, after a prosperous reign of three hundred years, saw that the land had no more room for his people and their herds. So Jamshid made the land one-third bigger, ruling his expanded clan for another six hundred years. When the herds expanded again, Jamshid made the land two-thirds larger than before, and the people found the land they needed. After nine hundred years, Jamshid performed this act of telluric inflation a final time.

The Avesta's ancient tale reflects a historical reality: horse breeding spread across the vast tracts of Eurasia. Within a period not much longer than the legendary eras of Jamshid, the horse breeders occupied the entire steppe, including steppe-like lands adjacent to the main Eurasian grassland, like the Hungarian plains and the high plateau of Iran. Interestingly, the colder and less hospitable grasslands of Mongolia, which we

sometimes think of as the homeland of steppe pastoralists, were settled last
of all, around 1300 BCE. This rich and unique environment was to become,
for the next four thousand years, the land of the horse breeders.

A Sea of Grass

The steppe extends over 3.1 million square miles—one-seventh of the
world's total landmass. By its very size, this part of the world was destined
to have a major impact on the lands adjacent to it, just like the oceans
determined the destiny of their shores. This is continental, as opposed to
maritime, Eurasia. It is a land of inland seas: the Caspian, the Aral, and
Lop Nor; of huge freshwater lakes: Balkhash and Issyk; and of endorheic
rivers—that is, ones that never reach the ocean.

In its core latitudes the steppe climate is temperate, providing a lush
spring that brings out wildflowers. The temperate steppe also has abundant
grasses for much of the summer, growing so high that a man without a
horse cannot even see where he is heading. The grassy steppe is characterized by pinnate feather grasses, fescue, absinthe, and other mixed grasses,
which vary according to the season. These shaggy, hardy plants are a preferred forage for horses. Horse breeders believe that their variety provides
a healthier diet than that in the feedbags of stabled horses. The best steppe
soil is fertile black earth, rich in minerals like selenium, calcium, and iron,
which contribute to the horses' bone strength and help oxygenate their
blood for speed.

The grassy steppe receives too little rainfall to support forests, but not
so little as to become desert. The little rain it does receive comes mainly in
the summer. The winter is cold and dry, cold enough so that some of the
world's lowest temperatures are found on the steppe. January's mean tem-
perature in Ulan Bator is minus 16 Fahrenheit, and it is not uncommon for
the mercury to show minus 40 Fahrenheit. High air pressure brings azure
skies and no rain.

Abutting the grassy steppe are zones of desert steppe, which can receive
fewer than two inches of rainfall per year. These include some of the world's
biggest and bleakest terrain: the Gobi in Mongolia, the Taklamakan in
western China, the Karakum and Kyzylkum of Central Asia, Afghanistan's

Dasht-e Margo and Registan, and Iran's Dasht-e Kavir and Dasht-e Lut. But despite the low rainfall and the extremely cold winters, the desert steppe supports the tamarisk tree, artemisia, the ubiquitous saxaul scrub, feather grass, and tussock grass growing up to six feet tall, which provide sustenance for many quadrupeds: onagers (wild asses), gazelles, and saiga antelopes. Snowmelt in the spring creates seasonal lakes in otherwise desert terrains, such as Sistan Province in Iran and Helmand Province in Afghanistan. None of these deserts is entirely devoid of grass or even animal husbandry. Brief seasonal grass allows some grazing, and the mountains are never far, enabling herds to escape the blistering summers. Foreign travelers over the centuries have wondered how herders survived in such conditions, but in reality the notion of a trackless, uninhabitable wasteland is misleading. The Eurasian Steppe comprises a mosaic of distinct territories, each with its own ecosystems, supporting many human settlements as well as some of the most varied flora and fauna in Asia.

The steppe is a kind of sea of grass in the middle of Asia, rather like the Mediterranean, that basin of water between Europe and Africa, and just as the Mediterranean connects to the Adriatic, Black, and Red Seas, the seas of grasses in the middle of Asia are connected to other, smaller seas of grass. Not all of these adjacent lands remain steppe today, as irrigation and intensive agriculture have expanded in modern times to feed hungry city dwellers. This has transformed the former grasslands of Punjab, the Jazira (as the headlands of the Tigris and the Euphrates Rivers are known in Arabic), the western slopes of the Taurus Mountains in Anatolia, where cotton is now grown, and the Puszta of Hungary, though horse raising is still practiced there. But much of the steppe remains almost as it was in ancient times, including the arid steppe of the Iranian plateau and the Arabian Peninsula, which helps to explain the very different histories of the Middle East and Iran as compared to India and China.

If the steppe is a vast inland sea, then the oases, such as Samarkand, Turfan, Herat, and Merv, are its islands. These oases played an important role in the early development of the herders' culture because they provided markets in which people could exchange meat and milk for bread. Some of these oases are just tiny gardens at the foot of mountains that tower seven thousand feet above them and whose snowmelt provides them with water.

The Eurasian Steppe

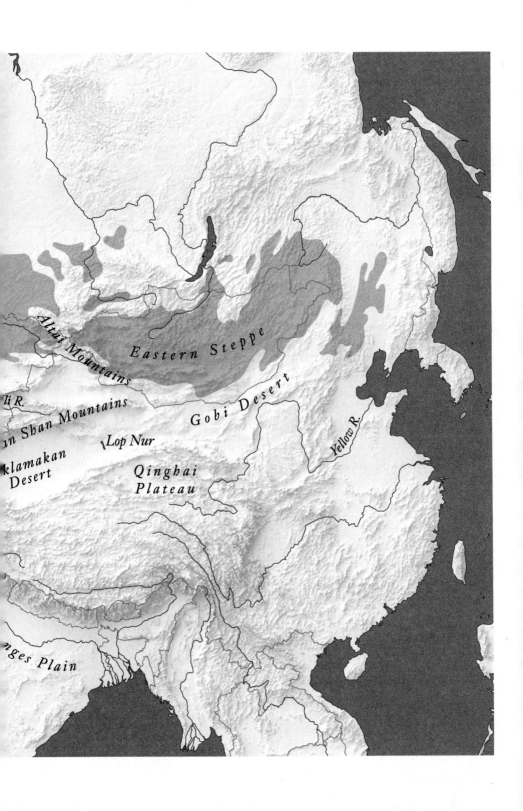

Others extend their green footprint with a delicate tracery of irrigation canals for miles in every direction.

The expansion of the herders into the vast sea of grass followed a clear geographic logic. Horses pastured primarily on lands that did not receive enough rain or benefit from irrigation to make them suitable for growing crops. The herders avoided lands that were intensively cultivated, in part because these were stoutly defended by local farmers, and in part because the land was too wet for their animals anyway. The Greek geographer Strabo noted in the first century CE that a farmer in the Crimea received a yield of thirty grains for every grain he planted, while in Babylon, the yield reached three hundred grains harvested for each grain planted. So, while one could raise crops on the Crimean steppe, the likelihood of drought or blight would have discouraged farmers from such a marginal land and encouraged, on the contrary, the pasturing of herds.

The steppe and, therefore, the land of horsemen extends deep into Europe. It is intersected by rivers: the Volga, flowing into the Caspian; and the Don, Dnipro, and Danube, flowing into the Black Sea, all of which appear to have been named by ancient horse breeders. The Dnipro, which passes through today's Kyiv, accompanies the steppe far to the north, to the frontier of the forest line. The Danube, flowing through Romania across broad plains, passes through a narrow valley between two great chains of mountains, the Carpathians and the Balkans, and enters the most western part of the steppe in Europe, the Hungarian plains. As a result of this geography, Hungary, Romania, Ukraine, and Russia have historically hosted large horse-herding populations. Horse herders came to play a major role in the history of these countries, as well as neighboring Poland and Lithuania.

The steppe, like other large natural zones on the planet, has undergone cyclical periods of wetter or drier climate. Paleoclimatologists have theorized that such changes have had a major impact on the horse population, and that this in turn may have resulted in some of the great migrations away from the steppe or of the invasions of settled lands by steppe dwellers. What is certain is that the steppe's volatile short-term weather, including sudden frosts and droughts, wreaked havoc on the horse population. The steppe often proves a harsh environment, requiring adaptability from the livestock herders, who frequently have to migrate to survive.

To the settled peoples attached to waving fields of grain, orchards, or vines, the trackless steppe appeared empty and frightening. For the horse herders, the steppe homeland came to be full of familiar landmarks. The Kazakh epic *Kozy-Korpesh and Bayan-Sulu* relates how the hero, obliged to abandon his ancestral pasture, bows down to bid farewell to his lakes, rivers, and hills. Everywhere the horse breeders looked they recognized signs, which were often the bones of their horses.

Afterlife

All across the landscape of Mongolia are scattered cairns, brick-sized stones stacked in piles to form knee-high landmarks. During my own journey through the steppe, the Mongols referred to the cairns respectfully as *ovoo*. On top of the ovoo, herders had placed the weather-bleached skulls of horses, which could be seen from a distance glinting in the sunlight. Our guides explained that each skull honored the memory of a faithful four-legged companion, as though from atop the cairn the empty eye socket and nostrils of the skull could still enjoy the wide sky, perfumed grasses, and blowing breezes, like a living horse. The practice is ancient.

The steppe is covered for thousands of miles in every direction with burial grounds containing human and equine remains. Most are simple trenches. Like today's ovoo, they often contain only the skull of the horse. It may be that horses were sacrificed for the deceased's funeral feast, in the way that Achilles sacrificed horses (and humans) at the funeral of his friend Patroclus. Indeed, we know from the fifth-century BCE Greek historian Herodotus that horse sacrifice featured prominently in the ritual life of the Greeks and Persians. Greek Hades itself, the underworld, was imagined as a pasture, κλυτοπολος, "famous for foals." In early India, the horse sacrifice was the most prestigious of all the ceremonies prescribed by the Rig Veda, the collection of religious hymns roughly contemporary to the Iranians' Avesta. Early horse-herding mourners feasted on the flesh of the sacrificed horses so that only the skulls remained to be buried. This is a testament to an ancient preference for horse meat, and at the same time to humans' veneration for horses.

In these ancient hymns, the horse is seen as the liminal animal par excellence, the vehicle for communicating between two worlds, as Philippe Swennen, an Indo-Iranian specialist, explains, "not only because it is used for transport, but because its stormy temperament means it can cross barriers suddenly, between day and night, between tamed and wild."

Later graves feature elaborate, raised vaults and multiple funeral chambers. Entire mummified horses, looking ready to accompany the human dead on their journey in the afterlife, have been found inside. In some colder steppe regions, permafrost has admirably preserved the buried horses. In any case, the horse is always the most important element in the grave, after the body or bodies of the humans. Bones of other animals also appear, but they represent the riches of the deceased or offer a store of food to be consumed in the afterlife. Sheep, goat, and cattle bones do not occupy the symbolically significant positions in the grave, while the horses are found close to the human remains or in a chamber above the human burial. "Our bones will lie together," the hero of one Mongolian epic promises his horse.

The ancient herders took pains to bury their dead, both horses and humans, in remote sites where they would not be disturbed. Herodotus confirmed that the steppe herders of his time maintained their ancestral burial grounds in great secrecy, far from familiar routes. Horses were used to trample down the excavated earth, and grassy turf was placed on top of the gravesites, as though the steppe had swallowed up the deceased. Thousands of years later, Genghis Khan was buried in a secret spot in Mongolia in just this way, with his favorite yellow horse. The mourners, it is said, were all killed, to prevent them from revealing the location. Many travelers have searched for this site, but none have ever found it.

Hidden graves appear to have been the privilege of great steppe chiefs. Ordinary graves, without valuable funerary goods, were marked by cairns and ovoo. Both kinds, sheltering human and equine remains together, gave the herders a sense of being at home in the vastness of the steppe. By their very remoteness, these places reminded them that without the horse, the steppe would have stayed empty. Though people are no longer buried with their horses on the steppe, the practice persisted through the nineteenth century, and the ovoo survive as a reminder of the entanglement between humans and horses, and the deep connection between the spirit of the horse and the vastness of the steppe.

The best-hidden burials, overlooked by grave robbers, tell us much about the early development of the domesticated horse, its DNA, its size, and its coloring. We have learned who the horse herders were, where they came from, what they ate, and, later, how they developed the practice of horseback riding. The archaeology that blossomed since the end of the Soviet Union, in 1991, confirms the intimate relationship of the horse with the ancient peoples of the steppe. The horse herders' way of life started when Ice Age hunters became obsessed with the animal's beauty and speed, intensified when the hunters adopted mare's milk as their primary sustenance, and turned into a unique way of life when the horse led them far into the grasslands, into a more exclusively pastoral existence. The horse filled such a powerful social, environmental, and emotional role among the early herders, and yet written history for so long did not take notice of this fact. It was the chariot that suddenly grabbed the attention of the great early civilizations.

Horses for Heroes

Horse herders enter the settled world, 2000–500 BCE

"**M**y lord should not ride a horse," advised the vizier of Zimri-Lim, king of Mari in northeast Syria, around 1760 BCE. "Let my lord ride in a cart or indeed on a mule, and let him honor his royal status." At that time, horse riding was not an accepted practice for a king. Odd as the recommendation to ride a mule seems to us, at least that sterile, horse-donkey hybrid provided a stately and reliable seat. The ancient Middle East, having long domesticated donkeys, had no reason to suspect that horse riding would have a portentous future. They probably viewed horse riding the way later peoples would view riding reindeer or yaks—as an exotic, ethnic form of transportation.

Second-millennium BCE inhabitants of Mari or Ur, on the Euphrates River in today's Iraq, or of Bactria, on the Oxus River in modern Afghanistan, had seen the occasional horse rider. Grazing their flocks on the steppe adjacent to those two great rivers, horse breeders would have ridden to the urban markets to exchange pastoralist goods—cheese, animal skins, horn, horsehair, and sheep's wool—for local products like bread and vegetable oil. The horse herders' visits elicited no special commentary on the part of the priestly scribes tasked with chronicling unusual events. Riding horses was not seen as particularly notable, but it was decidedly not, as per the vizier, noble.

The donkey cart recommended for Zimri-Lim figures frequently in the iconography of grand processions of this era. A famous example is the royal standard of Ur, dating to 2500 BCE; this artefact of wood, lapis lazuli, and seashells features five four-wheeled carts bristling with armed warriors, who are driving a team of donkeys. They are depicted slaughtering their enemies. But in a real battle, such slow-moving carts did not represent the formidable threat of the later war chariots drawn by horses. Donkeys, hardy natives of the desert, never grew very tall or very swift. They lacked the fight-or-flight reactions of the horse that made the latter so combative. Mules inherited most of these limitations. Other Afro-Arabian equids, like the zebra, the onager, or their hybrids, were also recruited for driving, without great success. The future of warfare belonged to horses and horse-drawn chariots.

The Chariot

We worship Mithra, who rules from a high-wheeled chariot. The powerful Mithra appears in a beautiful, lightweight, golden chariot drawn by four eternal, fast, white horses with golden and silver hooves. And all of them are harnessed under the same yoke, with ties on the beams, and a drawbar attached with a hook.

So proclaims the Avesta's hymn to Mithra, the god of herds and pastures. As with the holy scripture's tale of Jamshid, these verses recall another momentous historic moment: the advent of the chariot. The precision with which the god's vehicle is described underscores the impact that the new chariot-driving technology had on human imagination. People saw this new form of mobility as the most fitting vehicle for the gods.

Chariots were indeed much faster than what had preceded them: the oxcart, which was common across the Middle East, Transoxiana, and the western steppe. One such heavy cart with four solid wheels has been found near the Oxus River, on the steppe frontier, dated to 2200 BCE. It probably served to transport the herders' tents, carpets, cooking pots, curdled milk, and drinking water. Given their familiarity with carts, the steppe people didn't need to reinvent the wheel.

They did, however, start to tinker with it over the course of the second millennium. From heavy wheels carved from a single piece of wood (originally tree trunks sawed into sausage slices), they invented the hollow wheel with spokes. They added a bronze rim and fittings at either end of the spokes, which numbered eight or ten per wheel. Tires were of leather. A big gain of speed came from reducing the wheels from four to two, though this made the chariot much more unstable than the cart, and harder to drive safely. The two-wheelers gained in maneuverability once craftsmen learned how to distribute the weight of passengers and horses along the central pole.

Improvements did not end with the wheels. The cart was lightened and strengthened with more bronze fittings, since metal provided a better weight-to-strength trade-off than wood. Bronze blocks allowed the axel to spin more freely. Wicker was used for the chassis to further reduce weight. Archaeologists have recovered an extremely light cart made mostly of birch wood.

We do not know what prompted steppe peoples to improve the traditional cart and to turn it into the speedy chariot, more than twenty times lighter than its predecessor. The initial impulse might simply have been for the fun of cart racing, a sport still enjoyed in rural areas. Perhaps craftsmen built lighter vehicles because they couldn't find enough hardwood on the steppe.

The biggest advantage of the lighter cart was that horses could be harnessed to it, delivering speed inconceivable with ponderous oxen. Horses could never have pulled the heavier carts, so this was the first time a harness was thrown over a horse's neck. As with riding, putting a horse into the harness would have been an act of aggression. The unfamiliar weight, the constraints around the throat, the noise of the rumbling wheels would have all contributed to sending the horse into a state of panic. Humans learned that when they harnessed two or more horses side by side, their affinity for companionship reduced their trauma and enabled the driver to control the team.

The steppe peoples quickly adopted this vehicle for hunting; it allowed a bowman to stand upright and shoot arrows at prey while a charioteer steadied the chariot's trajectory. Since in that era the steppe abounded in game, the chariot must have been an extremely welcome addition to the herders' arsenal of weapons. Perfecting their driving and archery skills on the hunt, the steppe peoples soon began to deploy their chariots for combat, initially in their internecine rivalries on the steppe—specifically, near the Ural and Altai Mountains, where metallurgy in bronze was highly developed.

One might have expected that a practice involving more hardware would follow one that uses less, and that steppe peoples would have ridden their horses into war before the invention of the chariot. Yet up until the first millennium BCE, they did not fight on horseback. It seems like putting the cart before the horse to insist that chariots preceded mounted combat by almost a thousand years. To reconcile ourselves to this counterintuitive sequence of events, we must bear in mind two points: mounted warfare requires more hardware than simple herding, and the early horses were not big enough to be ridden into combat. Chariot driving ultimately addressed both of these deficiencies.

Firstly, hardware: driving brought innovations not only in carts and wheels but also in horse tack. From 1800 BCE on we begin to see increasingly sophisticated horse tack in the archaeological record, including bits, cheek pieces, and buckles that once held leather bridles and reins. These appear to have been invented specifically to drive horses. While the bareback riders used nose ropes or other simple tack made from organic materials, which left little archaeological trace, the charioteer needed more precise and sensitive means for directing or slowing down the horses. It is likely that herders gradually adopted chariot tack, as these articles became more common, to improve their horseback riding as well. This enabled the kind of riding required for mounted combat.

There are historical examples of fierce warriors riding bareback without any tack—the Comanche and the Apache come to mind. But these raiders practiced a very different form of warfare from that of cavalry in ancient and modern times, who rely on elaborate tack to get them into and safely out of hand-to-hand mêlées. The Amerindians also rode horses that would have been unavailable to the early steppe peoples.

Hence the second point: a horse of the second millennium BCE was not big enough to carry a heavily armed rider on its back, but a team of such horses had no difficulty pulling chariots. A passage from Herodotus, written fifteen hundred years later, illustrates this point. The Greek historian expressed surprise that the Sigynnae, a horse-herding people in today's Bulgaria, raised tiny, shaggy-coated ponies, "not strong enough to bear men on their backs. When hitched to chariots, though, they are among the swiftest known." Measurements of ancient chariot wheels and reconstructions of their harnesses convince scholars that ancient chariot horses were no higher than eleven to twelve hands. The Sigynnae continued to drive chariots and raise small horses in an age when most of their opponents had long abandoned those vehicles for mounted combat. The Sigynnae had, for some reason, not been able to breed the strong-backed steeds that succeeded the lighter horses of the chariot age. Herodotus found this peculiarity of the Sigynnae sufficiently archaic to take note of it. Lack of riding skills and lack of horses to carry them, then, ensured that steppe people entered recorded history as charioteers and not mounted warriors.

The Charioteers

Royal attitudes toward horses changed in the thousand years following the time of Zimri-Lim. A Chinese ruler of the ninth and eighth centuries BCE, King Xuan of Zhou, declared to one of his vassals,

> I confer upon you: a chariot with bronze fittings, with a decorated cover on the handrail; a front-rail and breast-trappings for the horses of soft leather, painted scarlet; a canopy of tiger skin, with a reddish-brown lining; yoke-bar bindings and axle couplings of painted leather; bronze jingle bells for the yoke bar; a main shaft rear-end fitting and brake fittings, bound with leather and painted gilt; a gilt bow-press and a fish-skin quiver; harness for a team of four horses; gilt bridles and girth straps; a scarlet banner with two bells. I confer upon you these gifts to be used in sacrifice and upon field service.

Elsewhere we read, "The king bestowed on him [another vassal] a team of four horses and herewith to support the king, and bestowed a bow therewith and brilliant scarlet arrows, and bestowed an axe herewith to subjugate the barbarian regions." The chariot-driving warriors had arrived.

The Bronze Age, roughly 3000 to 1200 BCE, named for its characteristic employment of that sturdy tin-and-copper alloy, saw the horse-drawn chariot take on the world during its latter half. Early literature, from Homer's

Iliad to the Bible, India's Mahabharata, and the Chinese *Book of Songs*, tells of the chariot-driving warriors.* Because of their ubiquity, scholars struggled for years to pinpoint their origin. Did chariot driving begin among the settled peoples of the Middle East or on the steppe? Did it spread through conquest or through a more gradual process? Discoveries in recent decades have provided answers to these questions.

Sintashta, an archaeological site just east of Russia's Ural Mountains, offers extensive evidence of the emergent practice of charioteering. Russian archaeologists discovered this site in 1978 but only really began to understand its significance after 1992, when accurate carbon dating confirmed the discovery of the world's oldest known chariots, dating to the early second millennium. Twenty sumptuously constructed and furnished funeral pits yielded sacrificed horses and their chariots, providing a vivid glimpse into the artifacts and ideology of the early chariot drivers.

The chariot horses were stallions, of uniform height and slimmer-limbed than the typical horse remains found elsewhere in the same period. This suggests that horses were already being selected for specialized tasks. Chariot horses were probably stronger and better winded than the herding horses. Since they did not trot—that pace emerged much later—they would have galloped in their traces, making a terrifying racket as they advanced. They were gaily decorated with bronze cheek disks (called *phalerae*), horse brasses on their harnesses, and bells. They must have been an impressive spectacle—all this clanging, jingling tack provided a form of exhibition dressage for the horse. The chariots themselves, whose ghostly traces have been recorded by their imprints in the surrounding mud, were narrow, single-passenger vehicles used for racing.

The fact that so many fine horses and racing chariots were buried together in these elaborately laid out burials is suggestive of the cultural role that horses and chariots played in the Sintashta people's lives. We can better reconstruct their culture in light of the hymns of the Rig Veda, one of the foundational scriptures of Hinduism. Like the Avesta, the Vedic hymns are hard to date but probably reflect oral traditions of the second

---

*   Irish legends also celebrate chariot-driving heroes like Cuchulainn and Fergus; see W. B. Yeats's "Who will go drive with Fergus now?"

millennium. The languages of both the Avesta and the Rig Veda are closely related, and they often refer to the same deities, including Jamshid, the Vedic Yama, and Mithra, the Vedic Mitra. Like the Avesta, the Rig Veda also contains hymns to chariot-driving gods. Its instructions for performing horse sacrifices resonate with Sintashta funerary rites.

The Sintashta people appear to have celebrated the funerals of great chiefs by organizing chariot races. The celebrants sacrificed the winning team of horses and carved, cooked, and apportioned the horseflesh to the hundreds, possibly thousands of guests attending the wake. The Rig Veda invokes the eagerness of the guests: "Those who see that the racehorse is cooked, who say, 'It smells good!' and who wait for the doling out of the flesh of the charger—let their approval encourage us." In Sintashta, the heads and forelegs of the sacrificed animals, all that was left over from the feasting, were then placed in the chief's grave together with their chariot and harnesses.

The Rig Veda calls for a goat to be sacrificed alongside the horse, and indeed the Sintashta site contains a goat buried together with a horse. Human sacrifices are rarely mentioned in the sacred scripture, but one hymn recalls a divinity who is beheaded, after which he receives a horse's head as a graft.[*] In Sintashta, a headless human skeleton lies with a horse skull on its shoulders. These parallels encourage us to see the Sintashta burials as the earliest tangible evidence of the chariot-driving peoples who later brought the Vedic gods and the language of the Rig Veda into India, where these later evolved into Brahmanism and Sanskrit, respectively.

For the chariot-driving people did not just stay on the steppe. Two hundred years after the Sintashta horse sacrifices, they sallied forth and introduced their new way of life to the surrounding settled peoples. One branch of these steppe charioteers gradually migrated from Central Asia into eastern Europe. Along this trail of migration archaeologists have found, in addition to chariots and horses, evocative horse-headed scepters, which first appear in the Ural Mountains around 1800 BCE, and by 1200 BCE in Greece. Homer's King Agamemnon of Mycenae may have wielded such a scepter in his war councils under the walls of Troy. The horse-headed

---

[*] Rather like the better-known example of Ganesh, who receives an elephant's head.

scepters show not only that these people raised horses but that the horse was for them the symbol of power par excellence. Because the horse herders entering Europe encountered preliterate societies, apart from archaeological evidence, we have only legendary accounts of them from many centuries later, like Homer's *Iliad*.

In the Middle East, on the other hand, the arrival of charioteers is well documented by the urban and literate societies that welcomed them, in contrast to the earlier silence about the first horses. The charioteers did not arrive as invaders; a handful of steppe chariot drivers could hardly have threatened the tall, walled citadels of the ancient Middle Eastern states. The rulers of the settled states quickly recognized the potential value of charioteering for racing, displays of power (remember those jangling harnesses), and, ultimately, for warfare.

To acquire this new technology speedily, rulers of the settled states recruited steppe people as grooms, drivers, trainers, and mercenaries, since only the steppe peoples knew anything about horses or charioteering. This pattern of recruitment from the steppes for equestrian know-how continued to be practiced in the Middle East, and later in India and China, for the next three thousand years. From this era, the horses of the steppe, along with their herders, became a fixture of life in the surrounding settled lands.

The Hittites, a chiefly city-dwelling people of the fourteenth century BCE who occupied much of modern Turkey, hired a man named Kikkuli as their chariot trainer. His instructions about feeding, cleaning, and training chariot horses are preserved on cuneiform tablets, acquired by German archaeologists in Turkey in 1906. Kikkuli probably spoke a language closely related to the languages of both the Avesta and the Rig Veda. He calls horses *assa* (compare the Sanskrit *aśva*), and himself an *assussani*, suggestive of the Sanskrit phrase *aśva-sana*, meaning "horse teacher." Later, the Assyrians would use this title to designate their cavalry marshals. Kikkuli gave specific advice for the horses' diet, as well as warm-up and cool-down procedures for either races or warfare. Although Kikkuli's manual is a unique artifact, hinting at the role played by experts from the steppe in diffusing chariot technology, frequent foreign names in the archaeological records of the Middle East demonstrate that this recruitment was indeed a widespread phenomenon.

The Expansion of Horses and Their Breeders

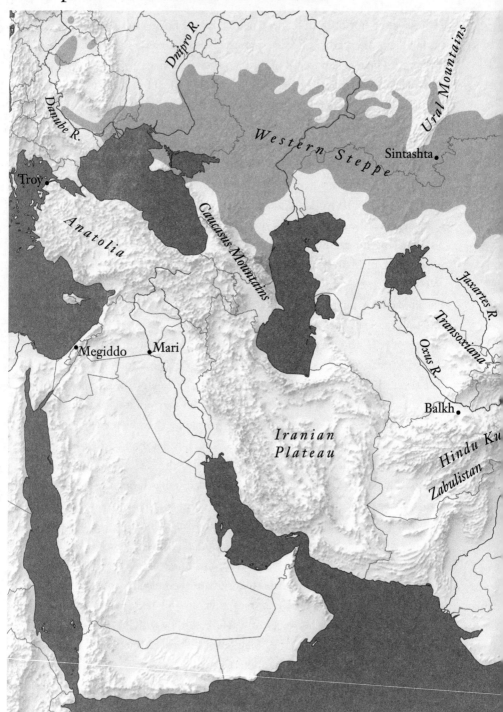

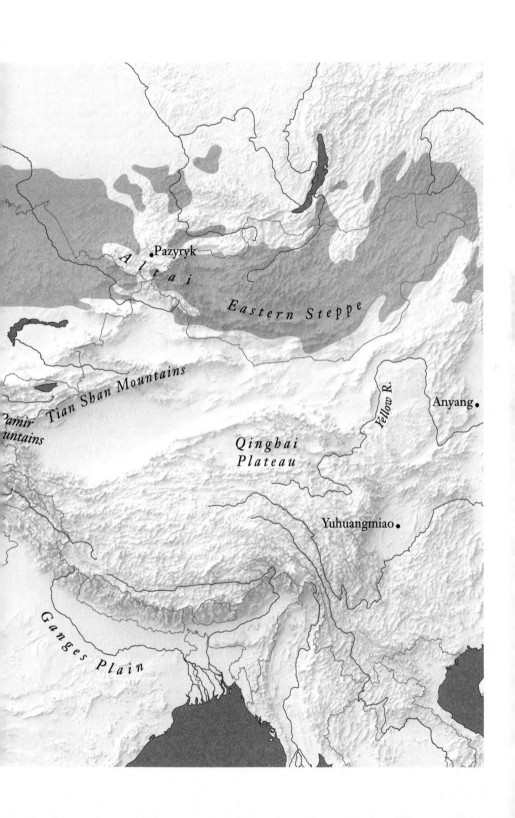

As the steppe horse herders entered into closer contact with the settled populations in this period, it is worth exploring in what ways they were different, and how they may have expressed those differences. While each of the settled peoples had their own distinctive cultures, the one common denominator is that, originally, they did not value horses, as the exchange between Zimri-Lim and his vizier showed. Outside of the steppe, the horse was an exotic animal, and marked the horse herders as different. The settled, farming peoples came up with a variety of negative descriptions for the horse herders. The Greeks called them nomads, from νομος, pasturage. The Chinese called them 胡, *Hu*, meaning "foreigners," or 行國, *xing guo*, "moving nation," as opposed to 土著, *tu zhe*, "staying put." In the Persian language, they are known as *khané be-dûsh*, "with their house on their backs." Today it is common to refer to these people as nomads, while anthropologists use the more precise term "nomadic pastoralists." That would have sounded redundant to the Greeks, since the two words meant the same thing to them. The word "nomad" can mislead us into thinking that the steppe herders were aimless wanderers, as the settled peoples often contemptuously characterized them. I have chosen to refer to them as "horse breeders," as this distinguishes them best from other peoples, including other mobile populations that did not raise horses.

The expansion of horses and chariots into new pastures connected the western and the eastern steppes of Eurasia for the first time in history, bringing the peoples of early China into contact with the Oxus civilization and even the Fertile Crescent. Tombs with rich chariot burials trace a path across the steppe, from the Urals of Sintashta to the heartland of ancient Chinese civilization. The "Sintashta moment" for China was identified thanks to the discovery of a grave of the Shang dynasty, circa 1200 BCE, in Anyang, Henan Province. Extensive archaeological investigations starting in the 1980s have brought to light the horse culture of the Shang, considered by the Chinese to be the first historical dynasty. These finds show that the chariot quickly became an important symbol for the Shang ruling elite, as chariots are found in all Shang prestige tombs. It is notable that the Shang chariots are almost identical in construction to those found in western Asia, underscoring the view that the horse and chariot were not phenomena that gradually spread into China but most likely arrived with a bang, fully formed. It is not until this period that we have extensive evidence of domesticated horses in China. The Chinese character for a cart or car, *Che*, is still clearly recognizable as the two-wheeled chariot of the steppe warriors, 車, and eerily resembles the earliest petroglyph renderings of the chariot one finds across the steppe. Some western scholars go so far as to speculate that the Shang dynasty itself came from the steppe. Evidence is scarce, but later Chinese history is full of dynasties with steppe origins.

Petroglyphs of steppe chariots resembling the Chinese character for vehicles, Mongolia, fifteenth to fourteenth centuries BCE.

One of the Shang tombs in Anyang tells an intimate story about the coming of the charioteers. The tomb of the queen Lady Hao, excavated in 1984, contained not only Chinese objects like ritual bronze vessels, jades, and ivories but also horse bridles and weapons typical of steppe people. This royal consort may have arrived at the court as part of an alliance between the Shang kings and chariot-driving steppe elites. The Anyang archaeological site lies on a distinctive ecological frontier between the steppe and the Yellow River valley, but the distinction between the barbarians of the steppe and the civilized Chinese, important to later Chinese historians, may not have existed in this early period. Through such marriage ties, perhaps, the Chinese naturalized the chariot and assimilated its steppe-born drivers into the mainstream of their culture and society.

This assimilation, in China and elsewhere, occurred rapidly because the chariot drivers represented a prestigious warrior elite. They became preeminent figures of what many traditions remember as their heroic age. Chariot-driving warriors practiced an aristocratic creed. They drove chariots to the hunt as well as to war and constantly trained themselves, under the exacting eyes of coaches like Kikkuli. They fought duels with opposing champions. It was considered improper for a mere foot soldier to engage a chariot warrior in combat, even if he proved victorious. This is the ethos practiced by Achilles and Hector as they battled before the walls of Troy. Hector, it must be remembered, was "the tamer of horses" and prince of Troy, "rich in horses."

Following the traditions of Sintashta's charioteers, elites everywhere considered the horse an essential element of the funeral ritual. This cult, practiced by the warrior heroes of the Trojan War and the Mahabharata, was shared by Shang dynasty aristocrats, whose burials reveal extensive horse and chariot remains, with the more important tombs holding up to fifty horses, as well as bronze and gold decorations for their train and chariots. Truly the Bronze Age is an age of horses, heroes, chariots, and the spectacular funerary rites that preserved so much for our discovery.

Over time the settled states scaled up their deployment of chariots, transforming them from aristocratic battle platforms to the equivalent of modern tanks. At the Battle of Megiddo in 1457 BCE, the Egyptians and Canaanites deployed one thousand chariots each, the biggest battle of its kind to date. Following the battle, recounts a victory obelisk at Karnak, the Egyptian spoils included nine hundred chariots and two thousand mares. We don't know if the mares were used to pull the chariots and, if so, how they survived combat. In China, the warlike Zhou dynasty replaced the Shang by relying heavily on chariots in massed combat. At their height, the Zhou mustered between four thousand and five thousand chariots, likely the peak use of chariots anywhere in the world. By that time, the early first millennium BCE, massed chariots were disappearing from the western Asian battlefield.

The eclipse of the chariot as a weapon should not surprise us. Accounts tell of generals preparing the terrain before hostilities by clearing away stones that might slow down or tip over their vehicles. The commanders had to choose the battleground carefully to avoid high grass, erosion, and gullies. Even in hunts—or perhaps especially in hunts, with their unpredictable chases—the instability of the chariot posed a clear danger. The earliest Chinese historical records tell of the thirteenth-century BCE King Shang Wuding and a certain Prince Yang setting off to hunt a rhino; the species then enjoyed a wider habitat than it does today. During the hot pursuit, the chariot flipped over. The king suffered minor scratches, but the unlucky Prince Yang had to be carried off the field. Chariots had their limitations, so there needed to be an alternative.

By the fifth or fourth century BCE, cavalry had replaced chariots as the decisive mobile arm in the Middle East, though chariots enjoyed a long afterglow. This is reflected by a model chariot of that era. Just eight inches long, it corresponds closely to the high-wheeled golden chariot described in the Avestan hymn to Mithra, hammered in solid gold and pulled by four miniature but powerful-looking ram-nosed horses, with reins of gold wire and wheels that actually spin. Perhaps a Persian prince played with this luxurious toy, preparing for a day when he might review his armies from atop a chariot. But his armies would have been cavalry troopers, armed with

Golden toy chariot from the Oxus Treasure, 200 BCE.

bows, lances, short swords, and maces. The transition from chariot combat to cavalry took place against a background of great developments in riding, in armament, and in the horse itself.

The War Horse

An ancient steppe legend, preserved among the modern Ossete people of the Caucasus, recounts how the hero claims his steed. In the chief's herd there is a young foal that stands only halfway up his dam's withers, but no one can master him. He rears, kicks, and bites furiously at the approach of any human. Undaunted, a young lad catches the foal by surprise, grasps hold of him by the tail, jumps on his back with no bridle, kicks his heels into his flanks, and after a brief but vigorous struggle to assert control, rides triumphantly away to show off his daredevilry to the chief. Seeing the horse and rider galloping up, the older man ruefully realizes that this youth is destined to replace him as the leader of the clan. The myths of horses for heroes, like that of Alexander the Great and his steed Bucephalus, began with the everyday heroism of the steppe horse breeders. Breaking in a strong, fierce horse required bravura: the fiercer the horse, the more heroic the rider. Around 1200 BCE, horses indeed became faster, fiercer, and stronger—the stuff of legends—and their riders became, like the young lad, more intrepid.

Breeding and riding powerful horses was a completely different occupation from climbing on ponies to help with herding. This new practice may have come about, like charioteering, out of love for the hunt. Hunting, for steppe people, was an important source of food, comity, and prestige. Ordinary horse breeders could not afford to build and keep a chariot, so only the wealthiest and most powerful of their chiefs enjoyed this sport. Hunting from horseback could be more accessible, as every family on the steppe kept horses, but it required maintaining careful control of the animal. Early riding entailed sitting over the horse's neck, guiding the animal by pulling on its mane. For any but exceptional equestrians, this did not allow for rapid turns or jumps. Moreover, when hunters were armed only with javelins, they had at most two opportunities to make the kill. In a sudden appearance, a lion or leopard could make quick work of both the horse and rider, after an unlucky missed javelin toss. Shooting the era's long bows, used by charioteers, proved cumbersome from horseback, as the horse's neck got in the way. These were the challenges confronting the common horse breeder when he watched, wistfully, his charioteering chief return from the hunt laden with game.

It took between 1800 BCE and 1200 BCE for horse breeders to overcome these challenges. Developments in horses, tack, and weaponry enabled the breeders to hunt but also delivered the cavalry revolution of the first millennium BCE, a historical event even more significant than the coming of the chariot. This era saw major changes in horses, their interactions with humans, and forms of riding.

Charioteering itself probably resulted in steadily stronger animals. Unlike the undemanding task of herding, for which any horse will do, chariot horses would have been carefully selected and, over time, given more opportunities to breed, to ensure their owners success at the hunt, in races, or in battle. The Sintashta chariot horses already had larger and stronger leg bones than earlier horses. They grew in height, gaining perhaps two hands (from four feet at the shoulders to five, more like modern horses). In this sense, chariot driving was the prerequisite for extensive horseback riding.

These physical changes came about slowly, since horse breeding in that era was fairly hands-off. Unlike Western breeders today, the steppe peoples did not set a stallion and a mare in a paddock and coax the stallion to cover the mare. As traditional breeders of Mongolia and Kyrgyzstan still do, they let stallions and mares couple while pasturing freely in the steppe. In this respect, the humans interfered very little in the reproductive process of the other species. In another aspect, however, they exercised an enormous influence over their horse herds. Gelding was and still is practiced on eight in every ten colts. Without limiting the number of stallions in the herd, the breeders could not have kept their herds together. Young stallions would have tried to establish their own herds and fought among themselves, resulting in many wounded horses as well as humans. For peoples who do not raise horses in stables or paddocks, gelding is an unavoidable practice.

Gelding practices in today's Mongolia offer clues about how ancient breeders influenced the evolution of the horse. Current breeders look at their two- and three-year-old colts and determine if they hold promise.

Muscles, speed, ability to go for long periods without water, and a good disposition are the signs of a horse worth breeding. If they feel the colt will grow into a mediocre horse, they geld him. In this way, the breeders practice rough-and-ready selective breeding of the male line. As a result of these ancient practices, between 1800 and 1200 BCE horses grew bigger, stronger, and faster.

Despite this selective breeding, ancient horses remained genetically very diverse. Herodotus ascribed to the steppe peoples the custom of giving and receiving horses as gifts between widely dispersed groups. In corroboration of this we have found burial sites with up to eighteen different brands detectable on the horses' remains. Each community had their own markings, rather like Highland clans of Scotland and their tartans. DNA analyses of horse burials of this period further confirm this preference for outbreeding. The DNA reflects a very low degree of consanguinity, showing that intensive selection based on a few foundational stallions was unknown. Genetic diversity was important to avoid injury and susceptibility to diseases, making the steppe horses much more robust than today's purebreds, who suffer, like many of our favorite domestic animals, from overbreeding. The ancient preference for outbreeding also suits horses' own reproductive habits. Left to themselves in the steppe, horses will not mate with closely related individuals.

After several centuries in which humans bred horses for hunting and warfare, a different animal emerged on the steppe: the warhorse. This powerfully muscled steed, long of leg and long of breath, could carry a full-grown adult with armor at a sustained gallop over great distances. But horses did not gain only muscle and endurance. Horses bred out of chariot stock developed more warlike instincts, losing some of the fearfulness of their hunted ancestors. Along with instincts for hunting and fighting, horses developed a deeper sympathy with their riders. Riders, too, learned how to understand horses' emotional states, and to communicate better through increasingly sophisticated and articulated tack, partly inherited from chariot driving.

The interspecies communication of horsemanship is at the heart of what makes the horse-human relationship unique. People ride oxen and donkeys, but neither for speed nor for distance, and not for races, hunting, or war. The horse forms a psychological bond with its rider; no other quadruped will jump over obstacles, pass through flames and explosions, or carry on when wounded. Through this bonding, horses overcome fears of dragging an encumbrance, loud noises, and water obstacles. Humans have weaponized the fight-or-flight instincts of the horse for mass cavalry charges, as well as single combat against another horse and rider. The increased use of the horse for hunting and warfare, more than its domestication per se, accounts for the almost mystical relationship that arises between a high-performance rider and their mount. Riding as an art, what we call dressage today, gradually emerged from these practices.

As they bonded more intimately with their mounts, riders started to give their horses names. It would have been impossible for a horse breeder to name every one of his horses grazing on the steppe; it also would have been unnecessary. He would have named a favorite riding horse—the one that won a race; the one that brought him safely home from battle. Already in the early second millennium, chariot horses' names were recorded by literate societies in the Middle East. Admittedly, some of these names were descriptive, but then, so were human names. A horse might be called "Dappled Gray," just as his rider might be "Stout" or "Baldy." Such names are found on cuneiform tablets, inscribed by clerks of the royal stables of Mesopotamia. Another indication of the increasing identification of the human with the horse can be seen in the discontinuance of ritual horse feasts, where prize horses were sacrificed and eaten. Today's Kazakhs and Mongols eat horse flesh, but they avoid eating the horses they have used for riding. The hero's horses came to be, as the Victorian English steppe explorer Thomas Atkinson wrote, "like members of an affectionate family."

The social connection between horses and humans deepened, starting around 1200 BCE. Elaborate burials of entire horses from this time suggest that horses were no longer butchered for sacrificial offerings but, instead, were interred as honored individuals in their own right. Pazyryk, a well-preserved burial site in western Siberia dating from the fourth to second centuries BCE, yields equine burials that seem to commemorate the horses as much as their riders. These horses were buried with humans, reflecting the lifetime relationship that had existed between the rider and the ridden. Such a horse would have had only one rider, and on the death of that rider, the horse would have served him in the afterlife.[*]

In this case, the afterlife looks astonishingly vibrant, as the permafrost of the Siberian soil preserves a unique glimpse of the vivid colors worn by horses and riders, including the oldest known woven pile carpets, silk from China, and embroidery from Iran. Many of the textiles used for riding look modern, like the shabracks (medium-sized saddlecloths) and seat cushions with rich, geometric shapes that remind one of today's Turkish, Mongol, and Tibetan horse coverings. What is most striking, though, is that each horse is buried with an elaborate caparison, or saddle blanket, including, in some cases, a head covering resembling those worn by horses in medieval tournaments. In a technique still common on the steppe today, the caparisons are made of felt, but these are brilliantly dyed and shaped into the most unexpected forms. One horse wears a mask shaped like antelope antlers. Another wears a mask in the shape of a leopard; the cat's forepaws wrap around the eye holes, and the hind paws curl around the nostrils. Scholars speculate that this horse had become famous for fighting a leopard; a subspecies was then native to the Eurasian steppe. This suggests special bravery, since the big cats are the horse's ancestral predator, and normally the smell of such an animal alone will send a horse fleeing. Compared to the timid horses bred on the steppe one thousand years previously, these animals were a fiercer breed.

The rich inventory of riding artifacts from these burials convinces us that the people who used Pazyryk as a burial site invented horsemanship as we know it. They were the first to adopt trousers for riding. They improved their seats by introducing padded cushions for the rider's thighs and coccyx This form of early saddle was light, designed so that a rider could simply throw it over the horse's back and vault into his seat. For additional stability, they fixed three girths, or bands, to keep the saddle in place, as well as a croupier attached laterally, from saddle to tail, and a pectoral band around the front. Many of the delicately molded gold appliqués found in the graves were once sewn into these bands, giving the horse and rider a

---

[*]   Indeed, in the folklore of the Ossetes, descendants of the Scythians, the dead ride their own horses in hell. See John Colarusso and Tamirlan Salbiev, eds., *Tales of the Narts*.

Horse's ceremonial burial mask of gold leaf
from Pazyryk, fifth to third centuries BCE.

brilliant allure. Moreover, these riders improved their horse tack with the snaffle bit. Replacing the simple cannon, or bar, through the horse's mouth, the snaffle bit comes in two connected pieces and gives the rider contact with the horse's tongue, lips, and cheeks, thereby enabling him to send more gentle signals to the horse, without damaging its mouth. Prior to the development of such bits, riding would have been tiring and dangerous for horses. These improvements reflected the need to control increasingly big and strong horses. Iron tack replaced bronze tack in this period, referred to as the Iron Age after the growing use of this metal. Though bronze is easier to work, iron is one hundred times more common than copper, and twenty-five thousand times more common than tin, the two main components of bronze. Using iron made horse tack more readily available to the ordinary horse breeder, whereas costly bronze had been the preserve of chiefs.

The riders of Pazyryk had another innovation to their credit, one that solved the problem of mounted weaponry. They invented the composite bow—and, with it, the next twenty-five hundred years of mounted warfare.

The Shooters

The ancient composite bow is often called "Cupid's bow." The little love god's weapon of choice curves forward at the extremities, increasing the power of the shot when the bowstring is drawn. In fact, it takes such strong deltoids to draw the string, it's hard to imagine Cupid wielding such a bow. It takes even more strength to string the bow—that is, to attach the cord to the two notches on each outward-curving end. A steppe creation myth tells of three brothers competing to rule their people by seeing who can string their father's bow. The oldest suffers a broken tooth when the bow snaps back in his face. The middle brother winds up with a broken shin bone. ("The slightest twist, and the bow wrenches out of the hand and delivers a reprimanding strike to the errant archer," observed Mike Loades, a learned British reenactor who specializes in archery.) In the myth, only the youngest manages to bend the bow far back, string it, and release it slowly into taut readiness.

The bow was a deadly serious business. Mounted archery represented the

Scythian trying to string a bow, on a golden bowl from the Kul Oba Kurgan, Ukraine, fourth century BCE.

final step that made the horse the first weapon of mass destruction. Full-length bows had been too unwieldy for mounted hunting and combat. The composite bow solved that problem by packing more resistance into a much shorter length, and using bone and sinews in addition to wood in order to increase the elasticity of the frame. Such a bow, assembled by a steppe craftsman from sixteen pieces, almost like a Stradivarius, could take up to three years to complete. Once strung, the bow could then be handily slung over the shoulder or tied around the horse's neck. This weapon became a fixture of steppe warfare, as noted by many later observers, allowing the archer to avoid engaging in hand-to-hand combat, instead overcoming the enemy at a distance, with arrows. Mounted archers carried two or three quivers, each holding up to a hundred arrows, and released three or four volleys immediately at the start of combat. Arrows account for 90 percent of all traumas found on human remains in steppe burials.

So significant was this new way of making war that it provided the name by which these people self-identified. We don't know what the Sintashta people called themselves, but we know what the people of Pazyryk did. In their own Iranic* language, they were the Scudra; the word is closely cognate to the English word "shooter." All the settled peoples who left written histories of the first millennium used some variant of this name: the Chinese, the Persians, the Hebrews, and the Greeks transcribed Scudra respectively as Sei, Saka, Ashkenaz, and Scythians. Today we call them the Scythians, following the Greeks. The Greeks also accurately referred to them as "mounted archers" (ιπποτοζατοι) and milk eaters (γαλακτοφαγοι), the latter suggestive of the cult of fermented mare's milk that survives to our times in Kazakhstan and Mongolia. Rather than walking anywhere, they always rode, and, more disturbingly to the Greek historians, women participated in hunts and sometimes battles. Their mounted way of life, if not a single, defined political organization, stretched from the Danube in the west to what is now China's Gansu Province in the east. It is from the Scythians that the peoples of the northeastern steppe, today's Mongolia— the Huns, Turks, and Mongols—learned to ride and to shoot.

Mounted archery is still one of the world's most challenging sports, for it

---

* "Iranic" refers to related peoples outside of Iran itself.

requires great power in the knees to maintain stability during a gallop after fleet game or the enemy, as well as an ability to hold one's torso and shoulders absolutely immobile, almost like a gun platform on a rolling battleship. Today's Japanese *yabusame* horsemen perform this feat, which appears to entranced spectators as nothing short of miraculous, but they have the advantage of stirrups, unknown to the early shooters. The faster their horses gallop, the less the rider is jostled. The ability to hit a target from the rocking back of a horse's spine requires months of training for both archer and animal. Horses must learn not to shy away at the loud twang of the bow releasing, and to gallop straight on when the rider drops the reins and reaches backward to retrieve an arrow from his quiver. How the steppe archers became so skilled is explained by the ancient Chinese *Annals of the Great Historian*, one of our major sources for early steppe history: "The little boys start out by learning to ride sheep, and shoot birds and rats with a bow and arrow, and when they get a little older they shoot foxes and hares, which are used for food. Thus, all of the young men are able to use a bow and act as armed cavalry in time of war."

Mounted archery as a form of combat became, then, the next innovation of the steppe peoples, after riding and chariot driving. Whereas chariot warfare had been the privilege of a few aristocratic combatants, like Homer's heroes, the mounted archer emerged among the simple horse breeders. Advanced metallurgy, involving sophisticated craftsmanship and valuable materials, succumbed to a practice that involved less technology: a rudimentary saddle, no stirrups, at most a more articulated bit and bridle.

The riding horse, as developed by the Scythians, became the critical enabler of mass warfare. Unlike chariots, which had to be produced one at a time and so were not scalable, horse breeding was exponential, since mares foal each year and bear up to sixteen offspring over their twenty-year lives. A herd with 100 mares could grow theoretically into a herd of 824,925 mares within those twenty years. Horse power is, mathematically, inexhaustible, as long as one has pastureland. This unique capability of horses, which enabled Iron Age rulers to mobilize on a previously unknown scale, had far-ranging implications for the future of the steppe peoples and their neighbors.

A further Scythian contribution toward making steppe cavalry a mass phenomenon came with the steppe people's preference to ride geldings into battle, instead of stallions. This surprised the settled peoples, who had grown accustomed to stallions pulling chariots, and who associated stallions with warlike behavior. The Greek geographer Strabo felt this preference for geldings to be so strange that it required a special explanation. He noted that the steppe horses were small but exceedingly spirited—so spirited that their breeders adopted the practice of gelding the horses to make them easier to manage and quieter on the march. Some other horse peoples rode mares for this reason, but the steppe horse breeders preferred not to use mares for warfare, because they needed them for milk and for breeding. Stallions were indeed avoided, because they required much more effort to control, both during peacetime grazing and on campaign. During military operations they had to be hobbled with anklet blocks to prevent them from running off, which meant one could not quickly leap onto the horse's back in case of a surprise attack. These were problems that had not arisen in the days of chariots. So, from the Iron Age through to the nineteenth century, geldings became the traditional mount of the steppe peoples. This enabled them to muster larger forces and raise hardier mounts, less subject to disease and injury; the geldings also required less time to be broken in. In this way the steppe archers were able to take to the field with many more horses than they could have done if they had ridden stallions.

Putting all these innovations together, the Scythians started a revolution that brought an end to one thousand years of chariot domination. One group of Scythians, recalled in the Bible as Gog and Magog, rode into the Middle East around 700 BCE and blazed a trail of destruction from the Caucasus Mountains to Egypt. These mounted archers enjoyed many advantages over the chariot warriors sent out to fight them off, including speed, maneuverability, and, importantly, the possibility of felling one's enemies without the shock of contact. Mounted archers could triumph without suffering casualties, an important consideration for the horse breeders, who were not the elite soldiers of a king but more or less free men. The settled peoples recovered from the Scythian invasion and came to similar conclusions about the relative benefits of chariots and cavalry.

Just as in the second millennium BCE the settled states of the Middle East had taken up the chariot invented in the steppe, so now in the first millennium BCE they adopted bow-armed cavalry, though not without hesitation. Riding a horse required more skill than driving a chariot. Cavalry entered the armies of the settled states, like chariot driving, via steppe mercenaries, before spreading to native-born riders.

The Chinese had experienced the chariot revolution with a lag of five hundred years compared to the Middle East. Their switch to cavalry occurred late as well, but it is well documented in a famous, if apocryphal story concerning King Wuling of Zhao, who ruled from 325 to 299 BCE. This king decided his army should adopt the new techniques, which he called "wearing the Hu attire and shooting from horseback" (Chinese: 胡服骑射), Hu being the generic Chinese term for the steppe horsemen. Wuling insisted that his soldiers replace the long robes and calf-high bottines of the Chinese court with tight-fitting tunics, elbow-length sleeves, high boots, and belts, for ease of movement on horseback; in the days before stirrups, riders had to jump into the saddle, and they also needed to be able to manipulate the bow without losing their hands in their sleeves. Wuling's conservative, Confucian-minded advisers warned against this adoption of foreign, barbarian ways, arguing that no good could come of it, but Wuling persisted, attending court in his steppe outfit and even making a present of one such outfit to his most stubborn adversary. The king's views prevailed, and the state accordingly formed and trained a cavalry arm. Even if this anecdote is a literary invention, it pinpoints a moment in time when the Chinese recognized the need to emulate the steppe warriors on the battlefield. Numerous examples of bronze belt hooks from this period demonstrate the adoption of riding breeches.

Clothes make the man, but the impact of Wuling's reforms was anything but superficial. The adoption of cavalry completely changed the nature of warfare. Until that time, mainly aristocratic warriors had dominated the battlefield from their chariots. Neither aristocracy, nor chariots, nor heroism were in limitless supply, even for a Chinese king. But horses and mounted archers could be raised and trained on a very great scale. Battles of the Warring States Period, from 475 to 221 BCE, dwarfed in size those of the preceding eras, and prefigured the massive armies of Genghis Khan. The armies of the ancient Zhou dynasty of 770–256 BCE had fielded four thousand chariots; Wuling could now deploy ten thousand cavalry troopers in battle.

These cavalrymen were probably mercenaries, possibly Scythians. Warring States Period tombs excavated at Yuhuangmiao, 220 miles south of Beijing, contain no typical Chinese articles but are rich in steppe-style art and horse accoutrements. This suggests that the local rulers raised their cavalry forces from a separate, homogeneous group of horse breeders, who retained consciousness of their distinct, non-Chinese identity even in death. To recruit a clan of foreign warriors would have been a quick alternative compared to training locals in steppe warfare. From China to western Asia, the cavalry were coming.

Cavalry changed the dynamic between the steppe horse breeders and the settled states. Though the horse breeders had invented the chariot, the settled states could produce more of them, and at no time did the steppe peoples threaten the settled states with their chariots. But with cavalry, the power equilibrium changed. The multiplier effect of mounted masses meant that even relatively small steppe nations could attack and defeat powerful settled states. This threat encouraged the emergence of great settled empires, which grew as a function of the amount and quality of horses they, in turn, could mobilize.

3

Engines of Empire

Iran and India, 500 BCE–400 CE

୨୦

First Empires

The prophets of Israel saw in the depredations of the Scythians the forces of Gog and Magog, harbingers of the end of time. A few years later the world had not come to an end, but a new enemy may have made many wish that it had. About this menace the prophet Jeremiah warned:

> They shall hold the bow and the lance: they are cruel, and will not shew mercy: their voice shall roar like the sea, and they shall ride upon horses, everyone put in array, like a man to the battle, against thee.

Jeremiah was describing the army of Sennacherib, the Assyrian king who "came down like a wolf on the fold," sacked Babylon in 689 BCE, and cowed Jerusalem. Unlike the Scythians, the Assyrians did not disappear after their attacks; they came to conquer and to control. Sennacherib's successors extended Assyrian rule to Egypt, covering a territory of 540,000 square miles between the Tigris and the Nile, thus creating the world's first great empire.

Horses acted as the engine for the Assyrian Empire, whose conquests were based on the speed and mobility of their cavalry. The empire's maintenance depended on the endurance of the post horse to connect its far-flung provinces. Yet the Assyrians neither controlled extensive pastures nor

Assyrian warhorses in a frieze from a palace in Nineveh, seventh century BCE.

mastered the art of horseback riding. Horse breeders on the frontiers of Assyria contributed their horse power to the empire's ascent. This set a pattern of relationships between the horse breeders and the settled peoples that lasted for centuries. Their interactions subsequently gave rise to three empires that far surpassed the Assyrians in size: the Persians in western Asia, the Mauryas in India, and the Qin in China.

It cannot be coincidental that these empires emerged following the horse breeders' migrations into the settled lands. The many wars that so embroiled the settled peoples made the horse breeders welcome suppliers of war horses, mercenaries, and auxiliaries, and the horse breeders were happy to help a select number of ambitious nations in their struggles for power over their neighbors. Scythian raids convinced the settled states that they had better equip themselves with cavalry, and encouraged the creation of large, multinational states with ever-expanding territorial ambitions.

In the seventh century BCE, the Assyrians, masters of the ancient capital of Nineveh in today's Iraq, acquired horses and recruited cavalrymen from the horse-breeding Medes, a people settled in northern Iran since the ninth century BCE, and closely related to the Scythians of the

steppe. This was the Assyrians' second bite of the apple, as centuries earlier they had tried, but failed, to expand their power beyond the valleys of
the Tigris and the Euphrates Rivers, though they did manage to conquer
Mitanni, whose charioteers had been trained by Kikkuli. In those days,
the Assyrians had had no cavalry; now, Median horses would power their
unprecedented expansion.

The Assyrian monarchs played up the terror that their cavalry inspired in
contemporary witnesses like Jeremiah. They proudly portrayed themselves
on horseback in the first known royal equestrian portraits. An alabaster
bas-relief from Nineveh depicts King Ashurbanipal mounting a superbly
harnessed horse. The Assyrians probably did not ride as well as the Medes,
since the native Assyrian cavalrymen are often depicted riding side by side,
with one trooper guiding both horses while the other wields his bow and
arrows, preserving the division of labor practiced by the charioteer and his
bowman. In other reliefs, one sees grooms, with the headdresses and trousers of Medes, bringing magnificent horses to the Assyrian king.

The Medes introduced the Assyrians to the finer points of horsemanship.
They rode with sophisticated harnesses, featuring jointed snaffle bits that
sat more easily in the horses' delicate mouths; elegantly sculptured cheek
plates (*psalia*), which connected the bridle to the bit, providing guidance
through the cheeks as well as the lips; and a martingale, a strap connecting
the bridle and the breast strap, which held the proud horses' heads down,
discouraging them from rearing. The martingales sported pom-pom-like
feathers that undulated with the movement of the horses' heads. Pectoral
bands and croupiers secured the saddlecloths. Scenes of battle, lion hunts,
and military parades show off the Median cavalry of the kings of Assyria in
all their equestrian splendor.

This dependence on Median riders proved to be the Achilles' heel of the
Assyrian Empire. The Medes revolted against their overlords in 612 BCE,
sacked Nineveh, and established their own empire. After suffering from a
revolt of their auxiliary Scythian cavalry, the Medes, in turn, succumbed to
Cyrus the Persian in 550 BCE.[*]

---

[*] In what follows, Persia will refer only to the empire founded by Cyrus. The country will
be called Iran.

The Persians hailed from Fars (originally called Pars, Hellenized as Περσία), in southwest Iran, where there is evidence of horse breeding since the second millennium BCE. The Persians quickly made themselves masters of Iran, absorbing a number of horse-breeding peoples between the Zagros Mountains in the west and the Oxus River in the east. Many Scythians pastured both within and without these borders. The ancient world considered the Persians, culturally cousins to both the Medes and the Scythians, consummate cavaliers. "To ride a horse," wrote the fifth-century Greek historian Herodotus, "is the first thing every Persian child learns." "God," asserts a monumental royal inscription, "has given me Persia, the land of good horses." The Persian rulers drank water only from the river Huvaspa, of "Good Horses." As with the Plains Indians of America, the ancient Persians often bore personal names referring to horsemanship, like Gushtasp (Racing Horse) or Siyavosh (Dark Stallion). Secure in their own equestrian prowess, the Persians pursued their ambition to rule a vast, settled empire without depending on cavalry from steppe horse breeders, who had provoked the downfall of both Assyria and Media. This became an ideological imperative.

The Persians are said to have invented dualism, with a religion that pitted good against evil. They projected this duality onto the ecological boundary between the settled and the steppe. The urban, agricultural Persian empire had to be defended against the pastoralists from beyond the Oxus. This duality appears in their earliest legends, according to which the gods themselves ride on white stallions and protect the lands of Iran against the forces of evil, mounted on black chargers. This sense of Iran as the "well-protected realm," to use one of the country's traditional epithets, and the steppe raiders as Iran's inveterate enemies infuses the later national epic, the *Shahnameh*, and the symbolism of good and evil carried through into court ceremonies, where it was expressed through horses. The king of kings rode a white horse. Sacrifices of white horses accompanied solemn occasions. Beyond such potent symbolism, horses were embraced by the Persians with bureaucratic thoroughness.

As the newly proclaimed king of kings, Cyrus implemented extensive governmental measures to sustain his horse power. A settled empire, if it did not want to rely on steppe horse breeders to furnish remounts from their unlimited herds, necessarily had to breed and feed its own horses with professional grooms and harvested forage—at great expense. Cyrus therefore ordered the creation of three stud farms, in today's Kurdistan, Azerbaijan, and Fars, under the watchful care of a full staff of guards, grooms, and veterinarians. Horses were grazed in herds of uniform colors—roans, grays, chestnuts, and jet blacks—to make them easier to track down if one should be stolen. The grooms also marked them with the imperial brand, the *nishan*. We do not know which *nishan* the king of kings used in this period, but extant royal sealing stones show bold geometric designs that recall the planetary signs of astrology, and that resemble later *nishans* used by subsequent dynasties in Iran. The notion that horses represented celestial forces was never entirely absent.

The elite Persian cavalry became famous for the Nisaean horses from Media, which appear stocky, ram-nosed, and powerful on the bas-reliefs of Persepolis, the capital of Cyrus and his successors, near modern-day Shiraz. Their manes are buzz-cut into a kind of brush that makes them look fierce and wild. Each forelock, the part that naturally flops down over the eyes, is knotted into a tuft, to make the horse look even taller. The tail is also knotted, as a precaution for combat. The tack includes a breast strap and a girth strap to hold in place the soft, Pazyryk-style saddle pad. On the bas-relief the horses' powerfully muscled bodies seem to be holding up the walls behind them, and after twenty-five hundred years, they still look ready to gallop up the triumphal staircases into the imperial courtyards. These horses are medium-sized by modern standards, at fifteen hands, but solidly built and weighing some one thousand pounds. The Nisaeans grazed on the pastures of ancient Media, near present-day Kermanshah, still the horse-breeding territory of today's Iranian Kurds. The Medes and Persians had to raise these heavier horses for chieftains and elite troopers, who wore armor and protected their horses against opposing arrow shots with breast plates, all of which would have added forty pounds to the weight of the rider. It was no surprise that the Nisaean horses' hooves "shook the earth," according to Herodotus.

The Nisaean and other Persian breeds enabled Cyrus and his successor Darius to build through conquest the largest empire the world had yet known, stretching from the Indus River in today's Pakistan to the Sardis in western Anatolia—twice as big as the preceding empire of the Medes, and four times larger than the Assyrian Empire. The Persians failed to conquer Greece, where sea power, and not horse power, played the decisive role. The rocky terrain of the Greek Peninsula inhibited the deployment of cavalry armies. In contrast, lands like Syria and Egypt offered little resistance to the Persian cavalry.

Horses enabled the Persians to govern their vast empire, as well. To connect the far-flung provinces with the imperial capitals of Persepolis and Susa, the Persians organized a system of relay or post horses, similar to that of the Assyrians. As echoed in the inscriptions in front of many U.S. post offices, neither sleet nor dark of night deterred these couriers from carrying messages to the ends of the empire. The word "post" originally referred to the wooden stakes to which the courier tied his winded horse and from which he released his fresh remount. A mounted messenger could gallop eighteen miles an hour, so with a change of horses at each of the one hundred-odd post stations, he could carry the king of kings' commands from Persepolis, in southwestern Iran, to Sardis, in nine days, a journey requiring ninety days on foot. This system of command and control proved essential for the Persian and later empires. Fifteen centuries later, to administer the largest land empire of all time, the Mongols instituted a similarly extensive system of post horses.

Cavalry and empire are like the chicken and the egg. Without cavalry, the Persians could not have conquered and maintained the empire they did. They and subsequent empires depended on the speed and mobility of horses to project power across great distances. Without an empire, maintaining such a large cavalry force off the steppe would have been impossible. The three horse stud farms, widely dispersed, each with several thousand horses, required a whole bureaucracy to manage. Cultivating alfalfa, a superfood for horses, and transporting it to the stud farms in the winter would have been another imperial challenge. The cost and effort to maintain such a cavalry force as the Persians fielded were beyond the capabilities of the smaller states of western Asia. Indeed, the Athenian Empire, with a larger fleet than the Persians, had just 650 horses in its cavalry.

Persian cavalry made an immense impression on the peoples of western Asia. From the era of Cyrus's conquest of Babylon in 539 BCE we find all

The Rise of Empires: Persia and India

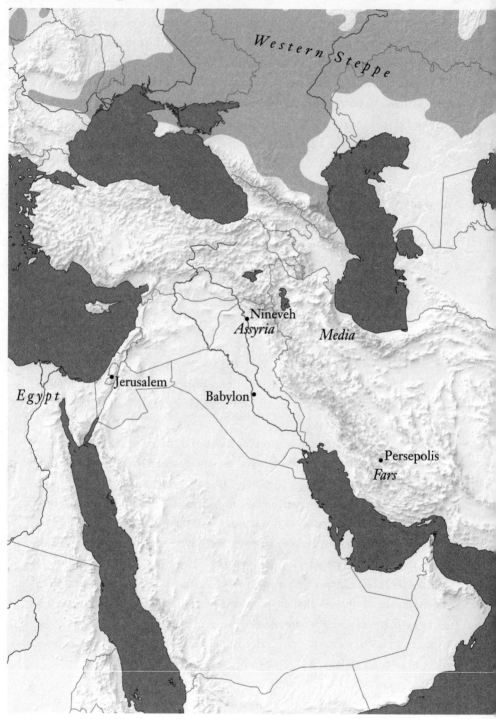

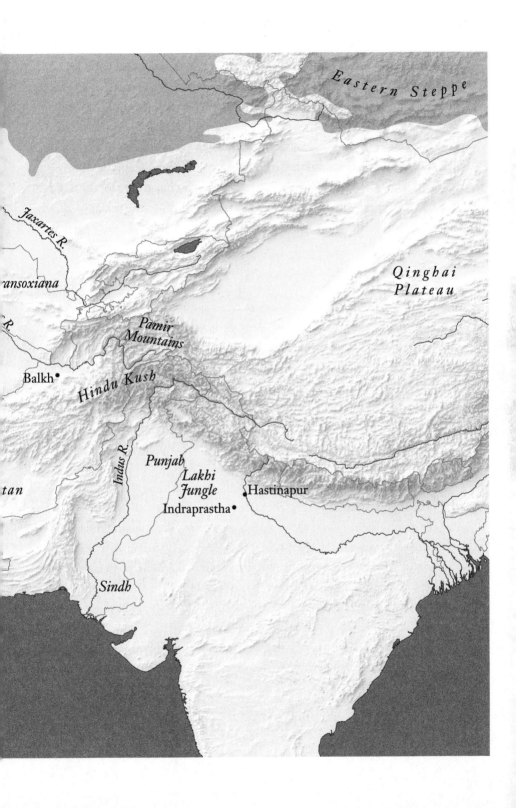

over the empire hundreds of terra-cotta figures of horsemen in traditional
Persian dress, armed with a short sword and a combined bow and arrow
quiver. These appear to be votary objects, which the local subject people
may have offered up to their gods. The Persian cavalryman appeared to
them as a powerful, prestigious symbol, worthy as a divine offering. This
may have been the origin of the toy horse, that tiny incitement for children
to dream about horses pounding their hooves in an imaginary race around
the nursery. These clay horsemen are a fitting legacy for the ancient world's
most extensive empire.

The Steppe and the Stable

Cyrus, the king of kings, enjoyed horse races as a means of celebrating and
demonstrating his immense power. Possibly for the spring equinox, the Iranian New Year, he turned out his entire cavalry, rather like the modern-day
May First parade in Moscow. First came his private stud of two hundred
horses, with gold-chased bridles, caparisoned in brocade. Three divisions
each of ten thousand Persian troopers followed his train. The cavalry of
the subject nations brought up the rearguard: the Medes; the Assyrians; the
Armenians; levies from Gilan and Gorgan, by the Caspian Sea; and, finally,
the independent Scythian auxiliaries.

Cyrus designated the course around an obstacle several miles distant,
and ordered the riders, nation by nation, to gallop at full speed around
this point and back. While this seems like a lot of riders competing at the
same time, the practice is not unusual in Asia, which still hosts equestrian
contests involving hundreds of participants, and where the whip is used as
much on the competitors as on one's own horse. Cyrus did not organize
races between the national teams, because this likely would have ended in
outright hand-to-hand combat. The Persians went first.

We owe the description of this horse race to Xenophon the Athenian,
who served as commander of contemporary Athens's pocket-sized cavalry
forces. He authored Europe's first manual on horsemanship, *Peri Hippikes*,
an otherwise dull book that has dismayed generations of schoolchildren
studying classical Greek. Xenophon reports that Cyrus came in first among

the Persians because of his diligent attention to horsemanship, not because his subordinates gave the king a generous handicap.

Each of the subject nations competed in succession. The winner of the Scythian heat was not a chief but a private trooper, who dashed around the course and crossed the finish line before his pursuers could reach the midpoint. Deeply impressed, Cyrus offered the young man a kingdom in exchange for his winning horse. The proud Scythian horse breeder refused the Persian king of kings. Cyrus magnanimously laughed off this affront—or was it a nervous laugh? Hero-worshipping Xenophon would have the reader believe that Cyrus had nothing to fear from the Scythians. In fact, they would be the death of him, in some versions of history.

Even when incorporated as auxiliaries into the Persian armies, the Scythians and their horses represented a threat to any empire, though less so than in the era of the Medes and the dangerously dependent Assyrians. The tale of Cyrus's horse race can be read as a parable for this rivalry, and it poses a question: Which proud nation had the best horses, the settled Persians or the steppe-dwelling Scythians?

This was not only a matter of racing and prestige; having the best horse was a matter of life or death, victory or defeat. Nations and riders strove to raise elite horses to prevail on the battlefield. An elite horse was more than a fast or a strong animal. It had great emotional intelligence. It anticipated the aims of its rider, whether attacking or fleeing. It learned to rear up and trample the enemy with its hooves, the caracole movement today performed in dressage events. In a mêlée going the wrong way, even a wounded horse would try to save the life of its rider. A good horse was indeed worth a kingdom.

Hence the care with which the warriors of this era chose their horses. The *Shahnameh* describes its greatest hero, Rustam, selecting his battle steed in an echo of the ancient myth of the Ossetes, though here the focus is on selecting the right horse: one that "can carry my steel mace, and will not shrink from the fray." The herds of Zabulistan, a horse-breeding region of southwest Afghanistan, are driven before the young hero; as far as the eye can see, the plains are covered with livestock. To try them out, Rustam vaults onto the back of horse after horse. Each one crumples under his weight, belly dragging on the ground, until one mare is led forth, powerful as a tiger. Her two ears are like steel daggers—that is, upright; her neck is thick, her flanks trim. Beside this mare trots a foal—black-eyed, narrow-barreled, well-paced—which does not run away, because the humans have tethered his dam. His body has firm flanks; his coat is rose-red with streaks of saffron yellow. In strength he is like an elephant, in stature like a camel. No man had ever been able to ride him until Rustam climbs onto his back. The fiery foal instinctively acknowledges his new master and becomes Rustam's faithful warhorse, named Rakhsh after his fire-red coat. When Rustam gives him his head to test his courage, strength, and blood, Rakhsh is able to carry rider, mace, and mail. In flight no deer could be swifter. He has a gentle mouth, foaming. He is light on the reins, clever, well-paced. In short, Rakhsh is the epitome of the superior warhorse.

Thomas Atkinson described the relationship between the warrior and his horse this way:

> [The rider] loves his horse. . . . When on a journey, the animal is teth-ered at night beside his master's earthy couch, and then he acts the part of a faithful watchdog. Nothing can approach without his giving notice, and by the snort or the tone of recognition his master knows whether friend or foe is at hand.

Indeed, the legendary Rakhsh defends the sleeping Rustam from nocturnal attacks by a lion, a snake, and, finally, a dragon before Rustam understands just how devoted to his safety Rakhsh is. Atkinson concludes, "The horse often possesses more intelligence than his master."

Both the Persians and the Scythians sought to raise horses like Rakhsh, and they perfected their distinct practices for raising superior, powerful horses—the original arms race.

The Persians had the advantages that money could buy. The imperial treasury supported the breeding and feeding of some one hundred thou-sand animals, and the stud farms sent ten thousand remounts a year for the king of kings' imperial needs. These were all or mostly stallions, of a height remarked upon by all the ancient sources. To grow such statuesque steeds, the Persians took care of both the foaling mares and the young, growing foals. While ordinary mares were allowed or encouraged to foal yearly, prize breeding mares were given longer rests between pregnancies. This yielded bigger and stronger offspring. The foals themselves pastured undisturbed for two or three years before the breaking process began, which allowed them to develop bigger and stronger bones and muscles. This was a costly and time-consuming practice that produced high-performance horses, suitable for highly trained cavalry troopers.

Since these young stallions were spirited and potentially dangerous animals, they required extensive training once they joined their regiments. The Persians most likely developed the exercises seen today in elite dressage events, including jumping and performing acrobatics on horseback. Stallions are more subject to accidents and disease than geldings, so they required constant attention by their troopers and grooms. The Persians did not let their horses graze on campaign, and instead hobbled them and hand-fed them alfalfa. This ensured that the horses did not fall sick pasturing on unfamiliar grasses, but it entailed a costly system of provisioning, and could not be indefinitely relied upon during a long campaign. This would matter when the Persians tried to chase the marauding Scythians back into their boundless steppe.

The typical Scythian warhorses, in contrast to the pampered horses of the king of kings, were tough and wiry, raised for speed, the ability to go without water for long periods, and resistance to cold. The total number of horses was limited only by rainfall and grass growth; compared with the Persians, they enjoyed an overwhelming advantage in sheer quantity. They did not limit the number of foals born each year, for their horses provided food as well as mobility. They did not wait two to three years before breaking their foals in, so their horses did not develop the height and strength of the Persian mounts. For steppe peoples, height and strength meant a horse that would always be hungry and, therefore, one that might not survive a harsh winter, when grass was scarce. Nor did the Scythians want to keep too many stallions—such horses would disrupt their herds—so they gelded most of their male colts. This also reduced their average size, but it made them easier to ride and required less elite training on the part of the masses of Scythian riders.

The Scythians also had elite horses, but here, too, the Scythians used the advantage of numbers. Horses, like people, are not born physically equal. Some have bigger hearts, which enables them to sustain faster speeds. Others have more powerful limbs or tougher feet. These are the innate differences that enabled the Scythian horse to win Cyrus's racing competition and caused others to fall behind. The Scythians identified equine talent out of an immense pool, just as Olympic trainers do in populous countries like the United States, Russia, and China. The ability to find such superior horses, fit for chiefs and champions, became the stuff of steppe legends.

In one such tale, a rider finds a horse skull bleaching in the steppe. He dismounts to pick it up and, upon examining the shape of the skull, detects signs of a superior horse—indeed, a great racing horse. He ties the skull to his saddle, and for months thereafter he rides around asking people he meets if they recognize the dead horse and if there are any surviving progeny. Though most people he meets conclude he has gone mad, one person indeed recognizes the skull and tells the horse expert where to find a foal sired by the dead horse. He acquires this foal, trains it with care, and carries off racing prize after racing prize.

The physical prowess of such horses could seem magical, since scientific breeding practices had yet to appear. The scale at which ancient breeding took place precluded micromanaging the mating rites of stallions and mares. Both Persian and Scythian horses roamed in open spaces, and nature took its course among them. Riders of this period attached a special significance to coat colors, associating them with celestial symbolism. The practice of herding particular coat colors together resulted in some pronounced genetic phenomena. Ancient riders appreciated leopard-spotted coats; Rakhsh's dappling was a variant of this. The gene for this coat coloring is closely associated with another for night blindness, which is to say the two genes are found close together on a chromosome, and so the two traits are likely to be passed on together from parent to offspring. There's speculation that early breeders appreciated this blindness, because it made horses harder to steal during the night.

After identifying a superior horse, the steppe peoples, no less than the sophisticated Persians, had techniques for rearing and conditioning their horses to produce winners. They accorded these horses gentler conditioning than that reserved for ordinary geldings. The elite horses benefited from better diets, particularly in the winter, when no expense was spared for the young horse to grow and develop its strength. Since the steppe people had no stables, the elite horses wore heavy blankets in the winter or would even escape especially bitter cold nights in the family tent. The horse breeders tended to give these horses unique names, while the run-of-the-mill horse was simply known by its color ("the bay," "the piebald"). The oral epics have a rich vocabulary of epithets for these horses: "doesn't sweat," "doesn't touch the ground" and "gazelle-fast."

Scythian elite horse-raising practices differed from those of the Persians, reflecting their particular ways of life. As Cyrus saw at his horse race, both the Persians and the Scythians possessed superior horses. Victory depended on choosing how to engage in battle.

Scythian-Persian Rivalry

Enjoying the impunity that their swift and hard-to-wind steeds afforded them, the Scythians frequently raided the lands of the Persian Empire and, later, the Indian subcontinent. As noted, an important duty of the king of kings was to defend the sedentary peoples under his protection from this predation. A rare painting of a Persian-Scythian battle scene from a tomb in southeast Anatolia provides a vivid snapshot of these conflicts. The Persian mounted archers on the right and the Scythian mounted archers on the left are arrayed against each other, discharging volleys of arrows from between the alert ears of their mounts. The Persian horses are bigger and stockier, and their riders keep a tight formation. The Scythians, on slighter animals, ride in dispersed order. The dismounted chief of the Persians, shown larger than life, deals a death blow to his adversary. This painting celebrates a Persian victory over Scythian raiders, either a historical or an aspirational one. Yet while the Persian cavalry was more than adequate to chase the Scythians back to the steppe, it was not enough to subdue the steppe itself.

Cyrus the Great felt obliged to respond to the Scythians' raiding by taking the battle into Scythian territory, in an attempt to subordinate them to his rule. He marched his army across the Oxus River, which separates today's Turkmenistan from Uzbekistan. The Scythians, under their Amazon-like Queen Tomyris, prudently retreated deeper into the steppe.

Cyrus offered peace and a couch in the imperial harem to Tomyris, who, unsurprisingly, refused. The Persian army then rode dangerously far from their base.

This was not friendly country for a large army with thirsty animals. The steppe beyond the Oxus River stretched for miles with scarcely any visible features. Only saxaul trees, with their needle-like leaves, interrupted the flat landscape. Goats could feed on the succulent bark of these trees, but there was little grass for horses, and especially not for a cavalry of ten thousand. Donkeys carried water and feed for them, but they, in turn, required provisions. Later armies crossed these steppes using camels in place of donkeys, which provided a much greater range of operations. But in Cyrus's time, his proud cavalry depended on the humble donkey and its limited capacity to survive without water.

The donkeys helped win Cyrus's first victories: the Scythian horses took fright at their braying in the Persians' immense baggage train and fled. After many days in the steppe, however, exhausted and short of supplies, the Persians succumbed to Scythian mounted archers. According to some accounts, Cyrus himself was slain, and Tomyris ordered that his head be brought to her. First she had it sewn into a drinking skin full of human blood, "to slake his thirst." Then she made a goblet out of his skull by sawing off the portion of the bone below the eyebrows, covering the pate with leather, and lining the inside with gold. Thereafter, whenever the queen hosted parties at court, the skull of Cyrus would circulate, filled with wine, and the story of his defeat would be retold.

The Persians, for their part, largely learned their lesson and refrained from future attempts to conquer the steppe. Even if the story of Cyrus and Tomyris is apocryphal, it served to justify more prudent policies. These included fortifying the eastern frontier against the steppe peoples and awaiting their attacks. The *Shahnameh* tells of legendary paladins, riding powerful steeds, chasing invaders back into the steppe. The opponents are well matched in horse power, so the conflict continues reign after reign. The *Shahnameh*'s tales of heroes and their steeds never lost their currency for the Iranians, who continued to confront steppe invaders in the form of Scythians, Huns, Turks, and Mongols. Two thousand years after Cyrus, another Iranian shah defeated an army of steppe invaders and turned their khan's skull into a drinking goblet, in an act of unconscious retribution.*

The Clash of Horse and Elephant

In another tale from the *Shahnameh*, an Indian ambassador to Iran brings a puzzle to test the shah's vizier, Bozorgmehr, famed for his wisdom. It consists of a cloth painted with alternate black and white squares, and two sets of tiny figurines, carved in ivory and teak. Bozorgmehr is given one day to study the components and explain the puzzle's significance in the presence of the shah and the Indian emissaries. After a long, studious night, he confidently declares that the Indian puzzle is, in fact, a board game, one that imitates the battlefield. The figurines represent opposing armies, each comprising a king, a vizier, elephants, cavalrymen, charioteers, and foot soldiers.

The game was, of course, chess, and the movements of each piece reflected their counterparts in the world of warfare. Foot soldiers, today's pawns, plodded forward. Charioteers, today's rooks (from the Sanskrit *ratha*, "chariot," via Persian), were posted on either flank and galloped rapidly in a straight line. Horses, or knights, attacked with flanking maneuvers. Elephants, the bishops of Western chess (once called fools, from the Persian *fil*, elephant), stood close to the king and the vizier (now the queen) and careened wildly at an angle. The vizier could use a chariot or an elephant, and so move in all directions. The puzzle gift of the Indian ambassador sent a warning that the Indian monarch's army had mastered all these means of warfare, so the Iranians had better treat him with appropriate respect. While the charioteer and the horseman had been imported into India from the steppe, the elephant was a particularly Indian phenomenon, and a worthy rival, in Indian eyes, for the foreign war vehicles. Nowhere else did another animal challenge the horse on the battlefield or inspire the symbolism of state power. Much of the difference in how horse power

---

* Unconscious because the Iranians did not rediscover the history of Cyrus until the nineteenth century, when a young Iranian student in England translated Herodotus into Persian.

played out in Iran versus India, the land of good horses versus the land of the elephant, can be explained by geography.

The Indian subcontinent is separated from the Eurasian steppe primarily by the Himalaya Mountains, which rise to twenty thousand feet on average, and to a lesser extent by the Pamirs and the Hindu Kush, farther west. This mountain barrier traps the moist air of the Indian Ocean over the subcontinent, creating both the dryness of the Inner Asian Steppe, favorable for horses, and the monsoon cycle in India. Horses do not thrive in the wet and hot climate produced by the monsoon. Though its heavy rains between June and September bring lush and abundant grasses, horses are picky eaters, and the rich flora of India holds too many unfamiliar or unappetizing surprises for them. Overabundant rain also leaches the grass of nutrients, depriving the pasturing horse of vital minerals, especially selenium. Monsoon rains soften the horses' hooves, making them fragile for riding over stony paths. In the following dry season, the sun is so strong and the evaporation so complete that the field becomes parched, and horses find nothing to eat. Much of fertile India teems with agriculture, so that even in places where conditions for horse breeding are favorable, the horse's expansive requirement for pasturage comes into conflict with the farmers' need for tillage. In many parts of India, therefore, horses are scarce on the ground.

The least-horse-friendly regions are heavily forested. The monsoon, spilling thirty to fifty-nine inches of rain per year, favors the growth of neem, acacia, pine, and creepers. They form a lush canopy that covers the northeast quadrant of the subcontinent. Today, India is home to three hundred thousand square miles of forest, a larger area than Texas. The aboriginal forest, before agricultural clearing, would have been much larger. Many incidents in Indian history and legend take the forest as their setting: this is where kings went hunting, where princes spent their exile, where hermits and holy men, like the Buddha, retreated for meditation. Indian classical and folk literature is remarkable for the omnipresence of forest animals, including monkeys, tigers, lions, snakes, and, of course, elephants. The Sanskrit epic the Mahabharata describes the ancient Ganges Valley, the site of titanic conflicts between two rival princely clans, as a region of dense forests. One clan clears the forest to build its capital, Indraprastha, later to become Delhi. The rivals hold court in a forest city, Hastinapur, its name meaning "Elephant City."

The elephant is the forest dweller par excellence, since its stomach requires 330 pounds of forage a day; that is 5 percent of its own body weight, as compared to 1.5 percent for the frugal horse, which requires only 20 pounds. This much food is available to a wild elephant only in its native forest, where it feeds itself for sixteen hours a day. In the first millennium BCE, when India's primeval forest abounded in elephants, their destructive presence frightened people and encouraged the rulers, the local rajas, to round them up and capture them. Once tamed, the elephants proved useful for transportation and warfare, in a domestication process similar to that of horses. However, unlike the horse, which can feed itself in suitable pastures, the elephant's feeding requirements are so burdensome on its owners that only the mightiest rajas, or maharajas, could afford to stable these powerful animals. Soon the very possession of elephants signified kingship, as it still does for Thailand's monarchy. Enticed by the warlike character of bull elephants, maharajas struck their coins with images of the elephant, and competed with one another to amass the largest elephant armies. Though they used horses to drive their chariots, they rode into battle on elephants.

As in the game of chess, both elephants and horses had useful military roles, depending on the terrain. The elephant was the preferred vehicle for war in the forest, where horses could not pasture nor large cavalry forces maneuver. The horse was in its element in the grasslands, where the elephant could not feed itself. As reported in a much later, thirteenth-century chronicle, some steppe warriors captured war elephants and turned them loose to pasture. To the warriors' surprise, the elephants all died of starvation. The steppe raiders of the fifth century BCE had little use for India's elephants, as they avoided penetrating too deeply into hot, humid, forested India. In the right terrain, the superior strategic and tactical flexibility of cavalry over elephants was demonstrated time and again, even if the fearsome combat ability of elephants and their majestic appearance continued to seduce Indian rulers into thinking they could beat cavalry with elephants alone. At the head of their powerful elephant-led armies, many an Indian monarch fell into the trap of accepting battle with horse-riding invaders on the open plains of the Indus and Ganges Valleys, after they had largely been cleared of forest. Horse-riding invaders of India, from Alexander the Great to the first Mughal emperor, Babur, owed their successes to the overconfidence of their elephant-mounted adversaries.

A big disadvantage of elephants as compared to horses is one of scale. Although horses can be bred in large quantities, elephants are typically captured in the wild, as they do not reproduce well in captivity. A mare foals every year, while an elephant cow calves once every two years. The cavalry armies of the Persians and the hordes of the Scythians contained tens of thousands of horses; the elephant armies of the Indian princes numbered in the thousands only. Indian elephants were good for defending the royal capitals, but not so useful for expanding the realm to distant provinces; nor could many of them be deployed at the same time, for lack of forage. As a result, during the fifth and fourth centuries BCE, when the Persians ruled from the Aegean to the Indus, India contained just a brace of smaller kingdoms, concentrated in the heavily forested center and east of India. With elephants alone, the Indian maharajas could not rival their western neighbors. The story of the chess game shows that they gradually became aware of this.

Relief showing horses and elephants in combat, Maheshwar temple, 1666.

The subcontinent is not uniformly inhospitable to horses. India enjoys a variety of localized climatic conditions, some of which are more than adequate for horse raising. The western marches—Baluchistan, Sindh, Punjab, and Rajasthan—form a natural extension of the steppe lands, stretching from Afghanistan in the north to the shores of the Arabian Sea in the south. They lie too far west to be subject to the monsoon's drenching. There are other islands of natural grasslands: the plateau of the Deccan, in India's hilly south, and the foothills of the Himalayas. At even higher altitudes, in Ladakh, Leh, and Nepal, hardy races of ponies flourish.

The dry and grassy plains of Punjab offered attractive pastures for Scythian horse breeders. Traditionally, these lands were considered a wild, scarcely populated frontier, far from the subcontinent's centers of power and population, so these pastoralists faced little opposition when they moved there in the middle of the first millennium. As in western Asia, steppe peoples migrating into India gained employment as mercenaries in the armies of Indian states located farther south and to the east; the newcomers probably formed India's first cavalry units. Centuries earlier, the Bronze Age chariot-driving steppe peoples had migrated into Punjab and brought the chariot revolution. Now Iron Age immigrants from the steppe would spark India's cavalry revolution.

In the fourth century BCE, when the Persian empire was already at its height, the first Indian imperial dynasty, the Nanda, had only just arisen in the Ganges Valley. As previous rulers had, the Nanda relied on elephants to dominate their base in the eastern, forested tracks of the empire. But it was necessary to adopt a new cavalry arm to hold their western frontiers against horse-mounted incursions from the steppe or from Iran. (Indeed, the fierce reputation of the Nanda cavalry persuaded Alexander the Great of Macedon to call a halt to his invasion of central India in 326 BCE, after his victory over the Persians.) The Nanda were able to conquer Bihar, Bengal, and Madhya Pradesh with their eighty-thousand-strong cavalry, in addition to three thousand war elephants.

A rival dynasty, the Mauryas, supported by Scythian, Macedonian, and Persian mercenaries, succeeded in overthrowing the Nanda Empire in 322 BCE. Details of this revolution provide the basis for the Sanskrit drama *Mudrarakshasa*, including much legendary material about the dynasty's founder Chandragupta Maurya and his wily vizier, Chanakya. What is sure is that Chandragupta, on coming to power, took pains to preserve the Nanda prowess in cavalry.

According to tradition, Chanakya, also known as Kautilya, compiled an extensive guide to statecraft for Chandragupta. This work, the *Arthashastra* ("Compendium of Principles"), devotes several chapters to horses and cavalry. Here Chanakya advised his ruler where to acquire good horses and how to raise them. He recommended horses from Kamboja (today's Hazara district in Pakistan), Sindh, or Aratta, the northern plains of Punjab. Horses from Vanayu, referring either to Iran or Afghanistan, and Balkh, now Mazar-e Sharif, in northern Afghanistan, also met with Chanakya's approval. Twelve hundred years later, cavalry general Firuz Jang recommended the same sources to his Mughal masters.

Raising horses in the inclement Indian environment required special care. For one, they had to be stabled. Chanakya addressed the psychological needs of stabled horse with insights that seem both quaint and modern: "Stables must include broad and airy spaces, which should also house monkeys, peacocks, red spotted deer, mongoose, partridges, parrots, and mina birds." This ensured that horses did not become lonely, antisocial, and hard to manage.

In the absence of fresh steppe grasses, the horses' feed demanded no less attention. Indian breeders preferred horses with glossy coats and a layer of fat under the skin, requiring an especially rich diet. Chanakya recommended that "horses should be fed clarified butter, flour and oil." For bulk, green wheat was mixed with chaff. Wheat or rice mixed with cow's milk, or even mutton meat with clarified butter, was provided. "A horse can adapt to different diets, even biryani, as long as it has time to get used to it," advises Indian equestrian and author Yashaswini Chandra. While the cost of feeding horses on such a diet would have appeared ruinous to the free-range Scythians or to the alfalfa-growing Iranians, compared to the feeding of gluttonous elephants, it must have seemed a bargain.

Besides stables and special diets, horses in the monsoon climate of India required constant medical attention. Scholarly pandits trained in veterinary science compiled extensive manuals about how to treat the diseases that afflicted horses. The post-Maurya, fourth-century CE *Aśvashastra*, or

"Compendium of Rules for Horses," described horse ailments and remedies in twelve thousand rhymed Sanskrit verses. This manual became a classic, read, commented on, and augmented for the next thousand years; it was even translated into Persian by the same Firuz Jang.

Finally, in addition to the proper sourcing and care of horses, the Mauryas, like the Persians before them, mastered the logistics required to maintain such a large cavalry force outside the steppe. They established a rigorous bureaucracy, with specialists in charge of forage, grooms, and specific services for horses, elephants, and baggage-train oxen. The state maintained a monopoly on the ownership of elephants and horses. For the elephants, this reflected a continuation of their traditional association with royalty. For horses, this reflected the difficulty of maintaining the stock in the Indian environment—only a powerful empire could afford such expense.

Maintaining these stables of costly horses and elephants contributed to the dynastic prestige of the Maurya rulers. They gloried in the power represented by both animals. Maharajas organized magnificent and gory battles between bull elephants in rut, which, when elephant combat spilled into the stands, were often more dangerous for the spectators than for the participants. By contrast, the biggest danger of popular horse races lay in the risk that already badly addicted gamblers would lose everything betting on their favorite champions. As an indication of the popularity of racing, Sanskrit has an expression for aphrodisiacs: "something that turns a man into a racehorse." The Kamasutra further warns, "A horse at full gallop, blinded by the energy of its own speed, pays no attention to any post or hole or ditch on the path—so are two lovers blinded by passion."

The size and prowess of the Maurya cavalry impressed the foreigners who wrote about India in the first centuries of the Common Era. The first-century CE Roman polymath Pliny the Elder estimated the size of the Maurya cavalry at thirty thousand horses. Corresponding estimates of elephant numbers range between three thousand and nine thousand, consistent with the greater scale of horse power versus elephant power.

The Mauryas did not maintain all these animals simply to assert their prestige. They were the first Indian dynasty to deploy horse power not only to repel invaders from the northwest frontier but even to conquer

Gupta racehorse and jockey, fourth to fifth century CE.

Punjab and Afghanistan in 303 BCE. There are no Maurya histories about
these conquests, for they preferred poetry to dry, annalistic writing. A
later, fourth-century CE epic by one of India's greatest poets, Kalidasa,
gives us a sense of how the Maurya campaigns probably unfolded. Their
campaigns may have even inspired Kalidasa. The poet's legendary hero,
Raghu, mustered his army of footmen, chariots, elephants, and cavalry, just
as in chess, to repel Scythian invaders. First, he chased them back across
the Indus River. Then, as the pursuit stretched into the Khyber Pass and
the Hindu Kush, the footmen, chariots, and elephants fell behind. Raghu's
cavalry army followed the Scythians into the chilly forests of chestnut
trees and snowcapped mountains. One thousand miles later, on the banks
of the Oxus River, near where Cyrus met his death eight hundred years
earlier, the Indian and Scythian cavalry locked together in combat. The
dust raised by the horses' hooves made it impossible for the combatants
to distinguish friend from foe, but for the distinctive twang of their bows.
Raghu's forces carpeted the ground with the bearded heads of the enemy,
whose bodies were riddled with arrows as though stung by a swarm of bees.

The Scythians doffed their helmets in submission, as their women, who had also ridden into battle, blushed in shame. The victorious Indian cavalry cooled their horses in the Oxus, while the Scythian chiefs surrendered gold and warhorses as peace offerings.

Whether the Indians really fared better than Cyrus against the Scythians on their home terrain cannot be known, but by securing Afghanistan—which was probably the objective of Raghu's legendary expedition—the real-life Mauryas did manage to establish a bulwark against steppe invasion. From the Mauryas in the second century to the Mughals in the sixteenth, and even the British Raj in the nineteenth, India's rulers strove to control Afghanistan to deprive the horsemen of their base of attack, and to use the pastures of Afghanistan to raise their own horses. Indian empires either succeeded at this and thrived, or failed and disappeared. After the fall of the Mauryas, steppe people resumed their raids into the subcontinent.

The speed and mobility of the horse turned it into a formidable weapon for the steppe peoples, and the adoption of cavalry coincided with the emergence of empire in Iran as well as in India. For the Persians, Scythians, and Indians, horse power meant the ability to conquer or to remain independent. Farther east, in horse-poor China, that competition for horse power played out on a continental scale.

4

Desperately Seeking
Heavenly Horses

China, 200 BCE–400 CE

⥀

China and Its Unruly Frontier

In the Year of the Horse, 770 BCE, a group of dissident courtiers plotted to overthrow King You, ruler of the three-hundred-year-old Zhou dynasty. They hit on the idea of recruiting foreign horse breeders to their cause. They asked the Dog Rong, a powerful pastoralist people, to attack the Zhou capital of Haojing (near present-day Xi'an) and depose the monarch. As an initial payment, they sent a cart loaded with gold and silk, and they also dangled the prospect of plundering the royal palace of its treasures. Delighted with this bargain, the khan of the Dog Rong mobilized fifteen thousand cavalrymen. This mass of horsemen, waving aloft their swords and spears, surged forward like a wave toward the unsuspecting and undefended city, surrounding it and cutting off its water supply. The city duly surrendered, and the Dog Rong thoroughly sacked it. They then, however, showed no urgency to ride back into the steppe.

The plotters realized too late that while it had been easy to recruit the Dog Rong to invade the Zhou capital, it was harder to get them to leave their new conquest. A combination of such steppe incursions and internal dissension is what gradually tipped China into the turbulence of the Warring States Period, from 475 to 221 BCE.

The Zhou had ruled a federation of chariot-driving, aristocratic clans by exploiting ritual and tradition more than hard power. The Dog Rong's attacks and deadly mounted archery destroyed the prestige of the Zhou and announced the obsolescence of the chariot. To defend themselves against the Dog Rong, the now-independent clans developed their own horse power. This was the moment when one of the now-nominal Zhou vassals, Wuling of Zhao, convinced his court to "wear the Hu attire and shoot from horseback," provoking an arms race among the clans as they fought with one another to secure hegemony over the rich northern plain of China. The attendant social disruption inspired the reflections of moral philosophers like Zhuangzi. As in Iran and India, so in China, the arrival of steppe horse breeders coincided with the emergence of the first empires. How these empires subsequently acquired and maintained horse power sufficient for their imperial ambitions furnished the material of durable legends.

There were a dozen or more groups of horse breeders along the thousand-mile frontier between the steppe and the Warring States. The Chinese knew these peoples by a variety of names, including Rong, Dong, Di, Wusun, and Yuezhi. It is often hard to attribute these names to a specific, identifiable ethnicity. The Dog Rong, named for their canine totem, may have been of Tibetan origin. Other horse breeders were the same Scythians who had, in the course of the first millennium, extended their pastures from the Altai Mountains all the way to Shaanxi Province, at that time the western frontier of China. Still others may have hailed from another ancient Central Asian people, the Tokharians.

To the north, in today's Mongolia, a people of unknown origin had adopted many Scythian habits in the course of the third century BCE, including herding the four heads, glorious metallurgy, hunting, and mounted archery. They referred to themselves as "those who draw the bow," the same meaning as the ethnonym Scythian; the Chinese called them the Clamorous Barbarians, or Xiongnu. As it is likely they were the ancestors of the Huns, I will use this later name for the sake of familiarity. These early Huns left behind relics that distinguish them from the Scythians. They used stone slabs for graves and placed petroglyphs of reindeer across their grasslands, prefiguring the later monuments of the Turks. Even their arrowheads differed from those of the Scythians, having just two blades instead of three. But in many other ways, the Huns resembled the Scythians, with whom they fought and cooperated, and whom they

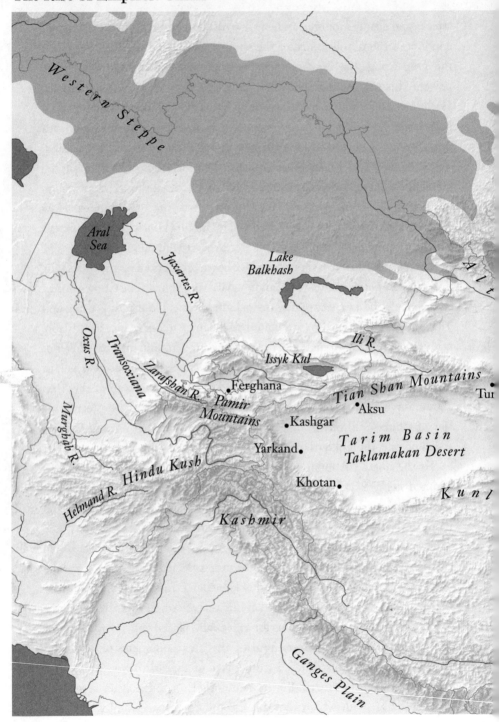

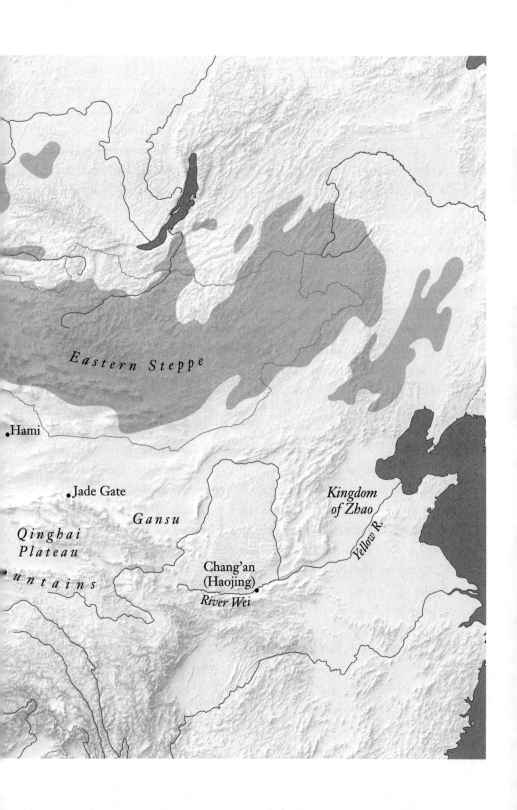

Hami

Jade Gate

Gansu

Qinghai
Plateau

untains

Eastern Steppe

Kingdom
of Zhao

Yellow R.

Chang'an
(Haojing)

River Wei

ultimately absorbed. Whatever their ethnolinguistic origins, these two peoples' horse-breeding activities made them both valued and dangerous neighbors for China. Over time, the Huns would grow to be the biggest and most powerful of the horse-breeding peoples on the frontier.

In addition to serving as mercenaries or raiders on their own account, the horse breeders also enjoyed brisk business in supplying warhorses to all the Warring States. Steppe tombs from this period are rich with silver and gold ornaments received in return for horses. The horse trading took place at walled fortifications erected by the Warring States out in the steppe adjacent to each of their territories. Sections of these walls would much later be consolidated into what came to be known as the Great Wall of China, but these early walls were simple, isolated forts of compressed earth. Still, they provided protection to local Chinese garrisons in their dealings with the steppe peoples. Proximity to these trading posts gave the western Warring States the advantage when it came to procuring horses.

The westernmost of the Warring States, Qin, may itself have been of steppe origin. Situated along the Wei River, the cradle of the Qin clan had hosted colonies of horse breeders for centuries. The Wei, a tributary of the Yellow River, formed an ecological frontier between favorable pasturelands to the north and wetter, more agricultural lands to the south. The seventeenth-century writer Feng Menglong noted that the Qin state's "customs differed little from those of the steppe peoples," like the Dog Rong, with whom they frequently fought. The founder of the Qin dynasty began his career serving the diminished Zhou court, for whom he procured horses. As a reward for finally driving the Dog Rong out of their now-ruined capital, the Zhou recognized him as the independent ruler of Qin. Of all the Warring States, Qin developed the reputation of being the most warlike—the Prussia of China—and developed the largest cavalry arm. The prince who succeeded to the Qin throne in 246 BCE embarked on a buildup of military power to knock out Qin's rivals once and for all, and in twenty-five years of almost incessant conflict he defeated and annexed the other Warring States, proclaiming himself in 221 BCE Shi Huangdi, 始黄帝, the "First Emperor." The ghosts of his massive army attract nine million tourists a year to his tomb near his ancient capital, modern Xi'an.

The Horses of the First Emperor

They stand respectfully beside their horses, their left hands gripping now-invisible reins. These cavalry troopers are tall, five feet ten inches in their knee-high boots and trousers. Their horses, many of them geldings, stand thirteen hands high, the size required by Qin cavalry regulations. The horses' ears stretch forward, awaiting commands. Their manes are cropped close, to facilitate mounted archery, their tails clipped for close combat. Their muzzles are thick, resembling today's Mongolian horses. They wear blankets on their backs, carefully attached with three girths, and low-slung, Scythian-style soft saddles.

These cavalrymen and horses belong to the terra-cotta army of China's First Emperor, part of his massive burial site, discovered in Shaanxi Province by farmers in 1971. The horses, like the rest of the army—thirteen hundred figures of which have been unearthed so far—were created in molds, yielding life-sized reproductions. After being fired in kilns at 1,800 degrees, the figures were incised and polished; this finishing gave each of

Terracotta horses from the First Emperor's tomb, first century BCE, Xi'an, Shaanxi.

the horses a different expression and variations in the eyes, nostrils, and set of the ears. The horses were painted in bright pigments—red, pink, and ochre—and their eyes would have looked lively, with white sclerae and black pupils. Finally, a lacquer finish was applied to preserve the colors. Alas, two thousand years of oxidation have turned the horses the uniform brown of terra-cotta.

The realism and detail of these figures enables scholars to distinguish close affinities with the horse tack of the Pazyryk burials. The soft saddle looks like it is stuffed with animal fur. The bridle system is the same as in Pazyryk, with a distinctive S- shaped cheek piece. The crenellated manes with square tufts recall the braided manes shown on Scythian metalware. The debt of Shi Huangdi's cavalry to the steppe horse breeders is unmistakable.

The monumental tomb, of which only 1 percent of its twenty-square-mile perimeter has been excavated to date, has yielded 116 cavalry troopers, 670 horses, and 516 chariots and drivers. The minuteness and faithfulness of the figures gives us a snapshot of what a third-century BCE Chinese army must have looked like, capturing a moment in Chinese history when rulers had not entirely given up on massed chariots but increasingly valued cavalry.

The tomb also reveals a change in attitude toward the horse itself and its use as a ritual object. Earlier burials contain tens or hundreds of sacrificed horses, as well as people. This tomb, so far, has yielded only four sacrificial horses, in a nod to the funeral practices of the Shang and Zhou dynasties. Although the site of the First Emperor was subsequently forgotten, later historians recorded the equine sacrifices performed at his interment: the horses all had coats of the same sorrel color and were buried alive, together with a bronze chariot and its team of small bronze dragons in the harness. From the Qin dynastic period on, we no longer find mass burials of horses. The horses had become a strategic resource for the state, which endured after the death of the emperor. Shi Huangdi used life-sized statues in place of the traditional horse and human victims. Subsequent dynasties, including the Han and the Tang, would also send off the dead with sculptures, no longer life-sized but of great liveliness.

In life as in death, the First Emperor marshaled his horse power methodically. Expanding on the bureaucracy he inherited from the Qin state, he instituted a Grand Stable, a Palace Stable, and a Middle Stable, each with its own criteria for animal selection, protocol, and carefully monitored grooms. The minimum size for warhorses, as reflected by both the tomb's statues and the equine remains, was set at five *chi* eight *chun*, corresponding to four feet five inches, or just over thirteen hands. While this seems small by the modern riding-horse standards of fifteen to seventeen hands, it corresponded to the average steppe breeders' horse. Keeping this cavalry up to strength required ruthless discipline. Severe punishments were meted out to state servants who failed to acquire sufficient horses or preserve them in good condition. This enabled the First Emperor to mobilize a cavalry army ten thousand troopers strong.

The extensive cavalry administration of the First Emperor survived his short-lived dynasty. When the Han dynasty seized power after a brief interregnum, they maintained and extended the imperial offices responsible for horse power. During the four-hundred-year reign of the Han, from 202 BCE to 220 CE, the chamberlain of the imperial stable, or chief equerry, held one of the great offices of state. Under him served directors for different departments, including the eternal stables of the inner palace, imperial mares, livery office, imperial hunting chariots, cavalry mounts, finest steeds, thoroughbreds, an office for requisition of military horses from the provinces for the capital, stables for fine horses of the left and the right (wings of the army), a directorate of dragon horses, more prosaically a directorate of horse corrals, and several directorates of pasturage. As under the Qin, grooms and stable hands were recruited from the steppe peoples. The tradition of elaborate hierarchy, with the chamberlain-equerry in the emperor's inner circle of government, persisted in subsequent Chinese dynasties and, indeed, in all subsequent Eurasian empires. This underlined the importance of raising horses for these great states.

During the five-year Qin-Han interregnum, however, these officers had responsibilities only on paper. The number of available cavalry horses plunged dramatically because of civil war and disruption. The great stables were abandoned, and the grooms rode home to the steppe with the horses

Han dynasty bronze chariot, first century CE, Henan.

under their care. There were so few horses available, reported the *Annals of the Great Historian*, that "the Son of Heaven himself could not find four horses of the same color for his chariot. Many of his generals and ministers were reduced to riding about in ox carts." Horse sacrifices had to be suspended. The Chinese empire, so dependent on horses, could not raise enough horses to replace their losses.

China's Troubles with Horses

When the Chinese first encountered horses, around 1200 BCE, during the age of chariots, the foreign animal enjoyed an aura of magic and mystery. Elaborate burial and divination rituals date to this era and continued through imperial times. Superior horses, it was thought, were not just foreign but celestial (天馬, *tianma*). This implied that breeding them was not something anyone could do. Nevertheless, the Chinese began to dutifully study the animals to see what they could learn.

The first Chinese hippology expert was Bole; though he may be a

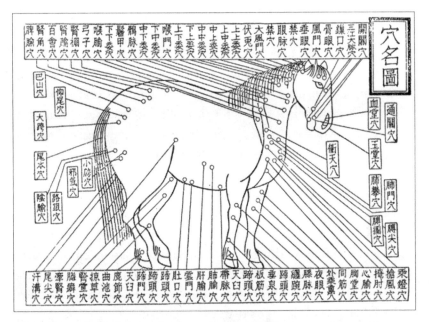

Hippology diagram inspired by Bole, seventh century BCE.

legendary rather than a historical figure, he is traditionally dated to the seventh century BCE. Later writers attributed to Bole the invention of physiognomy (想馬, *xiangma*), as the key to unlocking the secrets of the superior horse. The many recommendations ascribed to Bole, collected in the Han dynasty annals, have an enigmatic ring to them:

> Chestnut horses with shoulders that are yellow marked with black, horses with coats like that of a deer marked with yellow, dappled horses, and white horses with black manes all are good horses. If there is a streak of white running from the forehead into the mouth, and servants ride this kind of horse, they die outside their own country. If a master rides it, he will be executed in the marketplace. A horse with white rear feet, left and right, will kill women.

Elsewhere, Bole is said to have advised: "The implantation of hair under the stomach should be in the opposite direction of the hair of the loins.

This horse can cover 1,000 li in a day. If not, the horse will only do 500 li."*
These assertions are puzzling, but similar statements were repeated over
the centuries in traditional hippology manuals across China, India, and
Iran. Modern researchers have investigated the correlation between whorls,
or hair-direction changes, in laterality, or left- and right-handedness. They
suspect that some horses have subtle laterality preferences, which, if the
rider is unaware of them, can cause accidents. Bole's empirical observations
may have alerted him to the potential danger of certain whorls.

These advisories surely also reflected the importance of the horse's
visual impact as much as its functionality. The emperor's chariot was always
drawn by horses of identical, auspicious colors and markings. It may be that
certain colorings were associated with more sought-after bloodlines.

For all that, Bole's writings and Chinese hippology in general offered
little practical advice about actually raising good horses, and for centuries
China struggled to do so. More than a thousand years later, the Jesuit polymath Matteo Ricci found the situation unchanged:

> The Chinese have countless horses in the service of the army, but
> these are so degenerate and lacking in martial spirit that they are put
> to rout by the neighing of the [steppe] steeds, and so they are practi-
> cally useless in battle.

Indeed, the Chinese word for warhorse, 戎 馬, or *rong ma*, literally means
"western foreigners' horse," recalling the Dog Rong and pointing to the
horses' origins as imports. But even after horses were imported from
the west, their offspring grew to be smaller and feebler than their sires,
to the surprise and frustration of those responsible for the imperial studs.

With the aim of improving the quality of horses in the imperial stud
farms, in or about the year 30 CE, the gruff General Ma Yuan (馬 援)
presented to the Han emperor, Guangwu, a startling memorial in the form
of a bronze statue of a horse. This was a bold choice, given the value the

---

* 腹下欲平,有 八 字;腹下毛,欲前向。腹欲大而垂結,脈欲多 大道筋 欲
大而直。(' 大道筋',從腋下抵股者是。)腹下陰前,兩邊生逆毛入腹帶者,行
千里;一尺者,五百里。(Yu Xin). One thousand li is approximately three hundred miles.

court placed on sagaciously composed, beautifully penned documents cit-
ing ancient sages such as Bole, but the battle-hardened veteran minced no
words in explaining that his statue was worth a thousand words of description. "His Majesty," he said, "needs to acquire more horses that look like
this one." Surely the courtiers were not surprised by this general's preoccupation with horses. His surname, Ma, meant "horse." His ancestor Ma Fu
Jun was the "prince who tames horses" (馬服君).

Though no trace remains of Ma Yuan's statue, a contemporaneous tomb
offering provides a glimpse of what the general would have envisaged as the
ideal horse. It shows powerful, symmetrical chest muscles and haunches,
both conceived as spheres, as Bole recommended. Its back and belly are
both delineated with straight lines, with no curve. Its limbs are long and
elegant. Its neck is held high; its ears are pricked up; its nostrils are huge;
its muzzle is squared above and rounded below, with a prominently round
jaw. Its eyes bulge out of their sockets. With one hoof on the ground and
its head rearing to one side, it gives the impression of flight. This "Flying

The Flying Horse of Gansu, second century CE.

Horse of Gansu" represented everything imperial China wanted in a horse but could not easily obtain.

Many factors contributed to China's poor track record with horse breeding. The first was an inappropriate diet. The heartland territory of the Han dynasty, including modern Shaanxi, Shanxi, Henan, and Shandong Provinces, did not provide the healthy, mineral-rich grasses that horses required for growth, so even the offspring of a sixteen-hand-high stallion might never grow beyond thirteen hands. Raising tall horses requires selenium and calcium, which the heavier rainfall of China leaches out of the soil and, thus, the grass. It was not easy to procure the superfood alfalfa. A scholar-poet from the ninth century CE, Liu Yuxi, tells the story of receiving a gift colt from a friend responsible for selecting warhorses on the northern frontier. "I fed it [ordinary] grass and straw," he admits. Later, he sells the foal to a horse-wise friend for mere pennies. The new owner ensures that the animal is fed alfalfa, is washed down and dried off, and has an immaculate stable. Before long, reports Liu Yuxi regretfully, the foal grows to be an exceptional horse, one for which the Imperial Dragon Stables offer a thousand pieces of gold.

The conditioning of imperial Chinese horses was also lacking. A Han dynasty mandarin complained in 177 BCE that "the territory of the Huns and the [horse riding] skills it demands are different from those of China. It requires climbing up and down mountains and crossing ravines and mountain torrents. The horses of China cannot compare with those of the Huns." Horses have evolved to be constantly moving; on campaign, a cavalry of stable-raised and fodder-fed mounts could never develop endurance to match the steppe cavalry; nor would the troopers be anywhere as intrepid. The only way to maintain first-rate cavalry mounts is to consistently use them for war and warlike activities like hunting and raiding. Paradoxically, it was only through constant conflict that the Chinese cavalry could maintain an edge, through sheer numbers. Periods of peace frequently ended in sudden military disaster, since both horses and men lost their conditioning and their spirit in idleness.

The Huns' horses also dominated those of the Chinese in battles of will, causing the latter to panic and flee. A stabled horse suffers from metabolic, digestive, circulatory, and even psychological weaknesses. Free-range horses develop greater aggressiveness and fewer fears than stabled horses. Again, Liu Yuxi sees where he went wrong:

I kept [my horse] in a dark and damp stable. When he pranced and jumped, I thought he was going to kick and bite, so I hit him with a beating whip, not knowing he was trying to ascend to the clouds. As for the way he breathed and snorted, I thought he was sick and diseased, so I merely threw him some medicinal grasses, not knowing he was trying to spout jade.

This scarcity of horse know-how handicapped the native Chinese rider, but citizens also feared that if they were too successful in breeding horses, the Imperial Dragon Stables would simply requisition the best animals, rather than paying one thousand strings of gold for them. This happened frequently enough to be a real risk. Even when the government officially encouraged the breeding of horses by the population, the prices paid for them compared to the cost and effort undertaken by the breeder often proved disappointing. There is a world of difference between raising an animal that will save your own life in war and raising an animal to offset your taxes.

The huge Han empire even had difficulties feeding its horses. The regions favorable for growing fodder like alfalfa—Gansu and Ningxia— were the very locations the emperor was hoping to transform into arable land for peasant farming, and indeed, before long, the government was ceding to popular pressure to turn the land over for cultivation. In addition, the transport of preferred forage to breeding stations presented logistical challenges. Feeding horses in this way remained an expensive proposition, compared to pasturing them. As in other settled empires, maintaining cavalry weighed on the state treasury. War, of course, would make it weigh heavier. Despite all their efforts, the Han, with their thirty-six stud farms, never managed to resupply their cavalry with adequate horses.

Chinese difficulties in raising good horses became proverbial, featuring as part of traditional Chinese self-deprecation. As much as the emperor demanded more and improved horses, those with civil and military responsibilities had to tactfully disabuse their ruler, with all the risks that speaking truth to power entailed. The Chinese were acutely conscious of the homesickness felt by horses for their native steppe. An elegy by the same Liu Yuxi laments a horse's decline and death as owing to nothing less than this:

He struggled in the wind and rain. He looked askance, not upward. My
horse, how could he survive like this? He walked with short steps, con-
tinually looking back. He stopped and tugged at his bridle. Each day
he drank and ate less. From lack of energy he grew sickly. He was mel-
ancholy in the cold stable. Tired, his coat became patchy. He pranced
when he smelled the [northern route]. He longed to gallop forward
into that scent. He made sounds that he wanted to go. Dispirited, he
could only go back to his home once dead. He was a famous horse of
the Yuezhi, his home in Central Asia. His destiny was to pasture daily.
He would have been happy to reach the west. Often people say this
breed needs grass. People say this color of coat is not found on the
Central Plains. They scrutinize the coat and they wonder who could
be its sire? The Han say, "In the Emperor Wu's mausoleum, there is
a spring, the dragon's source." I cast your bones, my friend, into the
dragon's spring.

Of all the settled empires, China suffered the most from its deficit in
horse power, even as it admired horses as the source of political supremacy
and for their almost supernatural beauty. China therefore developed a
dangerous dependence on the steppe peoples to supply superior horses—
a dependence on the very raiders with whom they struggled for control over
the thousand-mile steppe frontier.

Gift Horses

Horses, because of their beauty and mobility, have always been a gift of
choice among steppe peoples. Originally they were not so much bought and
sold as offered in an intricate protocol of gift giving and receiving, as in the
age of the chariot warriors. From these early contacts between the steppe
and the settled, the steppe practice of offering gifts of horses to the Chinese
persisted for centuries, this ritual disguising what was in effect the state
procuring resources from their enemies.

Already in the third century BCE, the growing Qin dynasty employed
its well-oiled bureaucracy to make this a highly organized and efficient
exchange. Qin officials arranged for regular deliveries of steppe horses to

the customs checkpoints nestled in the gates of what would become the Great Wall.* Because of the Qin's high demand, neighboring breeders secured horses from other breeders farther out in the steppe. When Qin officials realized that they were now dealing only with middlemen, they annexed the neighboring territories so they could receive horses directly from the more distant but more productive breeders.

Following the practice of the Qin, the Han court continued to promote state-to-state exchanges that entailed elaborate gifting rituals. In this way, for example, the king of Yarkand, one of the cities of the Tarim Basin, offered horses to the Han court and received a chariot, gold, bright silks, and embroideries in return. The Chinese were buying not only horses but also loyalty. The Han court also tried to bind the chiefs among the horse breeders into the imperial family with opportunely offered, well-born brides.

The steppe missions to China frequently occasioned violence and disorder, another reason why the Chinese sought close control over their suppliers. Individual horse breeders tried to join official trade missions, so that the missions' size became unwieldy and their presence on Chinese territory threatening. The Han emperors were particularly punctilious about limiting access to high-level official exchanges. Around 35 BCE, after one diplomatic imbroglio, Emperor Chengdi of the Han complained: "Kashmir regrets its former actions, and comes to us as suppliants, but among those who make offerings there are neither members of the royal family nor nobility. They are all traveling merchants and men of low status who wish to trade in the markets under the pretext of offering gifts." This emperor's angry rebuke about low-born people attaching themselves to the embassies reflects a concern that gift quantity could replace gift quality. Later chronicles speak of trade missions two thousand strong, despite repeated remonstrances from the Chinese government to limit the number to fifty.

The Han state was also haunted by the knowledge that exchanges with the steppe dwellers enriched their opponents and even facilitated their military ambitions. The Han were in effect dependent on a strategic weapon, horses,

---

* Fortifications on the steppe frontier were already a feature of the Warring States Period. The Qin built up and connected these barriers even more extensively, leaving an example followed by many later dynasties, including the Han and the Ming, the latter of which built the wall we see today.

supplied by their adversaries. Freer access to supply horses inside the Great Wall, which the horse breeders eagerly sought, would have given them a precise idea of the state of the Han cavalry, providing valuable military intelligence for planning their forays. It is not surprising that the Han remained reluctant to open up access beyond the Great Wall to the steppe peoples.

As much as the Chinese valued the steppe peoples' ability to breed horses, they found them grasping and greedy, always eager for more Chinese products, like mirrors of silver, lacquer, and silk fabric. The Chinese hoped that accustoming the horse breeders to luxury would make them soft, inoffensive neighbors, without understanding how they actually used these valuable and easily transportable objects.

For the Chinese failed to see that the horse breeders' khans gave away everything they received from China as quickly as they acquired it. They were not seeking to accumulate stored wealth, since, in any case, they had no place to keep it. They distributed the gold and silk to neighbors farther out in the steppe to buy their political loyalty. The more gifts a khan could provide, the farther his influence extended. Far from weakening the khan's bellicosity, the gifts made him more powerful. He used his influence to ensure peaceful coexistence among the horse breeders and their flocks, and to resolve conflicts over kidnapped brides or cattle rustling. If challenged to military action, the khan could call on his gift-receiving allies for support in the field. Since the khans had a limited ability to impose their decisions on their fellow horse breeders, unlimited generosity was more effective than violence. A khan who could extract luxury goods from China could maintain a powerful network of loyal followers; one who could not was quickly abandoned or replaced by another. Chinese objects are found far into the steppe, signs of alliances formed between distant groups of horse breeders. For these reasons, the khans made inexhaustible demands on China, earning themselves a reputation for avarice.

The horse breeders had another motivation for constantly seeking to sell more livestock to the Chinese. Breeding led to expanding herds. The horse breeders could eat only so many of their own horses, whose population grew much faster than their own. Extra horses had to be sold, and if the Chinese would not buy them, the horses could be, and had to be, used for war. War, in turn, stimulated Chinese demand for horses, creating favorable conditions for raising even more horses. This insight appears to have escaped the otherwise perspicacious and observant Chinese historians of the Han and even some later dynasties, as the dynamic of raiding and trading across the steppe frontier persisted for two thousand years, in many rounds of tit-for-tat conflict.

Whenever the gifts offered were inadequate or the number of horses procured too low relative to supply, the horse breeders launched raids to encourage the Chinese to offer a better deal. Hostilities also resulted when the Chinese imposed embargoes to punish the horse breeders for bad behavior. At other times, the horse breeders embargoed China. Managing these unruly neighbors was an unceasing challenge, and the subjects of horses and gifts, war and peace, constantly came up during the deliberations of court ministers. China's dependence on horses from the steppe continued to grow with successive dynasties. But their unwillingness to allow free exchange with the steppe had an unexpected—and, for them, perilous—consequence. It gave birth to the first steppe empire, that of the Huns.

The Huns Monopolize Horses

At the end of the third century BCE, a young man from a powerful Hun clan on the Chinese border was sent as a hostage to the Scythians, many thousands of miles away. There, through observation of the Scythian-Iranian rivalry, he learned much about statecraft and warcraft. Later, he escaped back to his own people, where he evinced a steely ambition. He gathered a war band around him, and to test his men's loyalty, he ordered them to shoot arrows at any target he designated, on pain of death for hesitation. He shot an arrow at his favorite horse, followed by a fatal volley from his followers. The young leader and his band then shot dead his favorite wife and, finally, his father. Modun, as the young man was called, took over as chief of his clan. But his ambition extended much further than this, and the Chinese practice of controlling horse procurement furnished him the means to realize that ambition.

That system amounted to what economists now call a monopsony, the power of a single buyer. The Chinese state used its position as the foremost buyer of horses to set the terms of trade between the steppe and the empire, mandating exactly what quality of silk or gold would be provided in exchange for a specified kind of horse. The horse breeders were frustrated by the lack of free access to the Chinese market; they knew that if they could ride into China and deal directly with a myriad of buyers, they could negotiate much better prices. Clans of horse breeders periodically went to war to try to "open" the Chinese market, but the Han were more than capable of dealing with these raids, and as often as not bought off the raiders with a few more gifts and brides.

For Modun, however, the existence of these tightly restricted markets provided an opportunity as well as a constraint. Modun knew that the Chinese acquired horses at only a few border points, making it easy for him to monopolize the supply of steppe horses. If he could create such a monopoly and impose himself as the sole steppe interlocutor with China, he would command as much power and awe as the emperor himself. It required only an adroit combination of military and diplomatic successes against both China and his fellow horse breeders.

So Modun proclaimed himself paramount leader, the *chanyu* (the title is equivalent to the later term *khaghan*). To face off with the Chinese, he organized his court with its own protocol and hierarchies, perhaps reflecting his experience among the Scythians and what he had learned about the old Persian Empire. Using a combination of generosity and aggression, the new leader subjugated all the steppe peoples and created a unified bloc of horse breeders in what is today Mongolia. Through sheer size and hegemony, Modun had the power to reward and punish as no earlier steppe chief would have imagined.

With a combined population of only one million souls but over a million horses, the Huns posed a threat to China, with its population of fifty-four million. China could not match the Huns' ability to mobilize quickly and concentrate their forces locally. Unlike the settled empires, with their specialized bureaucracy and slow-moving decision-making, Modun's army and civilian administration were one and the same. Generals of the left wing, the right wing, and the center ruled over the tents and camps assigned to their wings, allocated pastures and migration routes, and organized hunting and war raids. Each of the army wings fielded horses of a uniform color: white for the right, westerly wing, blue gray for the left, easterly wing, and golden palomino for the center. Geomancy determined these colors and augured world dominion for such an army. Whereas the horse breeders had previously only raided the Han, Modun's ability to unite 240,000 cavalry troopers put them in a position to invade western China. At the dawn of the second century BCE, the cycle of steppe empires challenging the Chinese empire itself had begun.

Serious fighting now broke out across the frontier, where the Great Wall proved to be more of a customs barrier than an effective fortification. The Han made a major remount effort, acquiring twenty thousand to thirty thousand horses, but after a particularly pyrrhic victory over the Huns, the emperor was again forced "to reduce the expenses of his own table, dispense with his carriage drawn by four horses of matched color, and pay out money from his private reserves in order to make up the deficiency." The Chinese nevertheless succeeded in repelling Hun raids but dreaded campaigning on the north side of the Great Wall. As one Han minister is reported to have said,

No profit comes to an army that has to fight a thousand miles from home. The Hun move on the feet of swift warhorses, and in their breasts beat the hearts of beasts. They shift from place to place as fast as a flock of birds, so that it is extremely difficult to corner them and bring them under control. Though we were to win possession of their land, it would be no great addition to the empire.

Indeed, as soon as one leaves the vicinity of the Yellow River, bent like a dragon's back toward today's Inner Mongolia, the Gobi appears, a tree-less, trackless land, carpeted with stones and pebbles, which makes walking painful, and riding dangerous for horses with hooves unused to such hard, sharp terrain. Though in springtime there is plenty of grass, in August, the summer heat toasts the land camel-pelt brown. There are a few water-courses, which can sustain a handful of horsemen with their flocks, but are not enough for a large army to slake its collective thirst.*

---

* Today, small Chinese farms are to be seen incongruously pitched out in the desert, their gardens of squash covered with a thin layer of sandy dust. Since Han dynasty times, these hardy farmers have been trying to make the desert bloom. Two thousand years later it is still too early call it victory or defeat.

Han Wudi ("the Martial Emperor of the Han"), did, however, manage to fight the Huns to a standstill. His victories were extremely costly. In 124 BCE, victorious soldiers earned prizes of more than two hundred catties* of gold each, and even the enemy prisoners were sent home with gifts, food, and clothing. Chinese losses in these victories, which included 140,000 horses, were four times greater than those of the Huns. The Han empire, though, outnumbered the Huns nine to one, so this war of attrition was costly for the horse breeders, as well. The Huns duly sued for peace.

The settlement reached between the Han and the Huns allowed, and indeed encouraged, the chanyu to maintain his imperial status. The transfer of so many costly gifts placed a heavy burden on the Han empire of 54 million people; so, one can imagine the hugely welcome impact these gifts must have had on the million people under Hun rule. The flow of gifts to the leaders enabled them to acquire the loyalty of countless lower chiefs, and to cement their control over the wide steppe.

This is the source of the splendid gold, ivory, and jade objects that have been discovered in the Mongolian steppe. Bridle and saddle ornaments figure prominently, decorated with images of horses, unicorns, and fantastic beasts imagined by Chinese artists as living in the uncouth north. The imagery of horned and winged ungulates perhaps recalls the ancient reindeer hunters of the Huns' ancestors. The vast quantity of these artifacts demonstrates the great power of the Hun empire and its success at extracting wealth from Han China.

Even after a peace agreement was reached, from time to time the chanyu launched large raids, equivalent to invasions, against his "older brother," the Han emperor. This occurred when he either wanted to direct his followers' energies against an external foe or needed to raise his prestige through successful combat. If the chanyu and the lesser leaders allowed peaceful relations with China to last for too long, younger or poorer Huns with little to lose and hopes of gaining some booty or reputation would continue to carry out raids against the Chinese without the chanyu's authorization. This led the Chinese to mistrust him. Perhaps he did try to end raiding

---

* Presumably awarded only as a significant distinction, since a catty weighs somewhere between one and two pounds.

when it suited his purposes, but he also tolerated raiding when the danger from internal discontent was greater than that of Chinese ripostes. The Chinese remained confounded by the Huns' lack of sincerity, a characteristically Chinese value that implies reliability as well as truthfulness. Yet the behavior of the chanyu and the Huns was anything but unpredictable.

Continuing to monopolize the relationship with China was key to the Huns' power. If the Han state could procure horses from multiple horse-breeding states, the position of the chanyu would be threatened, and so the Hun confederation expanded to the west, in order to absorb as many potential rivals as possible. Rebellions were put down with fearful cruelty: rivals were boiled alive or tied to wild stallions, always as a warning to others. There was no natural frontier to the west of the Huns; all the horse-breeding peoples of Central and Inner Asia were potential horse suppliers. Accordingly, the Huns extended their empire eighteen hundred miles to the west, to the Aral Sea, including much of modern Kazakhstan. They controlled 3.5 million square miles, making their empire far larger than that of the ancient Persians, previously the largest empire in history. Far more structured than the realms of the Scythians, the Hun empire provided the model to which later steppe peoples aspired, including the Turks and the Mongols. From his tents filled with gold, silk, and slaves, the chanyu's efficient war-making machine gave the Han emperor sleepless nights.

The Blood-Sweating Horses of Ferghana

By 111 BCE, that most martial of the Han emperors, Wudi, had been fighting with the horse-breeding Huns for thirty of his then forty years on the throne. Pained by the superior quality and numbers of his foes' horses, he strove to improve the Han cavalry. Consulting the *Yi Jing*—the *Book of Changes* (in English, traditionally called the *I Ching*), often used in his court for divination—Wudi lit on an encouraging oracle that "divine horses are due to appear from the northwest." Then, from Han emissaries, word came to him of fabulous, blood-sweating horses abounding in a distant kingdom, Ferghana. The emperor determined to acquire these "foals of the dragon" for the imperial stud at any price. A court poet accordingly rhapsodized,

A gift from the Great Unity,
The Heavenly Horse descends,
Red sweat pearls on his neck,
He perspires in ochre foam.
He advances free and easy,
His nature untrammeled, strange,
He treads lightly upon fleeting clouds,
He vanishes in his skyward gallop,
With his muscled form,
He covers ten thousand li.

Chinese sources praised the wonderful properties of these unusual horses. One advantage was that "they are able to gallop over stones." Since in ancient times horses were not shod, except with straw or leather, and since horses bred upon the plains wore out their hooves on long journeys, mountain-bred horses with firmer hooves that could travel farther without needing rest for their feet to recuperate would give a decided advantage to Chinese cavalry. Because of their endurance on the march, the Chinese also called them "horses of a thousand li in one day." Due to their speed, the voyager "who rides in a carriage drawn by them must bind his head with floss in order to avoid becoming ill with the wind." Grandiose, they stood an improbable twenty hands tall, with manes reaching to their knees, and tails sweeping the ground. They may well have belonged to a bigger, bonier breed. Their height could also simply reflect different diet and training. In the distant country of the west, horses were raised on abundant alfalfa. Their riders, unlike the Huns, did not break them in until their bones had matured, so they grew bigger. Their hooves were as big as a man's clenched fist. But most remarkably, their sweat oozed from pores behind their front shoulder blades, blood-red in color.[*] No wonder their fame reached all the way to the imperial capital in Chang'an (modern Xi'an).

---

[*] Extensive literature exists on this topic. Sinologist Victor Mair sums up the two main theories: either the small blood vessels just under the skin burst when the horses broke into a gallop or parasitic worms, common on the steppe, provoked bleeding nodules on the horse's coat. In either case it would have looked like the horse was sweating blood. See Heather Pringle, "The Emperor and the Parasite," *The Last Word on Nothing*, March 3, 2011.

These horses were reared by Scythian horse breeders in the Ferghana Valley, in today's Uzbekistan, very close to the current Chinese border but twenty-two hundred miles distant from the Han capital. The Han were well informed about the valley, based on reports by intrepid emissary explorers. Some of the horse breeders in this region had once been friendly neighbors to the Han, before being chased away by the Huns. Yet the logistical difficulties the Han faced to even consider procuring horses from so far away were daunting. Moreover, any attempt by the Han to send a mission to far-off Ferghana would raise the suspicions of the peoples through whose lands they would have to travel. The Huns, especially, could be counted on to oppose their transit. Even at home, the emperor's coveting of distant, possibly mythical horses earned the disapproval of his risk-averse courtiers.

The emperor overruled his conservative advisers and ordered an imperial mission to distant Ferghana to bring back the blood-sweating horses. The party was stopped in neighboring states, delayed, disabused, and sent back empty-handed. Next, merchants more familiar with steppe life and customs offered to journey forth, risking their own capital, and purchased letters of accreditation from the state. Yet successive merchant missions also failed: either they did not make it all the way to Ferghana or they were rebuffed in their request for the horses. Finally, adventurers sought to bluff their way across the steppe, without any official endorsements, in hopes of enjoying the emperor's largesse in the improbable event of their success. One particularly undiplomatic emissary reached Ferghana only to be murdered after egregiously insulting his hosts. Although the emissary was not, in fact, accredited, Wudi saw this as an affront to Han prestige and vowed revenge.

Accordingly, in the fortieth year of his reign, Wudi organized a final expedition to bring back the blood-sweating horses, led by the emperor's own brother-in-law General Li Guangli. He assembled one hundred thousand soldiers and a baggage train of one hundred thousand oxen, thirty thousand horses, and many smaller pack animals. The size of such an army meant that most of the pack animals carried forage only for other pack animals. It was one of the greatest undertakings of any imperial state, perhaps of all time, dwarfing the unsuccessful attempts of the Persians to conquer the steppe or the campaigns of Raghu to repel the Scythians. The Chinese expedition was not even one of conquest or defense. They simply wanted to bring back the horses of Ferghana.

The general's army marched from Chang'an across the Yellow River and around the Yumen, or "Jade Gate," a still impressive, thirty-two-foot-high mud-brick fortress planted at what was then the western frontier of the Han empire. Beyond this portal stretched more than six hundred miles of shifting sand, the Taklamakan Desert. Here no water could be had, certainly not for the thousands of pack animals and sheep, who could travel at best sixteen miles a day. Later travelers in this desert would use camels almost exclusively as pack animals, because they can survive without water for a week or more. Yet even in the early twentieth century, travelers well provided with camels still described the crossing of the Taklamakan as the most terrifying expedition of their adventurous lives. The intrepid General Li marched his one-hundred-thousand-strong army ever westward, losing animals and precious supplies to thirst.

Chenhai, an adviser to the Mongol army in the thirteenth century and a later traveler across this route, explained the difficulties in these terms:

> It is a field of death. At one time a whole army perished there by exhaustion; no one escaped. Whoever crosses the desert in the daytime and in cloudless weather will die from fatigue, and his horse also. Only when starting in the evening, and travelling the whole night, is it possible to reach water and grass on the next day by noon. We have to travel more than 200 li [approximately 60 miles] to reach the end of the sandy desert, where we shall find plenty of water and grass.

Since the time of the Han, the Taklamakan Desert has hosted several oases, nestled in the piedmont of its enclosing mountains. Collectively these are referred to as the "six cities," today's Kashgar, Khotan, Yeni Hisar, Aksu, Yarkand, and Turfan.[*] Some thrive on underground irrigation systems, which channel snowmelt waters into their orchards and melon patches. The oases are still famous for their fruits and vegetables, especially their melons

---

[*] Some authors include Hami, Kuche, or other cities on this list, depending on the era, as the relative importance of cities fluctuated.

and raisins, which are reputed to be the sweetest in the world. These oasis cities delighted the Chinese expedition after the grim stretches of desert.

After a pause in the oases, General Li's expedition embarked on the next stage, which entailed crossing high mountains. The Chinese would have been familiar with the relatively gentle elevations of the Khingan, Sayan, and Jehol Mountains, rising six thousand to ten thousand feet in Mongolia and Manchuria, but as they moved west they encountered the Tian Shan (Heavenly) and Altai (Golden) Mountains, whose peaks soared to twenty-five thousand feet. To cross over from the eastern to the western steppe, Wudi's expedition had to climb to a pass at ten thousand feet that was open just three months a year, with snow falling as late as June, leaving a narrow summer window for caravans. The mountain chains of Central Asia did not prevent east-west travel but did impose their rhythm, just as the trade winds determined the departing seasons for sea travel for sailing voyages.

After the waterless sand and freezing snow, the western-facing mountain slopes provided welcome greenery, with alpine meadows beginning at five thousand feet, excellent pastures, and flowing streams for horses and pack animals. Snow melting from these mountains fed the great rivers, including the Oxus, the Jaxartes (today known as the Syr Darya), and the Ili. Unlike Europe and central China, where long, navigable rivers open the interior of the continent to the oceans, few of Inner Asia's rivers are navigable or give access to the ocean. These endorheic watercourses flow deep into heart of the continent. Some drain into large, freshwater lakes and salt seas, such as Issyk Kul and Lake Balkhash, the Caspian Sea, and the Aral Sea (before it disappeared in the twentieth century). Other rivers, like the Herat, the Helmand, and the Murghab, peter out in swampy marshes. The lack of relief means that these rivers meander and often change their course. The Oxus used to flow into the Caspian Sea before switching its course to the Aral Sea. This part of the steppe is inhospitably dry but doesn't experience the spring and fall melt, which makes the more western part, today's Ukraine, impassible twice a year. Here the steppe provides a more reliable surface on which to travel, and fulfills the role in Asia that the great rivers, including the Rhine and the Danube, play in Europe. This is what allowed the Han caravan to reach Ferghana.

Ferghana can best be described in the words of its most famous native son, Babur, who would become the first Mughal emperor of India in the sixteenth century:

> Ferghana is a smallish province. Grain and fruit are plentiful. All around are mountains, except on the western side, and so, aside from this direction, foreign enemies cannot penetrate. Melons and grapes are excellent. During the melon season in the fall, it is customary not even to sell them at the melon patches [but to give them away]. There are no pears better than the local pears. There are game and sporting birds. The pheasants there get extremely fat. It is said that not even four people can finish eating a stew made from just one pheasant.

Horses thrived in the Ferghana Valley, with its dry and temperate climate, mineral-rich grasses, and plentiful watercourses, fed by the Naryn and Kara Rivers, tributaries of the Syr Darya. Alfalfa flourished there, and still does. Even before the Chinese arrived, the Persians, Macedonians, and Scythians fought for control of this territory.

When the massive Chinese army appeared before the Scythians' fort, they demanded and were refused the blood-sweating horses. Prepared for this refusal, General Li organized a siege of the camp. Engineers diverted a river that supplied water to the Scythians, and so after a few weeks obtained their surrender. In a sign of submission, the Scythian elders put their chief to death and delivered his head to the besieging Chinese, along with thirty blood-sweating horses and three thousand superior horses. General Li returned triumphantly to Chang'an, after two years' absence. Again, the court poet reacted to this miraculous event with celebratory verses.

> The heavenly horses are coming,
> From the distant west,
> Crossing the sand dunes.
> The barbarians submit.
> The heavenly horses are coming.
> Born in flowing springs,
> Their backs striped like tigers,

Changing directions like spirits.
The heavenly horses are coming,
Crossing the grass-less waste,
Across thousands of miles,
Taking the road east.
The heavenly horses are coming.
Who could master their turning and climbing?
The heavenly horses are coming.
The august moment is come,
Who will give the command to receive them?
The heavenly horses are coming.
Open the gate!
I reach the Mountains of Kunlun
The heavenly horses are coming,
Peers of the divine dragon.
I reach the Gate of Heaven.
*I see the Jade Terrace.**

The emperor was delighted with these additions to the imperial stables and richly rewarded his brother-in-law Li. Nevertheless, the cost of maintaining an army of one hundred thousand soldiers for over two years on such an expedition weighed heavily on the Han treasury, and all for just thirty blood-sweating horses. The Chinese did manage to compel the Scythians to provide an annual gift of two additional blood-sweating horses each year, but even these new bloodlines were insufficient to improve the imperial stud or provide the Han with horse power equal to that of their steppe enemies. It is said that the famous Ferghana horses soon died, despite the care lavished on them.

Later, Wudi himself made a tour of the western region and personally selected horses of the best coats and colors, but they also wasted away in their new, unfavorable habitat. Their offspring did not reach the height of their sires. Provisioning the imperial stables of China continued to

---

* The concluding lines of the poem refer to the emperor's belief that the heavenly horses would bring him to the abode of the gods, where he would enjoy immortality.

challenge successive dynasties for the next sixteen centuries. Later historians of the great expedition tallied up its costs and benefits and found much to criticize in Wudi's obsessive pursuit. The episode became a morality tale of imperial hubris.

The Ferghana expedition did demonstrate, however, both to the steppe peoples and to the Chinese themselves, that Wudi would stop at nothing to obtain the horses he coveted for his cavalry. China would not be an also-ran in the arms race for superior horses. Wudi knew that some of his advisers harbored a cultural pessimism about horses and believed that China would never master horse power. The emperor's massive expedition was meant to challenge that pessimism and to encourage officials to raise strong, fast war-horses, as good as those of their Hun rivals. His efforts in this respect were only partially successful. This is not where we have to look for his legacy.

Although in one sense Wudi's expedition for the blood-sweating horses of Ferghana was a costly folly, indirectly it led to the final defeat of the Han's longtime enemies, the Huns. In the wake of this titanic undertaking, the Chinese established a diplomatic presence to the far west, in the Tarim Basin. This provided them a platform from which they could watch and influence the politics of their steppe neighbors and procure horses from a variety of trading partners, instead of being dependent on a single, potentially dangerous partner. China made alliances with those distant nations willing to risk the wrath of the Huns, weakening the Hun monopoly over horses. China also cultivated rival princes within the chanyu's own court, in order to encourage the latent divisions among these steppe leaders.

Hun power ebbed. The Chinese took advantage of the situation by enforcing a less rewarding gift-exchange relationship. Deprived of wealth and patronage capabilities, the one-hundred-year-old Hun empire slowly dissolved. The Chinese encouraged the rise of new hegemons, one of which succeeded in killing a Hun chanyu in battle, carrying off his skin as a trophy. A faction of Hun forces fled to the west, where they continued to practice trading and raiding, offering their services as mercenaries and extorting protection money from the settled states of western Asia, including Iran and Rome. Later, from a new base on the Hungarian steppe, they raided as far away as Paris, where Saint Geneviève used prayers to convince them not to sack her city. The Chinese exercised a policy of divide and rule, so that for some time no steppe empire arose on their frontier. What remained was an unwritten playbook on how to operate a steppe empire, to be put into practice by the next Modun. With the Huns out of the way and the Chinese eagerly buying horses on the western steppe, new traders entered China's market.

5

Silk Road or Horse Road

China and India, 100 BCE–500 CE

ॐ

The Masters of Horses

When General Li Guangli burst into Central Asia in 102 BCE he encountered old friends of China, the horse-breeding people called the Yuezhi. Forty years earlier, they had pastured in today's Gansu Province, not far from the Han capital of Chang'an. "China is famous for its great population, Rome for its treasure, the Yuezhi for their horses," went one saying. They had dared, in spite of the Huns, to supply horses directly to the Han, who appreciated the fine specimens they could provide. Such a move threatened to undercut the Hun monopoly on the horse trade, unraveling their web of control. The Huns, then at the height of their power, turned on the Yuezhi and punished them with characteristic cruelty. From a letter of the Hun chanyu to his "elder brother," the Han emperor, we learn:

> By the good fortune of Heaven, by the good quality of our officers and soldiers and by the strength of our horses, our general has destroyed and exterminated the Yuezhi. He has completely beheaded and killed, subdued and vanquished them.

The chanyu's general fashioned a wine goblet from the Yuezhi king's skull, in good steppe fashion.

The Yuezhi were forced to flee from their pastures. Some 150,000 souls embarked with their flocks on a trek of nine hundred miles to the Ili River in modern Kazakhstan. One can imagine the challenge of such a migration, and the resistance posed by the other horse breeders whose pastures they had to cross. When the Yuezhi reached the Ili River, they suffered another military setback and had to trek once more across the Oxus River into modern Afghanistan, a farther thousand-mile stretch. These migrations marked them for two generations, turning them into a formidable fighting force, inured to hardship and desperate for their place in the sun.

Yuezhi in combat as depicted on the Orlat plaque, first to fourth centuries CE, Uzbekistan.

In northern Afghanistan their luck turned. They fought and conquered both their own Scythian cousins and the Greek city-states left behind two centuries earlier by Alexander the Great. The Yuezhi were enjoying the horse-rich pastures of Balkh when the Chinese expedition arrived in pursuit of the blood-sweating horses, unfurling their banners beneath the snowcapped canopy of the Pamirs. The Yuezhi jumped at the opportunity to renew their relationship with the Chinese, petitioning for and receiving the right to send horses to the Han. This recognition by the Han in their new homeland, and the flow of valuable gifts that ensued, turned the former fugitives into a force to be reckoned with.

After their epic march of two thousand miles, the Chinese proved to be eager buyers of horses, to replace the animals lost on the outbound journey. On top of that, to secure the newly conquered Tarim Basin, General Li left behind garrison troops, for which remounts were regularly required. Elite horses, meanwhile, were sent all the way back to Chang'an, in the tracks of the blood-sweating horses. Again, Chang'an reacted with joy at the delivery of these horses:

The Heavenly Horses come forth from the [Yuezhi]
Their backs marked with tigers' stripes, their bones are dragon wings.

Assured of Chinese support in case of retaliatory attacks from the Huns, the Yuezhi continued to supply horses to their new allies, growing prosperous and powerful. Out of this alliance ultimately emerged both the Afghan people and their ancestral business, the international horse trade.

On the other versant of the Pamirs, the Indian kingdoms eagerly sought to buy horses as well, tens of thousands each year—as many or more than the Han acquired. Moreover, unlike the imperial Han, who once slaughtered an army of Yuezhi during a short period of disagreement, India lacked a hegemonic state, leaving open all sorts of raiding, ruling, and trading opportunities for the enterprising horse breeders.

Scythians had long migrated over the Pamirs into Gilgit and Baltistan and, later, farther south into Kashmir and Punjab. Petroglyphs from the second and first centuries BCE discovered alongside the Karakoram Highway, which connects Central Asia and the Indian subcontinent via today's

Pakistan-controlled Kashmir, show Central Asians, characteristically clad in caftans and boots, leading horses over this fifteen-hundred-foot-high pass. From here they established small, Indo-Scythian kingdoms, often in conflict with their Indian neighbors to the south, as echoed in the epic of Raghu. Other times, they sold horses to the Indians.

As in China, Indian rulers had no choice but to acquire horses from the very frontier tribes who menaced them. The mighty Mauryas had exerted control over Afghanistan from 322 to 185 BCE and monopolized the procurement of horses from the Scythians, but the Mauryas were long gone by the first century BCE, when one of the Yuezhi clan leaders, known as the Kushan yabgu, decided to cross over the Pamirs. The small Indo-Scythian kingdoms occupied this strategic gateway into India; the Kushan yabgu realized that if he could federate the Indo-Scythians and the different peoples of Central Asia and Afghanistan into a single polity, he could dominate the horse trade of India, in the same way his old rivals the Huns had monopolized the trade with the Han.

The Kushan rulers followed the Hun playbook and united the horse breeders from the Tarim Basin and the Chinese frontier to Punjab and Kashmir. They were the first of many groups in Indian history that parlayed horse trading into a huge empire. Controlling the renowned pastures of Ferghana, Balkh, and Punjab, they dominated the trade with India, provided horses to China, and fought with the Iranians to keep them and their fine horses out of the market.

The far-flung nature of the Kushan trade is striking. From their cockpit in the Hindu Kush, they could pivot in any direction. Their domains lay at the intersection of three great civilizations—the Chinese, the Indian, and the Iranian—and two of the largest markets for horses. They maintained winter capitals on the plains of Peshawar in today's Pakistan and in Balkh in Afghanistan, on the opposing versant of the Hindu Kush. In the summer they migrated up to the cool of the Bamiyan Valley, where later the two giant rupestrian Buddha images arose, one 180 feet tall, the other 125 feet.[*]

For the hard-riding Kushans became enthusiastic patrons of Buddhism.

---

[*] Dynamited by the Taliban in 2001.

The Horse Road

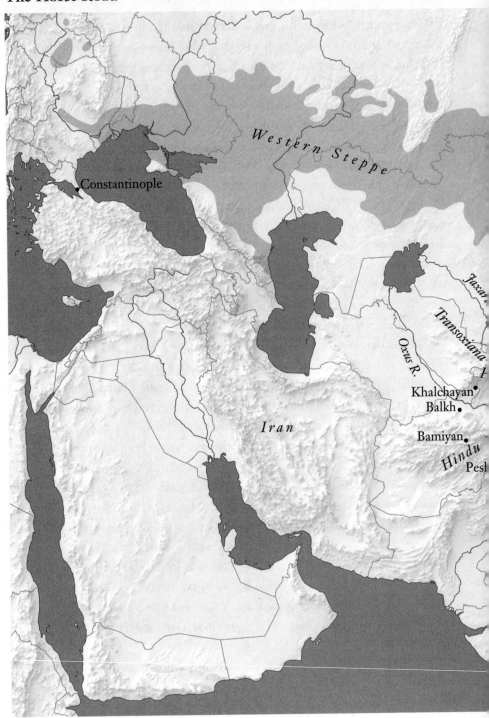

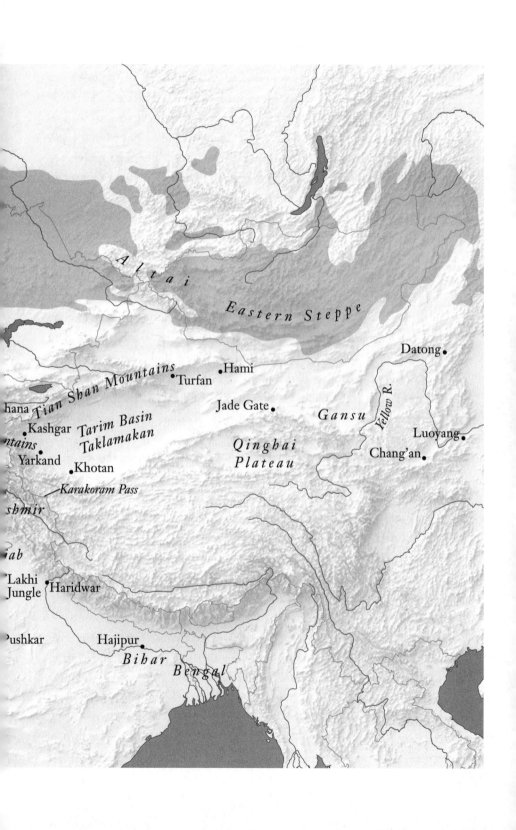

Altai

Eastern Steppe

Datong.

.Hami

Tian Shan Mountains .Turfan

hana

.Kashgar *Tarim Basin* Jade Gate.

Taklamakan *Gansu*

Yellow R.

Luoyang.

ntains *Qingbai* Chang'an.

.Yarkand .Khotan *Plateau*

Karakoram Pass

shmir

ab

'Lakhi .Haridwar
Jungle

'ushkar .Hajipur

Bihar

Bengal

Their embrace of this religion occurred in characteristic steppe-raider fashion. Some of their horsemen kidnapped a famous Indian poet. On their ride back north, their prisoner began to sing a song to their horses. The song described how the Buddha, Prince Gautama, took flight from his palace on his horse Kanthaka, and rode into the forest. There he renounced his princely life and bade Kanthaka farewell. The horse died of a broken heart but was subsequently reborn in human form and became the Buddha's disciple. When the poet finished reciting, the Kushans saw that their horses, having attained enlightenment, had turned into Buddhas. Forever after they called the poet Aśvaghosa, "the man who whispers to horses." His poems in Sanskrit have been found as far north as Turfan, in the Tarim Basin, transported, surely, in Kushan caravans.

Whether or not the legend contains any truth, Buddhism spread quickly among the Kushans and their trading partners. With its well-established scriptures and relatively simple worship practices, Buddhism was a more portable religion than that of the Brahmins, so it spread over Kushan trading routes to Central Asia and China. The White Horse Temple in Luoyang, a later Han capital, commemorates the Kushan horse that brought Buddhist sutras to China for the first time.

For all their impact on world religion, we knew little about the Kushans until the early twentieth century, when archaeologists began to catalog and study their elegant, Hellenistic carvings in gray schist stone, the legacy of their cultural fusion with the descendants of Alexander the Great's colonies in the east. The Kushan Buddha images are dressed in subtly draped cloth, an Indian *dhoti* or a Greek *chiton*, but when the Kushans portray themselves, they are unmistakably dressed for horse riding. The headless statue of their greatest ruler, Kanishka, confronts us with his caftan, belt, and riding boots, looking like he is about to leap onto his horse's back. Other rulers of the dynasty proudly represented themselves on their coins riding powerful horses, holding the reins in their left hand and resting their right hand menacingly on their arrow quivers—the essential equipment of a steppe horseman. A frieze of feasting warriors from Khalchayan, Uzbekistan, excavated by the Soviets in the 1960s, shows Kushan warriors looking for all the world like a band of modern Cossacks with their baggy trousers, wide-skirted cherkeskas, and big boots. They are either celebrating a successful hunt or having a drink before saddling up. The Kushans, despite their building of Buddhist stupas and monasteries, never gave up their highly mobile lifestyle, as they migrated throughout the year from the Indus Valley to the Hindu Kush, then down to the Oxus, all the while driving back and forth their caravans of horses for sale in Indian and Chinese markets.

Situated at the center of the Asian horse market, the Kushans contributed much to the evolution of the modern horse. In the rich, temperate pastures of the blood-sweating horses, the Kushans could raise taller, stronger, and consequently hungrier horses than those they rode in their ancestral Gansu. Demand for bigger horses came from the increasing use of horse armor in combat. Kings and princes gloried in these animals, which could lift their knees up high or kneel down in carefully choreographed displays. Raiders and adventurers appreciated sleek, lean horses that could sprint away from danger. Other buyers, like the Buddhist monks undertaking pilgrimages, sought horses that were comfortable to ride, with hard hooves for mountain travel and low water consumption for the deserts. Some of these traits could be produced by conditioning: a horse trained in mountains or deserts acquired the appropriate resistance. But others, like speed and gait, appeared mysteriously innate, though not consistently passed on from the sires and dams to the foals. This led the Kushan-era horse breeders, confusedly at first, to create the first distinct breeds.

Color, above all, was an important criterion for buyers; the Chinese liked dappled grays; the Indians avoided piebald horses as inauspicious. By raising several generations of horses and keeping the bloodlines apart, breeders found that the occurrence of undesirable colors tended to disappear over time. This preference for predictable coloring was the first step in creating breeds. Highly bred horses tended to sport a uniform coloring, except for white markings on the face and forelegs. In contrast, less intensively bred horses bore black markings, like their feral cousins. Color became a kind of branding and marketing tool, to ensure that a foal looked like its famous sire or dam, and as a promise that the foal would grow up with the same desirable traits its parents possessed. This period probably saw the emergence of what we consider equine beauty. In a phenomenon also seen in domestic canines, breeder selection resulted in paedomorphism, the persistence of cute, infantile features in the mature animal. The long eye-lashes, dish-shaped cheeks, and elongated nose of the Akhal-Teke, Arab, and Thoroughbred are modern examples of this physical type, in marked contrast to the stocky and blunt faces of Mongolian ponies. As with car manufacturers today, breeders created certain styles that buyers associated with desirable traits, even if those traits served no useful purpose. Indeed, the flat face of the Mongolian pony makes this horse a more efficient grazer than his long-nosed, aristocratic cousins.

On a more practical note, the Kushans also bred horses for comfortable riding. Ambling, a pace not all horses can manage, is an attractive characteristic that breeders in this era learned how to preserve from a single, random mutation. Bravery for hunting, racing (which was more of a contact sport in those days), and war also depended heavily on breeding.

This increased focus on desirable traits led early selective breeders to use a smaller number of stallions to cover the mares, resulting in decreased male Y-chromosome diversity, compared to the variability detected in earlier Scythian and Hun burials. DNA studies suggest that in the Kushan period the horse began to acquire its modern characteristics. Since the Kushans bred horses for much of Asia at that time, the modern equine haploids can be traced to them. But until very recent discoveries of specific genes responsible for desirable traits, breeding remained an art and not a science.[*] The very lack of predictability added an element of luck, as well as wonder, to the appearance and performance of an extraordinary horse.

The success of the Kushans' horse-breeding business attracted Iranian jealousy. After many attempts, the Iranians finally defeated the hard-riding Kushans, whose last monarch disappeared five hundred years after their flight from China. Yet the Kushans were not entirely forgotten in later centuries. The Arab historian al-Mas'udi, writing in the tenth century, called the Kushan kings "the second-greatest masters of the horse," the greatest ever being the khaghans of the Turks, who ruled the steppes a hundred years after the Kushans. An Arab geographer of the late twelfth and early

---

[*] The emergence of a specific gene for speed, called MSTN, linked to a large heart that efficiently oxygenates blood, did not occur until about a thousand years later, so whether a given foal could win as many races as its sire was a hit-or-miss proposition, and not a product of bloodlines, as with today's racehorses.

thirteenth centuries, Yaqut, noted that the Kushans were the masters of dragon-bred, celestial horses. Such was their fame for horse breeding that it echoed with these Arab scholars centuries after their disappearance. The Indian, Sanskrit-language sources referred to these horse breeders of the northwest as Aśvakas, likewise meaning "masters of the horse." This is at least one possible origin for the ethnonym Afghan, and it is generally agreed that today's Afghans, who likewise played a huge role in India as both horse dealers and conquerors, are the descendants of the Kushans. Their legacy persisted for centuries in the caravans that crisscrossed Asia.

Caravans

From the Kushan era right up to modern times, Afghans have led horse caravans from the heart of Asia to distant but eager buyers, across the two-thousand-mile route taken by General Li to Kashgar, and from there to the Jade Gate and China proper. During the reign of powerful emperors, those travelers were received in spacious caravansaries offering free room and board. During turbulent episodes, the caravans had to navigate geopolitics in real time to avoid danger from rebellions and invasions. When a civil war broke out in the Tarim Basin in the tenth century, a great horse caravan dispatched scouts to take the lay of the land; they discovered that their next planned halt had been occupied by rebels and that war was raging across their path in still another direction. So they turned around and made a big arc with their animals across the windswept Qinghai Plateau, adding a year to their journey into China. The resulting delay did not spell financial ruin for them, however. Their inventory fed itself on grass along the route and didn't lose value; on the contrary, a hint of warfare promised higher prices. Caravans enjoyed a kind of political and ecological sustainability, which is why they flourished for so many centuries.

Simultaneously herders and traders, the resourceful horse dealers looked for other ways to earn their living. Carrying goods in their caravans, besides horses and other livestock, could be lucrative. But the horse dealers were not professional merchants. Rather, they recruited merchants to join their caravans into China and India. To transport the merchandise, they provided camels for hire; they avoided using horses as pack animals so as not to wear them out. The horse dealers also charged merchants for the protection of traveling in their caravans.

A caravan could offer this protection to merchants because of its impressive size: five thousand or more people, ferrying ten thousand horses, sheep, goats, and camels. As a twentieth-century journalist, Joseph Kessel, described one such procession:

> Their flocks numbered in the tens of thousands. Opulent, powerful, proud, they moved forward fully armed. . . . The caravan without end emptied from one end of the valley, and slowly, majestically advanced toward us. The herds filled the entire surface of the road and overflowed up to the flank of the mountain on one side, and down the river on the other. Ferocious dogs and armed horsemen guided the progression of this sea of beasts.

Another one of the horse traders' talents, then, was the ability to organize and coordinate such a huge procession. If their numbers alone did not dissuade hostile intentions, the caravan had other means to protect itself, as Kessel hinted.

It was sometimes hard to tell the difference between a caravan and a military campaign, for the horsemen bristled with weapons. Sentinels stayed saddled up all night in case robbers tried to drive off their horses. In rugged, forested territories, heavily armed locals tried to shake them down for protection money, or to plunder them, or both. Even under the Kushans, there were insurgents in the Hindu Kush who made life difficult for traders crossing the passes. The caravanners responded to local attacks by organizing even bigger, better-armed caravans, making themselves ever more dangerous and threatening to their unwilling hosts. Caravans to India and China acted as schools of war for horse traders, who learned to apply military discipline on their annual expeditions. This would have fateful consequences for both destination countries in the centuries to come.

The Afghans called these traders *Kuchis* or *Powindahs*, meaning "those who travel." Unlike the migrating pastoralists, who traveled with their herds of horses and other livestock in an annual cycle between ancestral pastures, these caravans traveled much farther, from Central Asia to distant

China or India, across the Gobi Desert or over the Karakoram or Khyber Passes. At the end of their long travels lay the great horse fairs.

Horse Fairs

Both China and India hosted these great fairs, but the political situation in each country shaped them in very different ways. The Chinese fairs took place in the shadow of what had become the Great Wall. The unwieldy size of the horse caravans and their potential for mischief caused China much concern, and so the emperors ordered the northern frontier to be hardened with a snaking line of fired-brick constructions, to serve as a customs barrier and to ensure strict control over the horse caravans' comings and goings. In case there should be outright hostilities, the Han built military fortresses and garrisoned them with soldiers. Linking the old trading posts together, they built the most extensive frontier wall, even longer than the current wall, which dates to the fourteenth century. It stretched from the Jade Gate in Gansu to the Korean border. Beside this Great Wall arose paddocks, stables, and inns at specific crossing points to house the horse dealers and their wares. These border points were simply called horse markets, 馬市, *ma shi*. Mandarins inspected the horses for quality and restricted the quantity to suit the requirements of various ministries for war or transport. Because of the cumbersome process of official trade, and the frequent disputes over prices and quality of on both sides—the Chinese complained that the horses were sickly and the breeders were dissatisfied with the prices offered—the Han emperor sought to limit the number of these troublesome fairs. The breeders frequently used threats or even outright violence to extort additional fairs from the Han.

Unlike the Mandarins, the common people of China welcomed the horse fairs. They flocked from the interior to the frontier to settle and to engage in petty trade with the caravanners. They sold garden greens that they planted in the semi-steppe climate, alongside spindly cherry and plum trees that reminded them wistfully of their more fertile homes in the south. At the same time, they acquired a taste for roast lamb and even horse meat, which remain characteristic of northern Chinese cuisine. The markets would have been colorful sights, despite the mandarins' efforts to impose order, with horse breeders, Central Asian merchants, and Buddhist monks or preachers of other religions mingling with the Chinese and haggling over bowls of tea or steaming dishes of sheep offal. Over time, whole cities grew out of these horse fairs, like Datong, now 1.8 million in population.

As in China, India's demand for horses ensured that the horse fairs would represent, for centuries, a big business. Since India had no hard border with the horse dealers, they established fairs in wide-open spaces all across the subcontinent. Compared to their impact on China, these freewheeling fairs produced more profound changes in Indian social and economic life.

The precise foundation dates for Indian fairs cannot be known with certainty. Already in the Kushan era mention is made of an important fair at Hajipur in Bihar, where once the Buddha preached. The biggest and most famous of these fairs took place twice a year in Haridwar, where the Ganges River courses out of the Himalayas in modern India's Uttarakhand State. Early modern visitors describe an institution that had probably changed little since the first horse breeders came to trade. Half a million buyers and sellers shared less than a fourth of a square mile with ten thousand horses, as well as camels and other livestock. Afghans brought horses from Ferghana and the Oxus, satisfying the appetite of buyers from Benares to Bengal for locomotion, military capacity, and ostentation.

The noise, the crowds, the butting, shoving, and dragging of livestock, the hungry looks of the dealers and the feigned indifference of the buyers, the animal odors mixed with the nervous sweat of brokers counting their money—such was the sensory overload of visiting a horse fair. One had to be on guard when buying a horse, ready to detect sickness, a girth that had been pumped up with water, or a coat made slick with lamb fat, and careful to avoid animals with wicked temperaments or who were potentially stolen property. Prices could vary by factors of two to ten, depending on the quality of the animal. Concerning the elite horses: if you had to ask the price, you probably could not afford it.

As in any great mercantile exchange, the price of horses is matter of great interest. In the first half of the first millennium, an ordinary horse sold for 70 ounces of silver, about 1,300 U.S. dollars at current silver prices. However, money bought far more then than it does today. A typical urban Indian household of that era needed a minimum of 42 ounces of silver a year to live. So one can think of a horse as costing nearly double what most people earned in a year. An exceptional horse sold for twenty times the average salary. Such transactions thrilled the crowd of visitors to the market, who noted with attention the arguments over conditions in the closing phase, like whether all the tack was included in the price.

Rough riders, acting as agents for the different armies and courts of India, ambled around, inspecting the animals. Each one would buy a string of four or five horses or place orders for similar horses to be delivered the following spring. The rough riders resold the best and the worst horses in the string, making good money on the side, and kept the remaining horses for service in their employers' cavalries. Some exceptionally deft rough riders managed to steal horses from their pickets for sale to fences. Thieves caught in the act had their heads skewered prominently on spears to discourage imitators.

Princely connoisseurs rode through the fair on their elephants, surveying the merchandise from their elevated vantage points, followed by the horses they had either purchased or they were selling. As at a modern art fair, the most valuable items for sale, such as Persian horses with gorgeous, silk-brocaded saddle blankets, were kept out of sight, and one needed an invitation to see them. Monarchs visited the Haridwar fair every year in person to get the first choice of the best horses, which they then distributed as gifts to courtiers and clansmen. This is how the royal houses of India got ahold of the splendid mounts brought from Central Asia we see them riding in later Mughal and Rajput miniatures. Whether simple rough riders or lordly maharajas, Indians rarely bargained for their purchases. They were expected to know the right value for each horse. The transactions lasted hardly more than a few minutes before gold and silver coins were produced to seal the sale.

Yet fine horses were not really the staple of trade in these markets, for there were not enough of them. Most traders made their living buying skinny horses and fattening them up. They let their hungry horses, worn out from the strenuous crossings over the Hindu Kush, graze at leisure during the lush spring season in the Himalayan foothills, before bringing them down to Haridwar to market.

Haridwar's success attracted more than horse buyers and sellers. Over time, preachers and teachers of different sects took advantage of the huge crowds to recruit adepts, who would then perform ritual ablutions in the holy Ganges River nearby. Eventually a major religious festival, the Kumbh Mela, took root in and around Haridwar.

The horse fairs grew to such an importance that they reconfigured the spiritual map of India. The Pushkar Lake in the deserts of Rajasthan provided another suitable location to assemble numerous livestock, but when horse traders established a fair there, its waters were deemed holy, giving rise to yet another major religious festival. Today Pushkar has become better known as a market for camels, yet it long served as a favorite market for horse-mad Rajput clansmen, who acquired the mounts that made them famous as bandits, warriors, and founders of kingly houses all over central India. In the east, Hajipur, in Bihar, continued to welcome horse traders, becoming, like Haridwar and Pushkar, another important center of pilgrimage. The big, international horse fairs brought together people from all over India; they mixed in the markets and bathed in the sacred waters while horse dealers from the north patiently waited for clients.

Besides the social impact of the horse trade, it profoundly transformed India's economy—from largely self-sufficient and agrarian into one of intense production, trading, and export. As the horse trade grew in size, it drained India of metallic money around 1000 CE, for India mined insufficient quantities of gold and silver. The subcontinent was famously rich in gemstones—sapphires, rubies, and diamonds—but these were difficult to use as exchange for large-scale trading, because of the expertise required to accurately assess the value of a stone. Searching for an export commodity that could finance their imports of horses, Indian states took to manufacturing textiles on what was, for the time, a grand scale. The horse trade thus catalyzed an early but profound industrial revolution in India, starting in the eleventh and twelfth centuries.

Not only did the horse trade stimulate Indian industry, it also pushed the Indians into establishing wider trade networks across Asia. The Indians couldn't sell their fine muslin cloth to the horse dealers—the virtually transparent bodices that the cloth was made into would have been impractical for horsewomen on the icy steppe. Instead, a three-way trade emerged:

cottons were sold to the Khmers of Cambodia and to rajas of Java and Bali, who, in turn, paid the silver that the Indians needed to import horses.

In India as in China, horse fairs ranked among the most important economic and social institutions for centuries. They left their imprint in the landscape in the form of towns and places of worship that survive to the present. They reshaped people's livelihoods and their way of life. This should come as no surprise, because horse trading was the biggest business of the era. But it is forgotten today—or, rather, mislabeled.

Silk Road

Afghans, driving forward fine horses destined for the Son of Heaven, the Chinese monarch, caravanning from the Pamir Mountains to Chang'an, were well rewarded at their journey's end. In particular, they delighted in receiving silk cloth from the Chinese. Formal silk robes, called *khalat* in many Asian languages (as well as in Russian), came to be a standard element of any diplomatic or commercial exchange.

Several explanations exist for the steppe peoples' enthusiasm for fine silk clothing. For one, they believed that silk wards off biting insects, especially bedbugs. For those who spend days and nights with animals, it was very desirable to have silk undergarments and bedding. The horse breeders also claimed that silk prevents battle wounds from becoming infected, leading warriors to wear it.

Silk has conventionally been placed at the heart of Asian trade, in a narrative that takes as its starting point the very moment when General Li Guangli arrived in Ferghana. In addition to making an alliance with the Kushans, he established diplomatic relations with the Iranians and Greeks, enabling, for the first time in history, a courier to travel five thousand miles from the Han capital of Chang'an to Antioch (Antakya in modern Turkey) on the shores of the Mediterranean. The conventional narrative further suggests that the Chinese were looking for a highway through Inner Asia to the Mediterranean world, in order to dispatch caravans laden with luxury goods—silk above all—to those distant markets.

Yet the amount of silk that China could have sold to the peoples of the

West would never have justified the titanic efforts of the Han to maintain its numerous soldiers in the Tarim Basin, two thousand miles away from the capital at Chang'an. Indeed, silk-clad caravan chiefs would have been surprised to learn that they were following the Silk Road. With their strings of horses, thousands at a time and tens of thousands annually, crisscrossing Asia every spring on their way to Haridwar and the Great Wall, they might have called their route not the Silk Road but the Horse Road. Horses were the true strategic commodity of the time, and the primary motivation for China's expansion into the Tarim Basin in the first place.

As we have seen, in the first century BCE, China needed horses. Locked in a 130-year-long struggle with the horse-rich Huns, they urgently sought alternative sources of remounts from farther afield, in the rich pasturelands of modern Kyrgyzstan, Tajikistan, Afghanistan, and Iran. While General Li's expedition to Central Asia is often cited as the beginning of the Silk Road, the general went to acquire horses, after all, not to sell silk.

Undoubtedly the routes through Central Asia were crossed by traders in silks, porcelains, and many other products, as well as by Buddhist missionaries and pilgrims, who created the fabulous cave temples that adorn the route from western China all the way to eastern India. Central Asia turned into a vast bazaar, where merchants haggled over fermented mare's milk, honey, musical instruments, carpenter's tools, wool carpets, materials for building yurts, pelts for lining silk khalats, and glue made from hooves. Most of these items would have been for local consumption. Highly mobile horses, on the other hand, were regularly driven over long distances. In any caravan, many other items—high in value, low in weight—were included in the horse dealers' saddlebags, and bulkier goods traveled between the humps of Bactrian camels, which followed the horses. And while the Chinese eagerly bought amber and frankincense from the west, emperors often frowned on such luxury imports, and ordered that traders bring more horses and fewer nonstrategic items. Luxury simply piggybacked on this vital trade.

Horses made up the largest component of trade by value on the Silk Road, in terms of both the high prices paid for them and the quantity of horses purchased, especially in times of war. Scholars have calculated that the Tang dynasty, which ruled China from 618 to 907, spent 10 percent of its state budget on imported horses. Indian princes imported as many as seventy thousand horses a year from the north, a number consistent with the size of Indian cavalry mentioned in contemporaneous sources as totaling two hundred thousand or three hundred thousand troopers. Though those sources don't provide any aggregate budget numbers, if we take an average price per horse in this era as 70 ounces of silver, then the annual imports amounted to the equivalent of $4 to $5 billion in today's dollars, after we make the adjustment for the greater purchasing power of silver money in the past. No other commodity matched the size of this market.

The horse trade was not restricted to long-distance caravans over the terrestrial Silk Road; it also included a maritime leg. In this case, Chinese ships set out not with silk but with another item exclusive to China and in demand everywhere: porcelain. The monsoon winds carried Chinese and south Asian junks laden with this precious and carefully packed product of kilns from Hangzhou and Canton to avid buyers in India, Iran, and even Europe. An important component of the return trade was horses, for the intrepid traders managed to ship their valuable cargo all around the Indian Ocean and back to Canton or Hangzhou. This seaborne trade gave Iranians and Arabs an opportunity to sell their horses to the east, blocked as they were over land by whomever controlled Afghanistan. Yet even in the maritime trade the Afghans were active. Chinese texts reported that "the Kushans shipped horses from Bengal to Cambodia and from there to China."

Surviving accounts by medieval travelers across the Silk Road nourish our illusion of a thriving long-distance trade in luxury goods, but this is because most of those who left us accounts of their voyages were diplomats, not merchants. They were indeed sent from Constantinople to Mongolia or from Chang'an to India, often burdened with costly presents for local rulers. It would take caravans over two years to accomplish such journeys. They brought with them merchants, who benefited from the protections offered by the diplomats' letters of accreditation. The diplomats also carried out trade on the side. However, only the official gifts were ferried all the way from the homeland to their distant, royal recipients. The accompanying merchants engaged in *colportage* and peddling—that is, buying locally and selling in the next marketplace. And even the diplomatic missions almost always included prized horses. Except for these official missions, few merchants traveled great distances. The absence of numismatic evidence supports this view; archaeologists, for example, have not found Iranian coins far beyond such bordering countries as modern-day Afghanistan or Tajikistan. Chinese coins in Central Asia are rare. This is where silk comes in.

Until the sixteenth century, when silver flooded in from Spain's New World mines, the Chinese were short of monetary silver.* Important trading items were instead assigned fixed values in silk, made into bolts of twenty-one by ten inches and weighing a standardized amount. A slave girl on the ninth-century frontier markets, according to some surviving records, fetched six bolts of silk; a horse, eighteen. That the horse had a greater value than a slave is telling, but this must have depended on supply and demand. In periods of war, slaves became abundant and therefore cheaper, while horses became scarcer and, consequently, more expensive. In one instance, horse dealers received forty bolts of silk for one horse. The Chinese maintained the fiction that horses and silk were exchanged as mutual gifts, but the gift ratio was fixed by the mandarins. The wages of Chinese soldiers and steppe mercenaries on the frontier were also paid in bolts of silk, which were easier to transport than other goods. The silk used as currency was not very finely woven, but like any legal tender it enabled the horse breeders to buy items they needed in the frontier markets. It is estimated that the ratio of silk used as money to silk clothing was ten to one.

Merchants ferrying silk from China to Rome were thus not at the center of this economic system. Moreover, when there was trade in silk, its direction was often the reverse of what the popular history of the Silk Road makes it out to be. To be sure, silk was discovered in China and silk weaving was invented there. But by the sixth century, the secret of silk weaving had ceased to be a Chinese monopoly. Thereafter both Rome and Iran produced beautiful silks, and, in fact, Iranian brocaded silk, a finely worked craft item, was an important part of the luxury trade, traveling from Iran to China. When emissaries from the steppe offered silk for sale to sixth-century Romans, their hosts showed them their flourishing mulberry orchards—mulberry leaves being the sole food of silkworms—to make the point that they had no need to buy the product on offer.

This is not to suggest that we get rid of the wonderfully evocative name

---

* This accounts for the experimentation with paper currency that so amazed Marco Polo.

"Silk Road." It reminds us of the discoveries of early-twentieth-century archaeologists who brought back to life the histories of the ancient caravans that crisscrossed Asia. They were the first to uncover bundles of silk squirreled away in long-forgotten monasteries and taverns, or buried in the sand. Now we understand that that silk served as currency, and that the road and the currency were both used to serve the horse trade.

The horse trade grew so large that it strained the economic capacity of even wealthy China. Like the kingdoms of India, it had to make gigantic efforts to accumulate enough tradeable commodities to purchase tens of thousands of horses annually. The ever-increasing demand for silk needed to pay for the ever-increasing number of horses led silk producers to offer a fabric that was thinner and more coarsely woven than before. Naturally the horse dealers countered by demanding more of this cheaper fabric for every horse, to a point where, by the ninth and tenth centuries, China was struggling to recruit enough delicate female fingers to weave the silk.

Desperate to find an alternative to silk to revive the horse trade, the Chinese stumbled on tea, which had the advantage for the sellers of being consumed more quickly than silk wears out, and the supply could be increased more easily than that of mulberry trees and silkworms. Tea bushes soon spread over the hills of Fujian and Yunnan Provinces. The horse dealers, who spent their winters in their chilly tents, welcomed this warming and stimulating beverage. The Chinese learned to pack tea into the form of cakes that could be stamped and branded for quality.[*] Tea wound up paying for horses all the way through the middle of the twentieth century, when caravans of tea were still departing from Yunnan for Tibet, to be exchanged for hardy Himalayan ponies. As in India, the horse trade persisted for a very long time, durably transforming China's political map and its markets.

Horses and silk have more in common than their rival claims to name the trading road. Depending on quality, both can be either commodities or luxuries. The tens of thousands of horses that ambled over the Khyber Pass each year and the bales of cheap silk Chinese money are examples of horses and silk as commodities. The Afghans also dealt in high-end horses,

---

[*] Lovers of tea today will see similar round, black, stamped Frisbee-shaped wafers of pu'er in traditional Chinese tea shops.

as other merchants dealt in costly silk brocades. Yet the wealthy courts of the settled states valued elite horses as much for their aesthetic pleasure as for practical employment. The horse, having transformed politics and economics, would come to transform culture, incarnating not only hard power but also soft power.

6

Equine Mania

China, the Turks, and the world, 500–1100 CE

ᘐ

The Tang Teach the Horse to Dance

Elite horses from Afghanistan and Central Asia filled China's imperial stables, but not just in preparation for war. The seventh emperor of the Tang dynasty, Xuanzong, who ruled from 713 to 756 CE, was famed for training elite horses to dance. He spent hours with them, watching their exercises. They, in turn, were so fond of him that when he rode past on another steed, they cast jealous glances at him from their stables. This equine corps de ballet featured more than one hundred horses. Not only grooms and trainers but also musicians contributed to this spectacle, with specially composed arrangements accompanying performances that took place in the grand reception court of the imperial palace on occasions such as the emperor's birthday.* The horses would step out, resplendent in their gold- and silver-brocaded saddlecloths, their manes wreathed with pearls and jade; grooms gave them wine cups to hold in their mouths, which they then set on the ground before the spectators. No one could recall anything as magnificent as this equine display, which, moreover, reflected much more than mere show.

The horse, from its origins as a herding or military resource, useful for securing wealth and power, had evolved into a potent symbol of power itself. It retained its ancient role as a link to the spiritual world but now

---

* The closest equestrian tradition of modern times to the horses of Xuanzong is the Spanish Riding School of Vienna, whose Lipizzaner stallions perform a caracole to the music of Schubert.

also inspired secular artists and poets. This evolution culminated under the Tang, who were China's, and perhaps the world's, most horse-mad dynasty. Together with their steppe rivals and sometime allies the Celestial Turks (also known as the Sky, Blue, or Gök Turks), they brought the horse, horsemanship, and associated symbolism to a new level, and on a continent-wide scale. While warriors, diplomats, and merchants vied for mastery of horses to deliver what we now call hard power, aristocrats and artists exploited the horse as soft power and created long-lasting cultural norms. Both of these pursuits punctuated the rise and fall of the Tang dynasty and the Celestial Turks, preparing the path for horses and horsemen to dominate Asia both politically and culturally for the next thousand years.

Compared with the Tang, no other imperial dynasty in Asia devoted so much attention to cavalry, which became the preeminent branch of the military. The official dynastic history recorded the prevailing view in the words of the old Han general Ma Yuan: "Horses are weapons of the state. If Heaven takes away these weapons, the state will be in danger of perishing." At their peak, the Tang marshaled the largest cavalry force that had ever yet existed. Seven hundred thousand horses grazed and ambled in the imperial studs and stables, representing a military, logistical, and bureaucratic achievement on a scale that can only be compared with endeavors like American naval ship building in World War II or the Space Race. To do this, the Tang asserted mastery over the steppe in a way that no previous Chinese dynasty had even imagined.

Initially, the Tang both competed for and uneasily shared power over the steppe with their neighbors the Celestial Turks. This horse-breeding people replaced the Huns, from the fifth century onward, as China's principal horse suppliers. They took their name from the great sky under which they herded, and which they worshipped in a theistic way.* They ruled a steppe empire as large as that of the Huns, extending west to the Aral Sea. Their numerous cavalry helped the first Tang emperor ascend to power in 618 CE, during one of those turbulent periods that occasionally interrupted

* Later, these people were ejected from their homeland and moved on to Iran, Ukraine, Romania, and Hungary, as well as today's Turkey. They came to be known by a host of other names: Turkmen, Kyrghyz, Kazakhs, Oghuz, Uyghurs, Kipchaks, Gagauz, Uzbeks, or simply Turks.

Chinese imperial continuity. Through the maternal line the Tang clan itself descended from the Turks. At first, in return for military support, the Turks extracted from the new emperor a pledge of fealty to their own khaghan, or supreme khan. The second Tang ruler, Taizong, went on to reunite China starting in 626 and used his new powers to turn the tables on the Turks, who were now forced to acknowledge him as the khaghan of the steppe. For the first time, but not the last, the emperor of China included much of the boundless steppe in his dominion.

Taizong enjoyed his role as khaghan and the lifestyle this entailed. It provided him with an excuse to escape from the cloistered palace and ride out to receive his Turkish allies. He had a passion for hunting on horseback, a pastime viewed dimly by the mandarins, but that he justified as a means of maintaining himself and his horsemen in a state of martial readiness. "It is true," he noted, "that the world is at peace now, but preparation for war cannot be ignored." Still, the civilian courtiers disapproved. They besieged the emperor with memoranda about time wasted at the hunt, chided him in guarded language for imitating the ways of the Turks, and argued that hunting was harmful for farmers, whose crops were damaged by riders. Taizong protested, "I hunt together with my entourage on our own estates, so that we do no harm to the farmers. What is the problem?" The real problem was that hunting on horseback kept the emperor from attending to matters of state, for his ministers and court eunuchs were not prepared to risk their necks by joining the emperor's hunts. The emperor's ailing principal wife begged him on her deathbed to give up hunting, forcing him reluctantly to accede. Taizong's attention to his empire's horse power, however, never waned.

First, he conquered and pacified the extensive grasslands beyond the Great Wall that had belonged to his erstwhile allies the Turks. One could raise horses in China proper, but it was less economical, and, as always, land-hungry farmers steadily encroached on any available pastures. It took the Tang's huge cavalry force to conquer this new, outer steppe land. This land, in turn, was required to feed that cavalry force. The army needed to renew 15 percent of its total stock annually, or ninety thousand remounts a year, to make up for age and battle losses. The emperor therefore established fifty-eight stud farms across the northwestern commanderies, in today's

China Expands into the Steppe

Western Steppe

Constantinople

Anatolia

CENTRAL ASI

Aral
Sea

Jaxartes R.

Transoxiana

Damascus

Oxus R.

E

N

Afrasiyab

Baghdad

Iraq

Iranian
Plateau

I

N

I

Rajastha

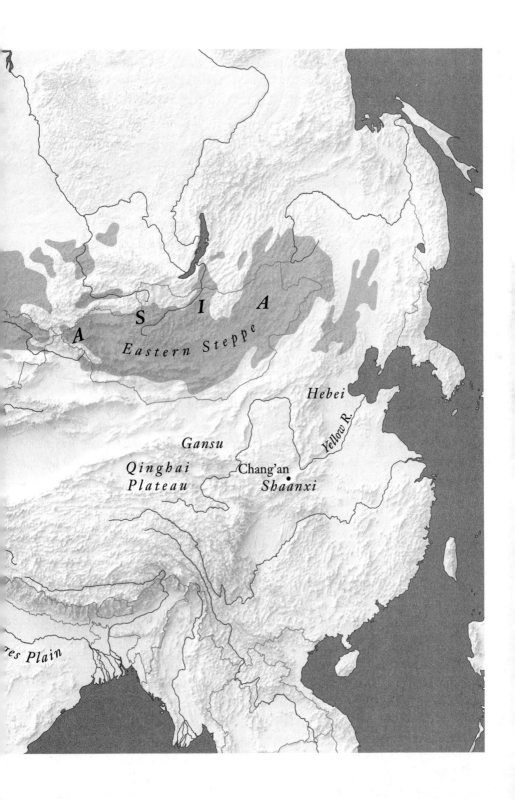

A S I A

Eastern Steppe

Hebei

Yellow R.

Gansu

Qinghai
Plateau

Chang'an
Shaanxi

...res Plain

Shaanxi, Hebei, and Gansu Provinces. Each stud farm hosted as many as three thousand horses on a regulation-sized three thousand acres of grasslands. Together, these stud farms probably provided forty thousand to fifty thousand remounts a year. Trade with the Turks contributed the remaining requirement, raised by thirty-four different clans, with each horse bearing the *tamgha*, or brand, associated with its clan of origin. Steppe horses were registered at the border, with severe penalties meted out to anyone who interfered with their transfer to the government.

In addition to land, the Tang needed competent grooms. The Chinese never developed enough familiarity with horses to breed them, break them, and train them at a sufficient scale. From the annals of later dynasties that used Chinese stable hands, we know that these stud farms never fulfilled their quota of suitable horses. The Tang resorted to Turkish grooms on a massive scale for this reason. The imperial stables employed more than five thousand personnel, and each stud farm had a staff of five hundred to seven hundred. In this period, more than one million Turks are thought to have immigrated into China, either as grooms or as cavalrymen.

The Chinese, like the Indians, endorsed keeping monkeys in the stables of high-strung stallions. This was not seen, as in India, as a way of giving the horse a companion. The Chinese felt the bearded Central Asians had a simian appearance, and that the horses would feel at home surrounded by hirsute primates. Grooms are depicted in countless Tang ceramic sculptures with bushy eyebrows, flowing mustaches, and beards, looking grimly comic. The grooms had the last laugh, as we will see.

The grooms played an essential role in preserving Tang horse power. These were men who had grown up in the saddle and could be trusted with the most valuable horses. Some had originally been prisoners of war or slaves, but because of their equestrian know-how and their allure on horseback, Chinese grandees employed them as outriders for their processions, and sometimes promoted them to important positions in their households. For the imperial studs the grooms performed a series of meticulous tasks, including evaluating the horses and marking them with special brands, depending on their potential. At two years the most promising colts received the brand *fei*, 飛, for "flying steed." After breaking the horses, the grooms trained them and added additional brands on different parts of the animals' bodies, like traditional Chinese chop marks, to certify their state of readiness. The fact that Tang studs acquired fodder for the winter and fed the horses in stables prevented the terrible winter losses of young animals suffered by steppe peoples. The Tang combined their extensive resources with Turkish savoir faire to raise superior horses on an unprecedented scale.

Following the grooms' evaluation process, the stud farms sent down horses to serve all the varied needs of the state. The superior horses, duly marked with the brand of the dragon, went directly to the imperial stables. The next best horses joined the cavalry as remounts. Medium-category horses entered the postal service, while ordinary horses were made available for civil servants to ride. Inside the Tang imperial palace in Chang'an, the Imperial Dragon Stables welcomed the empire's most precious horses, sourced either as choice gifts from the Turkish khans or from the best graduates among the *fei* of the studs. The Imperial Dragon Stables contained six corrals, each with its own distinctive name, including "Flying Steeds of the Right Wing," "Flying Steeds of the Left Wing," "Left Ten Thousand," and "Right Ten Thousand," a nomenclature that had grown only more elaborate since the days of the Han. Despite these aspirational names, the total number of animals in the palace never exceeded ten thousand, but this is still an impressive number of superior horses to be mustered together in one place, always ready for the emperor's commands.

Such a vast system with so many players required a fanatical attention to detail and to discipline. There was much temptation for lowly farmhands to resell fodder or turn a blind eye to livestock rustling by neighboring Turks. To counter horse stealing, for any horse reported dead, the stud farmhands had to provide the carcass to government auditors. Punishments were severe; Emperor Taizong controlled the stud system with an iron hand. When he learned that a prize stallion imported from Ferghana under a previous regime had gone missing, he ordered an investigation throughout the country to find it. It is said that they found the horse blindfolded and operating a grain-grinding mill. The emperor had him brought back to the imperial studs, where he sired five "thousand-li" foals. Taizong's attention to minute detail allowed him to keep seven hundred thousand horses, compared to the one hundred thousand of previous regimes and the three hundred thousand maintained by his less rigorous successors. This horse

A favorite warhorse of emperor Taizong, Zhaoling Mausoleum, seventh century CE, Shaanxi.

power, in turn, ensured the Tang's preeminence among the steppe peoples and kept China at peace.

Taizong commissioned a magnificent mausoleum to receive his mortal remains, for when the time came, and had it decorated with six life-sized portraits, in bas-relief, of actual horses.* This kind of bas-relief was unusual for China but resembled the horse carvings in the ancient Iranian capital of Persepolis. (It is possible that artisans from Iran assisted with the mausoleum, for, as it happened, some Iranian princes in Taizong's service were also interred in there.) The emperor's testament explained: "Since these war chargers carried me in every battle against the enemy's lines and rescued me from danger, their true images should be portrayed on stone and placed to the left and right of my tomb." Three of the horses are depicted

---

* After the abandonment and looting of the mausoleum, the carvings were carted away in 1912. Four of them wound up in a local museum, but two found their way to the University of Pennsylvania's Penn Museum, where they delight most visitors; the exception is the Chinese, who dearly want them back.

in a flying gallop, with all four hooves off the ground. Four are shown pierced with arrows, reflecting actual wounds they had received in battle. Each horse sported a different coat—bay, shaggy yellow, yellow and white, piebald, black, and brick red—and each bore a proud name, some of steppe origin, including Tekin and Ishvar (both meaning "prince") and Shad ("ruler"). The images were so realistic that visitors speculated they could magically come back to life.

These horses' crenelated manes and tied-up tails recall the steppe style of grooming. Incidentally, here is an early example of horses equipped with stirrups, simple iron rings suspended from the saddle. For Taizong, horses were the seat on which emperors could firmly sit; in this age, riders experimented with new ways to sit more securely on horseback. This included improving their horsemanship.

The Art of Horsemanship

The era of conflict between Chinese, Turks, Scythians, and Huns that had preceded the long Tang-imposed peace witnessed major improvements in available techniques for fighting on horseback. Cosmopolitan-minded horse trainers and cavalry generals alike paid great attention to innovations in horsemanship, whether these came from east or west, enemies or allies. Knights-errant wandered back and forth between the palace of the Tangs and the tents of the khans, and between the court of the shahs of Iran and that of the Roman emperor in Constantinople, perfecting their horsemanship, showing off their elegant accoutrements, and participating in equestrian competitions.

To ease long journeys on horseback and to provide a more effective combat platform, horsemen adopted physical improvements to the saddle. The Turks are thought to have invented the saddle tree. This consisted of a wooden frame fitting lengthwise on either side of the horse's spine, to distribute the rider's weight laterally rather than vertically, and over more equine vertebrae. The saddle tree provided more comfort and stability for the rider, as well, and replaced the Scythian saddle, which simply padded the horseman's seat with pillows. Saddlemakers now built up the front of

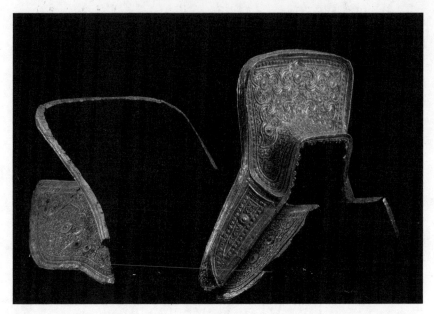

A gold-plated, Turkish-style saddle, possibly Khitan, twelfth to thirteenth centuries CE.

the rigid saddle with a pommel and the back with a cantle, producing the characteristic bucket shape of the Turco-Mongol saddle.[*]

The rigid saddle allowed riders to move their torsos more freely, since it provided a solid support for the thighs in the front and the coccyx in the back. This led cavalrymen to slowly begin to equip themselves with the characteristic curved saber, for slashing at their enemies in close quarters, this weapon replacing the short, stabbing sword of antiquity. Cavalrymen also abandoned throwing javelins, with limited reuse, in favor of lances, behind which they could now put their whole body weight without being pushed backward out of the saddle.

The more rigid tree saddle facilitated the use of stirrups, perhaps beginning in the fifth century. Scholars debate when horsemen first adopted this piece of equipment, and where it was invented. Today it is an indispensable

---

[*]   You can go to the bazaar in Kashgar today and buy a bare wooden saddle tree, similar to that of the Tang period, and ask the saddler to apply leather and brass decoration to suit your tastes and pocketbook. A more discerning equestrian will ask the saddler to custom-fit the tree to her horse's back.

means of mounting a horse, but early horsemen simply took hold of the horse's mane and vaulted onto its back. Wearing a full suit of armor made this more difficult, let alone while carrying the ubiquitous sword, cumbersome lance, hefty mace, bow, and arrow quiver. At first, grooms helped heavily armed warriors into the saddle. Single stirrups may then have come into fashion as an aid for mounting, and with time, riders found that using two stirrups allowed them to travel more comfortably over long distances. As with any invention, some riders resisted the stirrups. (Unlucky riders know that getting thrown from a horse with one foot caught in a stirrup can be very dangerous.) Hard evidence for the emergence and growing popularity of stirrups is scarce, since the earliest equipment may have been carved in perishable wood, not forged in iron. So this transition may have unfolded over a long period, from the twilight of the Scythians and Huns in the third century to the coming of the Turks in the fifth century.

Stirrups traveled to Europe with the incursions of eighth-century steppe invaders into the western steppe and the Hungarian plains. These invasions made the emperors of Constantinople and the principalities of eastern Europe familiar with the steppe peoples—Scythians, Avars, or Turks—whom they often recruited as mercenaries and auxiliaries. Characteristic steppe graves with horse sacrifices and riding tack have been uncovered across Russia, Ukraine, Poland, Hungary, Slovakia, Romania, and Bulgaria. The steppe style of riding and warfare prevailed across eastern Europe, as in China.

In other respects, however, horsemanship of this period did not prefigure modern riding. The Turks typically did not shoe their horses, since in their native habitat horses' hooves needed no such protection. Later, for warfare, horseshoes came into use to protect horses from the use of spiked obstacles deployed by the enemy. Spurs, too, were unpopular with Asian riders, who used the whip to provide horses with additional signals for maneuvering.

Warhorses of this period often wore protective armor, sometimes of hardened leather, more rarely iron plate, and most often a simple padded or felt skirting. Even the latter provided some defense against arrows, for which horses were always easy targets. Some of Emperor Taizong's favorite steeds had received six or seven arrow wounds each. Before battle such protection could be rolled up and carried in front of the saddle. These accoutrements were often works of art by themselves: the saddle blankets of brocaded silks; the stirrups and chamfrons (head protection) of guilloché or niello metal; the saddle decorated with lapis lazuli or turquoise. Such, then, was the mounted perfection of the Tang, Turkish, or Iranian heavy cavalry.

We can see just such mounted warriors depicted on the walls of the seventh-century archaeological site, in the suburbs of Samarkand, known as the palace of Afrasiyab, a legendary Turkish ruler. These paintings celebrate the Turks, who were then at their apogee, welcoming embassies from China, India, and Iran. It was indeed common for mercenaries, diplomats, hostages,[*] and horse traders to travel from one end of the steppe to the other, enjoying a standard reception protocol concerning guests, participating in a ritual gift exchange, and competing in games, inevitably equestrian: racing, hunting, polo, and archery.

The feasting horsemen of the Afrasiyab paintings recall the literary heroes of this age, like Lu Bu in *The Romance of the Three Kingdoms*, Tariel in *the Knight in Panther Skin*, David of Sassoon in the Armenian epic of that name, Digenes Akritas in the Anatolian Greek epic, and Siyavosh of the *Shahnameh*. Each of these paladins rides a famous warhorse endowed with quasi-magical powers: Red Hare for Lu Bu, David's Kourkig Jalali, Siyavosh's Shabrang. These warriors are also described as gifted horsemen who wander from court to court in search of adventure and exploits.

In real life as in literary epics, heroes showed off their horsemanship and courtly manners in polo games. In the fourth-century *Life of Saint Qardagh*, the shah of Iran invites a rising young athlete to participate in a polo game. His physique and fine horsemanship win accolades from the shah and his courtiers. After Qardagh wins a chukker (inning or quarter), the shah appoints him on the spot to the rank of provincial governor.[†] Similarly, the *Shahnameh*'s Siyavosh, wandering in exile, is invited by the Turkish khaghan Afrasiyab to show off his skills in polo. Siyavosh tactfully suggests that he play on the Turks' side, and not against them, but Afrasiyab will have none

---

* In those days, royal houses often exchanged hostages as part of their diplomatic activities. In the best case, hostages enjoyed hospitality consistent with their dignity.

† Later, Qardagh converts to Christianity and meets martyrdom at the hands of the same shah; hence his sainthood.

of it: "I have heard your mallet is invincible," he taunts. Both protagonists pick their teams and set to. Afrasiyab sends a ball soaring through the air; Siyavosh intercepts it on the fly and knocks it even higher. The passion for the game gets the better of the Iranians, and Siyavosh has to temper his side, yelling in Persian, "This is a game, not a battlefield. Let the Turks get possession." He realizes it would be dangerous to actually beat his hosts. After throwing the game, the exiled Iranians enjoy the hospitality of the Turks for months to come.

The game of polo is the most salient example of the shared equestrian culture in this era of knights-errant. No one can say for sure where the game originated, since it probably developed out of the traditional horseback competitions played by steppe people, like today's *buzkashi, kokpar,* or *kokboru.* It is thought that the Iranians were the first to play polo as a royal pastime, as well as for military training. Until modern times, contestants did not ride specially bred polo ponies but, rather, played with the same powerful animals they used for combat. The horses were, accordingly, as fierce or fiercer than the players. The game spread across Asia as the wandering mounted paladins sought fortune and adventure.

The ubiquity of polo is evidenced by the number of playing fields known to have existed. One of the Turkish khaghans built a pitch in Kashgar and held public games there. In Constantinople, the Roman emperor situated the polo field just below his palace, where today's Orient Express enters Istanbul's Sirkeci train station. The caliph of Baghdad, al-Mahdi, provided for a playing field outside the city's Halba Gate, where his Turkish slave soldiers excelled in the game and were eagerly followed by the enthusiastic, non-horse-riding public. Of these many fabled royal polo fields, we can still visit the Maidan-e Shah,* in Esfahan, one of the world's most glorious public squares, with marble goalposts still standing at either end.

The Tang, naturally, built the world's most spectacular polo field, inside the palace compound. The walls, we read in one description, were covered with satin; the grounds, plastered with a mix of eggs and sand, were said to have resembled a mirror's brilliance and smooth, even surface. Both Taizong and Xuanzong promoted this game. We can still watch Tang polo

---

* Since the 1979 revolution, the square has changed names. It is now Naqsh-e Jahan Square.

players on the walls of the tomb of Tang Prince Zhanghuai, where the lithe
and agile play of the horses is recorded as if they were in flight. The players, twenty of them, wear uniforms and caps and carry lacrosse-like sticks
with crescent-moon blades. The goals were one hundred paces apart. Like
today's elite athletes, horsemen were recruited to play for wealthy spon-
sors. Wandering Iranian players, like the legendary Siyavosh, are thought
to have brought the game to China.

Ladies of the court, assisted by handsome Turkish grooms, also learned
to play polo, but one authority recommended that women ride donkeys
rather than horses in order to reduce the risk of serious injuries. Indeed, the
sport occasioned more than its share of injuries, as well as deaths. When
his favorite player died in an accident during one match in 844, Emperor
Wuzong ordered decapitation for the remaining players—another source
of danger. Later, Emperor Taizong of the Jin dynasty[*] used the violence
of the polo game as cover to have his political enemies killed. No wonder
the civilian members of the government criticized this game, just as they
criticized hunting.

Playing a game like polo requires, on the horse's part, a careful educa-
tion. The horse breeders must select the most promising colts or fillies,
those that show intelligence and empathy. Such a horse doesn't shy away
from the dangers its rider confronts, and anticipates the dangers the rider
may not notice—taking the rider where he needs to go, either into combat or out of danger. Highly conditioned by constant exercise, the horse
can easily change its lead (switching from leading with the left foreleg to
the right foreleg or vice versa) and can collect itself to change directions
on a dime, without losing its balance or throwing its rider. If a *manège*, or
enclosed training area, is available, the horses will be made to practice riding in circles or figure eights. Horses also have to learn to ride in formation,
with each animal leading with the same foreleg and maintaining the same
degree of collection, so that the group can turn in the same direction at the
same time. Without this training, a polo game cannot be won. In war, a

---

[*]   Confusingly, there were three emperors named Taizong, one each in the Tang, Song, and
Jin dynasties.

Polo-playing ladies of the Tang dynasty, seventh to ninth centuries CE.

cavalry army without the necessary discipline quickly becomes more dangerous to itself than to the enemy.

For all the cosmopolitan exchange among the paladins, different riding schools reflected the unique character of each horse-breeding environment. The steppe peoples—the Turks and, later, the Mongols—raised their horses in semi-liberty, letting them graze freely on the open steppe, winter and summer. The Turks coaxed foals into discipline rather than forcing them. The Mongols, on the other hand, broke their two-year-old colts brutally and efficiently, lassoing startled animals out of the herd and riding them bareback to exhaustion. Thereafter, both Turk and Mongol riders controlled their horses with voice and hands, via the reins or the whip, which the Mongols used freely. They rode with their knees up on short-hooked stirrups, like modern jockeys, protecting the horses' flanks from their legs so as not to impart any lateral movement to their mounts. The goal was flat-out speed. Their horses neither trotted nor ambled, so rides of thirty to fifty miles a day took place at a gallop, two hours at a time, the riders raising their haunches off the saddles to avoid being tossed around like a ball on a string. The steppe horses maintained their conditioning by being constantly ridden in races and hunting, an approach to horseback riding that suited a people living in the saddle, where every man was a soldier, and where one could not afford to invest too much in a horse who might not live through a bad winter.

Settled peoples like the Iranians fed their horses fodder during the winter. Their horses grew more powerful as a result, and more headstrong. Iranian stallions in particular required a much lengthier period of training and more skill on the part of the rider, compared to the geldings of the steppe. Iranian riders had to use extra strength and dexterity to master their mounts. They rode low in the saddle and used their whole body, including their legs, to guide the horse. This gave them more flexibility when engaged in a mêlée with enemies coming at them from all sides. Because of their technical sophistication, the Iranians tended to look down on the rough-and-ready approach of the steppe peoples. The Chinese followed Turkish riding styles; the Indians, the Iranians.

Another school of riding came out of Arabia, where horses played a very different role in daily life. There, the camel had its natural habitat. This animal served as the battle platform of the Bedouin for their massed attacks and hand-to-hand combat. The horse, by contrast, was a rare and much sought-after possession. A Bedouin would not risk his precious horse in open combat but rode out on nocturnal raids upon a mare, prized for her silence and speed. As the tenth-century Arab poet and adventurer al-Mutanabbi wrote of his stealthy raids, "I am known for the night and the horse and the spear."* Arab horses were treated like spoiled children, fed delicacies from the owner's meals, and often bedded down inside the rider's tent for warmth and safety. They thus acquired the strong sociability trait that so endears Arab horses to their owners today. The Arab horse also developed a powerful sprinting ability, since they were used for only short bursts of speed for raiding. When a horse is fleeing rather than attacking, its most natural instincts are brought out, making them unbeatable over brief distances. This is the trait that attracted the interest of European racing enthusiasts centuries later. But Arab mares were just one of several breeds that vied for the affection of horse-mad aristocrats in this age.

---

*   الخَيْلُ وَاللَيْلُ وَالبَيْداءُ تَعرِفُنـي
وَالسَّيفُ وَالرَّمحُ والقِرْطاسُ وَالقَلَـمُ

A cosmopolitan gathering of horse admirers in eleventh-century Damascus enjoyed debating the pros and cons of different horse breeds. Some praised the steppe geldings of the Turks. Other prized the stabled and highly trained Iranian stallions. Still others acclaimed their pampered Arab mares. The Turks, though, won the argument with the following horse tale, recorded by the princely dilettante and horse lover Mubarak Qasim Zangi.

A Turkish prince once brought a horse from beyond the Pamirs as a present for the caliph of Baghdad. The courtiers found it very ugly, but the prince explained that this was a mountain horse, one whose dam had been left picketed beside a hot spring. Out of the hot spring came a fiery sire, which covered the mare and engendered this half-wild animal with a gray coat, a black spine stripe, and zebra-like coloring on the ankles. In the manner of his breeding, this horse recalled the dragon horses of ancient legend. Despite this wonderful bloodline, the caliph accepted the gift horse with barely feigned condescension.

Undaunted, the Turk proposed a race to demonstrate the true value of the horse. The caliph assented. The Turk saw the wisdom in the betting man's adage "horses for courses," so he adroitly selected the kind of course that would favor his horse. The four-legged contestants were conveyed the night before the competition to a distance of fifteen leagues, or forty-five miles, from Baghdad. This long distance gave an outsized advantage to the steppe-raised horse. The race began at the break of day, and before the morning prayers were said, the Turk's horse had arrived at the finish line. The horse then started off again and completed another fifteen leagues. In contrast, the caliph's Arabs pranced to the finish line in the early afternoon, while the Iranian horses, joked one wit, completed the race like the horse pieces on the chessboard: they had to be pushed forward by their riders. The caliph was so impressed by the steppe horse that he ordered the Turk back to the Pamirs to acquire more such animals.

Later the caliph asked Hizam al-Khuttali, the son of his Turkish chief equerry, to compile everything that was known about Turkish, Persian, and Arab horses into a treatise; the man did so, producing *al-Furusiyya wa'l Baytara* ("Of Horses and Veterinary Sciences"), which preserved much of Baghdad's equestrian lore for generations of horse enthusiasts in the

Arabic-speaking world. The court of Baghdad held horsemanship in high
regard. Indeed, the very word for horsemanship in classical Arabic, *siyasat*,
سياسة, came to mean "politics," since riding a horse involved, both metaphor-
ically and literally, matters of state.[*]

Yet for all the perfection and sophistication that the Turks, the Tang, the
Iranians, and the Arabs brought to the art of riding, the ancient sense that
horses were not entirely of this world persisted.

The World of the Unseen

As we've seen, humans have a relationship with horses unlike that with any
other animal. Canines are too docile to engender the kind of complex emo-
tions that horses do; dogs suffer from too much familiarity. We live in such
close proximity with them that they are just another member of the household. The horse, on the other hand, is both an intimate and the other. The
horse is unpredictable. The horse needs space. Identifying a good horse is
much more difficult than selecting a dog. The horse's strength, endurance,
robustness, intelligence, obedience, and beauty are all mysteries that we
must explore and uncover. Having chosen a horse to ride, then mastering
it, gives rise to a special relationship between rider and horse. The cultural
traditions of both steppe and settled peoples offer ample evidence of this
deep bond. This is a journey that begins at a very emotional level and takes
us to the realm of spiritualty and connoisseurship.

The journey began as soon as people experienced the speed of the horse,
directly, as riders. The sensation of galloping on a speeding steed is as close
as our ancestors ever came to flight. A fleet horse will gallop at twenty-five
miles per hour. An exceptional horse can attain fifty miles per hour. The
Turkish bard Dadaloğlu evoked this cult of speed:

> *The horse cocks his ears and stares,*
> *Like a drake that swims in the lake;*

---

[*]   The words *siyasat* ("politics") and *riyasat* ("statecraft"; see p. 229) both derive from words
for horses. In English, the verb "to govern" originates from the Greek κυβερναω, "to steer"
or "to pilot." For Europeans, sailing ships, not horses, provide the metaphor for ruling.

He tosses his mane like scattering antelopes.
The horse races like a flood, worthy of a hero. *

From the beginning, people associated fast horses with winged animals, birds but especially dragons, who were thought to slumber in hot springs and lakes. Ancient steppe nomads, like those buried in the Scythian tombs of Pazyryk, draped their horses in death with dragon costumes. The medieval Turks continued to clothe their horses in such a manner. From these ancient times arose the practice of knotting horses' manes with tufts of silk to recall the dragon's spiky back. A Mongol legend recalls a hero who lassoed three gray heavenly horses. In order to placate the gods and obtain an heir for the childless clan chief, the hero wove five colored silk scarves into each of the horses' manes and set them free. The effect of the bright patches of cloth down the horses' necks transformed them, in a shamanistic way, into galloping dragons. Other legends attribute this practice to Genghis Khan himself.

Another steppe legend tells of a people grazing horses by the shores of a lake, from whence emerged aquatic monsters that covered the mares. This recalls the steppe practice of allowing wild stallions to breed with domestic mares, to improve the hardiness of the breed. It also brings to mind the many legends about primal horses arising from watery, cosmological chaos. This association between dragons and horses continued for centuries. Both animals figure on the exquisitely carved tomb of Alauddin, a thirteenth-century Turkish ruler of Konya, in Anatolia. The exhilaration that galloping on a dragon-like horse produced remained a large part of the horse's attractiveness to humans. But the cult of the horse embraced more than speed and near flight.

The veneration of the horse also speaks to an interior transformation within the rider. Horses are prey, not predators. Along with eyes on the sides of their heads and ears that can point backward, they developed a

---

* *At kulağın dikmiş de göz süzer*
Gövel ördek gibi göllerde yüzer
Çırpındırır yele, ceyrândir tozar
Atin eşkini seldir, yegite gerek
(From www.zdergisi.istanbul/makale/at-mitleri-304.)

powerful hind-leg kick to dispatch their pursuers, not to attack—and yet humans ride them into war. In this case, the anxiety of the mount finds its echo in the anxiety of the rider. Buddhists imagined the horse to be the image of the human soul: fearful, flighty, yet ultimately obedient. They saw the conflicts raging inside the animal as parallels to conflicts that erupt within us. Milarepa, an eleventh-century Tibetan sage, welcomed the possibilities of this spiritual journey:

In the temple of my breast
The horse which is my mind flies like the wind.
He gallops on the plains of great bliss.
If he persists, he will attain the rank of a victorious Buddha.
Astride such a horse, one attains the highest illumination.

This sentiment is echoed both in the Avestan hymns and in Plato's *Phaedrus*, showing the persistence and power of this metaphor.

To tame a horse, one asserts human will over the animal world. Anyone who has ridden a recalcitrant horse has had to surmount the same fears as the first riders, for the horse remains partly wild. For this reason, the act of mounting a horse became entwined with chiefly rituals. Prior to the introduction of stirrups, a newly elevated Turkish khan would leap into the saddle and be led around the encampment by his followers, who trudged beside him on foot. Later on, the Turks of Anatolia performed a more elaborate version of this ceremony when the new sultans made a journey of several days, accompanied by their dismounted entourage, into their capital, Konya.

The chief on his horse was more than just a figure of political power. The horse became a cosmological symbol, representing space and time. The Turks and the Chinese, like the ancient Huns, mustered warhorses according to their coat colors: the red sorrels, the black, the blue gray, the white, and the palomino. These corresponded to the five cardinal directions of the steppe and of Chinese cosmology: south, north, east, west, and center. This formation symbolically associated the cavalry with world domination.

The rider dominated time, as well. When a ruler mounted a bucking black-and-white stallion, those colors symbolized the succession of night and day; the fierce bucking suggested the unpredictability of destiny; the stallion represented the speed with which time passes. The very act of mounting such a horse awaited the recommendation of astrologers, who would choose the auspicious moment when the rider could become the lord of time. A fourteenth-century Turkish poet, Mustafa Darir Erzeni, described the scene this way:

The king no sooner set his foot in the stirrup,
Than he mounts the piebald steed,
And from the horse's neighing,
The army knows its royal horseman. *

Finally, the horse came to represent time and nature not just for khans and sultans but for ordinary people. Like any part of the natural world, the horse embodies the cycle of the seasons and the years. Mares foal in spring or summer, when grass abounds. Then, during the dry winter, they survive by foraging on roots and scrub. In the twelve-year zodiacal cycle of animal signs observed by the Chinese, the steppe peoples, and the Afghans, the Year of the Horse is traditionally thought to have an important influence on the climate and on men. Because horses like cold weather, the Year of the Horse foretells bitter winters, and because horses are intimately associated with war, its year presages conflicts. Children born in the Year of the Horse will always be on the move, in war, on the hunt, or traveling. Those born in the first six months will become, like the horse, companions of kings, good-looking, brave, and intelligent. Those born in the latter six months will be stubborn and bad-tempered. In this way, countless generations were born and lived according to the influence of the horse.

These emotional, often unconscious associations between the rider and the horse gave rise to the belief that horses are numinous, that they are a

* *Koydu ayağını rikâbina şâh,*
Tâ ola suvâr ablaka nâgâh.
Gäş olunup sahîl-i ablak-i şâh,
Çehsuvâr oluşuğunu bilirdi sipâh.
(Mustafa Darîrî Erzenî, "Yüz hadisler tercümesi," Alî Emîrî Library, manuscript from Çer'iyye no. 1154, fol. 133.)

vehicle for divine communication. The most important and persistent role
of the horse was to be the vehicle for the hero into the next world. The
ancient Turks placed horses on the funeral pyres of the deceased, like the
Scythians and, indeed, like Achilles in the *Iliad*. The fourteenth-century
traveler Ibn Battuta commented on the burial practices of the Turks, who
had accepted Islam five hundred years earlier:

> The khan who had been killed was then brought, and a large sepulcher
> was dug for him under the earth, in which a most beautiful couch
> was spread, and the khan was with his weapons laid upon it. With
> him they placed all the gold and silver vessels he had in his house,
> together with four female slaves, and six of his favorite mamluks, with
> a few vessels of drink. They were then all closed up, and the earth
> heaped upon them to the height of a large hill. They then brought
> four horses, which they pierced through at the hill, until all motion in
> them ceased; they then forced a piece of wood into the hinder part of
> the animal till it came out at his neck, and this they fixed in the earth,
> leaving the horses thus impaled upon the hill.

The Turks in Anatolia continued to entomb heroes with their horses as
late as the fourteenth century. Later, when stricter Islamic orthodoxy discouraged such rites, the monarch's riderless horse would follow his funeral
cortege with his saddle facing backward, a tradition that has passed into
Western practice, as evidenced in the funeral corteges of American presidents Lincoln and Kennedy. On the steppe, the more elaborate sacrificial practices lasted until the middle of the nineteenth century. Until very
recently, Central Asian Turks would mount a sacrificed horse's tail on a pole
erected over the deceased's grave; such markers can still be seen today.[*]
    The horse occupied a profound space in the imaginations of the Tang
and their contemporaries. From the sky above to the waters of the underworld, from the soul to the state, from enthronement to interment, the

---

[*]   Later, these banners became a sign of military rank. In the Ottoman Empire, the sultan
was preceded by six or seven horsetail banners. A pasha, or general, could have one, two, or
three horsetail banners, depending on his importance.

horse represented the journey of life itself. Those who honored the horse, therefore, took great pains to capture its essence.

Capturing the Essence

The steppe people had the most at stake when it came to understanding horses. The horse was their livelihood, their family pride, their political survival. They believed their knowledge of the horse superior to that of the sedentary peoples. Yet even within steppe communities, some knew more than others. There arose a profession: individuals with quasi-magical insights into horses, the *synšy*. From looking at a foal, these horse experts could tell its age, its sire, and whether it would grow to be an ambler or a galloper; they could even predict the properties of a foal in a mare's womb. One famous synšy made a fortune by buying horses with hidden talents on the cheap and then racing them to victory. Another synšy bought a foal that was about to be butchered and turned it into a prize racer. Still another synšy worked for six years training a warhorse for her husband to ride. One day, his friends called on him to ride off to war. They asked his wife if his horse was ready; she answered, "Tell my sultan [her husband] the horse will be ready in forty-three days," and so they put off their campaign for just so many days. Such were the ways of the steppe horse experts.

The Chinese sought, in their own way, to capture the essence of horses. They followed the tradition of Bole, according to whom the outward appearance of the horse had to be understood as balance of forces, of yin and yang: "On a thin horse one should be able to see the flesh; on a fat horse one should be able to see the bones." A kind of platonic essentialism should be visible in the animal's form: "The best horse has square bones, as if planed by a carpenter, where they should be square, and where they should be round, round like tossed on a potter's wheel."

Following Bole, Tang-era artists strove to bring these dynamics to life with ink on silk or paper. The court painter Han Gan's portrayal of Xuan-zong's horse Night-Shining White is strangely distorted in order to show-case the different desirable attributes on a two-dimensional surface. Han emphasizes the circles in the subject's shoulders and haunches, rendering them as idealized forms around which the horse's outline is designed. The

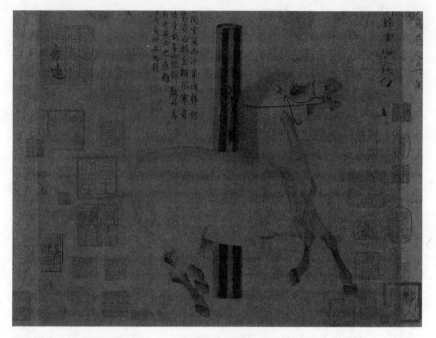

Han Gan's famous equestrian portrait, Night-Shining White, *ca. 750 CE.*

details, too, conform to what Bole would consider an ideal horse: his ears erect, his eyes bright, the eye socket curved above and round below, the muzzle squared above and round below. Han's masterpiece[*] was copied many times and provided a model for many subsequent painters of horses.

Tang-era painters mostly drew horses, not riders on horseback, unlike later European equestrian portraitists. They sought not to glorify the rider but to penetrate the essence of the animal. "Those who are good judges of paintings of horses will look for the essential spirit and muscular strength of the work," advised Liu Daochun, an eleventh-century connoisseur of horses and a noted art critic. "If the essential spirit is complete, then emotion emerges, and if the muscular strength is hardy, then powerfulness comes forth, and this must begin with the mouth, eyes, nose, ears, hooves, and joints." As with the bas-relief horses decorating Taizong's mausoleum,

---

[*]   Now in the collection of New York's Metropolitan Museum of Art.

the goal of the artist was to make something that could, with enough magic, come to life.

In fact, exceptionally for this period, artists drew their subjects from life. Only the quick-drying brushstrokes of the Chinese painter could capture on silk and paper the liveliness of the horse in movement. The greatest of the Tang poets, Du Fu, memorialized a painting session by one General Cao:

> *The late emperor had a heavenly steed,*
> *The Piebald Jade Blossom.*
> *Before the imperial throne,*
> *In front of the palace,*
> *Towering skyward, it posed for you.*
> *The imperial presence, smiling, filled*
> *Your hands with gold.*
> *The grand equerry and the palace guard looked on, dejected.*
> *Your student, Han Gan*
> *Grew by leaps and bounds*
> *In ability, in horse portraiture,*
> *Of remarkable appearence.*
> *But Han only drew the muscles,*
> *While you painted the marrow.*
> *For how could that fine horse*
> *Vanish with no trace?*
> *General, you paint expertly,*
> *Your art reflects genius.**

Without this element of live portraiture, the pure formalism of Bole's aesthetic criteria would not allow the Tang horses to leap off the page.

While engaged in a very metaphysical exercise, painters also had a mundane motivation to paint these exceptional horses: such portrayals supported the horse's application for admission into the Imperial Dragon

---

* The other imperial servants were dejected to see the emperor's largess go to the painter. Du Fu apparently esteemed General Cao as a better painter than Han Gan.

Stables. If a horse gained entry, its portraitist would receive a generous tip in reward. These painters acted as Chinese synšy, providing insights into the promising future of the horse.

In contrast to the great ink paintings that show only horses, or occasionally horses with dismounted grooms, Tang artisans produced models of both horses and riders: elegant women playing polo, intrepid hunters, or weary travelers. These sculptures in terra-cotta were glazed to yield three stylized colors: green, brown, and yellow (called *san cai* in Chinese). The oven firing yielded strikingly lifelike figurines, and the shimmering glaze recalled the animal's sleekness and sweat. Some examples have lost their glaze and come to us in bare terra-cotta. Even then, these barrel-chested steeds, with powerfully muscled legs, look ready to gallop away. These coveted objects accompanied Tang dignitaries into their tombs, ensuring the support of these numinous horses in the afterlife.

Inevitably Tang artists and poets contributed to an appreciation of the horse as a thing of beauty, as an object of desire in itself, beyond its utility for statecraft or war. Tang equestrian portraits have been collected for centuries, and gave rise to emulation as far away as Shiraz and Delhi when travelers brought back copies, or when visiting artists from farther west viewed Chinese collections. The tendency toward aestheticizing the horse was not necessarily a healthy one, however. Later Tang emperors spent too much time admiring their horses, or even paintings of their horses, rather than riding to hunt as Taizong had. Xuanzong's overly aestheticized horses hinted at the danger of focusing on the horse's soft power over its hard power. The dancing horses of Xuanzong could not save his reign, as new conflicts menaced both the Tang and the Turks.

Dropping the Reins

The Tang were lulled into thinking that the dangers of the turbulent steppe belonged to the past and that China would now live securely in its hegemony over the horse breeders. But this required living on a knife's edge with a court full of Turks of doubtful loyalty.

The Turkish khans, too, had enjoyed many decades of peaceful coexistence. The increasingly luxurious lifestyle of fine horsemanship and courtly contests gradually alienated the khans from their unruly herdsmen. But wary voices from the steppe warned against enjoying too fully the pleasures offered by China. It was as though the Tang had weaponized China's glamour in order to compromise the steppe chieftains, keeping them too distracted to organize raids or to plot against China. From being a military threat to the China from outside, the Turks became adventurers and intriguers on the inside.

In 755, when Xuanzong, the longest-reigning Tang emperor, believed life could get no better for him as he enjoyed his amors in his Palace of Eternal Youth, his own master of horses, An Lushan, started a fatal revolt. An Lushan himself was half Turk, half Iranic by birth, one of those foreign grooms who had risen to a high military rank. After much bitter fighting, the Tang managed to put down the revolt. It was said that the six horses of the long-dead Emperor Taizong magically appeared on the battlefield to quell the rebels—guardians of the Taizong mausoleum even reported seeing the statues of the six horses sweating and out of breath. But now not even magic could not save the Tang.

Tang horse and foreign groom, Tang Dynasty, 618–907 CE.

Quashing the rebellion forced the Tang to make a strategic retreat from the steppes, thereby abandoning most of their fifty-eight stud farms. In their desperation to acquire sufficient remounts, they bought on credit from distant steppe horse breeders. Their subsequent bankruptcy definitively brought down both the Chinese dynasty and their steppe allies, and an anarchy of competing horse powers swept over northern China. Turning their backs on the steppe, various successors to the Tang struggled to reconstitute an empire. The dancing horses were dispersed to military units along the border, among the ordinary warhorses. They were recognized, however, by their tendency to break into dance at the sound of military music.

The turbulence unleashed by the fall of the Tang reverberated across Asia. The Tibetans surged out of their frosty plateau and occupied much of the vacuum in Central Asia left by the retreating Chinese. Other steppe horse-breeding clans, having lost the huge Tang market for their services, either pushed deeper into China in search of buyers or plunder or, fleeing the Tibetans, set out for the west to try their luck in India, Iran, Anatolia, and eastern Europe. They sought new lands to raid, new kingdoms to rule, new markets for trade.

7

Hunting for Supremacy

Eurasia, 900–1200 CE

୧୬

A Serious Pastime

In the turmoil following the collapse of the Tang, horse-breeding peoples lost lucrative markets and China's protection. Worse, they lost their ancestral pastures to rivals. In search of better fortune, some migrated deeper into China. Others wandered westward.

Wherever they went, they hunted. Even if they had lost their flocks in their forced exile, with the remaining horses they could sustain themselves for months at a time, running down swift-footed antelopes and onagers, tens of thousands of which grazed on the steppe. When choosing new territories to inhabit, errant horsemen took into consideration the abundance of game as much as the availability of grass. When their wandering came to an end, the horsemen continued to hunt.

Hunting, though, was more dangerous than herding. Big game like elk and bears often turned on their pursuers. Apex predators—lions and tigers—sprang from the long grass to jump onto the backs of unwary horses. The dangers of the mounted hunt drew horse and rider into a deeper bond. An equally deep bond developed among the hunters, and hunting became their passion.

Heroes of *The Book of Dede Korkut*, a Turkish steppe epic dating back to the tenth century, thought of little else. "Brothers," says one, "hear my words. We have been sitting so long our backsides hurt; our spines have dried out from inactivity. Let's go hunting. Let's shoot birds with arrows and chase deer." The longer the hunt the better. Those horsemen rose and departed for a seven-day hunt. Elsewhere, *Dede Korkut* recorded, "When

360 braves set out for a hunt, they would be gone for months." This was possible because camp routine depended on women and children minding the flocks, milking the mares six times a day, foaling, and gelding. The men otherwise had nothing else to do, a fact remarked upon by Marco Polo when he visited the steppe in the thirteenth century.

In preparation for a big hunt, the local chief would send his followers out to prepare a campsite near a riverbank or in a forest where game was likely to hide. Such sites could be many days' ride from home, so tents were brought along for shelter. Some men were tasked with raising brightly colored silk tents on lofty polls. Others made ready cooking pots and spits for the expected game meat. Cool stream water was stored in jars for refreshment, along with fermented mare's milk and red wine. The more elaborate the preparations for the hunt, and the more hunters invited to join, the greater the fame of the chief organizing the hunt.

The hunters rose at dawn, a full day in the saddle ahead of them. *Dede Korkut* describes a scene of great beauty spread out before them, with mountains "dark, and beautiful-breasted." Horsemen and horses were almost intoxicated by early morning scents of wildflowers just opening in the sunshine.

With the sun high in the sky, the hunters then began to flush out the game, transforming the tranquility of nature into a flurry of fur and feathers. Hunting hounds barked themselves into a frenzy at the scent of the prey. The riders, blinded by the dust raised by the horses' hooves, galloped madly after the baying hounds.

To conserve their arrows, and to show off the speed of their horses, hunters often captured their prey by throwing their lassos around the fleeing animals' necks. *Dede Korkut*'s hero Begil used his bowstring to catch deer. If the animal turned out to be too thin, he contented himself with notching its ear, so that his companions would know that Begil had trapped it. If it was fat, he slit the animal's throat and swung it over his saddle to bring it back to the campsite.

Some wealthy chiefs set out with tamed cheetahs, who rode gamely behind the rider on the horse's croup. The big cat and the horse were ancient enemies, but the hunting horse had learned not to fear the feline. When the alert cheetah spotted prey, it leapt off the shabrack, or saddlecloth, and bounded across the steppe after the deer or onager. The horse, bearing the hunter, followed behind with pounding hooves. A poet, Asadi Tusi, likened the cheetahs attacking the antelope to thieves falling on a caravan. Hunting with cheetahs combined the raw violence of beast-on-beast predation with the sustained effort of the steeplechase.

Besides hounds and big cats, other horsemen rode with majestic falcons, perched proudly on forearms well-padded against the raptors' fierce grip. With these they hunted migrating geese, a difficult target for even the most sharp-eyed archer.[*] Large raptors even brought down antelopes for their masters.

Hunting horsemen also pursued big and dangerous game, at great personal risk. "The hunter does not get a jackal every time he hunts. One day a leopard may eat the hunter," according to Sa'di Shirazi. A particularly dangerous yet sought-after trophy was the dominant bull moose. This brawny animal acquires a harem of females during the mating season, emitting an unearthly braying that penetrates for miles. Hunters would ride up close to the bull moose, disguised with a moose head, and imitate its mating call, driving it into a rage. Fast and powerful, with enormous antlers, the bull moose would then charge, which could be fatal to a hunter who did not draw the bow swiftly and accurately. Hunters learned to retreat in the face of such an attack, while twisting their torso backward in the saddle to let loose arrows at the pursuing beast. This allowed the rider to keep a distance between the target and himself, while also offering him an opportunity to bring the animal down. The same technique applied in combat is known as the "Parthian" shot. Though the name recalls the wars of an ancient Iranian dynasty against Rome, the rear-facing shot was practiced by all the steppe peoples with deadly effect against their targets, animal and human.

At dusk, the hunting party rubbed down their horses and wrapped them in blankets against the cooling evening. Around the campfires, reclining on colorful bolsters, the hunters refreshed themselves with kumis or red wine and feasted on freshly stewed or grilled meats and fowl. A bard recited ballads, recounting tales of other hunts.

In the steppe epic tradition, the hunt is where adventures and misadventures

---

[*]   In modern Kazakhstan and Kyrgyzstan, this form of hunting is still practiced.

began—including quarrels occasioned by hunting. In another episode of
Dede Korkut, Begil's jealous khan stirred up a feud by wondering aloud, "Is
the skill in the horse or in the man?" Those present said, "It is in the man,
my khan." The khan insisted otherwise: "No. If the horse does not do his
work, the man cannot boast. The skill is in the horse." Begil abandoned his
service to the khan over this affront. Quarrels could turn into blood feuds,
and rivals used the cover of the hunt to shoot down other participants—
their deaths could conveniently be attributed to attacks by wild beasts.
Many hunters lost their lives this way. Meanwhile, unfaithful wives plotted
against their husbands while the latter were absent hunting; the clan's enemies took advantage of a prolonged hunt to attack the flocks and kidnap the
women left to guard them. These bardic stories functioned as a warning to
horsemen and chiefs alike to keep their jealousies in check.

By inviting horsemen to join him on the hunt, a local chief could constitute a larger following. He showered hospitality on his invited guests, making sure they enjoyed the best position in the cavalcade to get the best shots
off, to kill the choicest game. Over time this ambitious chief could vie with
others for leadership over the horse breeders. His hunts would grow bigger,
involving as many as three thousand or even five thousand horsemen.

For a great chief with thousands of dependent households dispersed across
the steppe, a big hunt provided an occasion to fraternize with his followers.
Chiefs regularly planned hunts in different corners of their domains in order
to refresh their personal ties with the local people. Just as the hunt helped
bind horses and riders together, astute chiefs could use hunts to bind horsemen to his banners. Both an outward symbol of power and a useful mech-
anism for sealing alliances, hunts were much more than mere displays or
sporting events. Great chiefs used hunting to establish vast steppe empires.

An Empire of Hunters

Silk scrolls, mural frescoes, and paintings of the Northern Grass School—
dedicated to recording their rustic way of life—celebrate the hunts of the
Khitans, a tenth-century steppe people from today's Mongolia. The official
histories of the Khitans confirm this visual record of well-attended hunts,
through which the great khans showed off their prowess in the saddle and

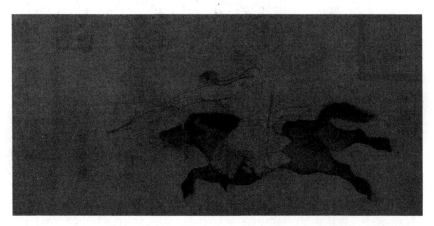

A Khitan hunter chasing his game, attributed to Huang Zongdao, ca. 1120.

with the bow. Unlike the courtiers of the Tang, who criticized hunting, the Khitan khans' entourages consisted only of other enthusiastic hunters. While no Khitan epics in the model of the Turkish *Dede Korkut* have come down to us, their historical records are full of information and rules about hunting. Their bards, too, must have celebrated epic hunts. Their nation itself evolved out of, and sustained and defended itself through, the hunt.

The Khitans were known to the Tang emperors as a people of hunters and horse breeders who reliably delivered tens of thousands of remounts each year to the horse-mad dynasty, then at the apogee of its power in the eighth century. The Khitans particularly impressed their Tang patrons with their fine horses, and this made their fortune. In recognition of their services, the Khitan khans received gifts and important-sounding Chinese titles. They also came to understand the workings and dysfunction of the Tang regime. When the Tang collapsed amid rebellion and bankruptcy, the trade in horses ceased; the ties between the Sons of Heaven and the khans frayed, and the khans' own power over the simple horse breeders faded, leaving clans and bands to seek their fortunes in the growing chaos.

In 907, a previously minor Khitan chief, Abaoji, took advantage of the chaos to seek and win election as supreme khan, or khaghan. One of his claims to fame came from having shot and killed a real live dragon, whose curious skeleton trophy graced, for a time, the khan's tent before being lost to history. Now he had become the man of the hour. He invited the other khans to celebrate his elevation with an elaborate hunt, following long-standing Khitan custom. After the successful conclusion of the hunt, we can imagine what Abaoji and his khans discussed over their campfires. How could the khans maintain the loyalty of the horse breeders without the largesse that used to pour forth from the Tang? Given the anarchy prevailing in China, who would profit from the opportunities for plunder and conquest, if not the Khitan people?

Abaoji grasped the nettle. He proclaimed himself emperor, something neither the chanyu of the Huns nor khaghan of the Turks had dared to do. He mustered first three hundred thousand cavalry troopers, then five hundred thousand, and finally one million. This snowballing of his followers reflected his ever-greater military success, as horse breeders eager for plunder rallied to his banners. He erected a walled city in the Inner Mongolian steppe, giving it the ambitious name Huangdu, or Imperial Capital. Immediately outside the walls he laid out a vast park with five banners in the five primal colors of geomancy: black for water and the cardinal direction north, white for the west and metal, yellow for earth and the center, red for fire and the south, and blue for the east and grass. This became the imperial hunting park. But Abaoji's ambitions extended far beyond his verdant enclosure.

Abaoji's hunts allowed riders to hone their combat skills in preparation for conquest, as the tactics employed in the hunt and in combat were very similar. As in war, so in the hunt: simply running hell for leather at prey—or the enemy—was not a successful tactic. Prey animals—deer, onagers, or wild horses—can run as fast as the hunter's horse, or even outrun it,

The banners of a Khitan khan evoke geomancy powers. From "18 Songs of a Nomad Flute," unknown artist, early fifteenth century.

since they are all equally well adapted for survival on the steppe. Instead, hard-riding steppe hunters had to deploy ruthless cunning to trap their fleet-fleeing prey.

The horsemen would form a wide, shallow arc around the just-spotted game. They would then ride forward slowly, forcing the grazing game, if possible, toward an obstruction, like a ravine or a cliff. As they approached their prey, they deepened the arc of the crescent, still advancing gingerly so as not to incite panic. Only when they were very close, so close the game animals became frantic at the smell of horses, dogs, and men, did they close the circle. The prey would rush madly forward to escape, but escape would no longer be possible. The trap was complete. It was customary to let one or two beasts escape initially, both to trick the others into a sense of false security and as an act of token clemency.

This maneuver is often called *nerge*, after the Mongol expression, but Western writers more commonly use the French term for hunting with beaters, *battue*. This can be misleading because, in European hunts, the beaters are on foot. The steppe battue, on the contrary, involved thousands of fast-moving mounted hunters and, accordingly, a much greater degree of organization than required by hunting with beaters.

A battue-style encirclement hunt, by Giuseppe Castiglione, between 1741 and 1754.

The *battue* is not just a flanking operation; it is also an exercise in self-discipline, calling for both control over the horses and psychological mastery of the prey. To organize and coordinate the two flanks, the individual horsemen must hold back from engaging in order to keep pace with their companions, despite the excitement of the chase. The horses also get excited when they smell prey, and can easily get carried away into a wild gallop without careful restraint.

The psychological element of the battue explains why the steppe armies utilized this tactic not only to encircle their enemies but also to dishearten and destroy them. Steppe-based armies surrounded their opponents, harried them from a distance with a shower of stinging arrows, and forced them into a progressively smaller space for maneuvering. Closed in, and increasingly in poor formation, the oppressed enemy would see the opening of the circle behind them. Those with the fastest horses made a break for it and tried to gallop out of the closing trap. This movement quickly caused their fellow combatants' resistance to melt away: they abandoned their weapons and armor in an attempt to flee more speedily. The steppe attackers would then pursue them mercilessly, shooting them down from behind. The defeat was crushing.

Maurice, a sixth-century Roman emperor and author of the military manual *The Strategikon*, argued that because the Scythians used this hunting tactic in war, the Romans needed to practice battue hunting as well. The emperor warned, however, that if the riders were inexperienced, they would find this form of hunting impractical. His best advice for fighting the Scythians was to attack them in March, before their horses had fat on them. Maurice's use of the term "Scythian" was anachronistic—by his time, the Romans were already encountering Turkish horsemen. But his analysis of the difficulty of performing the battue and the danger this maneuver posed to the Romans was prescient.

Today we would call the battue a dual-use technology. One contemporary scholar of Inner Asia, Dan Mureşan, quipped that for the horsemen, "War is the continuation of hunting with the same means," paraphrasing Prussian general Clausewitz's dictum that war is a continuation of politics with different means. Abaoji's son and successor, the tenth-century Khitan ruler Emperor Taizong of Liao, famously observed, "Our hunting is not simply a pursuit of pleasure. It is a means of practicing for warfare." A century later, at the other end of Asia, Farrokhi, a Persian poet, expressed the same idea in praise of his patron: "You are a king hunter, and when no kings are left, of necessity, you hunt lions. . . . Since hunting resembles war, out of passion for battle, when you are resting from war your thoughts turn to hunting." Sometimes a khan's hunt switched from pursuing game to going after human prey. Big hunts often immediately preceded military campaigns, and acted as a kind of warm-up for the troops. The Khitans ultimately went hunting not only for game but also for kingdoms.

At the head of one million horsemen, Taizong, who took the same throne name as the great Tang emperor, seized northern China from the newly constituted Song dynasty and moved his imperial court from Inner Mongolia to the site of Beijing, then known as Youzhou, or "Peaceful Place."* Taizong then hunted the Song even farther south. The Song, with no assured supplies of horses from the steppe, were already on their back foot, and what resistance they offered succumbed to the Khitans' battue tactics. They withdrew behind the walls of their cities and grimly watched the Khitans devastate the countryside. Khitan horsemen soon discovered, however, that the lands south of the Yellow River offered poor campaign conditions for horses. Eventually, disgusted by the hot and humid climate, they told their khaghan-emperor that they were riding back home. Even Beijing got too hot for Taizong, who spent summers in the cool of the Yanshan, or Swallow Mountains, one hundred miles to the east.

The Khitans' conquest included a Chinese population outnumbering that of the horsemen. Khitan emperors promoted Buddhism and erected splendid stupas across their domains, and the Khitan state replaced the Han and the Tang in the imaginations of many peoples to the west, who were unaware of the existence of the remote Song dynasty. Most of Asia and Europe came to identify the Khitans as China itself. Another form of their name, Khitai, passed into Russian, with Китай as the word for China in that language, and into several western languages as Cathay. The Khitans kept the Song dynasty in check to the south and compelled their Turkish, Tibetan, and Manchurian neighbors into submission. The khaghans'

---

*   This was the first time the city served as an imperial capital.

hunting had been a success. Now they would also have to herd their new flocks, the urban and agricultural Chinese under their rule.

Ruling from Horseback

Despite their conquests in China itself, the Khitan khans initially maintained their steppe lifestyle. They lived in majestic tented cities, where soaring tent poles, gilded and vermilioned, held aloft enough silk cloth, decorated with spiraling designs of dragons, tigers, and wispy clouds, to launch a sailing ship. In times of peace the tents would be aligned with the sun, with the tent of the principal consort on the eastern end, and each successive wife in order of rank to the west. In times of war the tents would be pitched in a circle, like the wagons of the American pioneers, with the principal tent in the center. The animals were pastured far from the tents; only riding and milking horses would stay inside the ring.

The great khan's principal generals would have had similarly appointed but smaller yurts, with each descending rank in the hierarchy more soberly housed, ending with the common horse breeder, who happened to pasture his herds near the tent of the great khan. A city of tents, it looked and functioned more like a weekly market than a Chinese imperial capital like Chang'an. Indeed, these great tented meeting places were thronged with merchants and merchandise, especially livestock.[*]

When the great khan traveled, the entire tent city would pack up and disappear into the whirlwind of dust raised by the departing caravan. This preoccupation with mobility demonstrated the Khitans' acknowledgment that their power flowed from the saddle of a horse. Only by maintaining one million cavalry troopers could they see off rivals from elsewhere in the steppe and keep the Song dynasty cowed behind its river borders.

Ever mobilized for war and with devastating strategic and tactical advantages, the Khitans feared no direct military challenges. Politically, though, their position was fraught. On the one hand, the Khitan emperor was the khaghan of the steppe. The simple Khitan horse brand, the tamgha,

---

[*] To this day Ulan Bator has suburbs of yurts, which must resemble these tented cities of old, were it not for the ubiquitous satellite antennae.

became the imperial seal. To maintain his power over the horse breeders, the emperor traveled around his domains, organizing the great hunts according to the best season for each territory. Since steppe leadership was never uncontested, the inherently egalitarian horse breeders needed to see their leader in the flesh, unlike the subjects of the Chinese empire, for whom the emperor had historically been a distant, intangible figure. The khaghan also had to recycle the wealth he had accumulated, sharing the profits from the great markets, which sprang up wherever he pitched his tented camp.

At the same time, the Khitan rulers increasingly felt responsible for the well-being of their Chinese subjects, a preoccupation that the horsemen did not share. The hunt itself became a source of friction between the horsemen and the Chinese. Like the Tang emperor who had protested that his hunts did not damage farmlands, the Khitan emperors tried to keep their hunters away from Chinese farms. They passed laws to protect agriculture from hunting and prohibited the hunt altogether during the harvest, and they personally carried out inspections to see that those laws were properly executed. Further, when visiting China proper, the Khitan emperor had to fulfill the duties of the Son of Heaven and perform all courtly rituals. The first emperors found this dual role difficult to fulfill; Taizong confessed after his conquest of northern China, "I find joy in hunting and feasting on meat. From the moment I set foot in the Middle Kingdom I never feel happy."

Gradually however, the predilections of the Khitan rulers changed. They spent more and more time in Beijing. They stopped making war on Song China. They began to lose their enthusiasm for the steppe. They found the manners, smells, and conversation of the horsemen uncouth and unappealing. It was not uncommon, for example, for a horseman to dismount from his horse and relieve himself on the ground, all the while carrying on a conversation with his companions. Far removed from this rough crowd 150 years after the great Taizong, the last Khitan emperor, Tianzuo, it was rumored, rode poorly.

The ever-more sinicized Khitan emperors were gradually abandoned by the politically alienated horsemen, who no longer identified their well-being with a khaghan who was, for all intents and purposes, a pure Chinese emperor. In the face of a long period of peace with Song China, and

The Steppe Expands into the Settled Lands

Moscow

Kyiv

Volga R.

Western Steppe

Sarai

Constantinople

Ankara

Anatolia

Konya

Manzikert

Azerbaijan
Mughan

Jazira

Khwarazm

Jaxartes R.

Otrar

Balasag

Oxus R.

Cairo

Damascus

Bukhara

Pamir
Mountains

Baghdad

Iraq

Gorgan

Merv

Zagros Mountains

Samarkand

Iran

Hindu Kush

Shiraz

Ghazna

Punjab

Ormuz

Indus R.

Sindh

De

Thar Desert

Oman

H

Aden

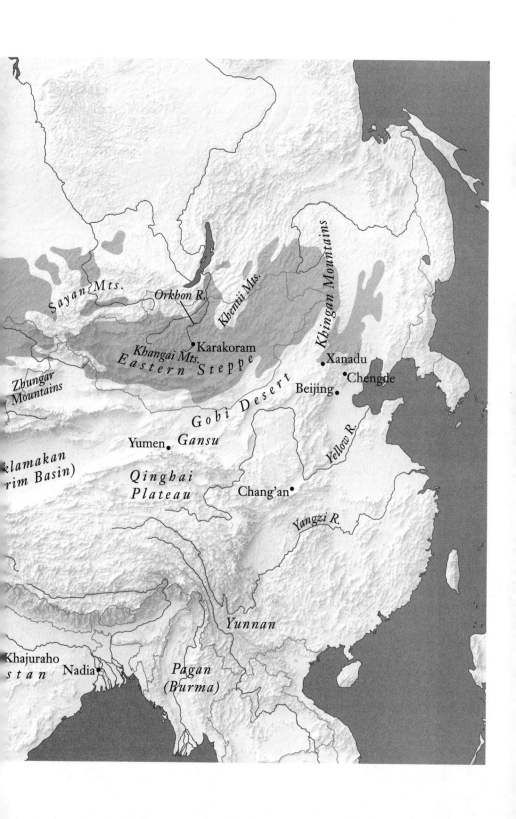

Sayan Mts.

Orkhon R.

Khentii Mts.

Khingan Mountains

Khangai Mts.

Karakoram

Eastern Steppe

Zhungar
Mountains

Gobi Desert

Xanadu

Chengde

Beijing

Yumen

Gansu

Yellow R.

klamakan
rim Basin)

Qinghai
Plateau

Chang'an

Yangzi R.

Yunnan

Khajuraho

s t a n

Nadia

Pagan
(Burma)

the resulting prohibition on raiding, the horsemen asked themselves what was in it for them, in return for loyalty to the khaghan. In 1125, a horse-breeding nation from Manchuria, the Jurchens, which had come to prominence supplying fine horses to the Khitans, revolted against their overlords and drove them out of Beijing, replicating the Khitans' own triumph two centuries earlier. The Jurchens, in turn, would succumb to the very same fate at the hands of Genghis Khan 109 years later. The Khitan collapse did not signal a revival by the Song Chinese, but simply the replacement of one flagging horse power by a fresher one.

Khitan conquests in China ushered in a new era, during which horsemen ruled extensive settled lands, not just in China but across Eurasia. During its golden age, the Tang had reckoned as its peers some of the most extensive and powerful empires the world had ever known: the Abbasid Caliphate of Baghdad, the Pratihara of northern India,* and the Byzantine Empire (or Eastern Roman Empire). Between 907 and 1071, all of those empires collapsed or retreated from raids by comparatively small bands of horse breeders. Steppe armies seized power over the northern portions of China and India and all of the Middle East, including Roman Anatolia. The Sons of Heaven, the maharajas, the caliphs, and the Roman basileis all lost power gradually, and then suddenly. The Tang dynasty had been a harbinger.

During the previous centuries of coexistence between the horse breeders and the settled states, the former thoroughly infiltrated the later. The elite strata of the settled empires dressed like, fought like, rode to the hunt with, and in many cases had been recruited from the steppe horse breeders. Moreover, in view of their equestrian accomplishments and their control of the all-important horse trade, horse breeders were the unavoidable candidates for high positions in procurement, stud management, and cavalry leadership within the settled states. It became only a matter of time before the steppe horse breeders ceased to be satisfied with ruling only over the steppe, like their predecessors the Huns, the Kushans, and the Celestial Turks. Centuries of comings and goings to and from the imperial courts of Chang'an, Baghdad, and Constantinople reduced the awe with which they held the rulers of the settled states. As in Tang China in the previous

---

* Best known for building the Khajuraho temples, with their graphicly erotic iconography.

century, steppe horsemen in high positions had worn thin the veneer of civilian power in many Eurasian states. It was almost as if the settled peoples were waiting for the barbarians.*

Steppe Breakout

The western steppe experienced delayed shock waves from the collapse of the Tang, as migrating steppe people reached the lands of Iran, India, Rome, and Kyiv in great numbers. The impact of this migration was greatest for Iran, then ruled by the Arab caliphs of Baghdad, and later Roman Anatolia. Both lands became unwilling hosts to millions of horses, with all the cultural and ecological change this entailed. This stands in stark contrast to China, which experienced little change under the Khitans and Jurchens. The divergent destinies of the eastern and the western settled people is suggestively reflected in the two great civilizational boundary markers, the Great Wall and the Wall of Gorgan.

Just as the Great Wall of China loomed over the hills of Shanxi Province to awe the horse-breeding peoples into submission, so the Wall of Gorgan dominated the open lands stretching 124 miles from the Caspian Sea to the Aladagh Range, the "speckled mountains," showing the determination of the ancient shahs of Iran to keep steppe peoples out of the nation's heartland. Covered by fired brick, with walkways six and a half feet high and in some places thirty-two feet wide, the wall rose sixteen feet above its dry moat. Thirty-six forts punctuated the wall at intervals, providing watchtowers and garrisons for thirty thousand soldiers, including cavalry. An elaborate system of hydraulics, including a dam three-quarters of a mile wide, provided the forts with running water. It must have been an extraordinary monument—certainly as imposing as China's Great Wall, far surpassing Hadrian's Wall and the Roman Limes in Germania. It is likely that the structure, visible traces of which remain today, was built by in the fifth

---

* "Because the barbarians are coming today
and the emperor's waiting to receive their leader.
He's even got a scroll to give him,
loaded with titles, with imposing names."
(Constantine Cavafis, "Waiting for the Barbarians," 1904)

century by the Iranian shah Peroz in defense against raiding Huns. A thousand years previously, an earlier wall may have been built by Cyrus the Great against the Scythians.

The wall separated two distinct ecosystems. South of the wall, the Gorgan River's willow trees let their branches droop into its fast-flowing waters. On the south bank grew rain-fed wheat, cotton, and even patches of oaks. North of the wall lay the steppe, dense with salicornia, a succulent herb rich in selenium. There pastoralism was the dominant form of land use.* Later Muslim tradition would marvel at the huge ruins of this wall, ascribing its construction to Alexander the Great, considered one of God's prophets, who shut out the hordes of Gog and Magog behind this barrier.

Those Muslim historians forgot who had built the Wall of Gorgan and, more important, why it had been built. In the eighth and ninth centuries, the caliph of Baghdad relied on powerful border lords to push the frontiers of their empire much farther into the steppe, for a time mitigating the need for a hard frontier. In China, by contrast, successive dynasties renewed and strengthened the Great Wall. Even the Khitans and Jurchens maintained it to demarcate the steppe from the settled lands. The Great Wall came to serve as a symbol of China's ability to exclude the steppe people, even though this was often an exception rather than the rule. Once the caliphal frontiers with the steppe faced the menace of new migrations, the lack of a hard border had consequences. The unenviable distinction of Iran and western Asia as a whole, as compared with the other great cradles of Asian civilization, China and India, was that steppe-like, arid, horse-friendly zones could be found throughout these territories, including western Afghanistan, Azerbaijan, Armenia, Georgia, and Iraq. Their rich pastures and even marginally grazeable deserts had attracted pastoralists since the days of the Scythians. Now the steppe horsemen leaving the frontiers of China discovered these pastures and began to migrate into Iran, first as a trickle, later as a flood.

One such migration started when the Khitans chased the Turks from

---

* And remained so until the 1930s, when irrigation works expanded the footprint of agriculture. Nevertheless, the line of the wall closely follows the modern border between Iran and Turkmenistan—a steppe legacy country par excellence.

Mongolia, even sending an army of three hundred thousand to turf them out of Kashgar, twenty-five hundred miles distant from Beijing. One Turkish band managed to establish a new Central Asian empire in what is today Kyrgyzstan, with its capital in Balasagun. Other bands of Turkish horse breeders had to flee farther, into Iran. The direction of flight almost always flowed north to south and east to west, because the biggest pastures were to the north and east (giving the peoples there more horse power), while the wealth of Iran attracted those fleeing. The Turks' new settled neighbors had the same appetite for steppe horse power as China, and provided opportunities for the horsemen similar to those they had enjoyed under the Tang.

The Turks entered Iran both as elite slaves and as freemen. The caliphs of Baghdad and their border lords recruited young horsemen as slave soldiers. To complement riding skills already acquired in their herding childhood, they underwent rigorous training in archery and swordsmanship. Bright candidates received further instruction in literature and the arts, which enabled them to rise to high positions in the army and in the court. But the name of their social class, *mamluk*, which means "owned," recalled their origins as enslaved individuals. The mamluks did not lose their connection with their herding kin, and often recruited family into their regiments. Being the mamluk of a powerful patron enabled one to seek favors for relatives, trading privileges, better pastures, and famine relief. With the right connections, a mamluk could install his birth clan on lands granted to him in return for service. Thus began the process of introducing the politics of the steppe into the military elite, as had happened earlier in Tang China, and of diluting the mamluks' loyalty to the caliph of Baghdad and the border lords.

The other route for steppe penetration arose when the border lords raised levies from entire clans. In return for protecting this or that segment of the frontier against still more hostile raiders, clans were granted pasturelands. In this way many more Turkish speakers began to flood in, as compared to the few, elite mamluks. Many of the immigrants arrived as desperate refugees. Droughts or cold waves often depleted their flocks and forced them to seek refuge in more fertile regions. Accompanying this settlement was a process of acculturation. While the mamluks were raised in the faith of Islam, the free steppe horsemen gradually abandoned their Buddhist,

Manichaean, or Christian practices for the new religion. Becoming part of the wider Muslim community made them aware that, once they crossed over the crumbling Wall of Gorgan into Iran proper, there was little to stop them before they reached the shores of the Mediterranean Sea. The newly converted horsemen came to be known as Turkmen; this ethnonym distinguished them from other, settled, Turkish-speaking Muslims.*

In 1035 a Turkmen chief of the Seljuk clan, Arslan Isra'il, petitioned Mas'ud, the ruler of Eastern Iran, or Khorasan, for permission to graze their flocks south of the wall.

> We number 4,000 families. If my lord were to issue a royal patent and allow us to cross the river and settle in Khorasan, he would be relieved from worrying about us, for there would be plenty of space for us in his realm, since we are steppe people and have extensive herds of sheep. Moreover, we would provide additional manpower for his army.

Mas'ud quickly regretted admitting the new guests. The Turkmen, who had migrated for decades across the empty northern steppe, had never lived in close proximity with settled peoples. They quickly fell to plundering the suburbs of walled cities, allowing their herds to trample crops and interrupt urgent repairs on the irrigation works upon which sedentary life itself depended. A chronicler lamented, "That region became ruined, like the disheveled tresses of the fair ones or the tearful eyes of the loved ones, as it became devastated by the pasturing of [the Turkmen's] flocks." After the failure of many punitive expeditions against the Seljuks to bring them to order, Mas'ud marched out to crush the unruly horsemen with his army of one hundred thousand mamluks and even elephants from India. Harried by the Seljuk archers on their fleet horses, the slower, heavily armed Khorasani horsemen could not come to grips with the enemy. After several days of battle in this particularly dry region, the hardy steppe horses held up better without water than their opponents' steeds. Mas'ud escaped capture

---

* The descendants of the horsemen are sedentary now, but they still raise horses and race them in the provincial capital, Gonbad-e Qabus. The horses are known by the names of the clans that traditionally breed them, the Yomut and the Goklan.

by riding off with a guard of one hundred elite riders as the steppe battue closed around his army. The Seljuk chief could hardly believe his luck when he seated himself on Mas'ud's abandoned throne. He and his clan really did not know what to do next.

After some hesitancy in the face of their new responsibilities, the Seljuks, like the Khitans in China, learned how to play the role of traditional rulers of settled lands, seeking to establish law and order within their realms and protecting agriculture and settlements. They constantly struggled to restrain their own horsemen, who used any excuse to return to plundering. The Turkmen gave rise to the Seljuk state but never ceased to be an existential threat to it. Unlike the Khitan state, which was neatly divided into two zones and two administrations, half according to the horse breeders' codes and the other half for the agricultural Chinese, the Seljuks found themselves, given Iran's geography, with rowdy Turkmen distributed throughout their territories, ready to plunder or to support revolts of local princes against their overlords.

The last great Seljuk, Sultan Sanjar, ascended to the throne in 1097 and became the subject of a popular fable that illustrates the difficulties this clan experienced in ruling Iran. Like the Khitans, the Seljuks were keen hunters. Practicing this pastime across the mixed steppe and farmland regions of Iran, hunters often found themselves in conflict with farmers. During one such hunt the sultan's entourage pillaged an old woman's farm. Catching sight of the sultan nearby, the crone seized the glittering bridle of his horse and hurled curses on the monarch. Bodyguards rushed forward to cut her down with their sabers, but the sultan raised his gloved hand to protect her. As the guards looked on stone-faced, she berated him for his inability to protect his subjects during the hunt. Sultan Sanjar heard her out and had the offending members of the hunt party executed. Iranians retell this story to this day to remind themselves that government relies on justice for its survival. This fable and its happy ending had less echo in the real world, however. Though Sanjar harnessed the horse power of the Turkmen, and used them to make war on his neighbors, ultimately he was unable to control them. On campaign to quell one of many Turkmen rebellions in 1156, Sanjar was captured and imprisoned. His realm fell to pieces during his captivity.

As with the Khitans, so with the Seljuks: another, fresh wave of steppe horsemen now conquered Khorasan. These were the Kipchak Turks, cousins of the Turkmen, under the leadership of the Khwarazm Shah, yet another mamluk warlord. The Khwarazm Shah then exhausted Iran with his military campaigns and wiped out several older power centers that could have acted as a buffer between Iran and the rising empire of the Mongols.

The Turkmen migration affected more than just Iran. The Seljuks encouraged their horsemen to raid the Christian Romans, Armenians, and Georgians; the difference in religion conveniently provided a legal justification for the lucrative business of enslavement. This activity also provided an escape valve to clear Iran of their troublemaking. It was at this time that Turkmen established themselves in Azerbaijan, northern Iraq, and Syria, where their descendants still live today. From there, they started to push farther into what was then Roman Anatolia.

In 1071, a hunting party led by Seljuk Sultan Alp Arslan stumbled into an ambush of Roman troops on the frontiers of Anatolia. With only one hundred retainers, the sultan could not offer resistance and was taken prisoner. The Romans did not recognize him, and he soon slipped away. A few days later the sultan and the Roman emperor Romanus IV met in the battle of Manzikert with their full armies. The Seljuks deployed a traditional hunting battue, forming a broad arc that gradually enveloped the Romans. Rome's own Turkish mercenaries, recognizing what was going on from their own familiarity with the battle tactic, decided to change sides. The Roman army was trapped, and Romanus fell, wounded with arrows, from his horse. The Turks dragged him before Alp Arslan, who sat in his saddle with a hunting falcon perched on one hand and the jeweled leash of a hunting hound held in the other, to remind the Roman of who was today's prey.

Alp Arslan's victory over Romanus IV ended Roman rule over Anatolia forever. Turkmen poured into this wide-open territory with their masses of quadrupeds. One band of twenty thousand warriors brought eighty thousand family members with one hundred thousand animals, including horses, camels, sheep, and goats. Anatolia had been a land of small-scale sheep and goat pastoralism, coexisting with farming since the Neolithic era; the Turkmen's four-head style of herding was unknown. Initially, the Turkmen pillaged towns and farms, causing markets to shutter and farmers to flee, when they were not enslaved. This was catastrophic for agriculture, and even when the violence subsided, the new style of pastoralism bore down on the land. Horses caused more destruction than sheep and goats. Abandoned and trampled, the farmlands of Anatolia declined precipitously. As in Iran, their nominal Seljuk rulers tried to reign in the Turkmen, but by the time they managed to assert some form of state control, agricultural, Roman Anatolia was well on its way to becoming Turkey, with a large horse-breeding, Turkish-speaking population. From these Turkmen raiders arose, a century later, the Ottoman dynasty.

The emperor Romanus was not the only European ruler to fall into the hands of Turkish horsemen. North of the Black Sea, Kyiv and its allied principalities also found themselves defending their lands against steppe incursions by the Kipchak Turks.[*] These horsemen had migrated west after the breakup of the Celestial Turk alliance with the Tang, and wound up raiding and trading with Kyiv. This immense,[†] prosperous emporium had been ruled previously by the Celestial Turks, before being conquered by the mixed Scandinavian and Slavic Rus around 880. Kyivan Rus grew to be, if not so prosperous as the Tang, one of the great states of Europe, ruling extensive territories bordering the steppe. In 1185, a prince of the Rus, Igor of Suzdal, launched a foolhardy retaliatory raid into the steppe, where the Kipchaks trapped his forces in a massive battue. They slaughtered his followers but made sure to capture the prince alive. To keep him entertained in captivity, they invited him to participate in their favorite pastime, hunting, and even gave him an especially fine horse to ride, fitting his rank. Taking advantage of the animal's speed, Igor galloped all the way back to Suzdal.[‡]

The Kipchaks continued to raid and trade with the Kyivan principalities, and with the kingdoms of Bulgaria and Hungary, while also serving as mercenary warriors and suppliers of cavalry horses. They did not settle in

---

[*]   Also known as the Pecheneg, the Patzinaks, the Polovtsi, Cumans, and Kun.

[†]   Medieval Kyiv had a population of one hundred thousand, at a time when London counted only fifteen hundred inhabitants.

[‡]   Furnishing a happy end to the thirteenth-century *Lay of Prince Igor* and subsequently Alexander Borodin's opera *Prince Igor*.

large numbers in eastern Europe, unlike the Turkmen in Iran and Anatolia, since Europe did not offer favorable horse-breeding conditions.* But the steppe peoples would leave a much greater legacy in the following centuries, above all in the Kyivan principalities.

Turkey, meanwhile, was not destined to remain under the sway of the Turkmen. In the fourteenth century, the Ottoman dynasty conquered the Balkans, providing a solid agricultural and maritime basis for their empire—one that was not powered by horses. In the sixteenth century, the Ottoman sultans brutally crushed Turkmen revolts in a way the Seljuks could never have imagined. By contrast, the Turkmen and other horse-breeding peoples continued to dominate Iran, politically and ecologically, until the twentieth century.

The migration of steppe horsemen in the tenth and eleventh centuries had varied impacts on the agricultural populations of China, the Middle East, and Europe. But across Eurasia, regimes based on steppe horse power experienced similar life cycles. After four or five generations, by the time the steppe rulers mastered the balancing act between pastoralism and agriculture, peaceful coexistence left the former conquerors with little fight in them, and the common herders felt increasingly alienated from their silk-gowned leadership. Steppe kingdoms then fell victim to a new wave of ambitious steppe conquerors.

In India, however, horse-breeding peoples neither overwhelmed the sedentary peoples, as in western Asia, nor did they remain restricted to the frontier, as in China and eastern Europe. The regime they established, along with a flourishing cultural synthesis, lasted a surprising three centuries.

Horse Dealers or Holy Warriors

Around the year 1020, the Chinese ambassador to Afghanistan described the impressive Turkish warlord to whom he was accredited:

---

* Exceptionally, the horse-breeding Magyars, chased from the western into the Danubian steppe by the Kipchaks, settled down and founded the Kingdom of Hungary. They preserved their equestrian traditions, fielding the finest cavalry in Europe, the original hussars.

The king's arms reach below his knees. He has one hundred head of warhorses, each more than 18 hands high. When he marches out, he alternates which one he rides; he shoots a bow that weighs several pounds, and even with the effort of five or seven men it is not possible to bend it. On horseback, he uses an iron mace, which weighs more than fifty pounds. All of Afghanistan and India fear him.

Such was Sultan Mahmud of Ghazna, who ruled for more than three decades, from 998 to 1030. He descended from a line of mamluk generals tasked by the caliph with defending Khorasan and Afghanistan from marauding Turkmen and Khitans. Mahmud found it easier to co-opt these horsemen and recruit them into his armies. Just as the Seljuks would encourage marauders to invade their western neighbor, Roman Anatolia, so Mahmud went after his eastern neighbor, India.

India presented a soft target for invaders from the northeast. Whoever ruled Afghanistan could cut off the supply of warhorses to the horse-poor subcontinent. India was, moreover, an attractive prize, with great portable wealth stored in countless gilded temples where Brahmins, Buddhists, and Jains worshipped. At the time temples functioned as banks, providing financial services to traders and rajas. That made them legitimate objectives for sacking and plundering under the normal rules of war, as happened during many local conflicts between Indian rajas. The opportunity was too good to be missed.

Sultan Mahmud perfected his military machine for invasion. Compared to his Indian enemies, he had crushing superiority in horse power, with both trained mamluk cavalry and Turkish and Afghan levies of steppe horse breeders. The former provided heavily armored shock cavalry, while the latter, more lightly mounted and equipped, proved to be formidable archers. The sultan was a military genius who mastered not only leading his men into battle but also the details of resupplying them. His raids into India covered as many as fourteen hundred miles, and he managed to attack sites separated from his base by the Thar Desert, the largest in India. It is no wonder he caught his enemies by surprise, since no cavalry army could have been expected to survive such a long crossing of this almost waterless expanse. Yet Mahmud carried out nearly thirty such campaigns, each one meticulously planned with adequate water and forage for his horses. On one expedition, thirty thousand camels carried water for thirty thousand cavalry troopers and fifty-four thousand steppe horsemen. Only once did his plans go awry, leaving him to ride out of the Thar Desert in disorder.

In order to finance these costly campaigns, as well as to satisfy his large mamluk establishment and retain the loyalty of his officers and steppe horsemen, Mahmud promised them generous loot (that word itself originated in India). Raiding and plundering left them no time for conspiracies or rebellions. The horsemen cared primarily about feeding their animals, however, so rather than occupying the conquered territories, his army returned to the cool of Afghanistan each summer, leaving India to recover from their attacks.

When not campaigning in central India, Mahmud organized hunts for his entourage, celebrated in Persian poetry by Farrokhi. One epic recounts his lion hunting in Punjab's Lakhi Jungle, where the well-hidden predators had every opportunity to leap onto his horse before he could bring his saber down on them. In another story, when chasing a deer, he uncharacteristically abandoned his prey after the deer admonished him, in Persian, for killing too many animals. Far from signaling a conversion to vegetarianism, this event only caused him to briefly rest from the hunt. Indeed, the sultan rode to the hunt every third or fourth day. In the same way, he never renounced his Indian raids.

Mahmud's courtiers praised him as a holy warrior fighting Indian idolatry, but it is anachronistic to see his wars in terms of religious conflict. His Indian opponents never referred to any religious animus, calling their enemies the "Turushka," which meant Turk, or else "Aśvakas," for masters of horses. They did not see Mahmud as any different a threat than that posed by the Kushans five hundred years earlier. Moreover, even if the sultan reveled in the title of holy warrior, he employed Indian troops as well as Turks and Afghans. Many of Mahmud's Indian allies came from the pastoralist populations of the Punjab where the Kushans had once grazed. Some of these peoples adopted Islam, notably the horse breeders of the Lakhi Jungle, but many others retained their ancestral faith.

Mahmud spent a lifetime in the saddle, but his heirs were unable to sustain his rhythm of campaigns, and their domains began to shrink. After 150 years the Ghaznavids succumbed to attacks by their former Afghan allies. The Afghans and Turks then formed an uneasy alliance under the leadership of mamluk generals, who ruled as sultans either via election or assassination. The mamluk sultans built a magnificent capital in Delhi. Like Beijing of the Khitans, the site of the new city was close enough to the steppe frontier to be easily resupplied with horses, the basis of the mamluks' power. Firmly ensconced, the mamluk sultans began to look after their Indian subjects just like traditional, sedentary rulers. In this their task was easier than that of the Khitans, Jurchens, or Seljuks.

For the mamluk sultans did not, like those other dynasties, bring whole populations of horse-breeding people into the settled realms they conquered; India was too hot and inhospitable for their flocks. Nevertheless, the wars of Mahmud and the mamluk sultans effected a change in Indian ecology and society. Although the subcontinent hosted no long-distance pastoralists like the Turks, hilly or desert-like terrain provided habitats for herders with flocks of sheep, goats, or cattle. Some of these groups now adopted hardy ponies, fit for the climate and not as hard to feed as the big Central Asian horses. This process may have begun as early as the time of Kushans, though we know much less about that earlier period. Now new powers based on cavalry arose in the arid zones, far from the traditional seats of power and prestige, Brahmin temples and ancient maharajas' courts. Horse fairs like those in Haridwar and Pushkar, as noted earlier, became new sites for religious pilgrimage, drawing devotees away from more ancient temple sites. New military capitals were constructed wherever pastureland was found. Rajas of the older, settled states often encouraged new local horse-breeding peoples—including Afghans in the north, Rajputs in central India, and the Nayaks in the south—to police the vulnerable, arid frontiers of their kingdoms and to provide defense against invasion.* These peoples alternately served as horse traders and mercenaries or practiced cattle thievery and highway robbery; enrolling them in armies and channeling their freebooting ways became an important aspect of Indian statecraft. Of

---

* They remain, to this day, fierce protagonists of Indian equestrian tradition.

course, many adventurers were only biding their time to become sultans and rajas in their own right.

Bengal offers a classic example of this kind of coup d'état. Its maharajas had long invited Afghans to fairs in their realm to ensure remounts for their "invincible and countless" cavalry, as the court laureates described them. One market day in 1202, an Afghan rode calmly into the center of the Bengali city of Nadia, the seat of an important maharaja, with eighteen companions. The crowd noticed nothing amiss in this cavalcade, since Afghan horses dealers visited the markets of Bengal regularly. The horsemen gathered in front of the maharaja's palace, situated to one side of the market, and then unsheathed their weapons. In the ensuing shock and confusion, the horsemen seized the palace, the maharaja fled, and the horse dealer made himself ruler in his stead. Muhammad Bakhtiyar Khalji, heretofore a wandering adventurer from Afghanistan, went on to conquer all of Bengal. He even invaded Assam to ensure access to the ponies of Tibet, since he feared the mamluks of Delhi would cut him off from Central Asian horses.

Many others similarly parlayed horse trading and its associated political opportunities to establish their own dynasties. Tughlugh Shah, the most outstanding of Delhi's mamluk sultans, rose to power from the position of master of the horse for his predecessors. He extended Delhi's rule over much of India, and was buried in a mausoleum built of red sandstone and white marble that hints at the synthesis of Islamic and Indian arts taking place under his rule. The political legacy of these swashbuckling horse dealers was to remake India as a checkerboard of competing horse-powered states, with the mamluk sultans of Delhi the biggest and best mounted.

Maintaining an advantage required importing horses, especially the bigger, more powerful animals from Central Asia and western Asia prized by the Turks and the Afghans. When war on the northwest frontier cut India off from overland trade, enterprising sailors supplied India by sea. Marco Polo remarked of this trade in the thirteenth century, when Delhi indeed faced a hostile neighbor to the north:

> A great part of the wealth of the country is wasted in purchasing horses. I will tell you how. The merchants of Kish, Ormuz [both in the Persian Gulf], Dhofar, Soer [both in Oman] and Aden collect

great numbers of destriers [warhorses] and other horses, and they bring them to this king [of Gujarat, western India]. Often the king purchased 2,000 horses at a time.

Later observers raised this estimate to thirteen thousand horses annually. A chronicler of the fourteenth century, Wassaf, claimed that two million gold dinars (almost $500 million in today's dollars, a colossal sum in preindustrial times) were spent to deliver horses to the Gujarati port of Cambay, paid for by the treasures of the temples and a tax on devadasis, the sacred courtesans. Maritime horses were more costly than the horses of Central Asia; it was not unusual for buyers to pay 1,000 rupees for a horse from overseas, while a good horse from Central Asia could be had for 500 rupees, and an ordinary one for 100 rupees. Despite the high cost, however, both the prestige of Arabian and Persian horses and the difficulty of procuring Central Asian horses kept the horse dealers of Arabia and the Persian Gulf busy for centuries.*

As long as the mamluk sultans could supply themselves with horses, either by land or, at much greater expense, by sea, their power over northern India faced no serious military opposition, and they occasionally prevailed in central India. The Indian subcontinent, meanwhile, had integrated these former steppe horsemen in a way that neither permeable Iran nor hermeneutic China had done. The mamluks imported horses, not turbulent horsemen, and so they avoided the herder-farmer clashes that so disrupted the Seljuks. While they became thoroughly Indian in culture, they kept their mamluk military traditions and their mastery of horsemanship, unlike the degenerated later Khitans. As a result of this distinctive synthesis, the regime of the mamluk sultans was one of few in Asia to survive the coming Mongol storm.

ILLUSTRATED BOOKS, mural paintings, and silk scrolls of this era depict the royal hunts of the Khitan khaghans and the Seljuk and the Ghaznavid sultans. Brilliantly bedecked horsemen fan out over meadows full of

---

* In the nineteenth century, Iranian and especially Parsi traders would lord over the Bombay Turf Club, an echo of their ancient role in supplying horses.

flowers. Painters emphasize the prowess of the monarchs, the beauty and power of their horses, the elegance of their harnesses. Amid these idealized and aestheticized images, gore pours out of the wounds of lions, tigers, and onagers. This contrast, between beauty and violence, is one duality of the hunt; another is its role as both sport and a rehearsal for warfare. The hunt also crystallized the wide cultural gap between horsemen and farmers. Hunting is one of the reasons steppe dwellers took to riding, converting the horse's instinct to flee into a love of pursuit. Farmers, on the other hand, diligently domesticated animals that were once game, including ducks and geese. They feared the riders galloping over their land in pursuit of bigger game, in groups of five hundred or even five thousand horsemen. A famous Chinese poem of the Han period provides a classic admonishment that might have been cited approvingly by the anti-hunting mandarins:

> *And yet,*
> *Galloping all day long,*
> *Exhausting body and soul,*
> *Wearing out carts and horses,*
> *Consuming the soldiers' energy,*
> *Running down the exchequer,*
> *Not with generous gifts,*
> *Busy with selfish pleasures;*
> *Without a thought for commoners,*
> *Forgetful of state affairs,*
> *Mad about game birds and hares;*
> *No virtuous rulers would do this!*

Steppe chieftains who conquered settled lands could not entirely ignore such advice. When a chieftain stepped up to fulfill the role of sultan or emperor, he needed to protect his farmers from the depredations of hunting. But he also had to keep his horsemen occupied with hunts or wars. The Khitans kept their horsemen out of China proper and warred against the Turks. The Seljuks tried, unsuccessfully, to keep their Turkmen busy attacking the Christians in return for internal peace. The Ghaznavids and Delhi mamluks raided central India. They all performed similar balancing acts, from Konya to Beijing, but their regimes were fragile, because their horse-breeding followers shifted their loyalties when a promising new leader appeared. Fortunes could change quickly, as in the hunt. *One day a leopard may eat the hunter.* While the khans and sultans hunted alongside their horsemen, events in Mongolia would soon turn them into prey.

8

As Far as Our Horses' Hooves Run

Genghis Khan's empire, 1206–1368

ᠥ

Legends of the Chanyu (1155–1215)

An illustrated Mongol history, produced long after the fact, shows Genghis Khan before the walls of Beijing, then known as Zhongdu, the "Central Capital." Accompanied by his horsemen, he shakes his mace imperiously in front of the city's main gate. The walls, nine miles in circumference, are empty of defenders. Though Genghis Khan's mounted archers cannot penetrate the fortifications, they are starving the city into submission, beating off relief columns sent by the Jurchen khan to resupply his besieged garrison. Genghis Khan impatiently circles the walls, waiting for the inevitable surrender of his enemies. On a fine June day in 1215, the famished surviving Jurchen defenders throw open the main gate and bring out their khans' treasure for the victors to inspect and inventory. As soon as Genghis Khan satisfies himself that the gold, silver, brocaded silks, and satins have fallen intact into his hands, he wheels about on his horse and rides to his home pasture in the Orkhon Valley, a thousand miles to the north.

Genghis Khan's capture of Beijing and his return to the Orkhon Valley followed the playbook of previous steppe invaders of northern China, including the Huns, Turks, Khitans, and Jurchens. Contemporaries probably saw this event as just the latest episode of such invasions. It would have been hard to foresee the revolution that Genghis Khan would unleash on steppe and settled peoples alike, or that by the time of his death he would have established the largest land empire the world has ever known. What distinguished Genghis Khan from the already legendary chanyus of the

Genghis Khan besieges Beijing, from a manuscript of Jami'u't-tawarikh, *Herat, 1430.*

Huns and the supreme khans of the Celestial Turks, Khitans, and Jurchens was how carefully he studied their successes and failures, and the discipline with which he applied the lessons he derived. Genghis Khan mobilized the horse power of the steppe as never before.

Twenty-five years before the siege of Beijing, ancestral enemies and rivals of the future Genghis Khan, then known as Temüjin, had reduced him to a fugitive, hunting marmots on the steppe to survive. He lacked even a horse. Temüjin's family, a prominent Mongol clan, had grown too powerful to suit the khan of the Jurchens in Beijing, who maintained peace on their northern frontier through a policy of divide and conquer. The Jurchen Wulu Khan encouraged the neighboring Tatar people[*] to weaken

---

[*] The ethnonym Tatar has changed meaning over time. Originally it referred to a group living in Mongolia who spoke Turkish and Mongolian. Then it came to describe all the Turks and Mongols in eastern Europe. Premodern European writers spelled the name with an additional *r*—i.e., Tartars, a play on the Latin name for hell, Tartary. This name is often found on old maps of Central Asia. Today Tatar refers to Turkish- and Mongolian-speaking Muslims and Buddhists of Russia, Ukraine, and Poland.

Temüjin's clan. The Tatars accordingly poisoned Temüjin's father, forcing his mother to flee with her small children and a single oxcart. Like many steppe leaders before and after, Temüjin's theft of a horse was his first war-like feat. Much of his youth passed in stock rustling, which earned him a reputation as daring and capable.

Shame, pride, desire for revenge, and intelligence impelled Temüjin to study the forces behind his family's humiliation. The Mongols then had no written language, but bards and storytellers crossed the steppe and were welcomed into the tents of the herders, fed and bedded for the night in return for an evening's entertainment. These bards accompanied their recitals not with a harp, like Homer's singers, but a bowed fiddle, the scroll of which was carved into the shape of a horse's head and strung with two cords made from carefully selected and braided horse hairs, one from a stallion and one from a mare. The sounds of the stallion's cord evoked the bass notes of the gallop, while the sounds of the mare's cord recalled the whinnying of the horse. From such performances, perhaps, Temüjin pieced together his understanding of the history and politics of the steppe.

In the time of Temüjin's grandfathers, the supreme Khitan khan, living in pomp and luxury in distant Chinese palaces, did not share his largesse with his horse-breeding subjects and ignored the pleas of his Khitan kin to go hunting on the steppes. His army of horsemen deserted him; the Jurchen, one of his subject peoples, attacked and captured him.

The Jurchen came from eastern Manchuria, and unlike the Khitans and other peoples from Mongolia, they did not have to migrate in search of water and grass. Dense forest covered their homeland. They practiced tree clearing in order to raise animals for the lucrative horse trade. An ambitious khan, Aguda, originally sold Jurchen horses to the Khitans, but in 1117 he entered into secret negotiations to supply the Song dynasty, which ruled China south of the Yellow River. The Jurchens sent these horses by sea to Hangzhou to avoid the notice of the Khitans, whose empire separated them from the Song. By agreeing to deal directly with Aguda, the Song cemented the Jurchen khan's authority and helped him to rally horse-breeding clans to his banner. He then challenged the weak but proud Khitan emperor Tianzuo to acknowledge Jurchen independence. When this was refused, Aguda invaded the Khitan Empire, which collapsed like a tent over its broken tent pole. Khitan horse breeders switched loyalties to the luckier, pluckier Aguda with no evident hesitation or qualms.

By 1142 the Jurchen had succeeded beyond their wildest dreams. Not only had their rivals, the Khitans, folded suddenly, but even their erstwhile patrons, the Song, had shown momentary weakness, allowing the Jurchens to occupy extensive territory below the Yellow River. These former horse breeders now ruled one-third of the former Tang Empire. Beijing became just one of three capitals for these peripatetic khans.

The Jurchens assumed the Chinese dynastic name Jin, meaning "gold." The steppe peoples accordingly called them the Golden Khans. To avoid the fate that had befallen the Khitans, the Jurchens visited the steppe regularly and paid a great deal of attention to steppe politics. They wanted to prevent the emergence of another Abaoji or Aguda at all costs, and to do so they instigated conflicts between steppe clans—leading to the death of Temüjin's father.

This is the story that Temüjin would have heard from the traveling bards, and the lessons for him were clear. The semi-settled Khitans had succumbed to the Jurchen. Now the Jurchen had, in turn, partly settled in China. The Golden Khans reinforced the Great Wall, rewarded horse-breeding chiefs for loyalty, and punished them for ambition. But at some point, Temüjin knew, the Jurchen would succumb to the next heaven-anointed ruler to muster the full force of the steppe. It was only a question of when—and who.

"Our Geldings Are Fat"

The Mongol term for vigor and power is *khii-mor*, a combination of the words for "wind" and "horse." Since the time of the Huns, the inhabitants of Mongolia have been crisscrossing its windswept steppe on their speedy horses. *Khii-mor* is an apt expression that evokes the pervasive horse power contained in this huge country.

Modern Mongolia corresponds roughly to the lands where Temüjin began his career of conquest. With six hundred thousand square miles of territory, Mongolia hosts three different ecosystems and types of herding. The Altai Mountains, in western Mongolia, and the forested Khangai and

Khentii Mountains, farther east and to the north, call for vertical trans-humance, as in Iran: arduous treks to drive livestock up to high altitudes in the summer, followed by descent into the valleys in the winter. In central Mongolia, where the steppe predominates, herders travel seasonally from northern latitudes to southern ones in search of fresh grass, often as far as a thousand miles. Snow is not an obstacle but, rather, a destination. In the unhospitable Gobi of southeastern Mongolia,* flocks graze on higher grounds in the summer and seek shelter from winter winds in gullies and ravines.

To exploit the vegetal resources of these lands, Mongolian herders kept each of the five heads: horses, camels, cattle, sheep, and goats, cited in the traditional order of precedence (the camel being an addition to the ancient four heads). All of these animals can survive in both the mountain and the desert ecosystems of the steppe, but with decreasing density. The minimum 250 acres for seventy-five sheep in the steppe feeds only fifty sheep in the mountains, and only twenty-five in the Gobi. Camels actually prefer the Gobi, their native habitat, because their metabolism requires its sodium-rich grass.

Herding horses was a low-touch activity, since the animals took care of themselves, little different from their feral cousins. They moved about constantly, nibbling as they walked and keeping their nostrils wide for the scent of grass. The stallions managed the herd; as a medieval Chinese visitor to the steppe observed, "The stallion bites [the lead mare] and makes her come back. If the stallion of some other herd comes and trespasses, then the stallion of the herd will kick and bite him and make him go away. They each distinguish their own." The stallion and the mare would take the herd in search of water and chase away predatory big cats and wolves. Observers today often remark that the Mongolian ponies resemble the Przewalski horse. This is not because the former descended from the latter but because they both live in the same habitat and have had to adapt to that climate. Watched from afar by the feral animals, the ponies dutifully carried their riders on the long migrations of the herd.

---

*   Gobi means "desert" in Mongolian.

The size of the thirteenth-century Mongol herd was essential for the rise of Temüjin. There is evidence to suggest that at that time, the horse accounted for 30 percent of Mongolian livestock. Another medieval Chinese observer of the Mongols noted, "When I travelled in the steppes, I never saw anyone walking. As for the army heads, each man rides one horse and has five or six, or three or four horses following him as a rule, to be ready for an emergency. Even the poor have to have one or two." The Mongols of that time kept many more horses than they needed for either herding, food, or transport, for they raised animals for the lucrative horse trade. Each of the Mongols' predecessors in Mongolia—the Huns, Turks, and Khitans—had depended on this trade to take them beyond subsistence herding. Mongolia, unlike Manchuria, Gansu, or Central Asia, lacked farming and towns, and so horses were the sole source of wealth for the Mongols. The Orkhon Valley, in particular, represented an important center for the horse and livestock trade. In Temüjin's youth, the wars between the Golden Khans and the Song Chinese drove up the demand for horses. The Golden Khans needed to import as many as eighty thousand horses annually, a value representing about $500 million today, to be shared among two hundred thousand households. This made the average horse breeder about twice as prosperous as the average laborer in Beijing.

With successive years of good weather, as appears to have been the case in the first decades of the thirteenth century, the herds grew very numerous. Historical estimates of the resulting horse population range widely, but we may take three million as a base. Of those, a third, or one million, would have been mature geldings, which the Mongols traditionally rode to war because they needed the mares for breeding and the stallions, as above, for herding. Geldings were tougher, more reliable, and less thirsty than stallions; not even Temüjin rode a stallion. The availability of so many well-fed geldings presented the Mongols with a challenge, however. They could not sell the excess to the Golden Khan. "Our geldings are fat," observed one of Temüjin's companions in arms—implicitly asking, What do we do with them? The rains, the grasses, and the geldings of Mongolia did not create Genghis Khan, but his conquests are impossible to understand without them.

Genghis Khan's Conquests (1206–1227)

When the Jurchens decided it was time to clip the wings of the Tatars, Temüjin was one of the local chiefs they recruited to their side. Temüjin eagerly hunted down his hereditary enemies, fully knowing that Beijing itself had instigated his father's murder. His successful campaign against the Tatars allowed Temüjin to assemble around him the most accomplished soldiers of his time, including former opponents. One enemy warrior, escaping from an earlier skirmish with Temüjin's forces, had launched a Parthian shot (over his horse's croup) at Temüjin's favorite horse, a chestnut with a white muzzle. The horse fell, dying, and the warrior got away. Later, pickets captured him and dragged him before Temüjin for judgment. "I was the one who shot your chestnut with a white muzzle," the warrior admitted, "but if you let me live, I will provide you with many such horses." Temüjin responded, "Such a man is worth having on our side. I will call him 'the Arrow.'" And the Arrow went on to become one of the most successful Mongol generals. In one battle, he captured several chestnut horses with white muzzles and presented them to Temüjin in fulfillment of his vow.

Genghis Khan's conquests brought into the Mongols' fold not only additional horsemen but the bigger, stabled horses of wealthy Khitan and Jurchen chiefs. This enabled him to turn his elite guard into heavy cavalry. Genghis Khan's general Bo'orchi was sufficiently inexperienced riding such spirited horses that the world conqueror had to warn him, "Don't use the whip, just stroke his mane with the whip handle."

With allies won on the battlefield, it took Temüjin a decade of campaigning to defeat his remaining rivals for power within Mongolia. In 1206, Temüjin convinced his new subject peoples to acclaim him as Genghis Khan, or "Universal Ruler," and predicted, "We will have an empire like that of the *chanyu* of the Huns, which has not been seen for thousands of years." A later dynastic chronicler described Genghis Khan's assumption of supreme power with an equestrian metaphor, "The Piebald Horse of Days is tame between the thighs of his command," recalling that a rider of a black-and-white horse symbolizes mastery of night and day, and of time itself, in steppe tradition.

Indeed, to signal his future ambitions, Genghis Khan exploited the cosmic symbolism of horses and their colors. Following the example of the Huns and the imperial Khitans, he ordered sorrel horses, representing the south, to ride on his left, and black horses, representing the north, to ride on his right. Blue-gray horses represented the east, and white horses, the west. In the center of his army, Genghis Khan rode one of eight gold palomino geldings. His cosmically aligned cavalry symbolized—and later, imposed—world dominion.

The most dangerous remaining enemy of the new Mongol Empire was the Golden Khan, Wanyan Yongji, who now intrigued with rivals of Genghis Khan to challenge his hegemony. It was time to act on the blood feud that existed between Genghis Khan and this clan, which had been responsible for his father's death forty years before. Initially his ambition was to reduce his rival's territory to a tax-paying subject state, but in the face of his repeated attacks, many Jurchens and Khitans abandoned the Golden Khan, who then fled to the south, leaving Beijing to its fate. The Mongols now added the Khitans, Jurchens, and northern Chinese to their new empire.

On the eve of Genghis Khan's phenomenal expansion, much of Europe and Asia had long been ruled by horse-breeding peoples. In what is today's western Russia, Ukraine, Moldova, and Romania, Kipchak Turks grazed their flocks. Alans, descendants of the ancient Scythians, lived on the steppe between the Black and the Caspian Seas.* Turkmen predominated in Anatolia and Iran. Afghans and Turks shared power in India. A patchwork of Turkish, Tibetan, and Mongolian nations occupied Inner Asia. The uniformity of the pastoralist lifestyle across this vast region made it easy for Genghis Khan to impose his rule. The region's fragmentation over the previous centuries into small, warring states facilitated his conquest.

In the west, Genghis Khan pursued Mongolian and Khitan groups who had refused to acknowledge his authority. The Turks of Balasagun wisely agreed to acknowledge Mongol overlordship without putting up a fight. This brought his empire to the border of Transoxiana, ruled then by mamluks of Kipchak origin. They were close cousins of the Kipchaks sparring at the same moment with Kyiv, but the more horse-friendly Middle East

---

* The settled descendants of the Kipchaks and the Alans are respectively known as the Gagauz, in Moldova, and the Ossetes, in the northern Caucasus.

afforded them a much greater role. Sought after as mamluk cavalrymen by rulers as far away as Egypt, the Kipchaks had rapidly developed dynastic ambitions of their own. They seized control of the oasis city of Khwarazm (modern Khiva in Uzbekistan), their rulers taking the ancient Iranian title of Khwarazm Shah. They built a powerful army based both on mamluks, painstakingly drilled in the arts of war, and levies of Kipchak horsemen from the steppe. In two generations the Khwarazm Shahs had replaced the Seljuks as the rulers of Iran and threatened the caliph of Baghdad with destitution.

Two such fast-growing states based on steppe horse power, Kipchak and Mongol, would have, in the best of circumstances, struggled to coexist; there were too many potential points of conflict, including plundered caravans, defecting clans, and horse raiding. The fact that these Kipchaks had accepted Islam,[*] and so regarded the shamanistic Mongols as primitives, was a further source of belligerence. The Khwarazm Shah, Alauddin, gave shelter to Turks and Khitans fleeing Genghis Khan, creating a climate of hostility. When the shah then had Genghis Khan's ambassadors in the Central Asian town of Otrar put to death, it was the final straw: in 1218, war broke out.

At the outset of this conflict, the winner would have been difficult to predict. The Mongols and the Kipchaks fielded similar cavalry armies of elite riders mounted on powerful warhorses protected by elaborate full-body armor, with more lightly mounted archers on small steppe ponies. Both sides had spent twenty-five years establishing huge empires: Genghis Khan in Mongolia and northern China, the Khwarazm Shah in Transoxiana and Iran. Alauddin had earlier driven off attacks by the Sinicized Khitans, so he felt sure he would dispose of the Mongols in the same way. Yet Genghis Khan prevailed against the Kipchaks in the field. Perhaps because they were operating so far from their native pastures, the Mongol army fought for its very existence, while Kipchak clans could and did switch sides when they saw battles going the wrong way for them.

---

[*] Unlike their kinfolk in eastern Europe, who practiced shamanism or, in some cases, adopted Orthodox Christianity. An earlier generation of Turks in that part of the world, the Khazars, embraced Judaism.

Sadly for the great cities of Transoxiana, their municipal leaders believed the Mongols to be just another raiding party from the eastern steppe, and decided to wait them out from behind their walled fortifications. They did not realize until it was too late that the Mongol cavalry army also included siege-warfare specialists recruited from China. The Khwarazm Shah's cities, Khiva, Merv, and Nishapur, fell one by one. Genghis Khan applied the then-accepted laws of war and put to the sword inhabitants of any city that had resisted. Even surrender did not save the cities from horrific scenes. After Bukhara opened its gates, the Mongols rode their horses into the cathedral mosque, mistaking it for a royal palace. "Our horses are hungry," they told the mosque attendants, "feed them." The mosque's library bookcases were hastily turned over and filled with fodder, serving as makeshift mangers. As holy books lay in the straw and filth, the doctors of Islam saw God's wrath at work.

Next, the Mongols reduced nearby Samarkand to ruins; the royal mahouts plodded out of the rubble on their elephants to surrender to Genghis Khan. "The elephants must be fed," the mahouts pleaded, assuming that Genghis Khan would be pleased to add them to his army. But this was not an animal for which Genghis Khan held any deep feeling. "What do you feed them?" he asked. When he was told the elephants ate grass, he ordered that the animals be let loose on the outskirts of Samarkand, where, for want of adequate forage, they died of starvation. Perhaps the khan could not conceive of an animal unable to feed itself.

Despite the compounding losses of horsemen and cities, the Khwarazm Shah refused to submit, holding on to the hope that at some point the Mongols would have to return to their distant homeland. He had not reckoned with Genghis Khan's determination to crush resistance before countenancing his return. With his still loyal mamluks, the Khwarazm Shah led the pursuing Mongols on a wild-goose chase through Central Asia, Khorasan, Afghanistan, and on into India. Such a cavalcade—even today, with paved roads and motored vehicles—is difficult to imagine. From Mongolia to the upper Oxus is three thousand miles; from the Oxus to the Indus, where Genghis Khan called a halt, another fifteen hundred miles. Even in the later stages of this campaign, the Mongols deployed at least a hundred thousand horses. They did not move like a modern army but, rather, traveled like a migrating herd, accompanied by families, tents, and flocks. Each warrior started the campaign with ten horses: five for combat, three for food, and two for herding. Including small animals, they brought one million head of livestock with them. The Mongols rode thirteen to fifteen miles a day, allowing the animals to graze along the way. To ensure that the same grass was not pastured by too many animals, they moved in a front ten miles wide. This also allowed the army to remain in a battue-ready formation, capable of enveloping any resistance. Seizure of grain and forage for these vast herds of horses inevitably resulted in the devastation and massacres for which the Mongol horde is remembered.

In 1221, still in pursuit of the Khwarazm Shah's son and successor, Jala-luddin, and now on the banks of the Indus in today's Pakistan, Genghis Khan heard rumors of revolt brewing in Mongolia. The army retraced its steps through Afghanistan and Transoxiana. Just the news of the great khan's return to Central Asia dampened any rebellious proclivities in Mongolia. Meanwhile, Jalaluddin escaped back to Iran, where he continued to harass Mongol armies until he was murdered by highway robbers. Genghis Khan's personal conquests were coming to an end, but his children and grandchildren continued campaigning at the far ends of the steppe.

Genghis Khan's Revolution

Genghis Khan's contemporaries called him "the world conqueror." No single leader or, indeed, nation had ever before succeeded in overcoming powerful rivals across China, Central Asia, and the Middle East. Though he saw himself as an heir to the chanyu of the ancient Huns, he had, in fact, led a revolution in steppe statecraft. For centuries the steppe horse breeders had enjoyed a degree of military advantage over the settled states, thanks to their constant training for hunting and fighting. This had enabled them to raid their neighbors and, opportunistically, to occupy territories, as the Seljuks, Khitans, Jurchens, and Kipchaks had done. But Genghis Khan's achievements were on another scale.

The world conqueror's armies were larger than those of the chanyu or the khagan of the Turks. Some modern historians have dismissed the pur-ported size of the Mongol armies as a storyteller's enthusiastic exaggeration, but there is no good reason to discount contemporary sources, which cite 600,000 warriors. Horse breeders constituted a nation in arms. A population of 1 million, like the Mongols, could muster 250,000 to 300,000 able-bodied, adult men, all of whom, because of their pastoralist lifestyle, were ready to take the field. If we consider that all the peoples of Inner and Central Asia were now federated into a great empire, an army of 600,000 warriors would not be a fable. What appears fabulous—and unprecedented—is how Genghis Khan forged the steppe horse breeders into a coherent political and military force. In doing this, he faced tremendous challenges.

Any leader of the horse breeders had to overcome their geographic dispersion across the steppe. A few families herding together occupied the space of a medium-sized city; Genghis Khan's Mongolia was vast. Communicating across the steppe took time. An event as portentous as the death of a great warrior took a month to reach his allies as a rumor, and a further forty-five days for an official confirmation.

Even after allies had been summoned, it took time for them to assemble and to marshal into armies. Campsites had to be designated, along with adequate pasture grounds for all the horses. This meant that the marshaling point had to be huge, generally the size of a province, in order to accommodate the tens of thousands of horses and the even greater number of other animals that made up the train. Observers were often surprised by the speed at which these armies moved, though perhaps they should not have been—like sharks, such armies had to move to survive. If they were to stay in any one place for too long, they would quickly exhaust the pastures available for their animals.

Horse-breeder armies had to ride away and conquer during a narrow seasonal window, starting in late spring, when the horses regained their reserves of fat and while the land still provided green grass on the march. By late summer the pastures were bare and could no longer support a marauding army. Winter often brought harsh temperatures and occasionally the dreaded *zuid*, in which the cold or the snow were so extreme that horses and other animals perished en masse. Such zuids could permanently end the campaign of a would-be conqueror. Dispersion, seasons, and weather meant that the horse breeders' forces needed to strike quickly and decisively to maintain their advantage.

Genghis Khan had to manage not just his troops but all of their families. With the men riding ahead in the vanguard, the women looked after the children and flocks. This required adroit horsewomen to steer the camp out of harm's way, moving swiftly backward or forward, depending on the success of the battle plan, and to organize the wagons, campsites, and animals in the same efficient manner as they did during the annual migrations. Occasionally women rode into battle. Given their heavy responsibilities, women enjoyed great prestige in Mongol society. Unlike their sisters in sedentary societies, women rode alongside their husbands and discussed military and political strategies with them. Genghis Khan needed to not only mobilize the men but also keep the women on board. His mother and his principal wife deserve much credit for Mongol victories.

A victim of betrayal and inconstancy in his turbulent youth, Genghis Khan was determined to introduce steely discipline into his inner circle. While other steppe leaders often forgave repeated betrayals, Genghis Khan implemented a policy of implacable punishment for failure to carry out orders or insubordination. Units that fled in the face of the enemy were killed, as were generals who failed to reach the battlefield.

Genghis Khan demanded direct personal loyalty to himself and to his enterprise of conquest. He spoke of his closest collaborators as "my horses," alluding to their seemingly instinctive loyalty as well as their courage and strength. He saw himself as the stallion that bites and kicks to keep the herd together. He sidelined traditional chieftains. He promoted strictly on merit, so that intrepid warriors from low or no lineage could aspire to command the sons of traditional chiefs.

Genghis Khan curtailed the dearest privileges of his followers. Like the Khitans, the Mongols liked to combine military expeditions with hunting. For short campaigns fought near their homeland, this posed no problems. For the long campaigns of conquest envisaged by Genghis Khan, however, too much hunting threatened to tire out both men and horses, leaving them vulnerable to counterattacks. "I am sending you across high mountains. You must ford wide rivers," he warned his forces. "You have to spare your horses." He ordered his generals not to let the troops chase after wild animals, nor to allow them to form a battue. "Hunt in moderation. This is a law. Anyone who transgresses this law is to be seized and beaten."

He further addressed the problems of traditional clan loyalty by organizing the army as mixed units of different nations. Although loyalty and identity had always involved a measure of politics, and not the reassuring myth of consanguinity, Genghis Khan was able to enroll peoples who had been warring with one another for several centuries and forge them into symmetrically arranged battle units of one hundred, one thousand, and ten thousand. The various peoples of Mongolia—the Jalayirs, the Naimans, the Keraits, the Tatars, and Genghis Khan's own people—all became Mongols; that name no longer identified a specific people but referred to the state led by him. As a concession to his own kinsmen, he renamed the close-lineage group of his ancestors the Borjigin, and this functioned as a royal clan within the greater Mongol state.

To make these new mixed units more pliable, he resettled them in military colonies at distant points in the empire. For example, elements of the Mongolian Jalayir people were moved to Iraq, while the Alans, descendants of the Scythians, were moved from their native Caucasus steppe to Beijing. This resettlement policy deprived occupied peoples of any realistic possibility for revolt or even escape, because people they did not know or trust surrounded them. Ancestral pastures were stripped from traditional leaders, and Genghis Khan rewarded and punished his followers using what mattered the most to them: access to grass and water. Dissidents could not simply melt away in search of pasture, because if they did, they were sure to encounter a rival, still loyal group claiming the same precious patch of green.

Intolerance toward any rival shaped Genghis Khan's policies. He pursued the ill-fated Khwarazm Shah for two years, not because this oft-defeated foe represented any military threat but to demonstrate that no one could defy the Universal Ruler with impunity. For the same reason, his heirs later pursued the Kipchaks of the western steppe and of Egypt. His assertion of universal sovereignty impelled him to attack any ruler who balked at paying taxes, including the Song emperors of China and the caliph of Baghdad. On the other hand, he left the mamluk sultan of Delhi in peace upon payment of a suitable sum.

Emptied of rivals, the steppe would witness no more games of musical chairs as had occurred in northern China when the Jurchens overthrew the Khitans. His Mongol forces would not assimilate into Chinese culture, like the Khitans, Jurchens, and Celestial Turks before them. Their capital would remain in Mongolia. Genghis Khan reinforced the horse breeders' traditional practices, enjoining them to live in tents, not in the conquered cities, and to practice animal husbandry, not to farm. He realized that the power of the empire depended on the horse above all else. Unlike the Seljuks, he did not try to replace his horsemen with slave soldiers, though he did recruit peasant levies from the settled populations, to serve as cannon fodder. With this formidable machine for making war, the world conqueror created the greatest empire the world had ever known. But with the backbone of this empire formed by horse breeders, it had well-defined ecological limits.

An Empire of Grass

The habitat of the horse determined the territorial ambitions of Genghis Khan and his heirs. Mongol leaders implicitly acknowledged this when they described their military objectives in terms of their own horses' need for space. Jochi Khan, the son Genghis Khan assigned to conquer the Kipchaks of eastern Europe, interpreted his orders in these terms: "[We will] ride from Khwarazm until the countries of Bulghar [on the Volga], and as long in that direction as the hooves of the Mongol horses will penetrate." Bayan, a general assigned to attack China, boasted, "Our horses will drink the waters of the Yangzi, and the river will dry up." Grandson Hülegü predicted, "From Azerbaijan to the gates of Egypt, the whole country is trodden down by the hooves of the Mongol horses." To hear them, it was the horses, not the riders, who dreamed of conquering an empire of grass.

Whether the appetite for conquest lay with the horse or with the world conqueror acting as the herd's stallion, much of Genghis Khan's statecraft showed obsessive concern for horses and their feeding. One of his first actions upon assuming supreme power had been to entrust his most loyal lieutenants with responsibility for horse herding. His personal bodyguard, which soon grew to ten thousand men, acted as herders and grooms for the growing herds of horses that belonged to the imperial stud.

Mongol war plans focused on the availability of pasture. Whenever the Mongols launched a new campaign, envoys sent ahead by the leading general were ordered to clear all livestock from the pastures, which were destined to be used for grazing by the invading army's animals. Any other use of the land, whether for gardens or for hunting, was also forbidden. As one Mongol general put it, "Most of the failure of our army is attributable to the death of animals that are neither watered nor fed." To ensure that enough water and feed would be available, the generals divided up their forces and sent them over different routes with a rendezvous date and place set in advance. Writers from the settled states, like the Arab historian Ibn Athir, thought that the Mongol army operated without any logistical support, because they did not have ponderous baggage trains of camels and elephants. In fact, the Mongols' logistical planning was meticulous. Army units traveled with the personal herds of their troopers and their families; in this way, seventeen million head of livestock were conveyed into Iran. Such migrations were strictly controlled and executed by the army and, indeed, formed part of the generals' responsibilities. The Mongols could securely conquer and rule any territory where pastoralists could flourish, since they both conquered and occupied the land.

Pasture often served as a casus belli. When a Turkish sultan brashly informed the neighboring Mongol general that he and his entourage planned to winter on the rich Mughan pastures (now divided between Iran and Azerbaijan), the Mongol, who considered Mughan as falling within his territories, was quick to take offense, but calculating in his response. He slyly withdrew his own camp from the Mughan and observed from afar as the Turks spread out, setting up countless gaudy tents, their jewelry-clad wives and concubines picnicking. A small Mongol force then surprised this unwarlike encampment, driving the sultan to flight and capturing many of the women, as well as their gold. The pastures themselves were the major prize, however. The Mongol general assigned the Mughan to his most loyal troops.

Pasture control lay at the heart of Mongol statecraft, especially as their horse power increased. The number of horses controlled by the Mongols rose from the original three million of the Mongolian homeland to ten million in the steppe empire, one-half of the world's total. At the same time, the Mongol empire now included large sedentary populations in northern China, Central Asia, Iran, and Afghanistan. How the Mongols managed conflict between the settled peoples and the herders would determine the durability of their rule, and also greatly affect their historical reputation, perhaps unfairly so.

The Mongols have been characterized as both ruthless and unprincipled in their relations with conquered peoples, particularly in their hunger for pasture. A fourteenth-century historian explained, "To some troops he gave places without measure on the borders of Khitan and Jurchen land, and in the borderlands of Mongolia." Here Genghis Khan simply annexed his enemies' lands and gave them to his troopers. In another campaign, his grandson Ariq Böke invaded the Ili region on the central steppe. He seized the farmers' crops and used it to feed his horses during the winter;[*] the farmers died of starvation. Whenever horses competed with humans for food, the horses came first.

The Mongols' approach to settling their armies differed sharply from the methods of previous steppe invaders, who had not, after the initial shock of invasion, executed an extensive plan of settlement. One hundred years earlier, the Seljuk rulers took over the land they needed for their immediate entourage but left the horse breeders who followed them to find whatever pasture they could. This led to much conflict and confusion, including the kidnapping of Sultan Sanjar; by the time the Mongols arrived in Iran, Seljuk power had collapsed completely. By contrast, following each Mongol conquest, the commanding general allocated specific pastures to their troopers, who continued to herd. William de Rubruck, a Franciscan missionary, reported, "Every commander, according to whether he has a greater or smaller number of men under him, is familiar with the limits of his pasturelands and where he ought to graze in summer and winter, in spring and autumn." Well-organized pastoralism served to keep the military units separate from the conquered population.

---

[*]   Seizure of grain was an extreme measure, as feeding it to horses could give them colic. This anecdote suggests that Ariq Böke had run out of grass.

At times the Mongols envisaged an even greater extension of pasture. When Genghis Khan overran northern China, overthrowing the Golden Khan, he initially planned to eradicate farming on these wide plains and convert the land entirely into pasture for Mongol horses. His Khitan and Jurchen advisers, descended from horse breeders who had once ruled northern China, convinced him not to pursue this genocidal policy, as the tax on agriculture would provide more than enough compensation to make up for the forgone pastures. Paradoxically, this decision probably sealed the fate of the Mongols in China; it meant that they would always be aliens in these lands. Had they converted northern China into pastureland, they might never have been evicted.

As Much Gold and Silver as They Fancy

The last horse ridden by Genghis Khan was known simply as Josotu Boro, "Reddish Gray." While hunting a herd of wild asses, the imperial entourage got caught in their stampede, and one of the wild asses hurtled into Josotu Boro. The animal reared and threw the aging khan. He never recovered from this fall. On his deathbed Genghis Khan encouraged the Mongols to choose as his successor his third son, Ögedei, a successful general, admired for his generosity and hospitality.

Ögedei's future difficulties in managing his father's conquests were vividly foreshadowed by the council called to acclaim him as supreme khan. So many Genghisid family members and officers with titles like *noyon, noker,* and *qurchi,* as well as slaves and hangers-on, came to attend this congress in Karakorum that its organizers ran out of food—a shocking lapse of Ögedei's legendary hospitality. Nor was there enough pasture surrounding Karakorum to feed all the animals. The council had to break up prematurely, with many participants vowing never to make such a journey a second time. Already the extent of the empire was becoming a problem. This did not discourage Ögedei from sending the Mongols on additional campaigns of conquest into Iran, eastern Europe, India, Korea, and China.

An expansive man ruling an expanding empire, Ögedei circulated for thousands of miles each year in his gorgeous tent city, meeting face-to-face with his subjects, an important piece of statecraft in an age where personal contact trumped laws and procedures. To instruct and confer with his far-flung Mongol generals, he relied on a network of fast post horses. Ultimately inspired by the ancient Persian system, the Mongol *yam* could bring a message from Armenia to Karakorum in one month.

The yam could deliver at this speed because of its density and size: between Ögedei's capital in Karakorum and Beijing, for example, there were thirty-seven postal stations, one every sixteen miles. According to Marco Polo, there were ten thousand postal stations and two hundred thousand horses in the system as a whole. Finally, especially fast horses, trained for sprints rather than endurance, enabled a courier to ride up to 190 miles in a day.

In fact, there were several distinct yam networks: the one described above rushed urgent diplomatic messages across Europe and Asia. A second carried only top-secret messages between members of the ruling family. The third conveyed heavy goods, like gifts, at a leisurely but secure pace. Local Genghisid princes frequently abused the postal system, using its horses for their own commercial deals. The Mongol rulers were increasingly engaged in big business: livestock and luxury markets sprang up on the otherwise empty steppe wherever Ögedei planted his tent city. By eliminating all rival rulers on the steppe and imposing a single tax at the frontier, the Mongols ensured that merchants would flock to Ögedei's court, supplying cheap and plentiful goods to his entourage. The Mongols had known poverty, but now they were going to enjoy wealth.

Early on, the Mongol court had formed business partnerships with prominent merchants. One such Central Asian merchant, Hasan Hajji, became an early associate of Genghis Khan himself, selling the khan fine horses from the west in return for sable and squirrel pelts. Hasan Hajji may have become an emissary or a spy for Genghis Khan, a role that horse traders frequently played in Central Asian politics. Successors to Hasan Hajji operated profitable trading houses for Ögedei and his family, borrowing money from them and sharing up to 70 percent of the returns with their patrons. Foreign merchants had to trade through the khan, and were forced to convert their silver coins into Mongol paper currency and use this paper currency to buy goods for resale.

As a result of these arrangements, immense wealth flowed through the hands of the great khan and, from there, showered down upon the Mongol commoners in astonishing displays of prodigality. Ögedei used to invite all and any to visit his treasury and ride away with as much gold and silver as they fancied. The khan still needed the loyalty of his horsemen, secured through gifts, more than he needed gold and silver. The Genghisid revolution in trade reoriented the wealth of Asia toward the Mongol people, and solidified their loyalty and political cohesion.

The newfound wealth of the Mongols turned them from sellers into buyers of horses. The Mongol elite keenly collected horses from Transoxiana and Iran. Bred in the more temperate climates of western Asia, these horses naturally grew up taller and stronger than those native to Mongolia. The chronicles referred to them as 異 (yi), or "extraordinary horses." Some of these horses were furnished by Mongol vassals as tax payments, but there persisted a robust merchant trade. Though the evidence is fragmentary, it is easy to imagine that five hundred thousand horses were traded across Asia each year, worth $1 billion to $3 billion in today's dollars. That amounted to a huge income received by the wealthy khans, and then shared among one million Mongols. The demand for extraordinary horses was such that horse dealers brought heavy-boned destriers all the way from France. Horses must have been by far the most valuable trade within the Mongol Empire. The Mongol revolution led to a huge diversion of trade from the settled periphery into the now wealthy, powerful, and pacified steppe.

Following Ögedei's death during an epic drinking bout in 1241, power ultimately passed to his nephew Möngke. Unlike the prodigal and bon vivant Ögedei, the new khan preserved the austere outlook of the traditional Mongol horse breeder. As an example of his probity, he insisted that the wealthy khans pay for private use of the yam. For all the prosperity they currently enjoyed, Möngke understood that only if the Mongols remained on the steppe could they keep their empire united and avoid the fate to which the Jurchens, Khitans, and Seljuks had succumbed: assimilation. He believed that the Mongols should rule from Karakorum and extract taxes from the settled peoples, but not settle among them.

In the mid-thirteenth century Möngke ruled over 4.5 million square miles—8 percent of the world's landmass, an area stretching from the Yellow River in China to the Danube River in the west, and from the Volga River in the north into Punjab in the south. Still, Möngke sent out his brothers Hülegü and Kublai to push those frontiers wider.* Perhaps it was good politics to keep these two ambitious leaders busy. Accordingly, Hülegü was sent to conquer the Middle East, and Kublai dispatched to fight the Song, now retrenched in southern China. The fate of both conquering brothers was emblematic, in very different ways, of the challenges of expanding Mongol power beyond the steppe.

In 1258, Hülegü consolidated Mongol control of Iran, where steppe-like conditions favored the establishment of Mongol military colonies. Then he decided to carry on the ancestral vendetta against another group of Kipchak Turks, those who ruled in Cairo and Damascus as mamluk sultans. The casus belli, was, as always, the refusal of these mamluks to hand over Kipchak refugees from earlier Mongol invasions. The mamluks mustered no steppe warriors, unlike the Khwarazm Shah. Their highly trained horsemen mounted fewer, better horses, all costly stallions acquired from Iran and Arabia. To match or overcome them, the Mongols had to rely on quantity rather than quality, providing each of their troopers with at least three or four mounts. Yet Syria lacked sufficient grass and water for the Mongols' one hundred thousand horses: the Mongols would have needed eight to fifteen square miles of fresh pasture per day, as well as 1.5 million gallons of water, to support such a force. These were simply not available. Unable to bring to bear their accustomed advantage in numbers, the Mongols suffered a searing military defeat. They returned to their pastures in eastern Anatolia and Iran, which Hülegü and his family ruled from their tented encampments for several generations. Hülegü had not succeeded in extending the empire beyond its environmental limits.

Kublai's campaigns in China, however, proved more successful than those of Hülegü in the Middle East, and wound up fundamentally transforming

---

* By 1279 the Mongols would rule 16 percent of the world's landmass.

the Mongol state. Möngke could not have foreseen, when he sent Kublai against the Song in 1251, that his younger brother would ultimately ignore Genghis Khan's dictum and abandon the steppe for a settled life.

Milking Mares in Xanadu

For decades following the conquest of Beijing, the Mongols in northern China remained aloof and geographically separate from the densely settled lands south of the Yangtze River, where the Song dynasty continued to rule a rump state known as the Southern Song. The supreme khan camped in Inner Mongolia, with Karakorum as the nominal capital for his peripatetic court, while the Mongol prince responsible for the Chinese provinces preferred the cool of Shangdu, Marco Polo's Xanadu, to the heat of Beijing.

The ambitious Kublai decided, however, that the complete conquest of China would make him by far the most likely contender for the top position in the Mongol Empire. Accordingly, he moved his administration from Xanadu 250 miles southeast to Beijing, naming it Khanbalik, the city of the khan, and declared himself emperor of China, the first of the Yuan dynasty. After sixteen years of making war, he had finally conquered the Song empire. In recognition of this accomplishment, following the death of Möngke, the assembled elders ultimately named China's conqueror supreme khan in 1264. His brother Hülegü, in faraway Iran, recognized him as the successor of Genghis Khan, Ögedei, and Möngke. Yet their cousin khans who ruled mainly horse breeders, in Mongolia, Central Asia, and the western steppe, hesitated. They foresaw that Kublai's desire to be simultaneously Son of Heaven and supreme khan would prove unworkable, and deleterious for the unity of the empire.

Publicly, Kublai showed his loyalty to horse-breeding traditions with displays that would have seemed ostentatious to steppe horsemen and impossibly foreign to his Chinese subjects, including drinking mare's milk. While the court escaped the summer heat in the cool of Xanadu, he gathered mares from his own personal herd and selected the fattest for milking. He had tents of felt erected to serve as milking halls, where he and the princes could watch the processes of milking the mares. In the winter, when the court gathered in Khanbalik, horses were driven down from

Xanadu for the milking ceremony. High-ranking officials personally fed the horses and prepared pure milk and ayraq, fermented mare's milk, for the imperial suite.*

The looming scission between Kublai and his steppe cousins was not about symbols, though; it was about resources. The Yuan emperor–supreme khan fought costly wars against the Song, the Koreans, the Japanese, and even the Burmese. The expense of these wars meant fewer gifts to be shared with the Mongols on the steppe. On the contrary, Kublai expected them to provide horses for his war efforts but offered to pay with paper money, a move that further alienated them. As his steppe subjects lost their enthusiasm for supplying horses to their citified cousins in Khanbalik, Kublai raided the uncooperative Mongol leaders, some of whom submitted, but without their followers or their herds. Precious remounts remained scarce; at one point Kublai managed to collect only seventy thousand mounts against the annual requirement of one hundred thousand.

Sometimes Kublai's commitment to his duties as emperor conflicted with the needs of the state for maintaining military might. At one point his privy council recommended allocating additional land in the suburbs of Khanbalik for pasturing cavalry horses. Kublai was about to assent to the proposal when his principal consort, Chaabi, joined the council. When she realized what was being proposed, she argued against it. "When we Mongols established Khanbalik, if we had needed this land for pasture, we would have expropriated it. Now the allotments are fixed for the army. Why should we seize new land now?" Kublai shelved the proposal.

The growing shortfall in horse power forced the Yuan emperor to impose measures that were as unpopular as any land requisition. Faced with the necessity of denying the Song resistance access to horses, he introduced a ban on exports and exclusionary measures over the right to own horses near

---

* The same pastures in today's Inner Mongolia are now managed by a major cooperative, Mengniu (Mongolian Cow). By adding sugar and fruit flavors, modern Mongols have managed to convince their Chinese compatriots to drink liquid yogurt (via a straw that has a poor record of actually penetrating into the Tetra Pak container). Twenty years ago, the Chinese consumed hardly any dairy products, so this represents, for the descendants of Genghis Khan, a small victory over Chinese culinary habits.

The Yuan empress Chaabi participates in a hunt,
by Liu Guando, ca. 1280.

the border. While Mongols were entitled and expected to ride, it became unlawful for many categories of Chinese subjects to even mount a horse: monks, scholars, imams, Uyghurs, Jurchens, Khitans, Koreans, tradesmen, workmen, hunters, merchants, and singing girls. Only Chinese officials with a government seal were authorized to ride. Rewards were given to informers, and the punishment for any infraction was death. The Mongols even sacrificed important economic activity dependent on horses, including turning millstones and hauling barges along the Yellow River.

The Yuan emperor then registered all the horses in China and requisitioned them for military purposes, which resulted in the corralling of a large number in Khanbalik without sufficient pasturage. The horses became a major nuisance for the farmers around the city. They could be fed with suitable crops, but that meant spending per cavalry trooper five times the amount as per foot soldier, draining the treasury. Horses could not be easily mobilized by a sedentary power, not even one that was Mongol.

The emperor also experimented with procuring horses from unfamiliar sources, Tibet and Yunnan. These were entirely different breeds, suitable for the mountains of Yunnan and northern Burma. This helped the Mongols conquer southern China, but even the Burmese kingdom of Pagan now had the capacity, with horses imported from Bengal, to resist. The number of horses available for each Mongol trooper dwindled from five, to three, to one. Eventually, a large part of the Mongol army had to fight on foot, enjoying no tactical superiority. By the end of Kublai's long reign, in 1294, Yuan China looked more and more like a traditional Chinese state, and not a steppe empire with limitless horse power.

Before long, the Mongols of Mongolia returned to the ways of their steppe ancestors: they raided Yuan China in order to secure more privileges from their Sinicized cousins. Weakened by dynastic feuds, crop failures, and a litany of other disasters that seemed to signal the withdrawal of the Mandate of Heaven, in 1368, the last Yuan emperor fled Khanbalik for the steppe in the face of a growing rebellion. The loss of China made it impossible for any Genghisids to pretend to the rank of supreme khan. The empire was finished. The Chinese pursued the Mongols through Inner Mongolia and burned down Kublai's famous pleasure pavilion in Xanadu, later sacking Karakorum. Within settled China, they proceeded, as far as was possible, to remove all vestiges of Genghisid rule.

The Mongol Legacy

Strangely, in today's Mongolia historical vestiges of Genghis Khan are scarce. But for the ruins of Karakorum, there are no visible monuments from the times of the Genghisids, and until very recently, there were no modern monuments to Genghis Khan. The location of his tomb remains a secret, though later dynastic histories claim it contains, in addition to the world conqueror, the remains of forty geldings and forty favorite beauties, richly arrayed with silk robes and jewelry. After the fall of the Mongol Empire, Mongolia reverted to the conditions that had prevailed there for centuries. New clans reemerged on the basis of the Mongol military colonies. Local chiefs came to power and fought among themselves, manipulated by foreign powers, as once the Jurchens had manipulated them. Paradoxically, the Mongols had the most lasting impact on their most distant conquests, Iran and eastern Europe.

The initial consequence of Hülegü's 1235 campaign in Iran was purely destructive. The Mongols campaigned ruthlessly, privileging pastures for horses over the survival of the local population; as the Franciscan missionary William de Rubruck informs us in his thirteenth-century account, "There used to be sizeable towns lying in the plain, but they were for the most part completely destroyed so that the Tartars [as he called the Mongols] could pasture there, since the area affords very fine grazing lands." Hülegü and his descendants stayed true to their steppe origins and ruled Iran from magnificent tented cities in present-day Azerbaijan, where the best pastureland was found, well watered by snow-covered mountains. They granted grazing rights to their armies in surrounding lands, and units of the Mongolian Jalayirs, Oirats, and Suldus, which the supreme khan had assigned to the invasion, found themselves herding in present-day Turkey, between the headwaters of the Tigris and the Euphrates, and in northern Iraq. Some of the assigned pasturelands had once been important centers of agricultural production. It is possible that the agricultural population had already declined due to war and disease, and the land was therefore empty. It is also possible that the Mongols simply pushed the old inhabitants aside.

The devastation occasioned by the Mongols exceeded that of the Seljuks because of the size of the Mongol army. The Seljuks arrived with four thousand families—perhaps twenty thousand people—converting arable land in Transoxiana and Khorasan into pastures. The Mongols brought many more horse breeders into Iran from Mongolia and Central Asia. One scholar estimates that one million pastoralists immigrated into Iran under the Mongols, while the settled population dropped from 2.5 million to 250,000, based on Mongol tax records. Impoverished peasants would have dropped out of the tax rolls, so the 250,000 figure does not necessarily cover the total population. Though there is no good population data for the subsequent centuries, estimates for the eighteenth century suggest that even after four hundred years, one million of Iran's three million inhabitants were pastoralists.

This explains why many of the districts of Iran with the most attractive pastures, including Azerbaijan (both in Iran today and in the Republic of Azerbaijan), the region of Gorgan, and parts of the Zagros Mountains, became Turkish-speaking. Turks in the invading armies outnumbered ethnic Mongols, whose language fell out of common use in the late thirteenth century. Many groups that would come to rule the Iranian state thereafter originated in Azerbaijan, including the White Sheep, the Safavids, the Afshars, and the Qajars. Farther south, the Turkish-speaking Qashqai later dominated the politics of Shiraz. Only in the twentieth century would the Turkish horse breeders cede political control in Iran to urban Persian speakers.

Today, many Iranians argue that the Mongol invasion was the most traumatic event in their history, though scholars are divided as to whether or not the Mongols permanently impaired Iran's agricultural potential. Iran lies in the arid zone, highly dependent on irrigation. As such, the country is vulnerable to the social and ecological disruptions that accompany large-scale warfare. It seems clear that the Mongol invasions damaged fragile irrigation infrastructure and caused agriculture to contract. It is hard to assess accurately if the horse breeders reinforced a longer trend toward desertification or whether they simply took advantage of marginal land slowly abandoned by farmers. Complicating the matter further, there are accounts of agricultural communities springing back after the initial, violent invasions.

For example, in the 1230s, the Mongol governor of Transoxiana, Mas'ud Beg, restored the cities that had been destroyed by Genghis Khan's initial invasion. He rebuilt the irrigation canals, established a new currency, and put a stop to raiding and plundering by the horse breeders. Some of this prosperity disappeared again during a period of fighting occasioned by the death of Möngke in 1259. A decade later, two of the younger khans competing for power in Transoxiana agreed that they should protect the cities from further destruction, and swore an oath on gold that "henceforth they would dwell in the mountains and plains and not camp near the cities, or graze their animals in cultivated areas, or extort the farmers." In the late thirteenth century Marco Polo noted that the Mongol garrison troops supported themselves from "the immense herds of cattle that are assigned to them and on the milk which they send into the towns to sell in return for necessary provisions." Coexistence was clearly possible.

The Mongols learned to govern Iran competently, raising taxes from farmers and cities to sustain their administration. Arable land was resettled, and irrigation was repaired. Gradually, the Mongols began to act less like foreign conquerors. They did not assimilate into the settled population of Iran; rather, they assimilated into and reinforced the region's existing horse-breeding population. Though they gradually broke up into bickering statelets, with the last khan losing power in 1357, the Mongols left Iran more than ever a land of good horses, an inexhaustible source of horse power for future conquerors.

In eastern Europe, the Mongol legacy differed from that of both China and Iran. Here they were neither ejected nor assimilated: they kept their horse-breeding traditions and remained separate from their conquered subjects. As a result, they survived for a much longer span of time, until 1783 by some reckonings.

Initially the Mongols campaigned with their proverbial brutality, relentlessly pursuing fugitive Kipchaks who had taken refuge in the Kyivan Rus* principalities, Hungary, Poland, and Bulgaria. Subsequently these lands registered sharp drops in population, as the Mongols requisitioned crops and plowlands in order to feed their horses. Moreover, the Mongols recruited auxiliaries from the conquered people—forty-three thousand Rus, for example, were sent to fight in China. It took decades for eastern Europe to recover. The kings of Poland encouraged immigration from western Europe to help rebuild ruined cities and towns.†

Eastern European rulers ultimately kept the Mongols at bay by paying heavy taxes. In any case, the conquerors never intended to settle among the conquered. They continued to pasture on the western steppe, where they were within striking distance of the subject peoples, and from where they could enforce tax collection and engage in trade. Ethnic Mongols formed

* The Rus are the common ancestors of Ukrainians, Belarussians, and Russians.
† This is the origin of the German and Jewish urban communities that later characterized multiethnic Poland.

a tiny minority of these Turkish-speaking herders, who came to be known, confusingly, as Tatars. Their ruling Genghisid khan traveled through his steppe realms in a great tent of white silk, the color white designating him as the lord of the west. The sun reflecting off the khan's tents gave rise to the name Golden Horde.* Under his rule, a numerically small number of steppe horsemen, perhaps 140,000, laid down the law for a much larger population of settled peoples, four to five million. This would change only when the descendants of the Rus learned to master horse power in their own turn.

With time, the Mongol presence in eastern Europe proved less destructive. The prosperity of a new principality, Moscow, would arise from the trade networks established by the Mongols. This commercial connection is evidenced by the Turco-Mongol vocabulary in the Russian language: *denga* (money), *yam* (postal services), *tamgha* (brands, but also customs duty and now the Russian word for postage stamps). The Moscow princes soon adopted these Mongol institutions, and over generations, people forgot that they were Mongol imports. They also adopted the Mongol word for horse, *mörin*, as their word for gelding.† Eventually, Moscow would develop into the most significant Mongol successor state.

The most important legacy of the Mongols, however, lay in the sheer magnitude of their achievements. Genghis Khan and his descendants mobilized horse power as no previous steppe rulers had done, even as they consciously imitated the earlier imperial ambitions of the Huns and the Turks. They achieved greater dominance than their predecessors by conquering great sedentary states, including Iran, Kyiv, Hungary, and China. The fabulous wealth the Mongols achieved and the enviable imperial lifestyle they led made Mongol rule the benchmark for future steppe ambitions. The Mongol collapse did not discourage successive attempts to restore their empire, as Iran, China, and even India would next experience.

---

* "Horde" comes from *ordu*, meaning camp or tent.

† Similarly, the French word for gelding, *hongre*, originally meant a Hungarian horse—e.g., a steppe horse.

Riding the Whirlwind

Timür and his descendants, 1370–1747

๛

The Horse Race

The horses might have quickened their pace, sniffing the road of return, as Tamerlane's cavalry rode back to the oasis of Samarkand in 1404, after seven years of constant campaigning in Armenia, Georgia, Syria, and Anatolia. Timür-e Lang, "the Lame," to use his Persian name, planned for them to rest and regroup in his rarely visited imperial capital. Under turquoise-blue fretted domes, the warlord unloaded his immense plunder and plotted his next conquest. His troopers relaxed and feasted in their tents, pitched beside the Zarafshan River—"flowing with gold," this Persian name recalling its eddies of gold-rich alluvium—among the orchards and mulberry trees of Samarkand's surrounding gardens. Their hungry warhorses also feasted on the immense stores of fodder that had been gathered for their return. Crowds of civilians strolled into the army's camps to admire the fine animals, and to enjoy the music of reciting bards and singing girls performing for the troops.

To further entertain the court and the people of Samarkand, Timür organized a *töy*, or festival, featuring horse races. The racecourse stretched twenty miles around, typical for Turco-Mongol games; a windmill barely visible on the horizon marked the far bend, while close to the dais of the noble spectators, a rope laid out across the ground served as the finish line. The flat field, golden under the autumn sun, bristled with plane trees. Invisible in the glare, irrigation channels crisscrossed the countryside. Clumps of spectators squatted on their heels throughout the course,

keen to see the winners up close and indifferent to the risk of being trampled. Those near the finish line were ready to rush forward and rub their
hands in the sweat of the winning horse, in hopes of acquiring some of the
animal's vigor.

These races were staged for every great gathering of princes and generals, as well as on holidays like Nowruz (New Year) and Bayram, the most
important Muslim feast. Bards reciting well-known steppe tales were sure
to recall famous races won or lost by ancient heroes. With epic exaggeration, one famous story told of a race that lasted three months. In another
tale, two heroes threatened to go to war with each other; their canny khan
sent them off on a race so long that the winner was never determined.
That race could have been a metaphor for Timür's own interminable campaigns, which had lasted, in all, for thirty years. Racing, like hunting, kept
the horses in fighting form. By organizing another töy upon his return to
Samarkand, Timür, then sixty-eight years old, signaled to his army that his
career of conquest had not yet ended.

The töy served yet another purpose, however. The best of Timür's
cavalry competed for prizes that included fine horses as well as saddles
embossed with silver. Turks, Tajiks (sedentary Persian speakers), Kurds,
and Arabs participated, each entrant riding a horse of his own country.
This put Timür's horse power on display before a select audience. From a
VIP stand, ambassadors from different lands enjoyed the spectacle; they
were sure to report back to their rulers, which included the king of Castille
and the mamluk sultans of Egypt and India. The race served to advertise to
all of Timür's allies and neighbors the invincibility of his cavalry.

One member of the diplomatic corps was conspicuously absent, though
Timür intended to send the strongest message to his ruler. A few months
earlier, the ambassador from Ming China had appeared in Samarkand on
a mission to remind Timür that the Ming had defeated and replaced the
Mongol-Yuan dynasty in China and that therefore Timür, as the ruler of a
former Yuan subject state, Iran, should pay taxes to and accept the primacy
of the Ming emperor, Yongle. The Chinese ambassador had added that
Timür was seven years in arrears with his taxes. In response, Timür had
ordered the Chinese ambassador and his suite to be chained with leg irons,
threatened to hang them, and confiscated their accompanying caravan,

which included eight hundred camels. Two centuries earlier, Iran's then ruler, the Khwarazm Shah, ordered the execution of the emissaries sent to Otrar by Genghis Khan, provoking a war that resulted in Iran's conquest by the Mongols. This parallel did not seem to trouble Timür.

For Timür felt himself unbeatable. He mustered close to one hundred thousand cavalry troopers, with perhaps half a million horses. Just as horse-rich Mongolia had provided the resource base for Genghis Khan, so now Iran, including Transoxiana and Afghanistan, provided a springboard for the conquests of Timür. As a legacy of the Mongols and their appropriation of agricultural land for pasturage, Iran abounded in horses in the fourteenth and fifteenth centuries. It had a more favorable climate than Mongolia, where icy winters regularly reduced herds. Neighboring states envied Iran and eagerly imported its horses for their own stables and stud farms. The sultans of Delhi alone accounted for tens of thousands of purchases annually. One Mongolian-speaking clan of Eastern Iran, the Nikudari, raised four hundred thousand horses for this trade, growing so wealthy and powerful in the process that they defied every overlord until Timür subdued them. Outstanding horses were even shipped to the court of the Ming emperors. Zheng He, the famous Chinese navigator, is said to have returned from the Persian Gulf with one hundred horses in his tall ships. Post-Mongol Iran had become a horse superpower.

The superiority of Iranian horses depended little on selective breeding or pedigree, which are modern concepts. Breeders kept no stud books,[*] and sires and dams were not recorded. Instead, the desirability of the horse came from its environment and the skill of the breeder as much as from the stock. Horses are highly mobile and outbreed naturally, and in his many wars Timür captured and added to his stud farms horses from Georgia, Kurdistan, Arabia, and the Volga, enriching the mix with no thought of purity or race. Horse-keen cavalrymen and traders recognized, however, the value of territory and training for the development of desirable horses.

The clan names of the breeders must have been as prestigious modern luxury brands. Each horse bore the tamgha of its clan on its haunches; this functioned as a kind of trademark for its breeder's particular excellence.

---

[*] A stud book is a registry of progenitures, sires, and dams of so-called purebred animals.

The breeders held festivities in the spring to accompany the branding of the young colts. The historians of Timür's time did not mention breeds by name, probably because these horses simply carried the name of the clan that raised them. Instead, traders referred to horses by their provenance: "Turki," from northeastern Iran, northern Afghanistan, and Transoxiana; "Persian" or "Kurdi" from western Iran; or "Arab," from Iraq, then part of Timür's empire. The Turki horses excelled primarily in speed, while the horses from mountainous Kurdistan had broader bodies with surer footing. Unlike Genghis Khan's cavalry, Timür's troopers often rode stallions— bigger, stronger, but more expensive to feed than geldings. Extraordinary horses were referred to as *arghamak*; this Turkish word was translated by the Chinese as "tall steeds." They were a superior class of horses among a herd that could already be seen as "the ultimate riding machines."

The images of Timür's horses have come down to us in a highly idealized fashion: the illustrations in the gorgeous manuscripts of his historians. The animals appear to fly, fairy-like, above the carnage of dismembered bodies and decapitated heads, their dainty hooves raised in graceful gestures of obedience to their riders. The coat colors of Timür's officers' horses are depicted handsomely: sorrel (red) with a white blaze and white forelegs; golden palomino, as in the stables of Genghis Khan; jet black, like the steed of the ancient Iranian hero Siyavosh; and silvery blue—Timür himself rode such a horse on his return to Samarkand. Art historian Sheila Canby argues that these pictures represent real equine portraits and prefigure the almost preternatural realism of the Mughal horse paintings. Or the artists may have simply varied the colors of their subjects to make for an interesting composition; even so, one is reminded again that these colors represented the cardinal directions, indicating the wide expanse of Timür's empire.

The Road Back to Xanadu

Timür's birth rank neither qualified him nor disqualified him for high leadership. His lineage was that of minor chiefs of Mongol horse breeders who had settled near the Oxus River in Genghis Khan's time. His success in raids earned him a numerous following, despite his being lamed during a daring raid. This brought him to the attention of local leaders, who began to use him for their own political ends; he served them dutifully, developing a reputation for competence and sagacity, and slowly expanded his circle of allies and clients. Between the 1350s and 1370, he outmaneuvered and double-crossed his former patrons, whom he forced into submission or exile; Timür soon had control not only of his own people but of a wider confederation of horse breeders and a firm base in Transoxiana and Khorasan. Starting in 1370, Timür had enough local horse power behind him to embark on the conquest of his Central Asian neighbors in eastern and western Iran, reconstituting out of fragmented Mongol and Turkmen statelets the Iranian empire of Genghis Khan's grandson Hülegü.

Like Genghis Khan before him, he brooked no rivals, going to extreme lengths to overawe or punish anyone who challenged him. The khans of the Golden Horde, ruling much of what is now Russia and Ukraine, had long contested the claim of Hülegü's descendants to Azerbaijan and Central Asia, and now they rejected Timür's. When the Golden Horde and their Russian vassals raided Timür's realms, he didn't simply chase them out; he launched his army two thousand miles into the western steppe, almost to the gates of Moscow.* Timür's expedition into what is now Kazakhstan and Russia provided an occasion for the Russian princes to declare independence from the Golden Horde, though Tatar khans later forced them back into submission. Russia remained subject to the Golden Horde for another century, before beginning its own expansion into the steppe.

The logistics of operating far from his base proved daunting. In the winter of 1391 Timür's army rode through drifts of snow as high as the horses' bellies. At one point the horses grew so thin that Timür had to send a third of them back to Samarkand, to ensure sufficient fodder for the remaining two-thirds. Unable to find the Golden Horde's army in the trackless steppe, he organized an enormous hunting battue to feed the hungry army. The horsemen rode down fat onagers, letting the thin ones escape. To further build morale, Timür organized a gallop-past, so the troopers could see him and his generals glistening with rubies, emeralds, and pearls on their horse tack, weapons, and armor. Musicians encouraged the galloping horses

---

* Some embellished accounts claim Timür sacked Moscow. It was his Tatar allies who were responsible.

Amir Timür pursuing the Golden Horde, from a
copy of the Zafarnameh, *1460.*

with heavy kettledrums and piercing reed instruments. "Since Genghis
Khan no one has seen an army such as this," claimed Timür's historian
Sharafuddin Yazdi.

Timür did more than provide morale-boosting spectacles. He kept his
troops motivated with the promise of plunder, and, indeed, his campaign
against the Golden Horde in Russia between 1391 and 1395 resulted in so
much booty that his soldiers could not carry all of it back. Horse expro-
priation was a standard practice of Timür's, as horses supplied their own
transport, and it was a way to strengthen the army while weakening the
enemy. Some who fought on foot managed to return with ten to twenty
horses, representing a big jump in their social status; those who fought with
a horse or two returned with a hundred. When Timür's forces sacked Delhi

in 1398, they left it a heap of ruins, and carried off the treasure that paid for remaking Samarkand into one of the wonders of the world in its time.

Timür went on to defeat and capture the eighth Ottoman sultan, Bayezid II, near Ankara in 1402, the Year of the Horse.* Yet following Mongol practice, Timür limited his outright conquests to territories with extensive pasture grounds, enabling him to recruit and maintain additional cavalry. Though he inflicted defeats on the Egyptian mamluks in Syria and the sultans of Delhi, he contented himself with extracting taxes from them, without annexing any of their pasture-poor territories.

Timür saw himself as the restorer of the Mongol Empire, and his victories overlapped with or exceeded those of the Mongols: Ankara, Delhi, Sarai on the Volga, and Baghdad. As ruler of Iran, he controlled one of the richest provinces of the old Mongol empire, with a cavalry force rivaling that of Genghisid Mongolia. From his homeland in Transoxiana, he could rapidly march in any direction, including across the Altai Mountains and into China. By the time of his triumphant return to Samarkand in September 1404, if anyone could claim the legacy of supreme ruler, like Genghis Khan or Kublai Khan, it would be Timür, not the newly enthroned Yongle Emperor in Beijing.

The Ming dynasty, even though it had succeeded in driving the Mongols out of China in 1368, was unable to exert control of the neighboring steppe the way the Tang had. By and large the Ming were content to strengthen and embellish the Great Wall in the form we see today, and to maintain the status quo on the steppe frontier using more diplomacy than warfare. Without a forward policy of engaging with the horse-breeding peoples, they struggled to maintain a cavalry force equal to their pretensions to collect taxes from Timür. And Timür knew this. Why, he may have asked the unhappy Ming ambassador in leg irons, should he accept Chinese suzerainty?† What would prevent Timür from reconquering Tibet,

---

* This defeat of the Ottomans' traditional Turkmen cavalry at the hands of the more professional Timürid army convinced the Ottoman Turks to similarly transform their army, creating the war machine that within a century would threaten central Europe.

† "Suzerainty" refers to indirect control by a more powerful state over another, less powerful one. Supporters of Tibetan independence argue, for example, that China historically exercised only suzerainty over Tibet, while the Chinese claim to have enjoyed full sovereignty over that country.

Gansu, and Mongolia, and making the Ming *his* subordinate state? There
is no evidence that Timür seriously contemplated invading the heartland of
China—something, he also knew, that had taken Kublai Khan more than
sixteen years to complete. Nevertheless, a signal defeat on the battlefield
in the western regions could well bring down the Ming dynasty, or at least
force it into submission. Timür would then extract taxes, just as Genghis
Khan had done with the Song dynasty. The wealth of China would serve to
build an even stronger army. The world would see a neo-Mongol empire,
as a court historian described it, "from Japan to the deserts of Syria and
Egypt, an empire more than a year's march from one end to the other. In
each province its princes possess innumerable troops and partisans, such
that the world is not vast enough to contain their soldiers and horses."

Horse power not only provided Timür with a means of making war;
it compelled him to do so. For the steppe army had lost its low-cost status in the era of Timür. This reflected the increasingly technical nature
of warfare, to which the steppe horse breeders now adapted themselves.
Genghis Khan had innovated with respect to previous conquerors, but
Timür made further improvements, all of which cost significant amounts
of money. While the Mongol army had fed itself on the hoof as it carried
out its invasions, Timür's army moved more like a modern one, with a
logistics train of camels carrying fodder for its animals. Genghis Khan had
conquered what was for him a blank slate, and could pasture his animals
wherever he as conqueror chose. Timür had to move through territory
belonging to his own subjects. He could tax them to provide supplies to his
forces, but could not simply drive them off their pastures, as the Mongols
had done. Moreover, by providing fodder to the army's horses, Timür was
able to stay on campaign twelve months a year, unlike the Mongols, whose
campaigns coincided with the availability of steppe grass. This increased
need for planning and administration would feature more prominently in
centuries to come.

Timür's cavalry was also more professionalized than that of Genghis
Khan. Each rank had the obligation to supply a fixed number of horses. A
common solider needed to muster two, a corporal (*bahadur*—a rank still
used in the Indian Army) five, a captain ten. Generals were obliged to provide 110 horses. The higher ranks needed more horses because they brought

more equipment with them; a captain needed a spare horse to carry heavy armor for the warhorse he would ride into battle, another horse to transport a tent. As with the Mongols, clan chieftains were replaced by officers appointed on merit. But unlike the Mongols, the army provided each combatant fodder sufficient for his horses. Their pay was in fact called *ulufat*, from the word for alfalfa. In addition, Timür's army drilled and learned to execute maneuvers beyond the traditional Mongol battue, to the rhythm of the deeply resounding kettledrums.

Timür's most visible innovation consisted of integrating artillery into his battle deployment. Artillery ensured that his 1398 invasion of India succeeded far beyond the attempts the Mongols had made a hundred years earlier. The impact of his cannons on the Delhi sultan's elephants was devastating, since these animals not only presented huge targets for scarcely accurate gunfire but also ran amok in their own ranks, causing terrible casualties. (Timür's cavalry had learned to cope with noise of gunfire.) To pay for all these innovations in logistics, training, and military hardware, Timür had no choice but to campaign decade after decade in pursuit of plunder and taxes.

Timür's staying in the saddle for seven years at a time served another purpose, too. Under his regime he faced few threats of rebellion from his inner circle—not even from his ambitious sons, who might otherwise have considered accelerating their father's retirement. Keeping everyone constantly on campaign ensured the adhesion of the Timürid army, troops, and princes to his rule, and thirty years of success in war made Timür the irreplaceable conqueror.

Sure enough, as Timür watched his cavalry proudly race across the meadows beside the Zarafshan, he announced to his entourage that they would soon prepare to invade China. The töy was, finally, not only to impress the foreign ambassadors but to give the participants overwhelming confidence in their invincibility, and motivate them once more for another seven-year campaign.

It took many weeks to muster the army. Horses, hay, and carts were assembled. The bellowing of camels and the bells that clanged at their necks added to the cacophony of the swearing drivers. Each soldier brought along two milk cows and two milk goats; when the animals stopped giving milk, they could be eaten. Timür informed his reluctant allies camped along the march route to be ready to provide the army with fodder. Pastoralists were expected to pay a tax on their horses and smaller livestock.

Intelligence concerning the routes and the weather was diligently collected. Timür himself interrogated the caravanners who had brought the unlucky Chinese ambassador. One merchant had spent six months in Beijing, probably as part of a horse-trading mission; he warned Timür that Beijing was twenty times larger than Tabriz, the ancient Mongol capital of Iran. He further noted that when the Ming emperor set out for war, he kept four hundred thousand cavalry in reserve to guard the realm, and that every nobleman in China had one thousand mounted retainers. Timür knew this latter information to be false, so it did not deter him, but he allowed it to be recorded in his histories in order to magnify the grandeur of his future victories. He understood that the Ming were vulnerable to invasion and subversion, given the fragile nature of the peace on China's steppe frontier and the Ming's lack of horses. He also knew from his own experience that success breeds success, and therefore if he could manage early victories on China's lengthy and porous steppe frontier, he could count on a wave of horsemen ready to join him.

The plan was to march his army northeast across the steppe, where the winter rains had lately covered the pastures with grass, reducing the amount of fodder needed. The year 1405 began unseasonably cold, but as the army headed north, they hoped for an early spring. The cold did not let up as they camped near the town of Otrar, 280 miles northeast of Samarkand. From there, a 620-mile march separated them from the Zhungar Mountains, the most accessible route from the western steppe to the eastern. Soon these pastures would provide excellent grazing for Timür's warhorses. From there, the northern rim of the Tarim Basin would be open to invasion. Though at this stage Timür would be far from Samarkand, the Ming armies would have to cover twice the distance, through less favorable pastures for their horses, in order to intercept him. He would be able to conquer much of the eastern steppe before the Chinese could even give battle.

In February, however, a snowstorm the likes of which no one could remember unleashed itself on Timür's army. The fields by Otrar became icy like pavements of marble or filled with snowbanks as fluffy as cotton, as Timür's historians described it. The streams looked like veins of crystal. As there was nothing to do except sit in the tents and wait for the thaw, Timür's inner circle enjoyed epic drinking bouts, entertained by singers and musicians. Did any of the singers retell the story of Otrar and the ill-fated ambassadors?

A few weeks later the weather broke. Some of the horse breeders camped along the planned march route greeted the spring with the first, fresh kumis of the year. Their elderly khan was much concerned about having to welcome Timür, the depredation that the passage of his army would cause to his pastures, and the taxes he would have to pay in horses and smaller animals. Anxiety caused the old khan to spill the ritual kumis on the ground. Just then, a horseman in white clothing mounted on a black horse galloped up. The guards could not prevent him from approaching the old khan's tent. "Amir Timür is dead!" he cried without stopping. "Wait, tell us the details!" the khan shouted. But the horseman galloped on to the next camp, outpacing the old khan's retainers dispatched in his pursuit.

The sixty-nine-year-old master of the steppe had died, either from too much drinking or from pneumonia. His war-weary heirs quickly called off the invasion of China. In 1419, they sent a delegation with fine horses—even Timür's own favorite horse—to make peace with Yongle, who received them in an overpowering spectacle in his newly built Forbidden City. By setting aside Timür's last planned invasion, his heirs hoped to enjoy the fruits of his previous conquests. They divvied Timür's empire up among sons and grandchildren, some of whom indulged in drink to the point that they grew too fat to sit on their horses.

Yet Timür had demonstrated once again what could be achieved with the power of the steppe; even the conquest of China could not be excluded. He would not be the last to try his luck.

"A Land of No Good Horses"

"Maybe *I* will conquer China," mused the nineteen-year-old Babur in 1502, as he rode sadly, with his faithful retainers, into exile. A great-great-great-grandson of Timür, he had just lost the kingdoms of Ferghana and Samarkand in Transoxiana to a horde of two hundred thousand horsemen, who had burst in under the banner of their Uzbek warlords to snatch power away from the now soft and unwarlike descendants of Timür. The loss of such a kingdom smarted. This realm had offered everything: temperate climate, sophisticated cities, and excellent pastures. Ferghana had been, after all, the home of the blood-sweating horses. As Timür had correctly judged, rulers of Transoxiana could not allow the horse breeders of the western steppe to become too powerful. His successors had sat idly by and watched the Uzbeks, an offshoot from the Golden Horde, do just that; Transoxiana was lost to the Timürids and to Iran forever. Iran itself then split again, into quarreling statelets.

Deprived of his throne, Babur became a *kazakh*, a freebooting warrior, wandering in search of an opportunity to restore his fortunes and reward his dwindling band of followers. Unlike a band of pastoralists, they traveled not in search of pasture but of plunder; *kazakh* also meant "bandit." In his memoirs, Babur himself refers to his raids as kazakh expeditions. For a prince of his lineage, there was no shame involved in living as a kazakh, as long as he could find a suitable kingdom to conquer. The Uzbeks themselves had started off as raiders, after all, and a branch of their original horde would proudly use Kazakh as their ethnonym. So even at this low point of his career, Babur did not think the conquest of China to be out of the question. It was simply a matter of assembling a sufficient number of horsemen. In the meantime, however, when his band of exiles sought safety from the pursuing Uzbeks in the distant Hindu Kush, they hunted not for kingly sport but because they needed to eat.

While hunting, Babur learned that the Kingdom of Kabul might just be the suitable opportunity he had been looking for. Kabul had earlier been ruled by one of his uncles but had fallen into the hands of an unpopular usurper. Milking his Timürid ancestry for what it was still worth, and invoking his powerful relatives, none of whom lifted a finger to help him, he put together a ragtag collection of Mongol[*] freebooters and snatched Kabul away from its upstart ruler in 1504. From then on, his dreams of

---

[*] "Mongol" was pronounced "Mughal" in Persian, whence the European name for Babur's future empire. The Mughals called themselves "Gurkani," or "of the Son-in-law," reflecting Timür's marriage alliance with a Genghisid princess.

conquering China faded. Babur fell in love with this little kingdom, a territory that corresponded to most of today's eastern and southern Afghanistan. He praised its fresh air, excellent fruit, swift-running streams, and plentiful game. It was also a land rich in horses, and had been since the days when the Kushans had immigrated from China and established their horse-trading empire.

However, in order to capture Kabul, Babur had made many promises, and to fulfill those promises he needed a bigger prize; Kabul was too small a conquest to retain the loyalty of the chieftains and their twenty thousand followers who had rallied to him. He knew that if he were to mount an invasion of India, he could count on any number of Central Asian chieftains and adventurers to join him for plunder, following the well-trodden path of invaders from the steppe. As in Timür's time, marshaling an invading army would cost a lot of money, and Babur incurred additional expenses by hiring professional artillerymen. Yet while Babur regretted leaving Kabul behind for the plains of India—"a land of no good horses," as he put it—that lack was precisely why he was able to conquer it.

Babur's foray into India was well timed because, as in Kabul, the Indo-Afghan Lodi sultanate was racked with factional conflict. In 1526, Babur and his comrades engaged in a huge set battle with the Lodis in the wasteland north of Delhi, near a locality called Panipat. Babur enjoyed a significant tactical advantage, with the presence of Ottoman gunnery masters overseeing his extensive artillery: at the time, the Ottomans had the most professional artillery service in Asia. Moreover, the determination of Babur's small band of Mughal warriors proved greater than the noncommittal attitude of the Lodis' Indo-Afghan generals, who waited to see how the battle would go before engaging. The Lodi sultan was shot off his elephant, and the battle was over. The riches of Delhi sufficed to reward Babur's old partisans, pay off the gunners, and also convert the local Indo-Afghans to Babur's cause. Like Genghis Khan's son Ögedei, generous to a fault, Babur gave away so much wealth he earned the nickname "the beggar."

Babur, king of Kabul and now emperor of Delhi, found a volatile situation among his new subjects. Several ruling clans originating in Afghanistan had fought one another for primacy in northern India over the last several centuries. They always had a supply of cavalry mounts from their

The Mughals in India

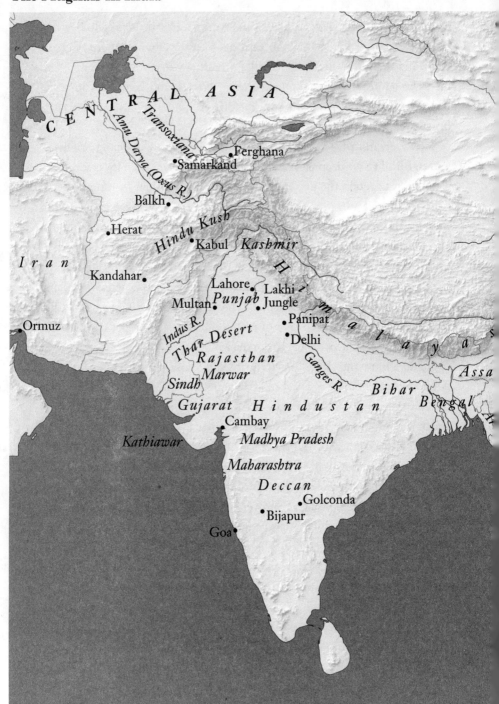

ancestral territories. Afghan horse traders, the successors, if not the actual descendants, of the Kushans, continuously operated caravans between Central Asia and the market cities of Lahore and Multan, importing as many as one hundred thousand horses annually. Between their business profits and military adventurism, some of these traders had carved out principalities for themselves. They formed a kind of military aristocracy of Indian-born Afghans, raising horses brought from their homeland in the foothills of the Himalayas. (Haridwar, the great horse market and Kumbh Mela site, lay in this district.) They enjoyed power and influence as far away as Bihar and Bengal, and Babur had to cooperate with them in order to rule his new kingdom. The Indo-Afghans tolerated Babur, since he appeared to have luck on his side and now controlled their homeland and their access to the horse trade. But even so, they looked for any opportunity to resume their independence.

Babur ruled over the combined dominion of Kabul and the former Delhi sultanate for only four years before his death in 1530, with his most notable accomplishment being the composition of his lively memoirs, *The Baburnama*. His empire could well have been no more than a flash in the pan, given his deeply flawed succession plan. His youngest son, Kamran, became king of horse-rich Kabul, while the older, peace-loving Humayun received Delhi. As Humayun planned no further wars of conquest, his retainers' loyalty melted away like Kabuli ice in the Delhi heat. The Indo-Afghans revolted, and Kamran spitefully withheld Kabuli horses from his older brother. Emperor in name only, Humayun fled across Rajasthan's Thar Desert in 1542 with his pregnant wife mounted on his horse, while he rode awkwardly on a camel.

In Iran, the recently consolidated Safavid dynasty gave him refuge. The Safavids, descended from both horse breeders and chiliastic holy men, mustered their Turkmen horsemen into a formidable, fanatical fighting force. The Iranian cavalry, it was said, took three whole days to pass in review. Moved by the plight of his fellow monarch, Tahmasp, the young and energetic new shah,* promised to help Humayun reclaim his throne.

The victories of Babur and the rout of his son Humayun demonstrated

* Tahmasp is a name from the *Shahnameh* and means "Powerful in Horses."

once again how easily a well-mounted cavalry force could invade a settled region, and equally how easily these conquests could slip out of a ruler's grasp without a secure supply of horses and prospects of further conquest to maintain the loyalty of followers. The son born to Humayun in the Thar Desert would revive Mughal control of northern India by establishing both, succeeding as no previous Indian ruler had before, and perhaps as no emperor of any settled state since Taizong, the Tang dynasty's greatest ruler, in the seventh century.

"His Majesty Is Very Fond of Horses"

Humayun's son Akbar succeeded him at age fourteen, less than a year after the exiled king had been restored to the throne of Delhi with the decisive help of Shah Tahmasp's cavalry. Akbar would prove to be one of India's greatest rulers, leaving behind an enduring legacy in the arts, philosophy, and statecraft. Due to his tumultuous childhood in exile, he never learned to read or write, but he developed an intense interest in the natural world and acquired a wealth of practical knowledge. He applied his talents to the machinery of warfare and government to a much greater extent than either his adventurous grandfather or his easygoing father ever had. He made sure to retain Afghanistan, and to keep his army constantly in the field. Above all, he focused on horse power. His chief minister Abul Fazl summarized this preoccupation:

> His Majesty is very fond of horses, because he believes them to be of great importance for government, and for expeditions of conquest, and because he sees in them a means of avoiding much inconveniences. His Majesty pays attention to everything which is connected with this animal, which is an almost supernatural means for the attainment of personal greatness.

One of Akbar's earliest and most far-reaching strategic decisions was to add to the Mughal and Indo-Afghan cavalry the Rajputs, who became his most loyal followers. Akbar had been born among the Rajputs, in the arid region southwest of the Ganges Valley. Here maharajas ruled over dusty territories from their severe-looking, impregnable hilltop fortresses: Malwa, Gwalior, Ranthambore. The origin of the Rajputs is subject to scholarly debate. Nineteenth-century British ethnologists imagined that the horse-breeding Kushans, once they assimilated into the Indian population, gave rise to the Rajputs. This is probably inaccurate, since horse breeding came late to the Rajputs, who first appear in history, in the twelfth and thirteenth centuries, as cattle and camel herders. Rajasthan lacked natural pastureland for raising horses, and camels were more suitable for crossing the Thar Desert. But in the thirteenth and fourteenth centuries, the Rajputs, a bit like the Arab Bedouins, discovered that horses outperformed camels for raiding their richer neighbors. The oldest Rajput ballads recount stories of banditry and horse rustling.

Prospering from plunder, the Rajputs acquired Arab and Iranian horses from the west and began to raise their own desert breeds. Today's Marwari horse has qualities typical of this dry environment; its distinctive tulip-shaped ears may reflect its desert heritage or the caprice of the maharajas of Jodhpur, who patronized the breed. Given the lack of pasturage in Rajasthan, these horses were raised in stables. Despite the cost that this entailed, the value of the horse in war and trade justified the new business of horse breeding. By the time of the Mughals, Rajput states like Amber, later renamed Jaipur, stabled fifty thousand horses—a huge proportion of India's total herd.

Unlike the Mughals and earlier Central Asian horsemen, the Rajputs did not practice mounted archery, riding into battle but fighting on foot. While the steppe warriors used flight as a battle tactic, the Rajputs developed a reputation for grimly fighting to the end, and their women, when they did not die in battle, committed suicide rather than fall into enemy hands. Akbar saw the value of these tough troops and, in a series of dynastic marriages, quickly incorporated the royal Rajput houses into his court and into his cavalry army.

The Mughal Empire now had three legs on which to stand: the Central Asian Mughals, who continued to immigrate into India to pursue military careers; the Afghans, established in the hill country for centuries; and the Rajputs of the desert. With these, the Mughals were able to gradually bulldoze their way southward into the subcontinent, conquering wealthy Bengal and Gujarat, which paid for the Mughals' costly cavalry and then some. The only place the Mughals struggled to advance was in the poor horse country of hilly Assam and forested Arrakan, on the Burmese border.

Akbar professionalized the Mughal cavalry to an even greater degree than his ancestor Timür. Officers were no longer paid with plunder, as in Timür's time; instead, agricultural land was set aside for their maintenance. Land revenues enabled the officers to feed and stable their own horses, in numbers proportionate to their rank. An officer with 5,000 troops had to bring 340 horses with him, in addition to the horses of his subordinates. Of the six categories of horses defined in the Mughal codes, the higher-ranked officers had to possess the right mix. Ordinary soldiers rode the lowest category of horse.

Paying for cavalry out of land revenue rather than plunder did not change the underlying challenge of mustering horse power—the Mughals still had to conquer new territories, just as in Babur's or, indeed, Timür's, time. In contrast to the Mongol Empire of Genghis Khan, however, the system allowed the Mughals to conquer India while feeding their horses on forage—something unthinkable to the pastoralist Mongols, and carried out on a much larger scale than what Timür had been able to establish.

Akbar organized the state stables with a meticulous attention to detail that reminds us of Tang Taizong, whose lore may have been passed down to Akbar as part of his Turco-Mongol heritage. The highest-ranking general, responsible for all the horses belonging to the state, held the position of *atbegi*, or master of the horse. Under him a series of officers, called *daroghahs* and *mushrifs*, and an even larger number of subalterns, saddlers, stable hands, vets, grooms, water carriers, and sweepers, all minded the stables with a dedication born of inherited obligation. Fierce punishments were meted out for dereliction of duty, especially if a horse fell ill or died. Horses, like officers, were inspected regularly by rank and by length of service, and accordingly promoted or demoted. Akbar's obsessive attention to his cavalry carried over to his heirs, Jahangir and Shah Jahan.

Jahangir, who ruled from 1605 to 1627, built a special stable for his own riding horses. Standing a hand higher than the rest, they came mainly from western Asia. These included personal gifts from his ancestral friend and sometime rival Shah Abbas the Great of Iran. The emperor regifted one of these horses to his Rajput brother-in-law Raja Man Singh, ruler of Amber. The raja was so delighted, reported the emperor, "that if I had given him a kingdom I do not think he would have shown such joy. At the time they brought the horse it was three or four years old. The whole of the servants of the court, Moghul and Rajput together, agreed that no horse like this had ever come from Iraq* to Hindustan."

The price of such horses was calculated not in silver rupees but in gold mohurs, a coin the same weight as the rupee but fifteen times more valuable. An especially desirable horse might command 50 mohurs, while the price of an average horse ranged between 10 and 30. Iraqi horses were expensive because, as the emperor noted, they had been shipped by sea to India, to speed the delivery of the precious cargo. Raja Man Singh's horse, if the raja had decided to sell it, might have fetched 300 to 500 gold mohurs, equivalent to $300,000 to $500,000 in today's dollars. Only the highest-ranking generals received such a gift.

The steppe tradition of gift giving was replicated by the Mughals on an imperial scale with bureaucratic efficiency. Each day, thirty lucky officers received a horse, an elephant, and jeweled dagger, a custom that explains the plethora of surviving Mughal daggers with jade hilts encrusted with rubies. In one year, ten thousand of these daggers and all of the imperial stable's twelve horses would have been given away. In this way, the Mughals secured the loyalty of jealous and ambitious cavalry officers.

Meanwhile, horsemanship came to be seen as a metaphor for Mughal rule itself. The same Persian expression, *riyasat*, ریاست, designated both equestrian practice and statecraft. Courtiers referred to the emperor as "the imperial stirrup," and when they attended court themselves, they were "present in the stirrup." On important feast days, like Dasara, the whole cavalry would muster before the court, another occasion for gift giving. From the most prestigious Persian horses ridden by the emperor to the

---

* Iraq here probably refers to "Iraq al-Ajami," meaning today's Iranian Kurdistan.

local nags of the water carriers, the hierarchy of horse quality echoed, and perhaps justified, the hierarchic nature of the Mughal regime.

In all, Jahangir's cavalry mustered two hundred thousand sabers, which must have represented six hundred thousand horses, as each trooper used on average three mounts. This underlines the biggest challenge for maintaining horse power in India: the expense, since the horses did not graze on empty land. As in the China of the Tang, the cost of this cavalry was tremendous, representing 50 percent of the state budget, or 51 million rupees. The cavalry also took up a lot of space. Forage for one horse, consisting of grass and vetch (a kind of leguminous plant), required between 2.5 and 7.5 acres of land. In all, the Mughal cavalry needed 270 square miles for their forage, about half the area of the Delhi Union Territory today, a little smaller than New York City, as well as a whole population of farmers to grow these crops. Since the Tang Empire, Asia had not known a settled state possessed of such a large and well-mounted cavalry arm.

To maintain their cavalry at full strength, the Mughals, like their Afghan predecessors in Delhi, extensively imported horses from Central Asia—sources speak of over one hundred thousand such horses each year. Turki horses were the backbone of Mughal cavalry, raised by Kalmyk, Kazakh, or Uzbek breeders and traded via Bukhara or Balkh. Traders were well rewarded for procuring good horses. Jahangir was so pleased with one piebald horse imported from Balkh that he granted the seller an honorific title, Tijarati Khan, "Khan of Merchants." The good riding horses were amblers, adept at this highly appreciated gait, which not all Mughal horses could manage and which made riding long distances more comfortable. Central Asian horses were reputed for their ambling.

The Mughal imperial family protected and promoted the horse trade. Jahangir's wife, Nur Jahan, built caravansaries to host five hundred animals at a time. Here, dealers hobbled the horses at night with leg blocks, partly to prevent theft but also to discourage the high-spirited stallions from fighting. Facilities on offer included farriers, feed, and, for the caravanners, dancing girls or boys. These caravansaries provided "places for horse dealers where they may without delay find convenient quarters and be secure from the hardships of seasons; by this arrangement the animals will neither suffer from the hardness and avariciousness so observed in dealers of the present time." Giving the caravanners some breathing room ensured that their horses "would not pass from the hands of well-intentioned merchants into those of others"—that is, speculators with ready cash—and gave buyers more confidence in the merchandise.

The Mughals also acquired native breeds, which had the advantage of being better acclimatized. Central Asian horses suited the purpose of ruling the Ganges plains, but the farther south the Mughals campaigned, the more attractive local breeds appeared. Equine historian Yashaswini Chandra estimates that the Mughals used up to 40 percent local horses in their cavalry. Old Abu Fazl had flattered Akbar on this point: "Skillful men of experience have paid much attention to the breeding of this sensitive animal, whose habits resemble those of humans, in so many ways. In a short period of time the horses of Hindustan rank above those of Arabia. One cannot even distinguish the Indian horse from the Arab or Iraqi breed. The horses of Kutch [also known as Kathiawar] are said to be the finest." It is doubtful whether Babur would have agreed with this statement; the emperors rode exclusively Persian or Arab horses.

Whatever the source of their horses, the Mughals had to learn much about the challenges of keeping horses well fed and healthy in the climate of India. From their steppe heritage, the Mughals knew as much about horses as anyone, but they were unfamiliar with local feeding practices and the common diseases of horses in their new lands. They worried that the climate itself weakened the animals' livers, and so affected their reproduction, making them less fertile than their steppe sires. Seeking local insights, they diligently translated thousand-year-old Sanskrit medical and equerry manuals into Persian, the language of the court and the army. From these ancient books, they learned to feed the horses ghee (clarified butter), jaggery (unrefined sugar), and sometimes red chili peppers, to better manage the balance of humors in the horse, a concept common to both Indian and Greco-Arabic medicine. Western historians of this era find such a diet inexplicable. Ghee probably served only to make the horses look fat and sleek on parade, but according to Chandra, an enthusiastic rider as well as an academic historian, it would not have harmed the horses, and jaggery merely needed to be burned off through exercise. For red peppers, beloved in Indian cuisine yet suspect as a risk factor for esophageal cancer in humans, scholars offer no opinions. The Mughal stables, though, seem to have flourished under this regime.

The Mughals also took great pains to divine the mystery of horses' coloration. Again, here, they combed the ancient Sanskrit texts for insights. One Mughal cavalry general, Firuz Jang, wrote an updated version of the Sanskrit *Aśvashastra*, enhanced with his own observations and Turco-Mongol equestrian lore. Firuz Jang could be long-winded and sometimes as obtuse as the Chinese hippologist Bole regarding color:

> If a horse has black hooves and white on its legs or white on two legs, it has to be avoided. The horse with . . . black on its upper lips, scrotum, hooves, tail, head, eyes and penis and white on other parts, will cause loss to the king.

On the other hand, a pearly-white horse is auspicious:

> The white that the Persians call silvery and the Hindus call "sit baruna" and the Arabs call "abyad," meaning in other words, the white that is like the pearl or cream or like the moon or silvery like snow. When the white horse is one color and the whorls are well conformed, that horse is priceless, praiseworthy and auspicious. In every household that owns it, the people are pleased and happy. and riding it in the day of battle you will be victorious against the enemy.

Firuz Jang's opinions, as with those of Bole, may have reflected observations about the connection between whorls and laterality, as well as behavior. Indian rulers agreed with Firuz Jang's advice, if the equestrian portraits we have of Mughal emperors and Rajput maharajas are to be believed. Curiously, Firuz Jang also advised against red coats, despite the fact that Iran's most famous horse, Rakhsh, was a sorrel. One of Firuz Jang's more practical pieces of advice was to avoid riding a piebald into battle. It had nothing to do with the auspicious or inauspicious properties of that coloration, but simply the fact that a piebald horse is an easier target for an archer or

A page from the Salihotra, *a Sanskrit manual of horses and horse-manship, translated into Persian as the* Farasnamah, *early eighteenth century.*

musketeer to hit. Off the battlefield, Mughal emperors enjoyed their pie-balds, and frequently posed for portraits astride them. Of the one hundred horses sent as a gift from the shah of Iran to Jahangir's son Shah Jahan, the icing on the cake was a handsome piebald that figures in several equestrian portraits of the builder of the Taj Mahal.

One of these portraits, by the court painter Payag, shows Shah Jahan riding a horse that has the dish-like cheekbones of the Arabs and a serpentine neck but a very solid body, reflecting the Mughals' preference for muscular horse flesh. His mane is tied up in knots of red silk, and he sports a yellow yak's tail on his ruby-and-emerald-encrusted gilt bridle. The embroidered shabrack, or saddle blanket, is of silk brocade. The emperor's stirrups are studded with crystals. He carries an embossed quiver with his bow but no arrows, which might otherwise make it harder to mount and dismount. His jeweled scimitar is fixed at his side by several straps of gold. One hand holds the reins and another his hunting spear. No finer portrait of a mounted

An equestrian portrait of Mughal emperor Shah Jahan,
by Payag, ca. 1630.

monarch can be found. Shah Jahan's reign, from 1628 to 1658, represented
the apogee of Mughal power and horsemanship.

As in Tang China, Mughal women as well as men enjoyed mounted
sports. Women frequently rode to the hunt, often with falcons elegantly
perched on their gloved and bejeweled wrists. Though elite Muslim women
in theory had to wear veils and travel in sealed palanquins, the daughters
of the steppe could flout convention and emulate their husbands, brothers,
and sons. Two begums of Humayun's court practiced mounted archery in
addition to playing polo. Normally, though, when attended by their retinue
of male servants, they rode draped head to toe in gauzy veils.

The Rajput women went one step further. Not only did they abandon
purdah, the practice of wearing the veil, to ride and to hunt, but on more
than one occasion they went into battle, even leading their troops. Painters

A Mughal couple enjoy a ride together, eighteenth century.

often portrayed these displays of womanly horsemanship and bravery in an idealized landscape of flowers and delicate clouds. Sometimes they showed lovers galloping across fields together.

The Mughals and the Rajputs indeed lived in the saddle, so men and women of the court had to ride, sometimes daily, from one beautifully appointed encampment to the next. Echoing the tent cities of ancient khaghans, the Mughals erected towering pavilions of silk cloth and rope, as imposing as palaces yet full of air and light. Like those steppe leaders of yore, the Mughal emperor hardly ever sojourned in the Red Forts of Agra or Delhi, but spent months on end traveling throughout India. This gave the court frequent opportunities to picnic and to hunt. The surviving portrayals of their life-style were not just idealized—the Mughals lived their ideals.

However refined their art, the Great Mughals never lapsed into too comfortable an existence. Horsemanship remained the ultimate symbol of self-control and instrument of political control, as Akbar had conceived it: "an almost supernatural means for the attainment of personal greatness."

Demonstrating daredevil bravery was as much a part of their culture as beautifully wrought saddlery. In a celebrated episode, Shah Jahan and his sons incautiously rode close to an exhibition of battling, rutting war elephants. One of the elephants broke free of its competitor, fixed the small eyes of its enormous head on the figure of Prince Aurangzeb, the youngest son, and charged him. Rather than wheeling his horse out of harm's way, the fourteen-year-old, conscious of the gaze of his father and the imperial court, charged the raging bull elephant and struck it below the eye with his spear. This act of foolhardy bravery impressed all the onlookers, and presaged that Aurangzeb would later triumph over his older brothers to succeed Shah Jahan on the throne.

A Perpetual-Motion Machine

Mughal rule depended on control of Afghanistan and continual conquests, the former to ensure the supply of horses, the latter to keep the horsemen

The young Aurangzeb battles an elephant in front of the whole court, ca. 1556–57.

occupied. The actions of the emperors all revolved around these twin imperatives. The fourth Mughal emperor, Jahangir, made a major demonstration of force to advertise his commitment to Afghanistan. He brought the extended imperial family to Kabul—many members of which had never before experienced the cool air of the Hindu Kush—and, in the manner of his ancestor Timür, organized a horse race down the main avenue of the city. The sultan of Bijapur, Adil Khan, then a Mughal ally, won the race on his bay-colored Arab and received a suitable prize, likely another priceless horse from Iran or Iraq to add to his string. While the court wistfully returned to the sweaty plains of Delhi, the emperor had sent notice to his challengers—Uzbek, Afghan, and Iranian—that the lands of the horsemen were his. The fifth Mughal emperor, Shah Jahan, went further and launched an invasion into Transoxiana, hoping to recover the lands lost by his ancestor Babur to the Uzbeks.

Unfortunately for the Mughals, while Afghanistan had always been a platform from which horsemen could invade India, it provided a poor starting-off point for their reconquest of Transoxiana. The Uzbeks simply enjoyed too much horse power, while the Hindu Kush, as in the times of Raghu and the Scythians, represented too great a barrier for Indian elephants, let alone for the artillery of the seventeenth-century Mughal army. Shah Jahan also battled with his sometime Iranian allies over control of Kandahar, in western Afghanistan. Historians see Shah Jahan's struggle for Kandahar as a fixation, and his pretensions in Transoxiana as mere nostalgia for the era of Timür. Yet this is to misjudge the emperor's foresight. He considered it axiomatic that possession of both Kandahar and Kabul were needed to head off an invasion of India from either Iran or Central Asia, and as a channel for importing Turki horses. The territories he coveted as his lost inheritance included some of the world's best pasturage. The Mughals had to abandon their campaign in Transoxiana, but they continued to contest Kandahar with Iran for much of Shah Jahan's reign. The emperor initiated his sons into leadership by assigning them to lead these campaigns, but even the brave Prince Aurangzeb failed to retake Kandahar from the Iranians. The Afghans took advantage of these lengthy campaigns to plunder Mughal supply lines and periodically revolt, foreshadowing the later loss of order that would be fatal to the Mughals.

Shah Jahan also continued to extend the empire south, at the expense of independent sultanates like Bijapur and Golconda. They managed to resist for a long time, despite the Mughal monopoly on Central Asian horses, by importing horses at great expense from Iran and Arabia. Here a European nation, the Portuguese, played an important and often overlooked role. At the same time as Babur entered India, the Portuguese were busy setting up their Estado da India and muscling their way into the flourishing horse trade, previously in the hands of the Iranians and Arabs.

The Portuguese are often thought of as players in the Maritime Silk Road, transporting Chinese porcelain and Ceylon's spices back to Lisbon and Antwerp, and they certainly did so profitably. But horses were the main source of the wealth of the Estado da India and its capital, Goa. As an official letter to king Dom João III in 1527 noted, "The most valuable thing your Highness has in India is the revenue from horses that come from Hormuz [on the Persian Gulf] to Goa." The viceroy of India, Afonso de Albuquerque, explained to the king why horses were so valuable: "Everyone who possesses a Persian horse can govern throughout the Deccan [southern India]." Each of the local powers wanted to import horses from across the Indian Ocean, to fight one another as well as to defend themselves against the looming Mughal threat. The Portuguese auctioned their cargo to the highest bidder. The Catholic Church tried to outlaw this trade as immoral, arguing that Christians should not profit from commerce with heathens, but the *fidalgos*, or the gentlemen class, found it too lucrative a trade to renounce.

The Portuguese exhibited in this trade the same knack for innovation that characterized their entire age of exploration. They built special ships that could carry up to four hundred horses at a time, while the competing Arab dhows could carry only seventy. In these floating stables the horses were secured in a standing position, padded against shocks. The floors were carefully cleaned to remove smells offensive to both the horses and the crew. The Portuguese also built special warehouses on the docks in Hormuz, at the mouth of the Persian Gulf. The survival rate of the live cargo probably improved compared to the earlier transporters using traditional sailing craft. To control prices, they issued trading permits to Indian or Iranian merchants on the condition that all horses should be imported via Goa. Any horse merchant without a permit or bound for another port, if stopped at sea by the Portuguese navy, forfeited his cargo.

Shah Jahan made it clear to the Portuguese that he would boot them out of India if they continued to supply horses to his enemies in the south. Under Mughal pressure, the Portuguese horse trade dwindled. The decline of the horse trade ended Goa's golden age, but not before the gold of Golconda had paid to gild the great shrine of Saint Francis Xavier.

The southern resistance to the Mughals sought alternative sources of horses as the Portuguese trade faded away. Paradoxically, the Mughal campaigns themselves produced a huge expansion of native horse breeding, just as the raids of the Delhi sultan had done centuries earlier. As bandits and raiders caused farmland to be abandoned, and the warring sides paid dearly for remounts, new actors emerged to raise horses on now-empty lands. The most successful of these new horse breeders were the Marathas. Occupying the Western Ghats, a mountainous spine running along the coast from Gujarat, past Mumbai, and all the way to Kerala, the Marathas originally lacked horses, just like the Rajputs. The Western Ghats are rugged and forested, not ideal horse country, and so the Marathas began their military history by fleecing horses from their wealthier, lowland neighbors, sultans and maharajas. From these animals they began to breed hardy ponies with thick hooves, good for scrambling over the Ghats. These were scarcely the animals to go head-to-head with the big Turki warhorses of the Mughals, but they were perfect for the lightning attacks and raids carried out by the Marathas. Their cavalry gained the reputation of being able to travel seventy miles a day, and to strike and disappear before the Mughals knew what had hit them. Initially, the Mughals considered the Marathas mere bandits. But once their horse power began to swell, their enemies could no longer underestimate them, especially after their leader, Shivaji Bhonsle, had himself crowned maharaja in an elaborate ceremony.[*]

---

[*] The airport and a raft of big edifices in Mumbai now carry his prestigious name.

Like many Indian rulers, Shivaji Bhonsle began his military career procuring horses for other local warlords. Over time he organized his own cavalry, suitable for the ruler of a large, conquering state. He established stud farms near the forts he controlled and offered land to farmers to grow fodder for his mounts. During the monsoon season, when military campaigning ceased, his horses fed at leisure on these farms. As soon as the rains stopped, at the festival of Dasara, he mustered his troops and set off to plunder the Mughals. With his increased riches he added prestigious Arab horses to his stud farms. While the Marathas could still not take on the Mughals in set combat, their raids turned rich provinces into wastelands, and made much of India ungovernable. In words that recall those of Genghis Khan's generals, one Maratha cavalry commander, Holkar, proclaimed, "My home is the back of my horse, and where his head is pointed is my country."

When Aurangzeb, the sixth and last Great Mughal, came to the throne in 1658, he sent one general after another to pacify the Marathas, without success. The threat posed by these daring horsemen increased, and they launched raids deep into Mughal territory. Aurangzeb decided to use diplomacy and gifts to neutralize the restless Afghans, so as to free up his entire army for the final conquest of the south. He also forbade rough riders to accompany their horses from Central Asia into India, to prevent any surprises from this traditional source of political troubles. For a time, he subdued the Marathas and the remaining independent sultans and maharajas, but putting down rebellions and retaking previously captured fortresses occupied the rest of his life. He never saw Delhi again, despite his courtiers' pleas to return to the comfort and relative cool of the north. Like his ancestor Timür, Aurangzeb knew that constant campaigning at the head of the army was his best insurance policy against internal rebellion. Also like Timür, he sought to reduce all his neighbors to satellite states, and to prevent them from amassing competing military power. Aurangzeb's campaigns in the south resembled a perpetual-motion machine, spewing out cavalry, camps, caravans, and sieges.

Aurangzeb succeeded in conquering the whole subcontinent except for the southernmost tip. A unitary India was the legacy of his empire, replicated by the British Empire and bequeathed to modern India.* Aurangzeb died in the saddle in 1707, at ninety years of age. His generals breathed a sigh of relief, hoping to retire in indolence. They forgot, like Timür's immediate successors three hundred years earlier, that it was as dangerous to arrest conquest as to try to stop a galloping horse.

Aurangzeb's heirs enjoyed thirty years of peace, but during this time, the army of three hundred thousand men lost the cohesion and conditioning it had attained under Aurangzeb's endless campaigning. Fatally, this generation of Mughals lost control of Afghanistan. In 1737, from Kandahar and Kabul, the age-old invasion route of horsemen into India, came a huge, hostile force of Turkmen, Uzbeks, Afghans, Kurds, and Azeris, 375,000 in all, under the leadership of the last great horsed conqueror, the Iranian Nader Shah.

The Last Conqueror

In the mold of Genghis Khan, Timür, and Babur, Nader rose to power during a period of conflict and chaos. Rebellious Afghans from Kandahar had toppled the flagging Safavid dynasty in 1722, creating a power vacuum across Iran. Iran's Turkmen, who once compared their shah to the Messiah, looked on with indifference as the Kandahari Afghans ravaged the country. The future conqueror, born into a humble Turkmen clan, began his career, like Genghis Khan and Timür, with petty raiding. He parlayed his bravura and success to become a local chief, a cavalry general, and then generalissimo in charge of mobilizing the tardy Iranian resistance to the invaders. After successfully driving them out of Iran, Nader arranged for the Turkmen chiefs to proclaim him Nader Shah. He went on to develop an elite professional fighting force, to launch on campaigns of conquest against the Kandahari Afghans, the Ottomans, the Russians, the Uzbeks, and, now, the Mughals.

Nader's army was hugely expensive to maintain, and he had exhausted

---

* Even without Pakistan and Bangladesh, modern India is still a bit larger than the Mughal Empire: 1.269 million square miles versus 1.2 million square miles.

his treasury supplying his soldiers with horses. Unlike the Mughal Empire, with its 150 million inhabitants, Nader's Iran had only 6 million people—little more than the steppe states of antiquity. No wonder opulent India attracted Nader's concupiscence. The Iranian upstart defeated the Mughal army sent out to intercept him, then entered and sacked Delhi, carrying back to Iran the Peacock Throne, the Koh-i-Nur diamond, and a financial indemnity worth $10 billion in today's dollars.

Mughal India never recovered, but neither did Iran benefit.[*] Nader Shah had done nothing more than ride the whirlwind. Even with the plunder from Delhi counted in camel loads, the cost of Nader's cavalry and mounted artillery tipped the kingdom into bankruptcy. Nader's only solution was to impose higher taxes on his few subjects and to drag his exhausted troopers into further, endless campaigns. They assassinated him in his tent in 1747, following which his heirs predictably killed one another off. Nader's death unleashed another period of chaos both in India and Iran.

On receiving the news of Nader's assassination, his quick-thinking cavalry commander, Ahmad Khan, snatched up the shah's treasure and gathered around him his loyal Afghan clansmen from Herat and Multan, long associated with the Powindah horse trade. He seized control first over Herat, Kandahar, and Kabul, then Punjab and Kashmir. Crowned as Ahmad Shah Durrani ("the Rare Pearl"), he is considered the founder of today's Afghanistan. Yet Ahmad Shah's conquests led not to the creation of a modern state but only, like the victories of Genghis Khan and Timür, to a situation of contingent loyalty to whomever appeared to be in the saddle at a given moment. The sudden rise of Ahmad Shah suggested that the cycle of mounted Asian conquerors would never come to a halt; indeed, up through the first two decades of the nineteenth century, it did not. Already, though, the initiative was slipping away from the

---

[*] Several decades later, Napoleon Bonaparte wrote, "Nader was able to conquer a great power, he triumphed over his enemies and reigned gloriously. But he did not have that wisdom which thinks both of the present and of the future. His descendants did not succeed him" (letter to the shah of Iran, Fath Ali Shah Qajar, dated March 1805; cited by Giorgio Rota, "In a League of Its Own? Nader Shah and His Empire," in *Short-Term Empire*, ed. Robert Rollinger, Julian Degen, and Michael Gehler (Wiesbaden: Springer, 2020).

horse-breeding nations of Central Asia, Iran, and Afghanistan, in favor of the great, sedentary empires.

In the traces of Timür and Babur, the newly proclaimed Ahmad Shah contemplated invading China in order to keep his restless horsemen busy. Calmer heads, who understood that the then-ruling Qing dynasty had cracked the horse-supply problem better than their predecessors, discouraged the king's ambitions. Peaceful trade with China, they suggested, would be a better option. So Ahmad selected four arghamak horses and dispatched them with an ambassador to Beijing. For the Qing emperor, Qianlong, these were more than beautiful horses: they were a symbol of the old "western provinces" of the Tang dynasty returning to the fold.

10

The Empires Strike Back

China and Russia, 1584–1800

꒦

Admiring the Four Afghan Steeds

The Qianlong Emperor of the Qing dynasty received Ahmad Shah's ambassador, Khwaja Mir Khan, at Mulan, his hunting estate in the cool mountains north of Beijing. The year was 1763. Khwaja Mir Khan presented the four arghamaks, the tall horses, each known by its coloring: Chao'er Lu ("Gray with Round Stripes"), Lai Yuan Liu ("Red Black"), Moon Bone Lu ("Yellow White with Red Hooves"), and Ling Kun Bai ("White with Red Hooves"). The emperor was delighted by their height, on average seventeen hands, with one horse said to reach twenty hands. Straightaway he ordered Giuseppe Castiglione to celebrate them with a suitable painting. A specialist in equestrian portraits, the Italian Jesuit had served as an official artist for decades, and had even chosen to live near the imperial stables in the Forbidden City so he could document the emperor's favorite horses. Qianlong felt a particular satisfaction that Ahmad Shah, a descendant of the Yuezhi and the Kushans, was now tacitly acknowledging Qing suzerainty over distant Afghanistan. The Qing emperor was less pleased with the uncouth behavior of Khwaja Mir Khan, who failed to kowtow, spoke tactlessly, and chewed his food with appalling manners.

In fact, the emperor received Afghan and other steppe emissaries in the imperial yurt in Mulan precisely because, he reasoned, they were mostly an outdoors kind of people who would be bored by the operas and stifling court audiences offered in Beijing. Here the emperor could be more relaxed, and his unrefined visitors posed less of a problem for protocol. The hunting grounds offered familiar entertainment to these steppe embassies. They were encouraged to hunt, to enjoy the music of bards, to show off their prowess in archery and wrestling, and to finish the day with deep drafts of fermented mare's milk. The emperor's camp, laid out between four colored banners marking the cardinal directions, allowed the horsemen to feel both at home and in the presence of the supreme ruler of the steppe.

Like Taizong, who presided over the apogee of the Tang dynasty in the seventh century, and to whom he explicitly compared himself, Qianlong was both the Son of Heaven and the supreme khan. His empire extended farther than that of Taizong, including the northern part of Xinjiang Province, Tibet, Inner Mongolia, Outer Mongolia (today's republic of Mongolia), and part of modern Kyrgyzstan. In all it was larger than today's People's Republic of China. In private, Qianlong was given over to self-satisfied observations, and scribbled praises to himself on priceless antiquities in the imperial collection. Castiglione's 1758 equestrian portrait depicts the

An equestrian portrait of Emperor Qianlong,
by Giuseppe Castiglione, 1758.

Emperor Qianlong receives tribute horses from steppe emissaries, 1757, by Giuseppe Castiglione.

emperor in resplendent armor, recalling Diego Velázquez's seventeenth-century painting of Spanish King Philip IV. His proud look and nonchalant pose reflect a European ideal of monarchy, very different from the calm, reflective, steady gaze of traditional imperial portraits, in which the monarch sits on a throne. No image better sums up the persona of Qianlong.

To be fair, by the time of Khwaja Mir Khan's visit, Qianlong was well entitled to look back on his three decades of reign with satisfaction: he had established peace on the once-untamable steppe frontier and put a stop to the cycle of raiding that had characterized these lands since the time of the Huns, two thousand years earlier. His policy toward the steppe peoples was based on a combination of ruthless repression of any attempts at independence and extensive efforts to support and protect the horse breeders' way of life. For the first time in Chinese history, under Qianlong's leadership, imperial authorities proactively intervened to reduce conflicts between the settled population and the horse breeders. Prior to Qing rule, famines and conflicts on the steppe had led to incursions into the settled areas. The Qing, however, provided reliable famine relief in the case of devastating frosts, which were frequent in the eighteenth century; no one would starve because of bad weather or cattle loss. Qing officials carefully monitored rainfall and grass height in anticipation of bad times for the herds. In 1748, little rain fell, and the Mongols lost 60 to 70 percent of their horses, which meant starvation for a people who depended on two bowls of mare's milk a day for their survival. But it also meant no riding horses for the Qing postal service, army, or other state institutions.

The Qing supplied food and animal support for starving Mongols fifty-five times during the reign of the Qianlong Emperor, mobilizing the

resources of China to pay for this largesse. Eighteenth-century China was sufficiently rich and well organized to be able, in effect, to subsidize the steppe in a way that previous dynasties had been unable. While the steppe population had scarcely increased above three to five million, China had grown from fifty million under the Tang to two hundred million under the Qing. This gave the dynasty a much greater pool of resources for controlling the steppe frontier. As a result, unlike the Tang and Kublai Khan's successors, the Qing never lost the support of the steppe horse breeders, who remained solidly anchored in China until the collapse of the dynasty in 1912. In this the Qing succeeded where all previous Chinese and steppe-based dynasties had failed. Through this alliance with the steppe horsemen, they were able to extend their influence to the borders of Afghanistan. Qianlong and the Qing had learned well how to govern the steppe. After all, for the Qing, it was their second attempt to get this right.

The Golden Khans Return

The Qing dynasty's affinity for the steppe horsemen reflected their origins: they were descended from the Jurchen nation, whose Golden Khans ruled Beijing a century before Genghis Khan. Just as the Song dynasty had encouraged the Jurchens at the expense of the Khitans in 1121, between the fourteenth and seventeenth centuries, the ruling Ming dynasty favored these horse traders as a counter to the potential revival of the hated Mongols. Thus the Jurchens reemerged from obscurity to become, once more, major suppliers of remounts to China. In the 1570s, a young Jurchen named

Nurhaci helped out his father and grandfather on their horse-trading expeditions to China, where, in reward for bringing the finest horses, they received honorary Chinese titles. The Ming allowed Nurhaci's clan to establish a marketplace for horse trading in today's Liaoning Province. This flourishing trade soon turned Nurhaci into a wealthy and powerful leader.

A redoubtable diplomat and strategist, Nurhaci maintained close relationships with the Chinese but simultaneously built bridges with the neighboring Mongols, forging marital alliances between his family and the Borjigin princes, descended from Genghis Khan. In return for brides and gifts, the Mongols supplied Nurhaci with horses, increasing his clout on the steppe. This growing power encouraged Nurhaci's son and successor, Hong Taiji, to take an imperial title when he came to power in 1636. He also changed the name of his people from Jurchen to Manchu, so that today we speak of Manchuria, the Manchu dynasty, and the Manchu people.

The new empire was, in fact, a condominium of Mongols and Manchus. Hong Taiji maintained strict equality between the two peoples. Each furnished eight banners, or brigades, with ratings of ten thousand to fifteen thousand, for a total of two hundred thousand troopers—an immense force for a territory that at first comprised only the modern-day Chinese provinces of Inner Mongolia, Heilongjiang, Jilin, and Liaoning. The banner organization originated out of hunting parties, used by the Manchu leadership to weaken the horse breeders' loyalty to their traditional chiefs. The bannermen constituted a first-rate cavalry arm with the discipline of Genghis Khan's warriors, making the new emperor a formidable arbiter of China's fate. The Ming dynasty was now beset by natural catastrophes, famines, and attendant peasant rebellions. When the last Ming emperor, besieged by rebels, committed suicide in Beijing in 1644, the young son of Hong Taiji, later known as the Shunzi Emperor, rode into the imperial capital, chased away the rebels, and proclaimed himself the new Son of Heaven, taking the dynastic name Qing, "the Pure," for his dynasty.

Once again, China succumbed to the rule of horse breeders, who saw themselves as the successors to both old rivals, the Golden Khans and Genghis Khan. The Mongol khans, descendants of the world conqueror, certified their allegiance to the new emperor by bringing him eight white horses and one white camel, and committed to bringing another nine white animals each year in perpetuity. The adhesion of the Mongol horse breeders had important implications for the ambitions and methods of the new Qing regime, whose strategy for ruling China embedded the lessons of Mongol, Jurchen, and earlier Khitan failures. All of these dynasties collapsed when the increasingly settled ruling class lost the loyalty and the horse power of their steppe cousins. The Qing emperors, therefore, carefully delineated the organs of the state that would serve to provide administration and justice in the steppe regions according to traditional Mongol and Manchu laws, while the Chinese provinces continued to be ruled by Ming law. The Manchu and Mongol bannermen formed the backbone of the army with additional, subordinate banners being raised among the ethnic Chinese. Initially, the Qing army comprised only cavalry and, in the time of Qianlong, still totaled two hundred thousand troopers. The garrison corps, with a higher proportion of Infantry, had four hundred thousand troops. It was the largest army in the world. Only Napoleon's Grande Armée briefly reached the same size, in June 1812.

To supply their need for horses, the Qing extensively exploited their control of the steppe land of today's Inner Mongolia, where they established their stud farms. They did not procure horses from independent pastoralists, instead hiring Mongol herders as ranch hands to manage the imperial herds. This ensured an adequate supply of horses without involving local politics, unlike the approach of the pastoralist Genghisids. In a return to the statist approach of the Tang, these horse farms represented a huge bureaucracy, including the Court of the Imperial Stud, the emperor's personal crown stud, and the studs of the various bannermen regiments. In total, 8,880 square miles were set aside for the grazing of forty herds, each of twelve thousand mares.

Later, when the Qing waged military campaigns on the distant steppe, provisioning horses from Mongolia proved to be impractical, so the army acquired horses from the Kazakhs, sixteen hundred miles to the west. This trade was strictly controlled by the state, characteristically distrustful of horse traders. The Qing set up a market pavilion in the far west, in Urumqi, that was closed to private traders during the state horse purchases. The Qing investment in horse power was so substantial, in fact, that it created a global shortage of supply, driving up prices. This made the Kazakhs quite wealthy, and made it harder for India to procure horses from Central Asia.

The Qing hoped that peace would now descend on China's traditionally turbulent frontier.

My Ten Famous Victories

This Pax Sinica did not satisfy everyone; it undermined the westernmost Mongols, the Oirats,* who were too far away from China to benefit from the Qing's patronage. In order to retain the loyalty of their own herdsmen, the Oirat khans needed to offer them something: either access to attractive markets or the opportunity to participate in lucrative raiding expeditions. The Oirat khans could satisfy these ambitions only if they federated the herders into a group large enough to menace China. Accordingly, the supreme Oirat khans alternately attacked Qing China for plunder and negotiated for improved market access, as once the Huns had done, seventeen centuries earlier. These raids proved intolerable to the Qing emperors, who waged extensive campaigns in the west to pacify them. In the 1720s, the Oirats obliterated a fifty-thousand-strong Qing army, captured one of the Qing's great stud farms in Inner Mongolia, and ran off with its twelve thousand horses.

Equally worrying, the Oirats flirted with the Russians and acquired modern artillery from them. Russia had, for centuries, peacefully traded Siberian furs for Chinese tea, and had never shown any aggressive intentions toward China.† The Qing knew, however, that at any moment the Oirats might declare themselves Russian subjects, thereby upsetting the balance of power on the steppe. Just as the Mughals considered Afghanistan key to their horse power, the Qing emperors looked on any threat to their control of Mongolia as an existential one. The Oirat problem had to be dealt with.

* Also known as the Eleuths and the Zhungars, each with a bewildering variety of spellings.

† While Russia and China had shared a Siberian frontier since the age of Ivan IV, the difficulty of travel through its forests made Siberia a poor jumping-off point for military aggression. Only when Russia built the Trans-Siberian line to the Pacific Ocean did it begin to covet Mongolia and Manchuria. Mongolia, under Soviet control, then broke away from China. Curiously, today, the Republic of China, on the island of Taiwan, does not recognize Mongolia as an independent state, but the People's Republic of China does.

Coming to the throne in 1735, Qianlong initially experimented with reconciliation. He made a point of inviting the Oirat leadership to join his annual hunts in Mulan, demonstrating the power of the Qing court and the equestrian prowess of the Manchu and Mongol nobility. This diplomacy on horseback, however, did not persuade the Oirats to abandon their ambitions. One of their khans defied Qianlong by refusing to respond to a not-so-optional invitation to the autumn hunt. Even worse, he conspired with the Dalai Lama to detach Tibet, a major source of horses, from Qing control. The emperor decided to destroy this chief, and also the Oirat nation.

Qianlong's ministers and war councilors, Chinese, Mongol, and Manchu alike, tried to talk him out of waging war in the distant steppe, using the same arguments the court had once employed with Wudi, the emperor of the blood-sweating horses. The Oirat pastures were more than two thousand miles away, across a waterless waste, and there was nothing to be gained by conquering that region. The courtiers reminded the emperor that the Han dynasty's first-century BCE expedition to bring the blood-sweating horses back from Ferghana had lost 60 to 70 percent of its troops and most of its horses. In the seventh century, the Tang dynasty had launched an aggressive expansion movement into the northwest, but Tang rule there remained unchallenged for only a short time. The Song dynasty, ruling from the tenth into the thirteenth centuries, had never ventured into the steppe: they had had enough trouble warding off threats to the northern China plain. During the Ming dynasty, the Yongle Emperor had launched five major, unsuccessful campaigns against the Mongols, from 1403 to 1424, and died in the middle of the last one. In 1449, another Ming emperor, Zhengtong, personally ventured west of Beijing against the Oirats and ended up their prisoner. In more recent times, the 1690s, Qing campaigns against the Oirats had run out of water after ninety days of riding through the steppe, and had been forced to return, almost losing the whole army and its horses to thirst.

But Qianlong would not be dissuaded. To ensure the success of his campaign, his final assault on the Oirats would be of a magnitude greater than anything that had been undertaken before. His Qing predecessors had mustered three armies each of thirty thousand troops for campaigns of ninety days. Now plans were finalized to maintain three armies each of

Russia and China Carve Up the Steppe

Poland

Grand Duchy
of Lithuania

Dnipro R.

Moscow

Moscovy

Kasimov

Kazan

Podolia

W e s t e r n   S t e p p e

Volga R.

Ural Mountains

Crimea

Tsaritsyn

Don R.

Sarai

Astrakhan

Caspian Sea

Khwarazm

*Kyzylkum
Desert*

Karakum Desert

Oxus R.

Jaxartes R.

La
Balkha

Balasagu

Bukhara

*Pamir
Mountains*

Kash

Samarkand

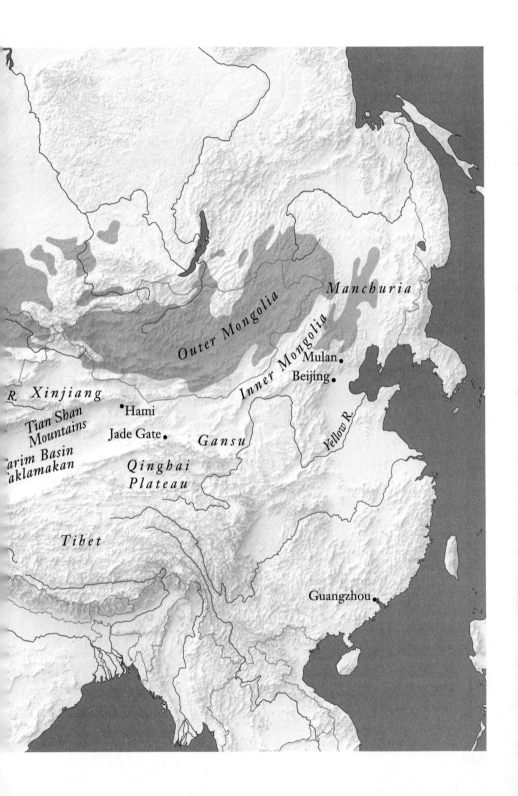

Manchuria

Outer Mongolia

Inner Mongolia

Mulan

Beijing

R. Xinjiang

Tian Shan
Mountains

Hami

Jade Gate

Gansu

Yellow R.

Tarim Basin
Taklamakan

Qinghai
Plateau

Tibet

Guangzhou

fifty thousand, capable of operating on the steppe for up to two years. The preparations read like passages from Rabelais's epic satire *Gargantua*: commissaries collected 1,322 tons of grain, 1,500 tons of noodles, 500 tons of bread, and 12,000 sides of mutton; 40,000 head of oxen and 20,000 head of sheep were slaughtered to yield 200,000 tons of dried meat. The cost of provisions was dwarfed by the cost of transportation. The army paid ten times more than the price of rice for haulage from the Grand Canal, the main artery of trade of the Chinese empire, to the distant oasis of Hami, in the Tarim Basin. For the final stretch, they benefited from the support of the local Turks, who, as Muslims, were alienated from the Buddhist Oirats by religious prejudices. With supplies securely stored on the frontier in both Hami and, even closer, Turfan, the range of operations of Qing cavalry would be only 120 miles, a march of two or three days.

The logistical achievements of Qianlong's campaign tower above those of contemporaneous European efforts. In the wars of Louis XIV, the French army essentially lived off the land, pillaging and starving the towns of Germany and the Netherlands through which they marched. They could not feed themselves if they stayed in any one place, as they carried no strategic stores. Napoleon's 1812 invasion of Russia likewise entailed a constant advance, since the army ate everything in its path. Napoleon's biggest weakness in this campaign, and the likely cause of his eventual defeat, was the lack of fodder for his horses. By the time he captured Moscow, he had no more cavalry. A key advantage held by the Chinese expedition to the Oirats was that the one hundred thousand horses of the Qing army, though they had to cover more distance than Napoleon's march on Moscow, could pasture part of the way, and otherwise be fed from the immense stores of food.

In two campaigns between 1755 and 1759, Qianlong's armies defeated the Oirats and occupied the entire eastern steppe, from the Jade Gate, in Gansu Province, all the way to the Ili River and Lake Balkhash, in today's Kazakhstan. The Qianlong Emperor was, characteristically, hunting in the game park of Mulan when he learned of the final, definitive victory:

> After several days of ceremonies, comes the time when the stags roar in Mulan. One thousand horsemen wait with bows and arrows. Heading north, the cold increases faster than one can add layers of clothing.

Mounted messengers bring good news from the west. This will be a good souvenir. Besides the autumn hunt, distant tribes will come to serve me as grooms.

It isn't clear how those tribes would provide grooms, given what happened next. The emperor gave unequivocal orders that the Oirats should be destroyed as a people. The Qing spread smallpox among the Oirats. Those who did not die of the disease or were not cut down in systematic massacres were taken into slavery by the Manchu and Mongol bannermen. By the end of the emperor's campaign, more than a million Oirats are thought to have perished. This was perhaps the first large-scale and historically attested example of genocide. It showed that there was no way to force a horse-breeding people into unwilling political submission, but by single-mindedly deploying the limitless resources of Qing China, one could eliminate them. Onto the now-empty steppe, the Qing moved new populations, including loyal Mongols, Kazakhs, ethnic Chinese, and Turks. They renamed the former Oirat lands Xinjiang, "the New Region." Later Russian ethnologists gave the Turkish speakers of Xinjiang the name Uyghurs, after a kingdom of the Tang era.

Reports of Qianlong's victories over the Oirats filtered back to the foreign merchants in Canton; the size of the opposing forces, the distances over which they had fought, and the fury of their battles seemed to defy description. Nevertheless, the tireless Giuseppe Castiglione and a team of European Jesuit and Chinese painters illustrated battle scenes, inspired by ten poems composed by the emperor himself to celebrate his ten victories. Like the terra-cotta army figures of the First Emperor buried near Xian, the sketches of Castiglione and his team portrayed dozens of individual troopers and cavalry generals of the Qing army, commemorating their bravery.

The emperor wanted to celebrate these victories widely: propaganda was an important part of his statecraft. So he looked favorably on an offer from the French Company of the Indies to create copper engravings of these drawings, which could then be duplicated and distributed throughout the empire. Along with other European maritime powers, France eagerly sought to curry favor with Qianlong in order to get better access to wealthy

China's immense markets. Backed by King Louis XV himself, the greatest engravers of Paris produced sixteen plates, taking over seven years to
complete the work. Between 1772 and 1775, the plates were carefully transported to Guangzhou, along with machinery for making prints, and from
there presented to the court in Beijing. Qianlong was delighted with the
unfamiliar copperplate technology. Louis XV retained one set for display
at Versailles. These are now in the Louvre.

   Ten of the sixteen plates, which have come to be known as the *Conquests of the Emperor of China*, illustrate Qianlong's commemorative poems.
One plate, *The Battle of Arcul*, focuses on the clash of Manchu and Oirat
cavalry. The Oirats field mounted dragoons, armed with muskets and
shooting from the saddle, but the Manchus enjoy the support of massed,
camel-mounted artillery. The Oirats then flee over the rugged terrain in
the face of unequal odds. A second plate depicts a dramatic episode, in 1759,
when the Oirats managed to bottle up the Chinese army in the oasis of
Yarkand. The Chinese commanding general is shown in the center of the
composition, surrounded by jagged mountains and clouds, suggesting the
desperate situation of the army. He wears full armor and gestures with
his horse whip, reassuring his beleaguered troops with his calm demeanor.

*The Qing armies defeat the Oirats, an engraving from the set "The Conquests of the
Emperor of China," 1770.*

On the horizon, reinforcements arrive to lift the siege of the Chinese and put the Oirats to flight. In *The Battle of Oroi Jalatu*, the Qing fall upon the Oirats, who are sleeping in their tents, and drive them naked into captivity or toward execution. At the final surrender of the Oirats, on the banks of the Ili River, they are seen falling to their knees, their muskets proffered in outstretched arms. Their sheep, cattle, camels, and horses huddle together. Several Buddhist lamas offer to intercede for the surrendering warriors, while a group of Oirats attempt to swim to safety across the broad Ili River. Manchu bannermen calmly trot up to receive the surrender.

This collection of prints is a fitting homage to the Qing empire at its height, and to the largest cavalry campaign ever waged. The Qing's victories on the steppe doubled the size of the Chinese empire and had lasting reverberations across Asia, as their neighbors measured up their options in the face of the new, supersized China. The fear of China's power was partly offset by an eagerness to do business. The Afghan Ahmad Shah, the Uzbek khan of Bukhara, and the Kazakh hordes all sought to profit from supplying the Qing with cavalry horses. The Qing's efficient mobilization of eighteenth-century China's immense resources and their alternately generous and ruthless dealings with their steppe neighbors guaranteed that never again would the steppe threaten China. Instead, the next danger to the empire came from an entirely unexpected direction, and had nothing to do with horses.

In 1793, at the age of eighty-two, Qianlong was still entertaining new embassies in Mulan, receiving them in his spacious yellow yurt. Turks from Bukhara brought beautiful horses, but on that same day, word arrived about an unprecedented seaborne embassy. These emissaries had come without horses and wanted to trade not at the Great Wall but via China's seaports. After a brief and awkward reception, the elderly monarch rejected their request to enter into a new trading arrangement. He signed his official response to the foreign diplomats with the traditional vermilion inscription, including the words "tremble and obey." The intended recipient was George III of Great Britain. This was the first of several unwelcome efforts by the British, and later the French and the Americans, to break into the Chinese market. The horse-breeding Manchus underestimated how hard it would be to keep these expanding maritime empires at arm's length.

The Qing dynasty held that defense of the steppe frontier was vital to their survival, since every successful conquest of China had originated there. In their view, the western seafaring nations would never represent an existential menace. So the Qing maintained a huge military establishment on the steppe, ultimately retaining these territories for China to this day.[*] And indeed, while steppe hordes no longer threatened, the expansionary policies of Russia, a major horse power, called for all of Beijing's vigilance.

Visiting the Treasure House

Russia, like China, had been conquered in the thirteenth century by the successors of Genghis Khan. Unlike in China, however, the Tatars of the Golden Horde, as the Russians referred to them, did not exert direct rule. They recruited local Russian princes to serve as tax collectors. This suited the Tatars, who did not want to govern the settled people directly or even migrate into the northern, forested lands, which were unfit for large horse herds. The Russian princes grew wealthy and powerful as loyal allies of the Tatars. They even raised armies to fight alongside the Tatars against their rivals, including, unsuccessfully, in the wars with Timür.

Timür's daring campaigns into the snowbound steppe in 1389 left the Golden Horde seriously weakened, leading to its split into the many smaller hordes and khanates of Crimeans, Nogays, Kazakhs, Uzbeks, and Turkmen. All these groups competed with one another for control of pastures and trade. Into this power vacuum stepped the princes of Moscow, former tax collectors, well schooled in the art of steppe warfare and diplomacy after 250 years of Tatar tutelage.

Horses lay at the center of Moscow's statecraft right from the beginning. A century after the Mongol conquest, Moscow operated the largest horse fair in the western steppe. It took place outside the Kremlin walls, on the banks of the Yauza River, where it made way for a busy tram station only in 1911. Just as the horse breeders of Mongolia sought to trade with Beijing,

---

[*] It is significant that the emperor entertained the British ambassador with a performance of an opera about the Turks' revolt against the Tang dynasty. It shows what his preoccupations were. See George Staunton, *An Authentic Account of an Embassy from the King of Great Britain to the Emperor of China* (London: W. Bulmer, 1797) 2:30.

and those of Afghanistan with India, the Tatars needed Moscow as a market for their horses and other steppe produce.

For the western steppe, just a few days' ride from the Kremlin walls, teemed with horses. The French mercenary Captain Jacques Margeret left a glowing account of the herds he encountered on his trips through Muscovy:

> The Nogay . . . horses can run for seven or eight hours without being winded. They are very wild and terrified of the sound of an arquebus [an early musket]. They are never shod. These are all white and spotted with black, like a tiger or leopard, so that one might think them painted. There are also jennets [a small saddle horse] from Georgia, very beautiful, but cannot compare with the Nogay for long wind, or speed, unless it just is a short run. There are Turkish and Polish horses, which they call arghamaks [i.e., very tall steeds]. All the horses are geldings.

Above all, Margeret appreciated the good value of the steppe horses: "A very beautiful and good horse of either Tatary or Russia can be bought for twenty rubles.* This horse will do more service than a Turkish arghamak, which costs 50, 60, up to 100 rubles."

The sheer number of Nogay horses brought to market astounded foreign visitors. An English merchant noted, "The Tatars raised so many horses that despite their own prodigious use of them for riding and food, there are brought yearly to Moscow thirty or forty thousand Tatar horses to be exchanged for other commodities." Margeret estimated the trade to be twice as big. The Moscow market was thus either half the size or the same size as the Indo-Afghan trade and the Mongol-Chinese trade; either way, it was enormous relative to the size of the then-modest Muscovite state. When the prince of Moscow wanted to reward loyal service, he awarded not agricultural rents, as in western Europe, but the right to collect taxes on the sale and branding of horses. As a sign of the horse's importance, Moscow struck coins with an image of a mounted horseman, armed with a

---

* A ruble coin of Ivan's time was worth approximately 6 rupees, so by comparison, a steppe horse in Moscow cost 120 rupees; in India, 400 rupees.

spear. The spear is a *kop'ye* (копьё) in Russian, so the coin came to be called a kopeck. Everyone carried in their pockets this image of the source of Moscow's growing power.

Moscow opened its horse market to win friends among the Tatars and to increase its political clout. It gave trading privileges to certain Tatars to induce them to become Moscow's allies, ready to defend it against common rivals, so that in most military campaigns, the fledgling Russian state could count on twenty thousand or more allied Tatar cavalry. That didn't mean the markets were without everyday tensions between the buyers and sellers. As with the Mongols in China and the Afghans in India, the steppe trading parties behaved like military expeditions. Referred to as "traveling bazaars" by the Muscovites, they comprised up to one thousand merchants and as many as nine thousand horses at a time. To control the horsemen, and to ensure that the state received first choice of horses at suitable prices, only Russian government officials were allowed to participate in the bazaar; private traders were banned. The horses were corralled into groups of one hundred, so that the officials could count them and collect a tax of four horses from each corral. The market governor, the *kon'iy prikaz*, extracted the equivalent of $12 million from these taxes for his own private income. Like the Chinese, Moscow restricted the sale of gunpowder, weapons, and iron implements to the horsemen, since individual Tatar bands could quickly switch from being trading partners to becoming hostile raiders.

To the Tatars, Moscow likewise represented both an opportunity and a threat. It offered them a market for their excess horses, but Russia's growing power robbed them of their political freedom of action. When the wealth and military power of Moscow became too great to ignore, the Tatars of more distant Central Asia suggested to their cousins on the Volga that they ought to jointly raid Moscow, as they had done in the past, and cut the Russians down to size. It was already too late. The Tatar khan of the Volga explained to his cousin, "You trade with Bukhara [from which horses were sold as far away as India]. I trade with Moscow. If I make war on Moscow, my people will be ruined."

Moscow acquired Tatar horses for its own cavalry, consistent with its growing military ambitions. The highest-ranking member of government was the *kon'iy boyar*, or grand equerry. This officer, along with the entire court, rode everywhere, never moving on foot, just like the Tatars. The cavalry was organized along purely Tatar lines in strategy, tactics, and even armament and tack. Cavalry troopers carried lances and sabers, like their Tatar counterparts. They utilized the Tatar bow and arrow well into the seventeenth century, at which point they gradually exchanged these for pistols, not because the firearms were more effective but because they required less training than the bow. Moscow mirrored the Tatars' military formations as well, deploying units of tens, hundreds, and thousands, divided into the left and right wings. The overall strength was eighty thousand troopers, who advanced, like Timür's horses, to the rhythm of kettledrums. Infantry constituted only a small portion of Moscow's troops, because battles saw mostly mounted armies fighting each other on the steppe. Even when Moscow fought against the Poles and Lithuanians, its western neighbors, the weapons and tactics on both sides reflected years of warfare against the steppe peoples. The armies of all of these settled groups shared the look and feel of their Tatar rivals.

Nothing better reflects both Moscow's affinity with the steppe horsemen and its ultimate success in overtaking them than the treasures stored up in the Kremlin armory. Here the princes of Moscow kept the precious gifts they received from their neighbors, eager to retain their support. These included a pair of iron stirrups, probably made in Constantinople, plated with gold, encrusted with pale blue turquoise and blood-red rubies, and hanging from straps made of cornflower-blue braided silk; a horse's noseband made of gold-plated silver niello work, each plate enclosing an enamel element or a ruby; a velvet shabrack embroidered with gold thread, stamped with tulips, hyacinths, and carnations; a quiver of arrows made of scarlet leather, annealed with silver and embroidered with gold and silver threads; a pair of saddles, one decorated with turquoise and rubies, the other set with pearls and emeralds.

In the early 1580s, the last years of his reign, Moscow's ruler, Ivan IV— "the Terrible"—invited the ambassador of England's Elizabeth I, Jerome Horsey, to admire these tangible proofs of his victories over the steppe horsemen. The now-stooped monarch led the Englishman through the glittering storerooms of the Kremlin to see the refined and elegant horse tack. Like Qianlong, Ivan had much to be satisfied about as he showed the

Tsar Ivan IV "the Terrible" showing Ambassador Horsey the Kremlin treasure rooms, by Aleksandr Litovchenko, 1875.

Englishman his treasures. Ivan's reign had culminated in the conquest of many of the successor khanates of the Golden Horde, including Kasimov, Astrakhan, and Kazan,* which provided Moscow with control of the trade along the Volga River. These conquests laid the foundation for Russia's emergence as a major Asian horse power, and, incidentally, made Ivan's Moscow significantly larger than Horsey's London.

A consummate master of spin, Ivan had twice abdicated from the throne, in both cases to catch his political enemies off-balance. The second time he abdicated in favor of a Tatar khan from Kasimov, whose claim to the throne of Moscow paradoxically derived from his Genghisid lineage. Ivan later returned to power and packed the Tatar off to a monastery. Ivan backed up his own legitimacy by asserting descent on his mother's side from Genghis Khan, a dubious genealogy that nevertheless underscored his ambition to take over where descendants of Genghis Khan had left off. To emphasize his lordship over the steppe people, in 1547 he took the title Tsar. This evoked not just the

---

*   Colorful Saint Basil's Cathedral, on Red Square, commemorates the fall of Kazan.

Caesars of Rome, from which the Russian word *tsar* derives, but also the way the Russians referred to the Mongol khans—for example, "Tsar Genghis." At his urging, the Tatar khans began to address him in writing as "the Great White Khan," and for generations afterward, tsars and emperors of Russia were called that by their Asian neighbors, including the shahs of Iran and the Qing emperors of China. "White" referred neither to a racial categorization of the Russians nor to the nineteenth-century color of their soldier's uniforms. In the ancient steppe tradition, white is the color of the western cardinal direction. Tsar Ivan aspired to be the Great Khan of the West, and by the time of his death in 1584, he had acquired the empire to go with this title.

Cossacks Versus Kazakhs

Though Ivan's steppe conquests proved durable in the long run, in the seventeenth century, fragmentary but still powerful remnants of the Golden Horde, located farther from the sphere of Moscow's influence, contested Russia's growing hegemony over the steppe and even raided the forested Russian heartland. Crimean and Nogay Tatars burned down wooden Moscow on more than one occasion. The attackers could cover a thousand miles in the course of a raid, surviving on mare's milk, appearing unexpectedly and instilling terror among the Russians. During Moscow's fifteen-year "Time of Troubles," following the death of Ivan's heir and the extinction of his dynasty in 1598, Tatar raiding parties carried tens of thousands of Russians off into slavery. Kazakhs and Kalmyks, the latter Buddhist and Mongolian-speaking, threatened Russian settlements on the Volga. In 1613, one of the urgent matters of business for Mikhail Fyodorovich, tsar of the new Romanov dynasty, entailed strengthening Moscow's defenses against the steppe raiders. He raised additional regiments of cavalry but could not match Tatar horse power. Grain-fed, stabled Russian horses lacked endurance for long campaigns in the steppe, and their cost limited the numbers that Tsar Mikhail could put in the field. Moscow had to acquire a much larger cavalry force, more suited to steppe conditions. This role was filled for Tsar Mikhail, providentially, by the Cossacks.

Cossack bands emerged during the period of decline of the Golden Horde. As the old steppe empire collapsed, their horse breeders set up on their own or in small bands. Like Babur and his followers, they called themselves *kazakh*, in the sense of "freebooter" or "bandit." The Russian equivalent, *kazak* (казак), originally designated adventurers and bandits of any ethnicity. Just as Tatars dissatisfied with their chiefs could take their flocks and look for new pastures, so, too, could fugitive serfs, defrocked priests, bankrupted landlords, and cashiered officers from Poland, Lithuania, and Moscow run away to the badlands beyond control of their former rulers and set up self-governing groups. The lawless territory where they established themselves came to be called Ukraïna, "the border." Here they lived off of livestock raising and plunder.

Cossacks and Tatar horsemen had much in common. They dressed in the same long cherkeskas, billowing trousers, and high boots. They both wore topknots, daring their opponents to cut off their heads and tie them to their saddles. The Cossacks fought on horseback with lances and bows, just like the Tatars. Their Don River geldings, like those of the Tatars, were small, tough, and resilient. The two groups even intermarried—or, at least, kidnapped one another's daughters.* But the Cossacks were Christian, speaking their own Slavic language, while the Tatars were mainly Turkish-speaking Muslims. The Cossacks were, in effect, the brother enemies of the Tatars, with whom they fought for possession of the borderlands, Ukraine.

The khans of Crimea led Tatar resistance to the Cossacks. The most powerful of the Golden Horde's successor states, the khanate enjoyed immense wealth derived from livestock raising and trade. These Genghisid khans alone possessed ten thousand horses and a quarter of a million other livestock; their closest retainers kept another fifty thousand horses. From these herds they supplied markets as far away as India, but still mustered one hundred thousand horsemen, more than enough horse power to command the respect of their neighbors.

But the Crimean khans had to protect their teeming herds on two fronts. To the east were Nogay and Kalmyk Tatars, who did not acknowledge the khans' supremacy and made frequent rustling raids against them. To the west, Cossacks were steadily encroaching on their pastures. The khanate's resistance weakened. Its horse breeders did not act in response to the

---

* Today, Kyrgyzstan is trying to eradicate bride kidnapping, but the custom is tenacious.

existential threat of the advancing Cossacks but, rather, resented the control of their own khans. By constantly revolting, they succeeded in overthrowing twelve khans in the sixteenth century, sixteen khans in the seventeenth century, and eighteen khans in the eighteenth century. As the khanate transitioned from being the bold attacker to defending its own pastures, khans could not secure the loyalty of their followers with plunder. Loyalty was contingent on reward, and Moscow and Poland-Lithuania could afford to be more generous with subsidies or bribes to dissident clansmen. Thus, in spite of their seemingly formidable horse power, the Crimean khans found themselves increasingly at the mercy of the Christian states.

The Poles and Lithuanians, who in the early seventeenth century occupied much of today's Ukraine, initially profited the most from the weakness of the Crimean khans and recruited Cossacks from as far east as the Don River. The Polish-Lithuanian state, like Moscow, had much in common with their steppe rivals, having spent the last three hundred years in constant contact with them, in both war and peace. Their nobility, the *szlachta*, raised great herds of horses on the steppe of Podolia, a region in today's Ukraine. The szlachta fostered the legend that they were descended from the ancient Scythians, who had roamed this same steppe two thousand years ago, to dress up their expansion into Ukraine as the return of native sons. Their dreams of steppe conquest ended abruptly in 1647, however, when their Cossack allies revolted, drove the szlachta out of their recently acquired estates, and tried to establish themselves as an independent power on the steppe under their own version of the khans, the hetmans.[*]

The common weakness of horse-breeding polities was the contingent nature of their subjects' loyalty to their rulers. If they so chose, horsemen could simply saddle up and abandon their chiefs. Autocratic Russia took advantage of this to ensure that no strong leaders emerged among its rivals for control of the steppe. Pretender khans, overproud szlachta nobles, and anarchic Cossacks all failed to organize themselves sufficiently in the face of Moscow's territorial ambitions. Tsar Alexei Mikhailovich subjected the Cossacks of Ukraine to Russian rule in 1654 in return for protection

---

[*] This is the context for Henryk Sienkiewicz's novel *With Fire and Sword*, and the catastrophe that befell Poland's Jewish community during this conflict.

against their former Polish-Lithuanian patrons. Russia emerged as the largest country in the world, while the frontier of independent horse breeders moved from the Don River to the Volga, 250 miles farther east.

Russia's settled population followed in the Cossacks' wake, cultivating newly available lands. As in China, the sheer demographic weight of Russia's population of nine million bore down on the horse breeders, whose numbers never exceeded half a million. Where horse breeding had been the predominant way of life since the time of the Scythians, now the steppe land converted to agriculture proved to be exceptionally fertile, attracting land-hungry farmers. Later these territories would make Russia and today's Ukraine major grain exporters.

In addition to the territories they conquered, the Cossacks delivered immense economic advantages to the Russian state. In return for Cossack privileges of self-government and grants of collective conquered land, the Cossacks provided military services and horses at a fraction of the cost of the regular army, which already consumed much of the state budget. The Cossack horses grazing on the steppe represented an essentially free resource, compared to the regular cavalry mounts, which had to be stabled and fed using agricultural lands. Like their Tatar rivals, the Cossacks could graze while on military campaigns, and so were freed from the logistic constraints of Russia's regular cavalry. Also like the Tatars, the Cossacks added to their income by breeding horses and selling them at horse fairs in central Russia. Even as the Cossacks gradually replaced the Tatars, they replicated their economic role as horse breeders for Russia, which continued to need steppe horses for military, civilian, and agricultural work.

Moscow's reliance on the Cossacks to expand the empire did not always result in smooth progress. The Cossacks frequently revolted and sometimes even made common cause with the Tatars against the tsars. In 1670, Stenka Razin, a Cossack warlord chafing under Moscow's rule, interrupted his combats with the Tatars to challenge Tsar Alexei, in an attempt to restore Cossack independence. With his army of seven thousand Cossack cavalry, he captured the two major trading cities on the Volga, Tsaritsyn (later Stalingrad and now Volgograd) and Astrakhan, and ravaged Russia's steppe frontier as pitilessly as any Tatar horde. Moscow had to mobilize all its forces to contain and ultimately defeat Razin. The rebellion ended with his capture and public execution in Red Square; to deal with the Cossacks formerly under Razin's command, Moscow sent them deeper into the steppe, thereby expanding the frontiers of the empire.

In 1717, continuing his predecessor's policies, Peter the Great launched the Cossacks, unsuccessfully, against the steppe oasis of Khwarazm, seventeen hundred miles distant. In 1720, Peter's Cossacks occupied Iran's Caspian provinces (from where Nader Shah later expelled them). The following year, Peter changed his title from the Slavic *tsar* to Latin *imperator* and formally proclaimed Russia to be an empire, a bold advertisement for his ambitions.

Russia Divides and Conquers

Under Peter's heirs, Russia's encirclement, like that of the Mongol battue, tightened ever further around the horse breeders of the steppe. Catherine the Great consigned to history Russia's old steppe rivals, exiling the last khan of the Crimea in 1783 and extinguishing the once-powerful Polish-Lithuanian state in 1795. The Cossacks built a line of forts both north of the steppe, in the Ural Mountains, and in the east, along the Volga River, and using both the pasture-hungry Cossacks and opportunistic alliances with Tatar groups, the Russians picked off their rivals' resistance one by one. Catherine aimed to make the Volga region as wealthy and populated as the Rhine or the Elbe, and even imported German agricultural colonists to settle there.

Opposing her designs were the Kazakh hordes. To contain the Kazakhs, Russia made an alliance with the Buddhist Kalmyks, whose powerful khanate extended from the Caspian Sea to the Ural Mountains, and who were major suppliers of horses to both Moscow and Beijing. Once the Kalmyks had cut the Kazakhs down to size, however, Russia failed to prevent the Cossacks from encroaching on the pastures of the Kalmyks. Consequently, in 1771 the Kalmyks renounced their Russian alliance and emigrated two thousand miles east into Chinese territory, where the Eighth Dalai Lama brokered an agreement with China's Qianlong Emperor to offer them pasturage. Both the Cossacks and the Kazakhs attacked the migrating Kalmyks, and only 66,000 of the 130,000 Kalmyks survived their trail of tears.

With the destruction of the Kalmyks, yet another threat to Russia's steppe hegemony disappeared. The flight of the Kalmyks was the last great migration of a steppe nation in history, and its disastrous result signaled the end of the era of independent steppe khanates.

No longer threatened by the Kalmyks, the Cossacks gave vent to their own anxieties about the transformation of the freewheeling steppe by both Catherine's German agricultural colonists and her ever more heavy-handed administration in faraway St. Petersburg. In 1773, Yemelyan Pugachev led the Volga Cossacks to revolt, just as Stenka Razin had a century before. He struck an alliance with his erstwhile Tatar foes and raised a cavalry army of twenty-five thousand troopers. The insurrection extended along the length of the Volga, nominally controlling the entire area of the former Kalmyk Khanate. His was the most serious political challenge imperial Russia had yet faced. Once again, however, the Cossack and Tatar horse breeders' preference for anarchic freedom doomed their movement. Catherine mobilized a disciplined and cohesive military, which overwhelmed the rebels, already undermined by Cossack-Kazakh rivalries, and, after two years of fierce fighting, suppressed the rebellion.

Chastened by Pugachev's rebellion, Catherine implemented new, more pragmatic policies toward her horse-breeding subjects, which ensured that the final pacification of the Kazakhs would be an anticlimax, compared to the turmoil that preceded it. With the destruction of the Kalmyks, and Russia's tighter rein on the Cossacks, St. Petersburg could afford to guarantee the Kazakhs peace and protection. Unlike the Crimean Tatars, whose herds had pastured in the rich, arable territory of Ukraine, the Kazakhs were better protected from encroachment by the aridity of their ancestral steppe. Moreover, Catherine extended the status of Cossack to many Kazakhs, incorporating them directly into the armed forces and acknowledging the essentially military character of steppe society. This provided Russia with a decisive advantage in its subsequent conquests in the Caucasus, Turkey, Iran, and Central Asia. In these campaigns, diseases devastated Russian regular soldiers, while the Cossacks, inured to life on the steppe, suffered relatively light losses.

Horses continued to drive Russian expansion deeper into the continent. As the nineteenth century unfolded, Cossack squadrons on the Ili River warily sized up the formidable Qing bannermen. At the same time, Russian scouts and explorers on the Oxus River noted that the British were steadily advancing from the south—for Britain, improbably, had replaced the Mughals in India. As the modern world emerged, two European empires found themselves competing in an ancient political game over Central Asian horse power.

The Great Game

British India and Russia, 1739–1881

༽

Anarchy Unleashed

Britain had not been the inevitable heir to the Mughal Empire, devastated by Nader Shah's invasion in 1739. Nader's return to Iran, with his caravans of plunder, left a power vacuum that rapacious Afghans from the north and ambitious Marathas from the south rushed to fill. Initially, the southerners managed to seize Delhi and turn Muhammad Shah, the thirteenth Mughal emperor, into a puppet. In 1747, however, the Afghan Ahmad Shah took over Mughal Lahore and used its huge revenue base to feed his ever-expanding cavalry, which ultimately numbered two hundred thousand. This enabled him to chase the Marathas out of Delhi, at least temporarily. They soon returned in force. In 1761, the rival armies sized each other up across the plains of Panipat, where another invader from Afghanistan, Babur, had vanquished Indian defenders centuries before.

The second battle of Panipat showcased, again, the importance of Central Asian horses as a source of power. On the Maratha side, Maharajas Scindia of Gwalior, Holkar of Indore, and Gaekwad of Baroda* hesitated before engaging Ahmad Shah's Afghans, who were equipped with "powerful horses of the Turkmen breed, naturally hardy, and rendered more so

---

* Over the course of the eighteenth century, Maratha power shifted from a single ruler, in the mold of Shivaji Bhonsle, to a confederation of warlords, each of whom took the title maharaja.

by continued exercise." Conscious of the Afghan advantage, Scindia urged caution on his fellow maharajas, but hotheaded councils prevailed, and the Afghans indeed crushed the lighter-mounted Marathas. Holkar and Gaekwad escaped the Maratha debacle on their superb Arabs. Maharaja Mahadji Scindia[*] fled from the field on his Kathiawar mare but was less lucky. As fast as Scindia could ride, a huge Afghan mounted on a tall Turkmen horse followed him in hot pursuit. The Kathiawar mare could deliver bursts of speed, but Turkmen horses never tired. Scindia made it a hundred miles before his mare stumbled in a ditch. The Afghan pounced on him, smashed his knee with a battle-ax, and stripped him of jewelry, clothes, and the mare. Surprisingly, he then rode off, leaving Scindia still alive but permanently lame.[†]

Ahmad Shah's victory at Panipat put an end to the Marathas' dreams of Indian empire, but the Afghans did not long enjoy their rewards. A few years later, a new horse power, the Sikhs of Punjab, drove them out of northwestern India. Having transformed from a purely religious movement into a formidable martial corps, the Sikhs rose up against Mughals and Afghans alike, and even pillaged the baggage train of Nader Shah as he returned from Delhi to Iran, laden with plunder. When Nader asked his local governor why he could not control these sometimes naked, sometimes saffron-robed holy men, he was told, "Their only homes are the saddles of their horses. They can last long periods without food and rest. They are known to sleep on horseback. We have put prizes on their heads, but their numbers keep increasing. They are never despondent, but are always singing the songs of their gurus." The elite Sikh cavalry, mounted on Lakhi ponies, were called the Nihangs, or "Crocodiles," for their ferocity.[‡]

The Sikhs were one of many contenders unleashed by the Maratha defeat and Ahmad Shah's exit. Cavalry armies sprang up that lacked any political

---

[*] Also spelled Shinde.

[†] As with Timür, however, lameness did not prevent Scindia from remaining India's foremost cavalry leader.

[‡] Nihang horsemen mastered a riding style that still thrills crowds, like the more familiar fantasia of Moroccan cavalry.

ambitions; they simply fought for subsistence. Otherwise poor communities found opportunities to cash in either as breeders and dealers or, riding their own horses, as bandits and cavalry troopers. The hill-country Indo-Afghans, always ready to act as middlemen, sold themselves and their horses to the highest bidders. The story of one Amir Khan is typical: he started off as a petty brigand with ten followers. Maharaja Scindia appreciated his ruthlessness and patronized him. Before long, he had five hundred troopers, then fifteen hundred, then thirty thousand. "Intriguing, cunning, avaricious, cruel and utterly lacking in personal charisma," he plundered everyone indiscriminately. His portrait in the Victoria and Albert Museum

Warlord Amir Khan sold his services to all sides in the free-for-all following the collapse of Mughal power, ca. 1820.

shows a robust-looking ruffian mounted on a powerful horse, its lower half brightly dyed in blood-red henna. His troops avoided regular battle but attacked baggage trains, burned down villages loyal to their enemies, and picked off straggler units. For decades, there was no power strong enough to suppress these troops, and many unscrupulous leaders were happy enough to employ them against their opponents.

The Kattra people, living in Gujarat's semi-arid Kathiawar district, similarly saw more opportunity in raising horses, trading, and raiding than in farming their infertile lands. In this period of anarchy, the Kattra took advantage of their horses and government weakness to become feared outlaws. They offered their military services to the Maratha warlords and flourished beyond what previous generations could have imagined.

The anarchy also incentivized India's settled states to invest heavily in cavalry, in hopes of acquiring former Mughal lands, which were now up for grabs. Tipu Sultan, who ruled the southern state of Mysore in the last two decades of the eighteenth century, is best known for his life-sized wooden tiger toy, which devoured a wooden Englishman to fiendish cries produced by its hidden sound box. To compensate for the lack of good grasslands in what is today's Tamil Nadu State, he subsidized horse breeding, paying out 100 rupees a year to feed a foal, 200 for a colt—this in a period when a good Turki horse cost 500 rupees up north. The total outlay for horse breeding came to 1.8 million rupees, while Mysore's annual tax intake amounted to just 400,000 rupees. The sultan could make up the difference only by winning wars and extracting indemnities. In other words, the Mysore cavalry had to earn 1.4 million rupees a year to break even. These economics explain well the endless wars of this era.

It was the Sikhs who proved the most successful of the new Indian horse powers. In the eighteenth and early nineteenth centuries, they carved out a state comprising Punjab, Kashmir, and Ladakh—which meant they controlled access to the horses of Afghanistan and Central Asia. Theirs was the last state founded in the saddle in India—and, indeed, the world. Looking back on his conquests, their greatest leader, Maharaja Ranjit Singh, confided to an English visitor in 1831, "All of my conquest had been done by the sword [i.e., cavalry]. I have never known the infantry or the artillery to be of any service." The magnificence of the maharaja's stables rivaled that of the old Mughals'. On the occasion of an ambassador's visit, the Sikh ruler passed in review thirty of his horses, all superbly caparisoned, their bridles laden with encrusted diamonds, emeralds, rubies, turquoise, pearls, and coral. Later, when two such bridles were shown at the 1851 Great Exhibition, in the Crystal Palace, they were insured for tens of thousands of rupees. As these ambling treasure carriers rode past, the maharaja could name each horse, its lineage of sires, and its strengths and weaknesses.

All told, the rivals for Indian supremacy mustered six hundred thousand troopers, with an annual cost of up to 20 million rupees in remounts and 80 million rupees for forage, nearly double what the Mughals had spent on their cavalry. India could actually pay for these expenditures, as well as for handsome dividends in plunder and tribute for the victorious. Unlike demographically declining Iran, which was scarcely able to afford the horse power of Nader Shah, India's population of two hundred million and growing produced enough surplus to sustain its perpetually warring cavalry armies.

The conflicts that engulfed India also swept up the European maritime nations that had been trading under Mughal protection. France and Great Britain began to back one or the other of the regional competitors, as proxies for their own global trading rivalry. The French encouraged the ruler of Bengal to drive the British traders from their lucrative trading post in Calcutta. Britain's riposte and subsequent victory over the French and their Bengali allies at the Battle of Plassey in 1757 left them masters of the subcontinent's wealthiest territories and turned Britain into a major contestant for paramountcy over India. With a cavalry of only five hundred troopers, however, the British were not yet a major horse power. The counting house clerks, from old commercial families, associated cavalry with aristocracy, and feared both the cost and the political influence of horsey people. Afghans, Indo-Afghans, Marathas, and Mysoreans warily eyed the mismatch between British wealth and its meager cavalry. In Mysore, Tipu Sultan's wooden toy tiger devoured its Englishman while the sultan himself planned to expel the foreigners from India.

British Raj and Its Enemies

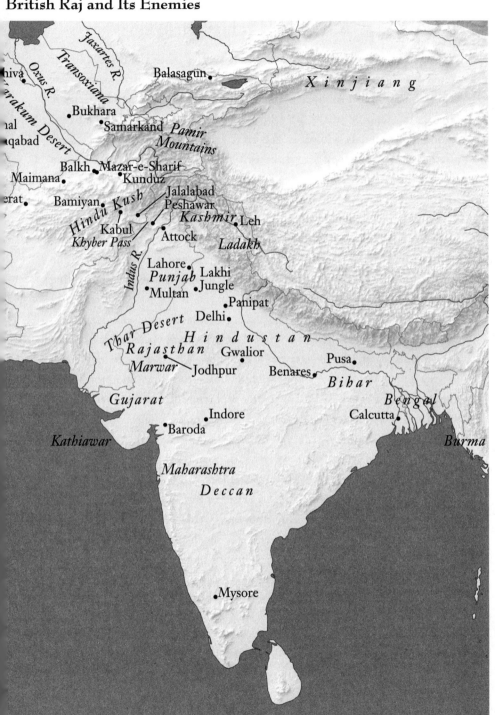

Jaxartes R.

Transoxiana

Oxus R.

hiva

Karakum Desert

nal

qabad

Balasagun

X i n j i a n g

Bukhara

Samarkand

Pamir Mountains

Maimana

Balkh Mazar-e-Sharif

Kunduz

erat

Bamiyan *Hindu Kush*

Jalalabad

Peshawar

Kashmir Leh

Kabul

Khyber Pass Attock

Ladakh

Indus R.

Lahore

Punjab Lakhi

Multan Jungle

Panipat

Thar Desert Delhi

H i n d u s t a n

Rajasthan Gwalior

Marwar Jodhpur

Pusa

Benares *B i h a r*

Gujarat

B e n g a l

Indore

Calcutta

Kathiawar Baroda

Burma

Maharashtra

D e c c a n

Mysore

A Costly Establishment

Mysore and the Marathas waged three wars each against the British. In one round of fighting, Mysore's formidable cavalry bested the British, and even captured the British Army commander. The Marathas inflicted a series of humiliating defeats on the British, using the same tactics they had used against the Mughals. However, the great Indian horse powers feared one another as much as they feared the British, and failed to make a common front against their shared enemy.* In 1799, the Marathas sided with the British to defeat Tipu Sultan. The Afghans and Marathas remained at daggers drawn, as did the Afghans and the Sikhs. Even among the Marathas, the Holkars and Scindias fought each other as much as they fought the foreigners. Finally, in 1803, Dawlatrao Scindia—the adopted son of Mahadji—and Yashwantrao Holkar agreed to combine forces against the British, fielding almost one hundred thousand cavalry.

What the British lacked in horse power they made up for with deep pockets. They played the different powers off one another, often bribing opposing generals to defect or at least to refuse combat. They recruited mercenary cavalry forces. While the younger Scindia made his preparation for hostilities, a half-English, half-Indian soldier of fortune, James Skinner, slipped away from Scindia's service to join the British forces under Lord Lake. He brought with him his own Indian troopers, who said, "We will only fight for Alexander the Great." This was what they called Skinner, taking his last name for the Persian "Sikander," or Alexander. Lake was impressed by the drill of Skinner's horsemen: "The usual exercise of shooting at full speed at a bottle on the ground, extracting a tent pin deeply embedded in the earth, single combat with spears, and swords and shields . . . would leave anyone versed in Indian history to believe Skinner's horse to be the descendants of the conquering Moguls of Timour," recalled Major Edward Archer, himself a cavalryman. The horsemanship and swordsmanship of Skinner's

---

* To be fair to the Indian statesmen of the eighteenth century, a durable alliance between Mysore, the Marathas, and the Sikhs would have made as much sense to them as one between Germany, France, and Italy before the creation of NATO and the European Union.

troopers, mounted on Turki horses, had the same effect on the Marathas as had Ahmad Shah's hordes at Panipat. Lord Lake defeated first Scindia and then the slow-to-mobilize Holkar. After fifteen years of conflict and a few strokes of military genius by Lake, Cornwallis (later defeated at Yorktown), and Wellesley (later victorious at Waterloo), complemented by adroit diplomacy and well-timed bribery, Britain had the better of its enemies. By 1818, the British controlled much of India, either directly or through treaties with Gwalior, Baroda, Indore, Mysore, and others. From maritime traders, the British had come into the inheritance of the Mughals, with an empire stretching from the Himalayas to the Carnatic tip of the subcontinent.*

As befitted the successors to the Mughals, the Britons now mustered respectable horse power. Their cavalry ratings increased from five hundred sabers in 1793 to six thousand in 1809, and to thirty thousand by 1819. Paying for all this weighed heavily on the profit-minded government in Calcutta. Once the Marathas surrendered, the British hoped to reduce the expense of the army and enjoy a peace dividend. They retired the Lieutenant Colonel Skinner and disbanded his regiment.

Yet concerns were soon raised that horses, for all their cost, were still indispensable to protect India from external invasion. The Sikh maharaja Ranjit Singh's thirty-thousand-strong cavalry threatened. Who knew if another Nader Shah would not arise in Iran, or another Ahmad Shah in Afghanistan? So argued General James Salmon, a veteran of the wars against Tipu Sultan and now the serving military secretary in Calcutta, the highest-ranking officer in India: "This immense Empire will have no protection against the predatory hordes of horse from the Punjab, from Afghanistan, or even from Persia or Tartary, except what it shall derive from cavalry." William Moorcroft, a veterinary expert brought out from London to improve Britain's horse-raising operations, warned that if India did not field sufficient horse power, "the prospect of a golden harvest may

---

* The status of the British in India fundamentally changed with William Pitt's India Act of 1784, from a trading body to an indirect branch of the British government. The notion of the trading body, the East India Company, survived until 1857, when the Indian government began to report directly to the cabinet in London and the last Mughal was exiled to Burma.

tempt hordes of Tartar cavalry and tribes of mounted Afghans to swell the flood of barbaric inroad upon British India."

Beyond these traditional invaders of India, farther north loomed another threat. Ever since the time of Peter the Great, Russia had harbored designs on the wealthy subcontinent. In 1801, the Russians dispatched a Cossack invasion force against India, expecting support from Iran as well Napoleon's France. And 1807 saw another Russian-French alliance aimed at India. Though these plans came to nothing, Russia's steppe conquests over the course of the nineteenth century brought Cossack squadrons ever closer to the Oxus and Indus Rivers. The British took these threats seriously. Their war staff in Calcutta prepared plans for the defense of India, and hawkish military leaders took preemptive actions in Afghanistan. This, in turn, only goaded the Russians to make faster advances. *"Ici il faut agir à l'anglaise, et cela d'autant plus que c'est contre les Anglais qu'on agit"* ("Here we must act English-style [i.e., boldly], all the more as we're acting against them"), opined General Count Vasily Alekseevich Perovsky, who led an unsuccessful expedition to the Oxus in 1839. The rivalry between the two empires for control of Central Asia was dubbed, with characteristic understatement, the Great Game.

Although the argument for a large cavalry force to defend their new Indian empire ultimately prevailed, the economical British struggled, over the entire course of the century, to obtain suitable horses at an affordable cost. When their forces were much smaller, the British could source remounts with no thought of the expense, bringing them from a stud farm in Dagenham, near London. Many perished on the long trip around the Cape of Good Hope, making the surviving horses effectively very expensive to import. The British also procured Arab and Persian horses from the Persian Gulf; these cost less to import but commanded higher prices than the English animals. As the cavalry grew in size, India's new rulers sought to replace the costly imports with local stock.

This immense territory, which only a few generations earlier had teemed with as many as six hundred thousand warhorses, suddenly experienced a shortage in supply. In 1809, the commander in chief of the British Army in India, Forbes Champagné, a French-Irish veteran of the American Revolution, complained about that shortage, especially the lack of larger horses:

In respect to Cavalry but little strength can be added to present numbers, the difficulty of procuring suitable horses for Europeans being
an unfortunate and insuperable obstacle to any great extension of an
arm so necessary and so formidable in a country so generally well
adapted to its operations.

All kinds of obstacles beset Champagné and his successors. The onset
of internal peace resulted in a steep decline in the number and quality of
warhorses raised by Indian breeders. Without profitable local wars, it was
simply not worthwhile for Indian breeders to produce the same quantity of
warhorses as they had in the turbulent eighteenth century. The Kattra people had risen out of poverty on their marginal lands by breeding exceptionally tough and fast warhorses. Now the demand for such horses had dried
up. Captain E. Wyatt, a British officer tasked with finding remounts, wryly
observed in 1814, "The decline of horse breeding amongst them [i.e., the
Kattra] is owing in some degree to a cause which cannot be regretted, that
is a check having been given to their plundering excursions by which until
very lately they almost entirely subsisted." Fifty years later, the Kathiawar
breed was almost extinct. Moorcroft, the veterinarian, judged the quality
of horses to be declining quickly, and feared that soon "the day of positive
scarcity shall arrive."

Disappointed by local breeders, the British tried their own hand at horse
breeding in India. In 1793 the government had established a stud farm
in Pusa, in the foothills of the Himalayas. The idyllic setting reminded
the British of home, with its cool air, greenery, and abundant pure water.
Yet this undertaking proved to be an even bigger drain on India's defense
budget than the imports. After ten years of operation, Pusa had consumed
406,427 rupees, while the value of the animals produced was only 262,966.
Annual operating costs exceeded 36,000 rupees, and yet the stud farm produced each year just thirty to forty horses suitable for the cavalry, at an
effective cost of 1,000 rupees a head—well more than the 400 rupees that
would buy a good warhorse from traders. Pusa's remote location and high
overheads contributed to these disappointing results. Another solution was
clearly needed.

A Mad Mission to Bukhara

Moorcroft took responsibility for the Pusa stud farm in 1809. A child of the Scottish Enlightenment, Moorcroft had a penchant for investigating everything from equine diseases to Tibetan yak wool. Quickly concluding that Pusa would never prove a viable source of horses for the army, he argued that the British must procure horses, as the Mughals had done, from Bukhara, that distant—and, in Moorcroft's time, faintly mysterious—oasis city in Central Asia. Here was the land of the blood-sweating horses of Han Wudi. No British merchant had visited Bukhara since the reign of Queen Elizabeth I: hostile Afghans, Sikhs, and Chinese barred the way. This did not deter Moorcroft.

Bukhara presented a tantalizing opportunity. Its Indian horse trade had once amounted to one hundred thousand horses a year. The arrival of the Portuguese in the Indian Ocean, followed by the British, French, and Dutch, had not led to a decline in overland trade or the impoverishment of caravan centers like Bukhara; in fact, Bukhara flourished throughout the nineteenth century. If fewer of its fabled horses were coming to market in India, this reflected not the decline of the trade but the eagerness of buyers among the Qing and the Russians, who diverted much of the region's business away from India. Moorcroft dreamed of reestablishing India's preeminence as the destination for Bukhara's horses.

As a first step, Moorcroft dispatched a discreet Persian secretary named Mir Izzatullah to gather intelligence. He found that the city held four fairs a week, compared to one or two in other trade centers. Each market day, traders would expose fifty to sixty Turkmen and Uzbek horses, the former bigger and more spirited, the latter having better endurance. Mares were rare, as owners preferred to keep them for breeding. Sellers asked between 200 and 300 rupees a head.* These prices were attractive, roughly half of that prevailing in India. But the market turned out to be less liquid than Moorcroft had imagined. With most breeders supplying Russia or China directly, attempts to buy on a large scale, especially with a single big order,

---

* Quoted as ten to fifteen tillas per head. A tilla was a miskal of gold, 4.25 grams, equivalent to 19 silver rupees at the then-prevailing gold-silver exchange.

risked driving the prices higher, before supply could be increased. Mir Izzatullah also emphasized that the superior horses sought by the British were actually quite rare, a state of affairs that had prevailed since the time of Wudi's expedition to Central Asia. Numbering at most ten or fifteen at a time, such horses were never shown at the open market but could be acquired only from a broker, on invitation, by a connoisseur willing to spend 1,000 to 3,000 rupees. The bulk of the trade in so-called Turkmen horses actually consisted of the less prestigious Uzbek breed, from Maimana and Balkh (today's Mazar-e Sharif). Traders often bought older horses that had fewer remaining years of useful life but could be marketed in India under the brand name "Turkmen" or even "Arab," if the horse looked fine enough.

Despite his secretary's misgivings, and ignoring the pleas of his immediate superiors to concentrate on horse breeding, Moorcroft persisted in his quest. He found one sympathetic sponsor in Calcutta and used that grandee's vague authorization to mount an expedition to fabled Bukhara in 1819. He interpreted the authorization in the broadest sense possible in order to indulge his wanderlust, exploring Kashmir, Leh, and Ladakh for two years before setting off on his mission proper. From Lahore, he planned to cross the Indus River on his way to Peshawar, continue through the Khyber Pass, then stop in Kabul, Bamiyan, and Bukhara. It was the return trip of the ancient Kushans.

In Lahore, Moorcroft paid an official visit to Maharaja Ranjit Singh to ask permission to transit the Sikh kingdom. After a ceremonial exchange of gifts, the maharaja offered an entertainment likely intended to be as much a dissuasive show of power, should the British have designs on the Punjab, as an exercise in vanity by the horse-mad maharaja. A single rider led a series of horses through their paces in the narrow enclosure of a palace garden. Horse and rider performed a gallop only to pull up abruptly, turn, and gallop off in the opposite direction. The strangely silent horses perfectly obeyed the slightest indications of the rider's hands. This display included local breeds from Lakhi and Attock, as well as horses from Bukhara for which the ruler had paid 1,700 rupees. "Beautifully made," observed Moorcroft of the Bukharans, "but below the knees too slight." A Persian horse that cost 7,000 rupees similarly struck Moorcroft as "inferior." Yet it was commonly agreed that Ranjit Singh commanded the finest cavalry in Asia, and he had collected hundreds of fine horses. "Every Sikh in the country," reported Moorcroft, "keeps a brood mare and reared colts for his own riding or for resale," with the maharaja receiving the finest of these as gifts. Perhaps Moorcroft belittled the Sikh horses in order to justify his risky expedition hundreds of miles farther north.

Ranjit Singh then consulted Moorcroft on the state of his own health, since Western medicine enjoyed a high reputation in nineteenth-century India. The maharaja complained that he could no longer consume as much strong drink as he used to. Moorcroft, the veterinary doctor, had no qualms about prescribing medicine, but he also stuck his neck out to recommend that the Sikh give up alcohol. The maharaja wanted to give him a horse as a present, but the Briton asked to defer such gifts until his return from Bukhara.

Moorcroft displayed a great deal of sangfroid. To cross the lands of the

Ranjit Singh, founder of the Sikh empire, still in the saddle, despite his age, ca. 1840.

Afghan Waziri clan, who were then no less predatory than in the time of the Kushans and of Babur, he put himself under the protection of a solitary venerable Sufi. Safe from the endemic highway robbery, he found time to admire the countryside: "At the time of our visit in March the desert was covered with a rich carpet of variegated colors from the purple flowers of the wild sainfoin and the yellow flowers of the marigolds and bugloss." He also admired the wiry Waziri horses, of which he bought two, one for 150 rupees, the other for 200. "The latter was in appearance precisely like an Arab and would have sold in Calcutta as an Arab for 1,000 rupees," he boasted. His enthusiasm for the local horses seemed to grow in direct proportion to the distance and increasing danger of his expedition.

In Kabul, the pastures of the Afghan cavalry, twenty thousand strong, met his approval:

I saw some shaftel or clover cut for seed and never saw ground so covered with hay of any kind. After the seed is threshed out this chaff mixed with wheat and barley is given to horses as winter forage. Almost all the troop horses of Kabul are wintered at Mydan [i.e., the *maidan*, or meadow] on this food and Lucerne [alfalfa] at the cost of two and a half rupees a head and come out of this feed in the spring in the most excellent condition.

Here was the secret to the superiority of the Central Asian cavalry over the Indian cavalry, and the key to the Afghan victory at Panipat: it cost them very little to raise big, powerful warhorses. Moorcroft wrote back to Calcutta recommending that Afghanistan become a British dependency— a policy pursued with disastrous results in the First Anglo-Afghan War, twenty years later.

Two years after departing from Lahore, Moorcroft at last reached his longed-for destination. Amir Haydar of Bukhara received him warily in audience. The amir feared British intrigue and was cautious not to put his trading relationships with Russia and China in jeopardy. After all, the Russians had been trading with Bukhara since before the times of Ivan the Terrible, China since the era of the blood-sweating horses. The newcomer set about procuring horses, with neither the amir's objection nor his endorsement. This proved no easier than his Persian secretary had warned him. Russian and Chinese purchases at scale meant few fine horses came up for sale at the public markets. In addition, a revolt of the Uzbek horse breeders against the amir, their nominal ruler, interrupted the flow of horses to the market. To pass the time in between frustrating shopping expeditions, Moorcroft documented his boundless curiosity in a diary, penning descriptions of an Armenian distillery, silk weaving, and the famous Bukhara grapes and pomegranates. Naturally, he recorded in great detail the Bukharan methods for breeding, feeding, and training their famous horses. A striking passage from his papers mentions the peculiar method the horse breeders used to keep their horses in top condition:

> A Goat . . . is placed and at a signal the Horsemen gallop forwards to seize it. The Man who first reaches the Goat, stoops lays hold of and having thrown it across his saddle goes at full speed towards a distant goal which having attained he returns at the same rate of exertion to the point from which he started.

It was the first description in English of the game of buzkashi.

Satisfying his curiosity about Bukhara, though, provided Moorcroft with only meager compensation for his failure to acquire prize horses. After five months in Bukhara, Moorcroft set out on his return journey to India with just a handful of horses, none of them of the size or pedigree he had so long dreamed about. Nearing the Afghan frontier, he tried and failed to acquire some of the much less rare Uzbek horses. How the intrepid vet felt about these final setbacks is unknown; he caught a fever and died suddenly in Andkhoy, in northern Afghanistan.

From the start, the improbable chances of success of Moorcroft's horse-buying plan has suggested to some historians that his real goal was espionage. The Russians certainly thought so, for they were as concerned about British designs on the Oxus as Britain feared Russia's move toward the Indus. Given the veterinarian's colorful character, his ill-fated expedition could very well have been motivated simply by a love of adventure and an enthusiasm for beautiful horses. Even so, Moorcroft's voyage to Bukhara is often considered the opening round of the Great Game.

Defeated by Sea, China Retains the Steppe

Moorcroft's failure to secure Central Asia's ready horse power weighed on the British military expenditure. The government reluctantly continued to pay for expensive imports and its unsatisfactory Pusa stud farm. Meanwhile, the Indian Army was engaged in foreign wars throughout the nineteenth century: the three Anglo-Burmese wars, the First and Second Anglo-Afghan Wars, and the First and Second Opium Wars against Qing China.[*] Britain annexed Burma, imposed a tutelary[†] relationship on Afghanistan, and demanded trading privileges from Qing China.

In 1793, the British embassy to Qianlong had not set off alarms in China about vulnerability along its eleven-thousand-mile maritime frontier, even though the Qing possessed no deep-water naval forces to mention. In 1860, during the Second Opium War, this gap in Qing defenses enabled two thousand British and allied French troops to disembark at Tianjin, where only a few days' march separated the invaders from the Forbidden City.

At the Eight-Li Bridge, ten miles from the walls of Beijing, they encountered the very spectacle made famous through Castiglione's engravings: the densely massed Manchu and Mongol bannermen in their steel armor, equipped with lances, sabers, and bows. The Europeans guessed there might be as many as twelve thousand cavalrymen. In fact, they numbered thirty thousand. Their commander, Sengge Rinchen, was a twenty-sixth-generation descendant of Genghis Khan's brother. As he deployed his steppe horsemen into the battue formation to surround and destroy the invaders, not a sound came from their serried ranks, for their officers issued orders by raising and lowering fluttering pennants. The horsemen bore down on the Europeans, showing complete indifference to their deadly rifle volleys. But Sengge Rinchen's steppe tactics could

---

[*]   These wars came in succession because each conflict left enough ill will—on the part of the Burmese, Afghans, and Chinese, respectively—as to make the next one inevitable. Mention should also be made of the two Sikh Wars and Britain's annexation of Punjab, following Ranjt Singh's death.

[†]   Off and on during the nineteenth century, Britain controlled Afghanistan's external relations and selected its rulers.

make no impact on the narrow front and the marshy terrain, crisscrossed by canals. His men simply did not have room to maneuver. After taking terrible losses, they withdrew in good order, and engaged no more with the invaders. The allied march on Beijing continued. The emperor fled to Mulan, leaving his brother to accept the European diktat to open China to western trade.

Qing horse power was not up to defending the country from its maritime foes. Sengge Rinchen's attack may have been a face-saving gesture, and his retreat a reflection of cool realism. In the coastal provinces of China where the Opium Wars were fought, horses had never played a decisive role. The Qing dynasty reluctantly extended what they rightly foresaw as temporary concessions to the maritime powers—these survived eighty-five years—but they preserved their bannerman cavalry to defend their steppe frontier, which now came under new threats.

News of the Qing defeat at the hands of the French and the British encouraged the Russians to launch Cossack incursions into Xinjiang. At the same time, revolts broke out in the province, where a certain Yakub Beg, claiming to be a descendant of Timür, declared himself amir of an independent state. Qing generals organized flying columns of crack bannermen with the same grim efficiency and determination as Qianlong's armies of a century earlier. The success of the Qing armies in storming into the cities of Xinjiang discouraged the Russians from recognizing Yakub Beg's regime. Resistance to the Qing soon subsided. St. Petersburg decided that it made more sense to find common cause with China, in order to control both sides' rebellious steppe subjects, than to risk war with an uncertain outcome against the bannermen.

Accordingly, the two powers agreed to draw a formal border, the first ever in the steppe. The surveying activity passed close to Balasagun, the capital of an ancient Central Asian Turkish empire. There, the stump of the Burana Tower was the only surviving trace of the ancient Turks. It had once attracted travelers from across the steppe, when it rose 150 feet, visible to caravans a day's march away. The pasture adjacent to the tower, deep with long grasses, was studded with stones engraved with ancient Turkish runes. This site had served as a meeting point and a place of burial for millennia. Now, in its truncated shadow, the Russo-Chinese border commissioners buried the political independence of the steppe peoples, formalized by the Treaty of St. Petersburg in 1881.

The Powindah's Twilight

The partition of the steppe between Russia and China slowed the flow of horses from Central Asia to India down to a trickle, just fifteen hundred in some years. Still, Indian buyers longed for these horses, as their allure and mystique remained undimmed since the days of Moorcroft. This demand kept the Afghan Powindahs, with roots going back to the era of the Kushan king Kanishka in the second century CE, in business. Rudyard Kipling's 1901 novel *Kim* is an elegy to this storied institution. The image Kipling evokes is deliberately timeless: there is

> a huge open square over against the railway station, surrounded with arched cloisters, where the camel and horse caravans put up on their return from Central Asia. Here were all manner of Northern folk, tending tethered ponies and kneeling camels; loading and unloading bales and bundles; drawing water for the evening meal at the creaking well windlasses; piling grass before the shrieking, wild-eyed stallions; cuffing the surly caravan dogs; paying off camel-drivers; taking on new grooms; swearing.

Here in the lively marketplace of Lahore's Kashmir caravansary, Kipling's young half-Irish, half-Indian hero, Kim, meets the Pathan[*] Mahbub Ali: "The horse-trader, his deep, embroidered Bokhariot belt unloosed, was lying on a pair of silk carpet saddle-bags, pulling lazily at an immense silver hookah." His magnificent mien and Old Testament features proclaim his tribal affiliation to the Suleiman Khel (clan) of the Ghilzai people. Kipling describes him as "one of the best horse-dealers in the Punjab, a wealthy and enterprising trader, whose caravans penetrated far and far into the

---

[*] "Pathan" is the Hindi and Urdu word for "Pashtun." "Afghan" was the Persian exonym (i.e., a name used by foreigners) for the Pashtuns. In the 1970s, the government of Afghanistan mandated that all its citizens be known as Afghans.

Back of Beyond"—that is, Central Asia. A call girl at the Kashmiri Gate is less impressed by Mahbub Ali, for she says, "That North country is full of horse-dealers as an old coat of lice." But Mahbub Ali is successful and well connected. He supplies remounts to the British Army and does a good business providing ponies to polo-mad officers who go into debt for the sake of their passion for the game.

Mahbub Ali is dismissive about the British ability to make a good trade at the horse fairs. There was that difference between a warrior buying a horse that would save his life and a remount major bargaining for a string of horses within his fixed budget. Whether a simple *chabuk suwar* (rough rider) or a lordly maharaja, Indians barely bargained for their purchases; they were expected to know the right value of the horse. The efficiency of local markets struck Charles Davidson, an English traveler. "I will tell you the truth, *bhai* [brother]," Davidson reported one Indian buyer saying, "I will give you 100 rupees." After a short discussion, the buyer and seller concluded the deal for 150 rupees and headed off to find a *shroff*, or banker, to get change and conclude the transaction. The British, by contrast, had a reputation for being cheap. Another British equestrian expert, John Pigott, admitted, "From the high estimation and great respect in which this horse is held by the natives, a Turkmen is rarely procured by Europeans, who, in general, decline them at [a] price equal to what a merchant can readily obtain from the opulent native." Dealers were reluctant to waste their time showing off their wares to British customers. A further difficulty faced the British: Indian buyers and sellers frequently resorted to secret hand signals during their negotiations or used a verbal code for numbers, so that only the dealers and customers in the know could follow the market prices. The Britons' ineptitude in open markets provided an opportunity for a trusted dealer like Mahbub Ali.

It was a source of frustration to the progress-minded British to be dependent on a people and culture they perceived as relics of ancient times. Afghan horse traders traveled constantly and mysteriously between Afghanistan and India. They could play the role of double or triple agent in the Great Game on behalf of Kabul, Bukhara, Calcutta, or St. Petersburg. Government officials of the Raj, as British India was called from 1858 until Indian independence in 1947, feared them, and sometimes tried to repress them. They knew that in the past, countless dealers, like Kipling's Mahbub Ali, had parlayed the horse business into a high position or even an empire in India. But such dealers were indispensable in providing these officials with precious insight into the politics of Afghanistan—over which the Raj exercised tutelary control—as well as up-to-date accounts of the menacing Russian advance toward the Oxus.

Kim takes place around the time of the Second Anglo-Afghan War (1878–80), when Russian advances into Central Asia were giving the British nightmares. In 1875, General M. I. Ivanin of the Russian General Staff did little to assuage British fears when he published a study of the campaigns of Genghis Khan, Timür, and Nader Shah, showing how a Central Asian army could conquer India. In that same year, the government in Calcutta got wind of a memorandum prepared by the swashbuckling Russian general Mikhail Skobelev, in which he proposed

> to organize masses of Asiatic cavalry which, to a cry of rapine and plunder, might be launched into India, as the vanguard, thus renewing the times of Timür. . . . The further operations of a Russian column from Kabul . . . might terminate in the presence of the Russian banners at Benares.

While the logistics of moving a modern army with its heavy weaponry and supplies across the steppe would be difficult—requiring up to thirty thousand camels—a cavalry force like that of Timür could still take India by storm. Calcutta did not know if their northern rivals would dare to launch such an audacious attack against them, but there were clear indications that the Russians aimed to conquer the sole remaining independent reserves of Central Asian horse power.

The Last Stand of the Turkmen

In 1875, one stretch of the steppe remained independent from the great settled empires: Turkmenistan. Here, horses as extraordinary as the blood-sweating ones of Wudi set off the final round of the Great Game.

Turkmenistan boasted some of the most inhospitable territory on the planet. In the previous century, a branch of the Oxus River had dried out before reaching the Caspian Sea, causing the land for miles around to turn into barren desert. The Turkmen expressly selected this territory for their homeland to avoid paying taxes to either the rulers of Khwarazm or the shahs of Iran. In such an environment, their only source of riches was slave raiding. They rode out into neighboring Iran or Russia, kidnapped villagers, tied up their captives behind their horses, and dragged them to the slave markets in Khwarazm, whose agriculture and handicrafts depended largely on enslaved workers. To carry out their cruel business, each of the Turkmen clans, the Ersari, the Yomut, and the Teke, bred their own exceptional horses. The most famous of these were the Akhal-Teke.

Travelers to Central Asia believed these horses to be descended from the blood-sweating horses of Ferghana. Raised by the Teke Turkmen in the oasis of Akhal, not far from the Iranian border, these extraordinary animals boasted "slender barrels, thick tails, handsome heads and necks and a particularly fine and glossy coat," according to the Hungarian explorer Arminius Vámbéry, who visited the steppe disguised as a Turkish dervish in the 1860s. A Russian equestrian expert went further: "They are a pure product of the desert, distinguished by their nobility, the beauty of their lines, well put together with excellent limbs, muscled, tall, 15 to 16 hands, and do good work under the saddle." The glossy coat, combined with their long lines and slender neck, reminded observers of a greyhound or a cheetah, both hunting animals. Because the breed was very lean, it did not require a lot of food to power itself. It could cope with the extreme climate of the Karakum Desert, where temperatures fell as low as minus 20 and rose to 120 degrees Fahrenheit. Raised in the family tents, the horse was "prized by the son of the desert more than his wife, more than his children, more than his life," added Vámbéry. As a result, the highly social Akhal-Teke was loyal to its rider. Stories were told of a wounded horse carrying two adult riders out of danger, even over shifting sands. In a horse race the animal would even try to bite and bring down opposing riders. The Akhal-Teke enabled the Turkmen to cross the waterless steppe, enter Russian or Iranian territory, and escape with their captives before anyone could catch up with

The Akhal-Teke's slender physique enables it to thrive in desert environments.

them. This more than compensated the Turkmen for the cost and effort of raising such a horse.*

In the face of the logistical difficulties and dangers of campaigning in the desert of Turkmenistan, Russia hesitated for a decade before taking action against the slave-raiding Turkmen. Worries about the British advancing from India spurred them into action. They knew that a British military mission in 1873 had explicitly recommended extending British protection over the Teke Turkmen, in order to secure superior remounts for India's cavalry. What's more, in 1878, Britain invaded Afghanistan in the Second Anglo-Afghan War, making the likelihood of their appearance on the Oxus ever more likely.

The ensuing Russian campaign of 1881, led by the swashbuckling

---

* The Akhal-Teke is still one of the world's most sought-after horses. Chinese president Xi Jinping, himself convinced that they are descendants of the blood-sweating horses of Ferghana, has collected fifty of them, mostly gifts from an admirer, the president of Turkmenistan.

Skobelev, set new standards for brutality, even for nineteenth-century colonial wars. The final stand of the Turkmens turned into such a bloodbath that Skobelev, the lionized hero of previous Russian victories, had to give up his command. But the Russians achieved their objectives: the last steppe horse breeders lost their independence; the prized Akhal-Teke and other prestigious Turkmen breeds fell into Russia's hands; the Great White Tsar won this round of the Great Game.

The loss of life and the high cost of these victories compelled the Russian military establishment to justify them. General Aleksey Nikolaevich Kuropatkin, governor-general of what was then called Russian Turkestan, argued: "The [Central Asian] horse will be, I am convinced, the jewel in the crown of Russia and its army. All the states of Europe will envy our [Central Asian] horse breeding, because none of them has the natural conditions favorable for a real war horse, and our country now has that in abundance with the infinite steppes." Whether Russia's bold steppe gambits would pay off as Kuropatkin expected, whether Britain's dogged persistence with Indian horses would pay for itself: these were questions that would await the twentieth century, with surprising answers.

March, Trot, Gallop, Charge

The last horse powers, 1890–1919

᠙

Breeding and Race

In the decades before the First World War, the armies of Europe were engaged in arms races of various kinds: warships, rifles, artillery, and, of course, horses—still absolutely essential to making war and projecting power. The Russians wanted to believe that the Akhal-Teke horse, and other famous Central Asia breeds, would give them an advantage in the competition for the best cavalry, a conviction that only increased when the Russians observed British buyers eagerly acquiring Akhal-Tekes in Iran and in Afghanistan. Even the Germans took interest in the Akhal-Teke, acquiring a prizewinning stallion as a stud for their cavalry in 1912. This made Russia all the more determined to develop the breed. In 1917, Prince Shcherbatov, chief of the imperial stud farm, grand chamberlain, and author of a book on Arab horses, introduced a stud book for the Akhal-Teke, the first of its kind in Asia. The Russian military tried hard to protect and promote their prized breeds, obtained with such expenditure of blood and gold, but they faced many headwinds.

For one, as the British had discovered with their earlier suppression of the Kathiawar raiders, pacification inevitably resulted in the deterioration of these breeds. Russia had conquered the Turkmen in part to put an end to their slave raiding. Once opportunities for kidnapping dried up, the rationale for raising such superior horses disappeared as well. "Only a tribe of plunderers and brigands needs to raise a horse like the Akhal-Teke," wrote one Russian animal husbandry expert. "It can save the life of its rider. It gives him power, influence, and riches. But when the country is pacified, there is no need for such a horse."

The Russians also exported too many horses from Central Asia to Europe. The coming of the railroad lowered transportation costs, so that by 1900, 360,000 Central Asian horses were sent west every year. Russian horse traders offered prices triple that of the local markets, which convinced many a khan to sell his otherwise favorite steed. This huge demand quickly depleted the stock of good steppe horses and threatened to ruin the local breeds.

Further, despite policies dating back to Catherine's time established in order to protect the horse breeders' way of life, Russia's late-nineteenth-century colonial practices systematically undermined the horse breeders. Russian agricultural colonies slowly took over steppe land, just as they had on the Don and the Volga one hundred years earlier. The price of forage increased. After a particularly bad zuid, in which large numbers of livestock died, many khans, unable to feed their herds, sold their best horses.

Faced with these threats to the newly conquered breeds, the Russian military came up with breeding schemes designed to preserve and even scale up the number of superior steppe horses. They hit on the idea of breeding rare Akhal-Tekes and other Turkmen stallions with the much more numerous Kazakh mares. The latter, raised in a semi-wild state, small, with long hair, a thick neck, and heavy feet, resembled tough Mongol horses, "seldom fed by hand, but accustomed to seeking subsistence in the pastures, summer and winter," as Vámbéry put it. But improving the Kazakh breed proved to be much more difficult in practice than it seemed on paper.

Initially the government established breeding stations on lands requisitioned from the Kazakhs, where they encouraged herders to bring their mares. These stations were few and far between, however; not surprisingly, the Kazakhs were unenthusiastic about traveling such distances. They also harbored reservations about a breeding program so different from their traditional ways. They were reluctant to let their mares be covered by pure-bred (i.e., heavily inbred) stallions, fearing that the crossbred offspring would be more costly to feed and less resistant to disease. The government tried offering a fee for each mare, to little avail, and then ordered the local khans to bring a fixed number of mares to each station. The khans complied by including mares that were either already pregnant or too young. Moreover, the ovulating mares were so unused to coupling in a stable that they refused to let themselves be covered by the stallion. The fertility rate of these breeding stations was only 5 percent, as compared to 50 percent in the open steppe. When the Russians tried to bring the stallions to mares in the pasture, instead of in the breeding stations, their efforts were equally unsuccessful. The stable-reared stallions, unused to the open space, fought with one another and lost weight without stable-provided forage. The Kazakhs also refused to bring in winter forage for the horses, since this was not their traditional way of managing the herds.

The Russians expressed bitter disappointment, attributing these failures to the "low level of civilization" of the Tatars. When the government sought to requisition Turkmen Yomut horses for breeding, instead, the Yomuts revolted and fled into Iran, where they live to this day. The government soon embarked on another effort, setting up its own stud farms. "The creation of these stables," wrote Count Vorontsov-Dashkov, a cavalry general and member the imperial privy council, "is to improve the local breeds by pairing mares with suitable stallions. By exploiting these mares, and the passion which the Kazakhs show for horses, we can hope to rapidly exploit a new source of remounts for our cavalry." The Russians created a stud farm in Ashqabad, the capital of today's Turkmenistan, to protect the Akhal-Teke breed, now menaced by uncontrolled crossbreeding and exports.

South of the Pamirs, decades of experimentation only deepened British disappointment with their own programs to breed warhorses. This reflected in no small part a prejudice that aligned with nineteenth-century scientific racism. The British believed as an article of faith that the Thoroughbred horse represented the ultimate degree of equine perfection. Thoroughbreds, whose stud books had been closed since the eighteenth century, were believed to be descended from just three storied racing stallions of Arab and Barbary stock. The English crossed the Thoroughbred stallion—valued for its beauty, intelligence, and speed—with sturdier mares to produce more workaday horses, like the Hackney, and so believed that a dose of Thoroughbred blood could improve any race. Early-nineteenth-century theories of racial inheritance taught that active stallions transmitted more of their traits to foals than did the passive mares, and that a good cavalry horse gained spirit from a high-strung and already overbred sire. Foreign buyers from France, Germany, and even Russia paid top prices for English and Irish racehorses, which confirmed the English in their sense of superiority.

Old India hands among the British knew that Sikh and Maratha maharajas considered their horses in no way inferior to those from overseas. In 1839, the British governor-general, Lord Auckland, asked the superintendent of the government stud farms, E. Gwatkin, to find a suitable gift for Ranjit Singh, the Sikh ruler and as fine a connoisseur of horses as anyone in India. This put Gwatkin in an awkward position, since Sikh and British tastes in horses were so different. The superintendent studied up on his subject, perusing Indian hippology manuals, most likely including the popular *Faras-nama-e Rangin, or The Book of the Horse*, written in 1795 by Sa'adat Yar Khan Rangin, a cavalry officer turned poet. Gwatkin might well have pondered Rangin's advice: different nations had their unique preferences when it came to horses. For instance, the Mughals feared feathers (i.e., whorls) on the forehead as inauspicious but saw a feather on the throat as very lucky; Rajputs disliked horses with a feather under the saddle, while Marathas considered a horse with a feather under the belly unlucky. Duly instructed, Gwatkin selected two horses from the stud farms under his care, explaining to Auckland that one of the horses had feathers "upon which Native Gentlemen set such a value." The other candidate "sported a *juwab* [a mole] on his near nostril . . . to render him valuable." Without these detailed explanations, Gwatkin feared, Auckland would find his two candidates highly unsuitable as diplomatic gifts, lacking barrel (too narrow-chested), and with short forelimbs. In the end, confused by the unfamiliar Indian criteria, Auckland decided that the safest bet for satisfying Ranjit Singh would be to present costly English carriage horses. The Sikh maharaja was delighted with their great size, calling them his little elephants, and gaily invited his entourage to come and admire them. But while the Indians might have appreciated the novelty value of these exotic gifts, the British never learned to appreciate storied Indian breeds like the Marwari or the Lakhi. Gwatkin even documented what he perceived as the shortcomings of Indian compared to English horses in a scholarly publication. The irony that Ranjit Singh had established an empire on Lakhi horses either did not occur to him or risked being irksome for his British readers.

To be fair, the British officers of the Indian cavalry needed bigger horses, as did all ranks in the European regiments* stationed in India. These riders were beefier than Indian horsemen, and they carried more kit: the former weighed in at 258 pounds fully equipped, versus 200 pounds for the latter. The British also rode long-legged in the saddle, so that on a small horse their stirrups risked scraping the ground. The Indian horsemen rode short-legged, like racing jockeys, so the size of the horse mattered less. British officers, who had to buy their own mounts, often went into debt to acquire suitably sized horses. A British lieutenant earning 273 pounds annually could expect to pay 50 pounds, or 800 rupees, per head; he often needed more than one mount. For the units recruited locally, like the reconstituted regiment of Skinner's Horse, troopers from horse-breeding backgrounds brought their own mounts, so the issue of size and cost did not arise. Maintaining heavier, costlier British regiments was a question not so much of racism as of internal security; their existence, however, was a constant reminder of India's dearth of locally bred big horses.

Throughout the nineteenth century, administrators of the Raj sought to bring British-inspired improvements to India, the livestock sector being no exception. A veterinary colonel, J.H.B. Hallen, successfully handled a dangerous cattle plague in Bombay, so in 1876, the Indian Army named him to the post of general superintendent of horse-breeding operations, with the mission of fixing the still underperforming, costly breeding program. Hallen's plan predictably echoed that of the Russians up north. The single, government-operated stud farm in Pusa would be replaced with a network of local breeders dispersed across the subcontinent. This would have the advantage of providing horses closer to various cantonments, rather than driving horses from Pusa, in Bihar, to far-flung regiments. The Afghan frontier, for example, was a thousand miles distant from the stud farm. This approach would also enable the British to exploit many

---

* In addition to the twenty-odd cavalry regiments raised locally but led by British officers, nine cavalry regiments from the United Kingdom were stationed across India, as were, indeed, several horse artillery units.

more Indian breeds, like the Kathiawar, the Marwari of Rajasthan, and the Lakhi of Punjab, as broodmares. Of course, large British stallions—Hackney or Thoroughbred—would be used for crossbreeding, and loaned to Indian breeders.

This scheme delivered meager results. The local agents responsible for managing government covering stations paid little attention to which mares would be allowed to mate. A prominent Rajput landowner could always use his influence to borrow the covering station for a time. Pairing large stallions with small mares worried the Indian breeders; traditionally, to ensure a safe pregnancy, a stallion smaller than the mare is preferred. The English, moreover, would not pay more for quality. Ultimately, they got the poor cooperation they deserved from the Indians and lost, in turn, their own enthusiasm about working with local breeders. Hallen, abashed, admitted in a scientific paper published in 1887 that it had all been an ill-judged fight with nature, and nature always wins.

For years, then, the Raj continued to import English stock into India at great expense, and persisted with unproductive crossbreeding efforts. They would have done well to recall Marco Polo's thirteenth-century observation that the Indian offspring of tall, foreign sires often grew to only middling height. It was the effect of the mare's heredity, overlooked by veterinary science of the time, as well as the diet and the breaking-in habits practiced in India. British racist assumptions about India and its horses complicated efforts to exploit India's local horse power.

An *Equus ex machina* saved the cavalry of the Raj. Already in the 1830s, the army had discovered that the bushwhackers of New South Wales, Australia, bred horses with many qualities desirable for patrolling the arid frontiers of Punjab. Descended from English stock, including Thoroughbreds and Hackneys, they grew strong bones on the calcium-rich soil of New South Wales and could go for long periods without water. Initially the Walers, as they were known, were as expensive to import as other foreign-bred animals. But as the steamship connection between Australia and India improved in the second half of the nineteenth century, the Walers proved to be a reliable and, at 600 to 700 rupees a head, competitively priced resource, especially when improved accounting revealed that the true cost of the government stud horse was close to 3,000 rupees per head. Imports of Walers to India rose from one thousand per year in the decade ending in 1870 to five thousand per year in the last decade before the outbreak of World War I. The imported Walers were geldings, which facilitated their transportation. The docile Australians put up with the long voyage with few complaints, no biting, and no kicking. On land they did not need to be hobbled, and they could feed without unbitting. But only the white troopers took to the Walers; local regiments refused to ride geldings, which they considered unmanly, ignoring, perhaps, the success of Genghis Khan on such horses. Walers soon became the backbone of the British cavalry in India, solving the decades-old problems of local breeding.

In one sense, even without racist attitudes, the Russians and the steppe peoples, the British and the Indians would always have been at cross-purposes in their horse breeding. The Turkmen and the Marathas found their horses suitable because they could manage long marches on little food. European cavalry was not expected to cover so much ground in one march but needed heavy, strong, and fast horses for the shock of the final cavalry charge—that nearly sacred event in the career of a cavalry trooper. In fact, the cavalry almost never actually ran into the defenders' line; it attempted to break the defense's morale with a superior show of force. This required heavy horses and perfect alignments. The European cavalry also strove to have each regiment mounted on only horses of the same color. This practice lapsed among the line cavalry, but among elite units, the uniform-colored mounts gave the attacking regiments the appearance of an invincible force of nature. And then there was always the matter of size. The Europeans wanted horses no less than fifteen hands high, while most Kazakh and Marwari horses stood under thirteen hands. Colonial attempts to exploit Asia's horse power foundered for the same reasons that colonialism itself failed. The colonial powers lacked the wisdom of Kipling's Mahbub Ali:

> The wise man knows horses are good—that there is a profit to be made from all. Now manifestly a Kathiawar mare taken from the sands of her birthplace and removed to the west of Bengal founders—nor is even a Balkh stallion of any account in the great Northern deserts. Therefore I say in my heart . . . each has merit in its own country.

Imperial High Noon

In 1900, Russia remained Asia's and the world's foremost cavalry power, despite disappointing returns from its costly conquest of the Turkmen horses. In this respect their experience was not so different from that of Wudi, whose pursuit of the blood-sweating horses signaled more his determination to assert hegemony than any tactical advantage of having better broodmares. Still, no one observing the cavalry of the Imperial Guard, superbly mounted on their rare and coveted Akhal-Tekes, could have any doubt about Russia's cavalry force. The Russian empire mustered two hundred thousand European cavalry and another two hundred thousand from the steppe heritage: Cossack and Tatar. Since the days of Qianlong, the Mughal Akbar, and Taizong of the Tang, no one had fielded as many mounted troops. The regular cavalry could count on seven hundred thousand horses plus fifty thousand remounts a year. These numbers had more than doubled in the fifty years since Russia had taken control of the steppes, meaning that their steppe conquests had at least made up in numbers what the equine connoisseurs considered to be a loss of quality. One of Russia's great horse experts, Sultan Kilich Giray, himself a descendant of Genghis Khan, boasted about the unbeatable combination of steppe breeds with English Thoroughbred blood. It was an exaggeration that expressed the sense of invincibility prevalent among Russia's cavalry officers.

The British Army in India aimed to hold off that fraction of Russia's overwhelming numbers that could be transported across Afghanistan in the event the Great Game turned into a major war. They fielded sixty thousand sabers with around a hundred thousand horses, resupplied with ten thousand remounts a year, about half of these from Australia. The cavalry was organized into twenty-nine regular, British-officered regiments; twenty regiments raised by Britain's former rivals, including Gwalior, Indore, Baroda, and Sikh Patiala; and an additional twenty auxiliary regiments mostly assigned to police operations. On top of this were the horse artillery units and British or Irish regiments on rotation to India.

Feeling confident in their ability to resist Russian invasion, the British rulers of the Raj spent the turn of the twentieth century asserting their claim to the legacy of the Mughal Empire. They restored the Taj Mahal, fallen into ruin after a hundred years of neglect, to send a strong message about the continuity between the new empire to the old. They transferred the capital of the Raj from commercial Calcutta to Shah Jahan's imperial Delhi. Finally, in 1911, they organized the state visit of King George V, featuring a Mughal-style court ceremony, the *durbar*, to which three hundred maharajas and nawabs presented themselves "in the stirrup" to salute George as emperor of India. The king-emperor rode into Shah Jahan's Red Fort on a coal-black waler. Many spectators, assuming the monarch would proceed on an elephant, like the Mughals of old, missed his entry entirely. The Indian princes came with their own cavalry regiments, integrated into the British Army but independently recruited and officered. All told, ten thousand horsemen, including a reconstituted Skinner's Horse, Holkar's Indore Lancers, and Scindia's Gwalior Lancers, "completely clad in chain armour and carrying spears like knights of old," churned up the dust of the durbar grounds. The march-past gave the public the opportunity to admire how finely the princely cavalry was turned out, in their brightly colored kurtas and turbans. The local breeds, Marwari or Lakhi horses, ridden by these regiments sported all kinds of coat coloring: piebald, white with pink points, and black with a white blaze, in contrast to the uniform chestnut or

Lancers on parade during the 1911 durbar.

bay color of the Walers ridden by British units. All trotted by in brigade formation, their sabers flashing, lance pinions flapping.

Following this display, select units performed the gallop-past, demonstrating the devil-take-the-hindmost spirit of both horses and riders. This could have resulted in life-threatening injuries, but in the end only two horsemen stumbled. The crowds cheered the teenaged maharaja of Jodhpur on his white Marwari horse in high Rajput riding style. The next day, polo matches and horse races pitted the British-officered units against the princes' horsemen. The British prevailed at polo, but the four-and-a-half-mile cross-country race was won by a rider from the maharaja of Patiala's Sikh lancers.

The irony was not lost on spectators that these princes' forefathers and their horsemen had not played polo against the British but, rather, fought many bloody battles against them. Though his great-grandfather Dawlatrao Scindia had been Britain's fiercest foe, the current Maharaja Scindia of Gwalior now sported the scarlet uniform of a British major general. An imperial aide-de-camp, the nawab of Rampur, traced his descent from the Indo-Afghan pillagers of the Mughal Empire. As their horsemen paraded in front of King-Emperor George, the Maratha maharaja Gaekwad of Baroda turned his back abruptly on the monarch, suggesting simmering resentment against British rule. The Raj was scandalized and later demanded a written apology from Gaekwad. A growing number of the Indian public, though, sympathized with the maharaja. They wondered why the British Army cost India 27 million rupees annually, almost double the cost of twenty years before—"the most expensive army in the world for the poorest people in the world,"[*] as His Majesty's opposition in Westminster put it. Already in 1903, the prime minister, Arthur Balfour, had admitted that the Great Game was just that, a game: "I think that a war between Russia and Great Britain is to the last degree improbable." Perhaps the Indian public wondered, What was this display of horse power for, after all?

---

[*] Despite India's great wealth, on a per capita basis it was one of the poorest countries in the world at that time.

World War I

The answer was not long in coming. By 1914, events in Europe had pushed Russia and Great Britain into an alliance against an aggressive Germany and its ally Austria. Their Asian cavalries would be deployed not against one another in the Khyber Pass but on battlefields far from Central Asia: Prussia, Galicia, Flanders, Iraq, and Palestine, the latter two theaters of operation resulting from Ottoman Turkey throwing its lot in with Germany.

In the years leading up to World War I, horses still held great value for the two empires. Despite predictions that the machine gun, the repeater rifle, and rapid-fire shrapnel artillery would banish the horse from the battlefield, the experience of warfare at the turn of the century suggested there would still be a role for horses. Britain's war in South Africa with the Boers in 1899–1902 and Russia's 1904–05 war with Japan had shown that cavalry could still act decisively on the battlefield, though more as a means of mobility than as shock troops; soldiers dismounted to use their weapons. Also, armies using artillery and machine guns required immense trains of horses to pull their ammunition wagons into battle. An army corps of seventy thousand soldiers required twenty-one thousand horses to move.

All in all, the Russians mobilized over a million horses in 1914, with over half of these coming from Cossack breeders and former steppe lands. The size of this cavalry force, and the number of Tatar troopers it included, gave the opposing generals in Berlin and Vienna sleepless nights as they recalled the invasions of the Mongols, seven hundred years before. They fearfully talked about "the Russian Steam Roller."

The Russians failed to steamroll over the Germans and Austrians, but this was not the fault of the horses. The irony of Russia's horse power was that it was ideally suited to a rapid campaign into Germany and Austria, but it took too long to reach the field. The Russian army needed weeks to mobilize its cavalry from the far-flung regimental depots of the empire and deploy them on the German border. Bringing a regiment of, for example, one thousand horses by train from the Volga region took as many train cars as one division of infantry, or twenty thousand soldiers. Russia's spectacular defeat at the Battle of the Masurian Lakes at the outbreak of the war was in part due to their advancing into enemy territory before the screen of cavalry—which an army needed in the days before aerial reconnaissance to "see" the enemy—was available. Even completely constituted regiments required at least six months for both horses and riders to reach conditioning for battle. The great steppe conqueror Genghis Khan had ridden to war when his horses were ready; by the time Russia's cavalry was ready, the opportunity for a rapid breakout had passed. Subsequently, much of the disappointing performance of cavalry in the Great War arose from the fact that it was long held in reserve, and so never attained critical physical conditioning. In Europe, as opposed to the steppe, horses were very expensive to feed, even more so when properly exercised. Wartime demand for horses also raised their price, from an average of 50 rubles to 2,000 in Russia—making it even more difficult to keep the cavalry arm properly mounted.

The British Army of India enjoyed somewhat more success with its cavalry in the First World War. Since the army had originally been created to defend India against Russian or Afghan invasion, at first there were no plans to deploy these forces outside the subcontinent. As hopes of a quick victory against Germany faded in the winter of 1914–15, however, the Indian Army received instructions to send contingents of cavalry to France. The Germans tried to instigate an Afghan attack on India in order to tie down this expeditionary force, to no avail, though Afghanistan's Anglophile Amir Habibullah was assassinated by factions hostile to the British.

With the western front already defended by four hundred miles of trenches and barbed wire, not to mention the mud and rain, the scope for a cavalry breakout was limited. After a few months of dismounted trench combat, the Indian cavalry subsequently received orders to redeploy to Iraq and Palestine, against Ottoman Turkey. On both these fronts, with room to maneuver and a suitable climate for horses, the Indian cavalry proved eminently useful.

Their finest moment came in Palestine in 1918, when Indian and Australian cavalry broke through Ottoman lines at the Battle of Megiddo, rode breakneck for forty miles, encircled the enemy, and entered triumphantly into Damascus. Named after the nearby site of an Egyptian chariot victory nearly thirty-four hundred years earlier, Megiddo was one of the last large, decisive cavalry engagements in history (it is also called the Battle of

Armageddon). In addition to the imperial cavalry, British ally Amir Feisal of Mecca deployed both horse-riding and camel-riding Bedouins for reconnaissance, sabotage, and harassment of the Turks, advised and assisted by Colonel T. E. Lawrence. Oddly for an ancient nation of steppe peoples, the Turkish cavalry played scarcely any role in these campaigns.

The Palestine campaign is notable for a much more significant event than this last cavalry battle—an event in which Lawrence had just as much a hand as he had in directing the Arab Revolt against the Turks, and one that would sound the last post for the horse in combat. Though popularly imagined as an atavistic dreamer charging on his Arab mare at the Turkish lines, Lawrence "of Arabia" harbored a deep fascination with modern technology. He experimented with aircraft to perform reconnaissance over enemy lines, and then learned how to coordinate aircraft bombing and cavalry charges simultaneously, in what later became known as combined operations or, indeed, Blitzkrieg. He even learned to fly. The Royal Air Force made a certain number of planes available to him. After the Battle of Megiddo, the RAF attacked the fleeing Turks from the air. Nine tons of bombs were dropped on the Turkish columns. "When the smoke had cleared it was seen that the organization of the enemy had melted away," wrote Lawrence in his memoirs, *Revolt in the Desert*. "They were a dispersed horde of trembling individuals, hiding for their lives in every fold of the vast hills." The innovative Lawrence also deployed armored cars as part of his Arab Corps. Palestine, with its deserts and blue skies, proved to be a better place to introduce modern technology than the western front, where mud, rain, and clouds made the early exponents of Blitzkrieg look like unrealistic visionaries. Lawrence later recommended to the Colonial Office, responsible for imperial security, that the RAF be used instead of boots on the ground to police Britain's Asian empire. The authorities took note.

The Last Post on the Khyber Pass

The guns had scarcely fallen silent in the Middle East when, in 1919, Skinner's Horse found themselves fighting off an invasion of Afghan Ghilzai warriors swarming across the Khyber Pass for the first time in more than a century. Skinner's regiment was not at full strength. It contained many recent, untried recruits as a result of suffering heavy casualties in France and Iraq. The Afghans knew this; it was for precisely this reason that they had decided to make their move now. The Ghilzai warriors were primarily interested in plunder and a chance to demonstrate their warrior bravado. In Kabul, the newly proclaimed king of Afghanistan, Amanullah, hoped to exploit the weakness of British India to redraw the political map of Asia and to avoid the fate of his father, Habibullah, who had paid with his life for his pro-British sympathies. Amanullah was supported by Soviet Russia, after informing their ambassador that he himself, a descendant of Ahmad Shah, was a Bolshevik. Kabul enjoyed the sympathy of the border clans, who had traditionally controlled access to the Khyber Pass and regularly raided British-controlled territories. In addition, Amanullah hoped that the ethnic-Afghan auxiliary troops in British pay would switch sides, just like their ancestors had in the eighteenth-century wars. If the Afghan invaders could provoke a general frontier uprising against British rule, they believed, they could achieve their aims, throwing off British influence over Kabul, recovering territories lost to the British in the nineteenth century,[*] and, perhaps, even provoking an India-wide revolt against British rule.

Skinner's Horse was deployed out of its cantonment, just sixty miles east of the Khyber Pass, and rode forward to engage the Afghans. After a hundred years of waiting for an invasion on the North-West Frontier, British India was finally defending itself against the descendants of Ahmad Shah, Nader Shah, Babur, and Timür. The role of horses, however, had changed since the times of the great Asian conquerors.

The Afghans could no longer surge into India like an unstoppable wave. In Ahmad Shah's days, two hundred thousand troopers had followed their ruler, mounted on superb Turkmen horses. But since the Russian annexation of Central Asia, Afghan trade and prosperity, based for centuries on the horse trade, had dwindled. Of the fifty thousand troops in the regular army, only half were mounted, and on inferior horses. They mostly fought on foot. That made sense in the mountainous terrain of the Khyber Pass, but dimmed any hope of a breakthrough on the plains. The Afghans had

[*]   More precisely, these territories, including Peshawar, were lost to the Sikhs and absorbed by the British. This remains a bone of contention between modern Afghanistan and Pakistan.

not seen combat against an organized foe since the Second Anglo-Afghan War, forty years earlier, so both discipline and conditioning were poor. The Afghans could not hope to achieve crushing victories like those of their ancestors at Panipat. The best outcome would be to make the British seriously lose face, and hope that wider disturbances undermine the Raj. This they nearly achieved.

While the British initially succeeded in driving the Ghilzai tribesmen back across the border, their base camp sat in an exposed position below the Khyber Pass, from where the Afghan army could rain down artillery fire. Pinned down, the troops were unable to riposte, but withdrawing to a safer position was unthinkable. Their prestige was at stake. The loyalty of frontier peoples under British control was wavering. Despite British tactical successes, their situation remained critical.

For victory in this conflict, Britain did not rely on cold steel or horse power, although afterward they would boast of having made one last combat charge. The RAF, following T. E. Lawrence's recommendations, had deployed to India several squadrons of BE2s.* These now bombed the exposed groups of Afghans on the hills around the Khyber. The bombing interrupted the distribution of weapons by the Kabul government to the Ghilzais, who then refused to concentrate in any number, reducing their combat effectiveness. Additional raids over Jalalabad demoralized the Afghans. Soldiers, officials, and civilians abandoned the ravaged city. Occasionally the sharp-shooting Afghans managed to bring down BE2s with rifle fire, presaging the exploits of their grandchildren against Soviet and American helicopters. The worst was yet to come for the Afghans, however. The RAF flew sorties over Kabul, three hundred miles from their base, and dropped bombs on the royal palace.

Although some Afghan forces made progress against the British at other points on the front, the experience of being bombed from the air, powerless to riposte, changed everything in the mind of King Amanullah. The aim of this war was to assert his prestige and to damage that of the British. Now, with his palace in flames in full sight of the people of Kabul, his very throne was at risk. The king and his counselors demanded a truce. The

---

* The BE-2 was an antiquated biplane that first flew at the time of the imperial durbar.

peace treaty that ended what would be called the Third Anglo-Afghan War led to very little political or territorial change, though Britain did renounce all influence over Afghan affairs. Afghanistan spitefully banned the export of horses to British India, a moribund trade since the Word War and the Bolshevik takeover of Central Asia.

And so, by the 1920s, Lahore's fabled Kashmir caravansary became a pale shadow of what it had been in Kipling's time.[*] A visitor of this period reported seeing the Afghan horse dealers still sitting beside rows of horses tethered in the courtyard, in the cool of the caravansary's walls, but only local breeds were for sale. One of the real Mahbub Ali's grandsons had been sent to Cambridge to study veterinary science, and returned to the family business in Lahore, but shortly thereafter the family firm went under. He was left with only stories about the lost splendor of the family fortune made famous by Kipling.

Twenty years later, in 1941, Skinner's Horse shuttled twenty-two hundred miles from the Khyber Pass to Burma, where they bade their horses good-bye and got acquainted with a new, mechanical mount: the battle tank. The age of horse power itself had ended, and petroleum, not grasslands, became the strategic resource that both enabled empires and was indispensable to their defense. Already in 1912, as First Lord of the Admiralty, Winston Churchill had decided to replace coal with petroleum in the British navy, committing Britain to a policy of controlling the world's petroleum supplies. This is why he was determined to fight the Turks for control of Iraq's petroleum in the First World War, and to defend Burma against the Japanese to retain the petroleum of Southeast Asia in the Second. Genghis Khan, Timür, and Nader Shah suddenly seemed as remote as the Paleozoic forests. In a fine irony, geologists found the new black gold underneath the old steppe lands in Iraq, Arabia, Iran, Kazakhstan, and Azerbaijan.

The children of the twentieth century struggle to imagine a transition away from petroleum, whose dominance looks to last for no more than 150 years. We can scarcely conceive, then, the upheaval that accompanied

[*] According to *Pakistan Today* (January 11, 2021), there is still a bazaar here. A few Afghan families live in the neighborhood. Central Asian merchandise has been replaced by Chinese mass-produced exports, brought over the Karakoram Highway by today's truck-driving Powindah.

the disappearance of our three-thousand-year-long reliance on the horse. Horses had powered the empires of Persia, India, China, and Russia. The horse trade had united the peoples of Eurasia in a vast market for livestock. Herders and aristocrats from one end of Asia to the other had shared the cult of the horse. Now the flow of caravans crisscrossing the steppes ceased. Central Asia, once a wealthy emporium, became one of the most isolated and impoverished regions on earth. Horse-riding aristocrats like Sultan Kilich Giray and Prince Shcherbatov had no role in Soviet Russia. The Qing bannermen sank into obscurity in Republican China. In 1971, India's prime minister, Indira Gandhi, would tip into the dustbin of history the maharajas of Indore, Gwalior, and Mysore. Only in one country did the horse maintain its social importance and economic value: the Land of the Horsemen, Afghanistan.

Epilogue

A royal Buzkashi game, 1950–1973

༄

D espite his smart British-style general officer's uniform, Afghanistan's King Zaher Shah, with his thick-lensed wire-rimmed glasses, looked more like the graduate of the Institut Pasteur he was than the steppe warriors from whom he had inherited his throne. He sat in the front row of the royal stand, smiling and peering out at the sports field, surrounded by courtiers in Astrakhan wool hats and dark glasses. Members of the diplomatic corps had brought their wives, whose bare arms and bright dresses contrasted sharply with the somber overcoats of the otherwise all-male spectators in the royal stand. On either side of the stand, Kabulis of every description thronged at the barrier to get a glimpse of the wide-open playing field. Most spectators sported traditional dress, ample tunics and trousers, though government officials and schoolteachers wore jackets over their tunics. It was better to be stuck behind an Uzbek, with his four-sided woven skullcap, than a Pashtun, with his voluminously folded turban.

They were watching an equestrian game, brought specially by the king to Kabul from the north of Afghanistan. He had sent buses to transport the players and their horses from steppe country: Maimana, Kunduz, and Mazar-e Sharif. The players were all hard-riding Uzbeks, breeders of superior horses, who had brought the game and the horses from their native Bukhara after the Soviets took over. The Kabulis were unfamiliar with this sport, but since public amusements in the 1950s and '60s were few and the presence of the king lent it prestige, eager spectators mobbed the entry gates. This was same game that William Moorcroft had described in Bukhara 130 years earlier: buzkashi.

Zaher Shah on horseback, 1940.

The king loved displays of horsemanship. During a royal visit to the
north, he had been so captivated by this traditional steppe game that he
had invited these competitors to Kabul in celebration of his October birthday. The game the king had enjoyed up north was more of a violent brawl
between hundreds of horsemen for control of an animal carcass, usually a
calf, not the traditional goat. That version was unsuitable for spectators,
because it had no rules and no defined playing field. Neither did it have
prizes or even teams. It was played like the children's game King of the Hill,
to show off which rider had more strength, which horse had more fight.

The polo-riding king and his court devised rules appropriate for a sport
to be watched and enjoyed by a more sophisticated public. The playing
field, laid out on the grounds of the Kabul Golf Club, was fixed at about one
hundred yards square, almost twice as large as a football field. At one end
stood a ring of ankle-high stones, known as the circle of truth. The flag of
Afghanistan, black, red, and green, flew from a mast at the opposite end.

The object of the game was to seize a 120-pound carcass off the ground in the circle of truth, gallop faster than one's pursuers with the carcass slung over the saddle, get around the flag, and return, depositing the carcass back inside the circle of truth. This resulted in a score. Two teams of five riders disputed possession of the carcass with their whips, and the horses' hooves and teeth. The team with the most goals after two parts of forty-five minutes each was declared the winner, and received handsome prizes from the king, including saddles, bridles, and other princely horse tack.

At first, the players did not understand these alien rules very well. Being confined on a playing field struck them as odd, since in their native steppe the play sprawled without boundaries. Hence, during the royal game, riders dashed over the barriers and plowed their way through the spectators, even though the royal attendants admonished them about the danger and the unsightliness of this behavior in the eyes of the king and the foreign visitors. The riders also felt uncomfortable wearing livery, or even being on the same team as other riders, with whom they had often battled to the bitter end in the free-for-alls that constituted their regional pastime.

The golf course venue, the rule book, the livery, and even the few women spectators showed how Zaher Shah hoped to impress on his people his success at marrying tradition and modernity. Twenty-one rulers had preceded him on the throne first occupied by Ahmad Shah Durrani in the eighteenth century, often for very brief reigns. That bespoke a political culture as violent and unpredictable as the cut and thrust of goat dragging. Now the royal throne wobbled between the insistence of the rural chiefs and religious leaders that nothing should change in Afghanistan and the aspirations of many urban Kabulis that everything had to change. Through spectacles like the buzkashi game, the king hoped to assert a common ground, a vision of Afghanistan with an ancient past, yet one whose beauty and courage could be admired by all.

The Afghans began to call buzkashi their national game, even though it had never been played by anyone but the Uzbeks in the north. Zaher Shah chose it because for all the divisions that racked and still rack this country with seven main languages, religious schisms, tribal vendettas, and increasingly unreconcilable political orientations, a love of horses united Afghans. After all, the Afghans, in the broadest historical and geographic sense, were the ancient Aśvakas, the masters of the horse. In the twentieth century, buzkashi alone expressed that two-millennia-old tradition.

Twentieth-century geopolitics had isolated Afghanistan and left it the only refuge for the horse breeders of the steppe. The once-fabled markets of Kabul no longer thronged with horse traders from Bukhara, Turfan, or Lahore. The British bombs of 1919 had destroyed the ancient caravansaries. The trade routes themselves had disappeared. The Soviets along the Oxus River, the People's Republic across the Pamirs, and Pakistan on the Indus had all shut their borders with Afghanistan. The country had for centuries thrived as a wayfaring stage for horses to cross the Hindu Kush with migrating raiders, rulers, or traders. Afghanistan was now reduced to a backwater.

The closing of the borders accompanied the suppression of pastoralism. The new Soviet republics of Turkmenistan, Kazakhstan, Kyrgyzstan, and Uzbekistan encouraged their respective horse breeders to become sedentary. Flocks of animals became state property, with only a few herders to watch over them. The Soviets believed that in the absence of clan conflict, there was no need to have so many herders per flock. The former herders were supposed to grow cash crops like cotton on new, ambitious irrigation projects. This eliminated the need for horses, which were sent for slaughter. Horse-breeding families had to learn to live without a horse, where before no one had ever walked on foot to get anywhere. The Soviets' collectivization experiment succeeded as badly for pastoralism as it did generally for agriculture. In the absence of the watchful eye of the mounted herder, guarding his own family's flocks, animals began to disappear. Wolves ate them. Soviet-American anthropologist Anatoly Khazanov tells of a Kazakh work group that received a prize for managing to migrate a large herd with four trucks. Khazanov reminded the foreman that in the days before collectivization, the same size herd used to be managed by a single horseman and his son. The foreman replied, without batting an eye, "But in those days the herd belonged to the horseman." Now that the animals belonged to everyone and therefore no one, the herders, too, butchered horses for meat.

The difficulty of following traditional migration routes without sufficient horses also led to mass livestock losses, and after a zuid, there was little incentive to rebuild the herds. The total livestock of Kazakhstan dropped from thirty-six million animals in 1928 to three million in 1932. Mongolia, thanks to Soviet advisers, had a similar experience. The horse breeds of Central Asia—Kyrgyz, Turkmen, Akhal-Teke, and Karabair—declined dramatically, in both numbers and quality, to general indifference. In Iran, a new regime founded by Iranian nationalists likewise tried to force the horse breeders to settle, not so much in order to impose collectivization but to break their political power. The khans were arrested, the horse breeders' weapons were confiscated, and poor farmland was hastily assigned to the herding families to plow. The results resembled those experienced by the Soviet Union. The pastoralists became impoverished, and Iran lost its livestock industry. Turkmen fled from Iran and the Soviet Union; Uzbeks and Kyrgyz fled from the Soviet Union and China. Afghanistan offered them a refuge.

Afghanistan alone, of the countries mentioned here, did not pursue any social engineering in the countryside, until the Communist-inspired revolution in 1978. The writ of the king lay very lightly on the border provinces. The refugee Uzbeks found their fellow horsemen installed on the steppe of northern Afghanistan, where they were welcomed. Having brought their prized horses with them, they made a living breeding and training them.

The buyers were no longer Indian maharajas but wealthy landowners, khans and beys, who increasingly drew wealth from the nascent modern economy of Afghanistan but for whom fine horses served as a precious reminder of their steppe traditions. The wealthiest men in the north competed to see who could raise the finest horses. These horses resembled the prized Turkmens praised by Vámbéry in the 1860s. They stood eighteen or even nineteen hands high, veritable giants. The prices of these horses rose to equally stratospheric heights, as much as 100,000 rupees (about $20,000 in the 1960s; in 2018, such horses fetched up to $100,000). It was not rare for wealthy breeders to keep one hundred such horses. Like the fabled blood-sweating horses of Wudi, like the Akhal-Teke, these horses were pampered, like children in a loving family. A dedicated syce, or groom, took them for exercise every day, watched over their diet, cooled them down after strenuous training, and calmed their nerves after combat.

The *chapandaz*, or buzkashi player, drilled his horses as exactingly as a soccer coach trains his players, and in much the same way. Horses practiced feinting, turning, defending, attacking. Sometimes the chapandaz galloped their horses into a copse and forced them to charge at trees, avoiding impact by swerving only at the last second, now to the left, now to the right. The horses underwent seven years of preparation before performing for up to twenty years. (Unusually for an athlete, the chapandaz at forty years old was considered at the peak of his career.) During the spring and summer, the horses put on fat and were ridden little. In the fall, they were switched to a rigorous diet and a high-calorie-burning, four-hour-a-day workout, to harden their muscles. After the workout they were given nothing to drink or eat until they entirely cooled down. This preparation produced superbly athletic horses who played the game with the same intensity and desire to win as their chapandaz.

Buzkashi has survived the Zaher Shah's exile in 1973, the Soviet invasion in 1979, the American occupation in 2001, and the return of the Taliban in 2022. In the land of the horsemen, the buzkashi horse, the arghamak, the blood-sweating horse, and the thousand-li horse remain deeply entangled with human beings in a way the rest of us struggle to imagine. We may even

Buzkashi competitors follow the play to the farthest horizons.

try to experience Afghan horsemanship up close, but this is easier said than done. If a Westerner tells you they played buzkashi in Afghanistan, in most cases that means that they watched the game played. Since in the countryside there is no field and no circle of truth, the only way to watch the game is to join on horseback. The difference between the spectator and the player is how close they get to the carcass. In the eye of the storm, thousand-pound horses hurtle themselves at you, biting and kicking, while raging riders strike each other and the other horses with their plaited leather whips. In this version of the game, the aim is for the rider with the carcass to cut his way out of the scrum and gallop free of any pursuers, before declaring victory by dropping the carcass back down. The game goes on as long as riders stay in the saddle: for many hours or even several days. Since the foreigners cannot keep up with these rapid horsemen, they are left watching the competitors disappear over the horizon with the carcass, the cyclone of flashing hooves, dust clouds, and cracking whips spinning and vanishing into the freedom of the limitless steppe.

ACKNOWLEDGMENTS

I would like to thank, first of all, Peter and Amy Bernstein for persisting in support of this project from its earliest stages, as well as Peter Gordon, who first suggested that the topic would make a worthwhile book, and Richard Bernstein, who stopped me from channeling Charles Doughty for my writing style. Jamie Greenbaum, Julie Sullivan, Luo Qi, Daniel Potts, and Wheeler Thackston have been unstinting in their support with Chinese and Persian texts and history. Alexander Morrison shared his views on Russia's expansion in Central Asia. Mike Barry reminded me that Afghanistan means "the land of the horsemen." Laerke Recht, Katherine Kanne, and Igor Chechushkov shared their enthusiasm for Bronze Age horses, while Araz Imamov, Ömer Karabey, and Ayako Kaiho conveyed their enthusiasm for horses they ride today. Assiduous readers and thoughtful critics included Joe Kolman, Charles Trueheart, George Foy, and Wiley Wood, who took time away from their own projects to provide thoughtful criticism. Librarians in the British Library, the Fundação Oriente in Lisbon, BULAC (Paris), the Bibliothéque Nationale de France, and the American Library in Paris all did what librarian do expertly: help you find the right books. I have been fortunate with erudite traveling companions, including members of the Royal Society for Asian Affairs during our 2018 trip to Xinjiang. Some companions are now missing: Roger Covey, founder of the Tang Research Foundation, together with whom I had hoped to explore Central Asia; Derrick Wong, tireless traveler to Azerbaijan and Uzbekistan; and, most poignantly, Marguerite Yates, *hayat yoldaşım*—my companion on the road of life.

APPENDIX: A NOTE ON MONEY

India, one of the largest markets for horses, used the silver rupee for centuries, a coin weighing approximately 10 grams, or .35 ounces. If an ordinary horse sold for 200 rupees, then we can express its value as follows:

- 2 kilos of silver, or 70 ounces
- USD 1,400 at silver prices at the time of writing
- a little less than double the annual income of an urban laborer's family in former times (1,200 grams of silver)

In purchasing power parity for today's equivalent household in India, an ordinary horse would be worth about USD 5,000.

For China during the Tang era, silk was used to buy a horse. Twenty standardized bolts of silk bought an ordinary horse. But one bolt also had a metal, monetary equivalent, about 20 grams of silver. Hence for Chinese horses we have the following values:

- 400 grams of silver, or 14 ounces
- USD 276 at current silver prices
- a little more than half the annual income of an urban laborer's family (744 grams of silver)

Monetary incomes were much lower in China than in India, so a horse, even at a lower price, was still worth a great deal in China. In purchasing-power parity for today's equivalent household in China, an ordinary horse would be worth about USD 4,400.

In sixteenth-century Russia, a horse cost 20 rubles; at that time a ruble contained 68 grams of silver, hence:

- 1,360 grams of silver, or 48 ounces
- USD 947 at current silver prices
- approximately the annual earnings of an urban artisan

This would be the equivalent of USD 10,000 to USD 12,000 at current purchasing power.

Sources

Ban Gu, *Food and Money in Ancient China: The Earliest Economic History of China to A.D. 25.* Trans. Nancy Lee Swann (Princeton, NJ: Princeton University Press, 1950).

Haider, Najaf. "Prices and Wages in India (1200–1800): Source Material, Historiography and New Directions." Paper presented at Towards a Global History of Prices and Wages, Utrecht, August 2004 (New Delhi, 2004). Available at http://www.iisg.nl/hpw/papers/haider/pdf. 2004.

Mironov, Boris N. "Wages and Prices in Imperial Russia, 1703–1913." *Russian Review* 69, no. 1 (January 2010): 47–72.

Naqvi, Hamida Khatoon. "A Study of Urban Centres and Industries in the Central Provinces of the Mughal Empire Between 1556 and 1803." PhD diss., University of London, School of Oriental and African Studies, 1965. ProQuest Dissertations Publishing; https://doi.org/10.25501/SOAS.00033929.

van Leeuwen, Bas, Jieli van Leeuwen-Li, and Reinhard Pirngruber. "The Standard of Living in Ancient Societies: A Comparison Between the Han Empire, the Roman Empire, and Babylonia." Working Papers, Utrecht University, Centre for Global Economic History, 0045. 2013.

TIME LINE

		Western Steppe	Sub-continent	Eastern Steppe	Horses
20,000 BCE	*Ice Age*	*Equus gallicus* roams around western Europe			11 hands high, more like an antelope, dun-colored
5000 BCE	*Neolithic*	Horses hunted on the steppe			
2500 BCE	*Bronze Age*	Horses domesticated			Coat colors vary, reduction in Y haplogroups
1800 BCE	*Bronze Age*	Chariot-driving warriors appear			12–13 hands high
1200 BCE	*Iron Age*	Mounted archers		Shang dynasty chariot drivers	
700 BCE	*First Empires*	Medes and Scythians serve the Assyrians	Scythians settle in NW India	Dog Rong fight the Zhou dynasty	
500 BCE	*First Empires*	Cyrus the Persian conquers western Asia			14 hands high, stabled, warhorses, equestrianism

		Western Steppe	Sub-continent	Eastern Steppe	Horses
400 BCE	*First Empires*	Persian Empire	Mauryan Empire	Scythians infiltrate the Warring States	
200 BCE	*First Empires*			The First Emperor unifies China	
100 BCE	*First Steppe Empire*			The Han and the Huns are rivals	
100 CE	*The Silk Road*		Kushans establish trading empire		16 hands high, specific breeding, reduction in Y haplogroups
700 CE	*The Great Settled Empires*	Caliphs of Baghdad rule much of western Asia	Pratiharas rule India	Tang China dominates the Celestial Turks	Hard saddles, iron stirrups
1000	*Steppe Conquest*	Turks settle Iran, Anatolia, establish Seljuk rule	Ghaznavids, Turks, Afghans rule northern India	Khitans rule northern China, chase the Turks west	
1200	*Mongol Empire*	Mongols conquer Iran, Anatolia, eastern Europe	Mamluk sultans push Mongols back	Mongols conquer Jurchens, then the Song	Further reduction of Y haplogroups
1368	*Mongol Successors*	Mongol successor states slowly fracture		Ming dynasty expels the Mongols	
1400	*Mongol Successors*	Timür reestablishes a neo-Mongol empire in the west, destroys the Golden Horde	Mamluk sultans pay tribute to Timür	Ming fend off Mongol attacks	

		Western Steppe	Sub-continent	Eastern Steppe	Horses
1500	*The Age of Gunpowder*	Moscow grows at the expense of the Golden Horde	Babur loses Samarkand, gains Kabul, then Delhi		
1600	*The Age of Gunpowder*	Moscow co-opts the Cossacks into its program of expansion	Great Mughals conquer India	Manchus allied with Mongols overthrow the Ming and reestablish a steppe empire	
1700	*The Last Steppe Conquerors*	Iran's Nader Shah invades Russia, Turkey, Central Asia	Nader Shah deals death blow to Mughal Empire	Qing dynasty clashes with the Oirats	
1800	*Colonial Conquests*	Russia conquers the western steppe	The British establish the Raj in India	The Qing dynasty conquers the eastern steppe	Origin of modern breeds, Arabs, Akhal-Tekes, Karabairs
1900	*The Age of High Imperialism*	Russia and Britain spar over Afghanistan		The Qing succumb to foreign sea power	
1914	*World War I*	Russian cavalry does not win the war	Third Anglo-Afghan War ends battlefield role for cavalry	Mongolia becomes a Soviet satellite	
1963	*Recent Times*		King of Afghanistan organizes first buzkashi tournament in Kabul		

GLOSSARIES

Places Cited in the Text

Afrasiyab Archaeological site from the seventh century CE; according to legend, the palace of the king Afrasiyab; in the suburbs of Samarkand

Akhal Locality in Turkmenistan where the Teke Turkmen raised the famous Akhal-Teke horses

Aksu One of the "six cities" of the Tarim Basin

Altai Mountain chain separating the western and eastern steppe; today's Kyrgyzstan, Kazakhstan, Chinese border

Alti Shahr "Six cities" of the Tarim Basin; traditionally Kashgar, Khotan, Yarkand, Yeni Hisar, Aksu, and Turfan. Some lists include Kuche or Hami.

Amu Darya The Oxus River of the Greek geographers; flows from the Pamirs into the Aral Sea. *See* Transoxiana.

Anatolia Peninsula that extends Asia into the Mediterranean world; much of eastern Anatolia is a natural habitat for pastoralism.

Anyang Site of an archaeological excavation located near the Yellow River

Ashqabad City in Turkmenistan

Azerbaijan Historic region including both the Republic of Azerbaijan and the Iranian province of the same name

Baghdad	Capital of the Abbasid Caliphate; many earlier capitals are located nearby, including from pre-Islamic Iran
Balasagun	Locality in Kyrgyzstan, former steppe capital of several peoples, site of the Burana Tower
Balkh	Ancient city in northern Afghanistan
Bamiyan	Valley in the Hindu Kush, site of the giant stone Buddhas
Bengal	The Ganges and the Brahmaputra made this an especially rich province, now divided between India and Bangladesh.
Bihar	Historic province of Bengal, now a state in India
Bijapur	Sultanate of the Deccan, now in Karnataka State
Bukhara	City of Transoxiana; replaced Samarkand as the regional capital in the sixteenth century
Burana	Tower or minaret in Balasungun
Cambay	Modern Khambat in Gujarat, western India
Central Asia	Typically refers to Kazakhstan, Uzbekistan, Turkmenistan, Afghanistan, Kyrgyzstan, and Tajikistan.
Chang'an	Modern Xi'an, in Shaanxi Province; site of Qin, Han, and Tang dynasty capitals
Chengde	The Qing summer capital, then called Jehol
Constantinople	Capital of the Eastern Roman Empire and later of the Ottoman Empire; modern Istanbul
Danube	Europe's second-longest river, long serving as a path for steppe nations, including the Huns, Avars, Magyars, Kipchaks, and Mongols, to penetrate into Europe
Dasht-e Kavir	Salt desert in central Iran, the twenty-fourth-largest desert globally; *dasht* means desert.
Dasht-e Lut	Salt desert in central Iran, thirty-third-largest desert globally
Datong	A Chinese city that grew up as part of the Great Wall
Deccan	Literally, "the South" of India, as opposed to Hindustan and Bengal
Delhi	Capital of the Mamluk sultans, occasional capital of the Mughals; the Raj moved here in 1911.
Dnipro	River flowing into the Black Sea; home to many horse-breeding people, most recently the Cossacks
eastern steppe	Includes Mongolia, the Chinese provinces: Inner Mongolia, Xinjiang, and Gansu.
Fars	A province in southwest Iran

Ferghana	Valley between the Tian Shan Mountains and the Pamirs, now mainly in Uzbekistan
Gansu	Westernmost province of Han China; the starting-off point for Han expeditions into the western regions
Ghazna	Former imperial capital, now a town in southwestern Afghanistan
Gilan	Iranian province beside the Caspian Sea
Golconda	Sultanate of the Deccan, near today's Hyderabad, in Telegana State
Gorgan	Historical region of Iran on the Turkmenistan border, the Hyrcania of the classical geographers
Gujarat	Province of western India with intense trade relations with Iran and the Persian Gulf
Hajipur	A horse market and pilgrimage site in Bihar
Hami	One of the "six cities" of the Tarim Basin
Haridwar	Site where the Ganges comes out of the Himalayas; formerly an important livestock market, now a pilgrimage destination
Hastinapur	Ancient settlement mentioned in the Mahabharata; "City of Elephants"
Helmand River	River in southern Afghanistan
Herat	City in western Afghanistan; traditionally an important livestock market
Hindu Kush	Mountain chain that dominates Afghanistan
Hindustan	Traditionally refers to northern India.
Ili River	River in Kazakhstan and northwestern China
Indraprastha	Ancient settlement mentioned in the Mahabharata; near modern Delhi
Inner Asia	Typically refers to western China, Mongolia, and Tibet—i.e., the steppe lands east of the Altai; *see* eastern steppe.
Iraq	Refers to both the modern state of Iraq as well as southwestern Iran, once known as "Persian Iraq," and Iranian Kurdistan.
Issyk Kul	Lake in Kyrgyzstan
Jaxartes	Syr Darya, a river flowing mainly through Uzbekistan
Jazira	The upper reaches of the Tigris and Euphrates Rivers, in modern Turkey
Jehol	Summer capital of the Qing dynasty, a hundred miles northeast of Beijing; modern Chengde

Jalalabad	City in eastern Afghanistan on the route to the Khyber Pass
Jodhpur	A city in Rajasthan, seat of a maharaja, home to the Marwari horse
Kabulistan	Historical region of Kabul and the neighboring Hindu Kush
Karakorum	Capital of the Mongols
Karakum	"Black Sand" desert in Turkmenistan between Iran and the Oxus River
Kashgar	One of the "six cities" of the Tarim Basin
Kashmir	Region in the far north of the subcontinent, historically an important trade path to Inner Asia and China
Kathiawar	A peninsula of Gujarat and home to a race of horses
Kazan	City on the upper Volga River, formally a Tatar stronghold
Kermanshah	City in western Iran
Khajuraho	A group of temples in central India built by the Pratihara dynasty
Khalchayan	Archaeological site in Uzbekistan, Kushan era
Khanbalik	Kublai Khan's name for Beijing
Khangai	Mountain range in central Mongolia
Khentii	Mountain range in northeastern Mongolia
Khingan	Mountain range in Inner Mongolia
Khiva	Ancient city on the Amu Darya; ancient Khwarazm
Khorasan	"Land of the Rising Sun"; refers to both western Afghanistan and the bordering Iranian province.
Khotan	One of the "six cities" of the Tarim Basin
Khwarazm	Ancient city on the Amu Darya; modern Khiva
Konya	City in western Anatolia, the capital of the Anatolian Seljuks
Kunlun	The "Cloud Mountains," separating Tibet from the Tarim Basin
Kyiv	City founded by the Celestial Turks; ancient capital of the Rus; called Kiev in Russian
Kyzylkum	"Red Sand desert," between the Oxus and Jaxartes Rivers
Ladakh	Himalayan kingdom, part of the Sikh Empire
Lahore	Cultural and economic capital of Punjab
Lakhi Jungle	Onetime scrub region in Punjab, formerly famous for horse breeding
Luoyang	One of the four ancient capitals of China, on the Yellow River

Madhya Pradesh	State in central India
Maharashtra	A state in western India, homeland to the Marathas
Maimana	City in northern Afghanistan
Manchuria	Forested, hilly region in northeastern China
Manzikert	Locality in eastern Anatolia
Marwar	A region in Rajasthan famous for horses; also called Jodhpur
Megiddo	Site of a battle mentioned in the Bible as "Armageddon"
Merv	Ancient city on the Amu Darya
Mughan	Rich grasslands divided between modern Iran and Azerbaijan
Mulan	Hunting park of the Qing Empire, near Jehol, modern Chengde
Multan	Important horse-trading center in the Punjab; the seat of Ahmad Shah's clan
Murghab	River in northern Afghanistan
Mysore	Sultanate in the south of India, in today's Karnataka State
Orkhon	River in Mongolia
Ormuz	Island in the Persian Gulf; important center of trade
Otrar	Town in southern Kazakhstan
Oxus River	*See* Amu Darya.
Pamir Mountains	A mountain chain that separates the Tarim Basin from the Indian subcontinent
Panipat	Locality north of Delhi
Pazyryk	An archaeological site of the fourth to second centuries BCE in the Ural Mountains
Punjab	Five rivers flowing into the Indus define this region, now divided between India and Pakistan.
Pusa	Formerly the site of a British horse-breeding farm in the foothills of the Himalayas, later that of an agricultural research center
Pushkar	A lakeshore city in the mostly dry region of Rajasthan; formerly an important livestock market, now a pilgrimage destination
Puszta	Steppe in central Hungary
Qinghai Plateau	An extensive highland region where yak pastoralism is practiced, in between today's Tibet Autonomous Region and Sichuan Province

Rajasthan	A state in northwestern India; homeland of the Rajputs
Registan	Desert in southeastern Afghanistan
Samarkand	Ancient city of Transoxiana, capital of Timür, now in Uzbekistan
Sarai	The capital of the khans of the Golden Horde, on the lower Volga, destroyed by Timür and superseded by modern Astrakhan
Sayan	Mountains in Mongolia
Shangdu	Kublai Khan's summer capital, called Xanadu by Marco Polo
Sindh	Province named for the Sindh (the Indus River), which flows through it; in modern Pakistan
Sintashta	An archaeological site from the second millennium BCE just south of the Ural Mountains
Sirkeci	Istanbul's main train station; the site of a Byzantine polo field
Sistan	Province in eastern Iran, on the border with Pakistan; ancient Sakastan, the land of the Scythians
Solutré	Archaeological site in the French department of Saône-et-Loire
Syr Darya	The Jaxartes of Greek geographers; a river flowing from the Tian Shan Mountains into the Aral Sea
Taklamakan	Desert zone in the Tarim Basin
Tarim Basin	Depression between the Tian Shan and Pamir ranges, site of the Alti Shahr and the Taklamakan Desert
Thar Desert	A desert covering much of modern Rajasthan State
Tian Shan	Mountain range in Xingjian Province separating the Tarim Basin from Zhungaria
Transoxiana	The land beyond the Oxus River (the Amu Darya); today's Uzbekistan
Turfan	One of the "six cities" of the Tarim Basin
Ulan Bator	Modern capital of Mongolia
western steppe	Ukraine, southern Russia, and western Kazakhstan; includes the Pontic Steppe (north of the Black Sea) and the Kipchak Steppe, as well as the Volga; extends to the Altai Mountains
Xi'an	The modern name for Chang'an
Yarkand	One of the "six cities" of the Tarim Basin
Yellow River	In Chinese, the Huang He; a historic frontier between agricultural China and pastoralist Inner Asia

Yeni Hisar	One of the "six cities" of the Tarim Basin
Youzhou	An older name for Beijing
Yuhuangmiao	Archaeological site south of Beijing, Warring States Period
Yumen	The Jade Gate, part of the Han frontier defenses in Gansu Province
Zabulistan	Ancient region of Iran; location of Ghazna, in modern Afghanistan
Zagros	Mountain range in southwestern Iran
Zarafshan	River flowing from the Pamirs to Samarkand and Bukhara; formerly a tributary of the Oxus
Zhongdu	a former name for Beijing; the "Central Capital"

People Cited in the Text

Name	Definition	Dates	Also known as
Abaoji	1st Khitan emperor	916–26 CE	A poa chi, Taizu of Liao
Afrasiyab	legendary Turanian king of the *Shahnameh*		
Afshars	Turkmen people in northeastern Iran, from whence came Nader Shah		
Aguda	1st Jurchen emperor	1115–23	A ku ta, Taizu of the Jin
Ahmad Shah	1st king of Afghanistan	1747–77	Ahmad Baba, Durr-e Durrani
Akbar	3rd Mughal emperor	1556–1605	
Alans	6th-century descendants of the Scythians		
Alauddin	13th-century Seljuk ruler of Konya, in Anatolia	1229–37	Kayqubad

Name	Definition	Dates	Also known as
Alauddin Khwarazm Shah	6th Kipchak mamluk ruler of Khwarazm and famous for provoking Genghis Khan's invasion of Iran	1200–20	
Alp Arslan	2nd sultan of the Seljuks of Iran	1063–72	
Amanullah	king of Afghanistan	1919–29	
An Lushan	leader of the rebellion against Xuanzong that broke the Tang dynasty	703–57 CE	
Ariq Böke Khan	briefly 6th supreme khan of Mongols	1259–66	
Ashkenaz	biblical Hebrew exonym for the Scythians		
Aśvaghosa	Indian poet	1st century CE	
Atkinson, Thomas	British explorer, painter	1799–1861	
Aurangzeb	6th and last Great Mughal	1658–1707	Alamgir
Avars	steppe horsemen who invaded Europe and sparred with Charlemagne	8th century CE	
Babur	1st Mughal emperor	1526–30	
Bakhtiyaris	Iranian pastoralists of the Zagros Mountains		
Bakhtiyar Khalji, Muhammad	13th-century conqueror of Bengal	1203–06	Khilji
bannermen	Manchu cavalry troopers		
Begil	legendary hero of a cycle of the Dede Korkut tales		

Name	Definition	Dates	Also known as
Bole	Legendary Chinese horse expert	7th century BCE	Sun Yan
Borjigins	The clan of Genghis Khan		
Bulghars	a Turkish people that migrated from the Volga to the Danube	7th century CE	
Burnes, Alexander	British explorer, diplomat	1805–1841	
Castiglione, Giuseppe	Jesuit, court painter to the Qing emperors	1688–1766	
Catherine the Great	Russian empress	1762–1796	
Celestial Turks	a dynasty of steppe rulers in the 6th century, contemporaries of the Tang		Blue or Gök Turks
Chandragupta	1st emperor of the Mauryas	324–295 BCE	
Cossacks	freebooting horsemen, later irregular cavalry in the Russian army		
Crimean Tatars	last state descended from the Golden Horde	1441–1783	
Cyrus	1st Persian king of kings	559–30 BCE	
Dede Korkut	legendary Turkish storyteller		
Di Rong	a horse-breeding people of northwest China	2nd half of 1st millennium BCE	
Du Fu	Tang dynasty poet	712–770 CE	
Durrani	dynasty founded by Ahmad Shah	1747–1863	
Ersari	a branch of the Turkmen people		

Name	Definition	Dates	Also known as
Firuz Jang	Mughal general	1649–1710	Feeroz Jung
Gaekwad	Maratha maharajas of Baroda, in Gujarat	1721–1949	
Gagauz	a modern Kipchak people living in Romania, Moldova, and Ukraine		
Genghis Khan	1st Mongol supreme khan	1206–27	Chengiz Khan, Temüjin
Genghisid	a descendant of Genghis Khan		
Ghilzai	a Pashtun people		
Giray, Sultan Kilich	imperial Russian cavalry expert, descendant of the Crimean khans	1880–1947	
Guangwu	2nd emperor of the Eastern Han	25–57 CE	
Habibullah	ruler of Afghanistan	1901–19	
Han Wudi	the "Martial Emperor" of the Han	141–87 BCE	Wu ti, Wu Emperor
Herodotus	Greek historian	484–425 CE	
Holkar	Maratha maharajas of Indore, in today's Madhya Pradesh state	1732–1950	
Hu	Chinese exonym for pastoralists of the western regions		
Hülegü Khan	Genghis Khan's grandson, conqueror of Iran and the Middle East	1256–65	
Humayun	2nd Mughal emperor	1530–40 and 1555–56	Homayun
Huns	an ancient horse-breeding people		Xiongnu, Hsiung-nu

Name	Definition	Dates	Also known as
Ibn Athir	Arab historian of the Mongol invasions, author of "The Complete History"	1160–1233	
Ibn Battuta	Moroccan jurist, traveler	1304–69	
Ivan the Terrible	1st tsar of Russia	1547–84	Ivan IV
Jahangir	4th Mughal emperor	1605–27	Salim
Jalayirs	originally a Mongolian nation, then a Turco-Mongol group established in Azerbaijan		
Jamshid	legendary Iranian king from the Avesta and the *Shahnameh*		
Jin	dynastic name of the Jurchen emperors of northern China	1115–1234	
Jochi Khan	Genghis Khan's oldest son, conqueror of the western steppe	1182–1227	
Jurchens	horse-breeding people of northeastern China		
Kalidasa	Indian poet, author of *Raghuvamsa*	4th–5th centuries CE	
Kalmyks	horse-breeding people of Oirat/Mongolian origin established on the Volga in the 17th century		Torguts
Kanishka	the greatest Kushan king	100?–150? CE	
Kanthaka	the horse of Prince Siddhartha Gautama, the historical Buddha		
Kashgari, Mahmud	scholar who wrote some of the earliest descriptions of the Turks	1005–1102	

Name	Definition	Dates	Also known as
Kautilya	minister of Chandragupta	375–283 BCE	Chanakya
Kazakhs	a branch of the Golden Horde that formed its own khanates in the 17th and 18th centuries		
Keraits	a people living in Mongolia in Genghis Khan's time		
Khalji	a Turco-Afghan dynasty established in Bengal	1290–1320	
Khazars	a 6th-century Turkish nation established on the Volga		
Khitans	a horse-breeding people of Mongolia, founders of the Liao dynasty		
al-Khuttali, Hizam	Abbasid horse expert	9th century CE	
Kikkuli	chariot horse trainer	1400 BCE	
Kipchak	a branch of the Turks established in the western steppe and eastern Europe		
Kublai Khan	5th Mongol supreme khan, 1st Yuan emperor	1264–94	Qublai Khan
Kushans	rulers of northern India and Central Asia in the 1st century CE; descendants of the Yuezhi, ancestors of the Afghans		
Kyrgyz	an ancient Turkish people; the name refers to the Kazakhs in the 19th century and the people of modern Kyrgyzstan		

Name	Definition	Dates	Also known as
Li Guangli	leader of the Han dynasty expedition into the Tarim Basin in 104 BCE	died 88 BCE	
Liao	a dynasty established by the Khitans in northern China	916–1125	
Lodi	a dynasty of Afghan horse dealers in northern India, overthrown by Babur	1451–1526	
Ma Yuan	Han general	14 BCE– 49 CE	Wen Yuan
Mahbub Ali	fictional Pathan horse dealer in Kipling's *Kim*	circa 1880	
Mahmud	1st sultan of the Ghaznavids; ruled much of modern Afghanistan and Pakistan	998–1030	
mamluks	enslaved steppe horsemen trained as elite soldiers throughout the Muslim world		
Manchus	inhabitants of Manchuria, formerly known as Jurchens		
Marathas	a people of western India, successors to the Mughals in much of India		
Mas'ud Beg	Mongol governor of Transoxiana	13th century CE	
Maurya	early Indian empire founded by Chandragupta with the help of Kautilya as well as Persian and Scythian mercenaries	332–184 BCE	
Mikhail Fyodorovich	1st Romanov tsar of Russia	1613–45	Michael

Name	Definition	Dates	Also known as
Mitanni	chariot-warring people living on the upper Tigris and Euphrates	mid-2nd millennium BCE	
Mitra	deity mentioned in both the Iranian Avesta and the Indian Rig Veda		
Modun	1st chanyu of the Huns	209–174 BCE	Motun
Möngke Khan	4th Mongol supreme khan	1251–59	
Mongols	originally Genghis Khan's people; the term now applies to Mongolian-speaking people		
Moorcroft, William	British explorer, horse expert	1767–1825	
Mouraviev, N. N.	Russian diplomat and explorer	1794–1866	Muraviev-Karsky
al-Mutanabbi	Arab poet and adventurer	915–965 CE	
Nader Shah	Iranian war leader, briefly shah	1736–47	
Naimans	a Turkish-speaking people living in Mongolia in Genghis Khan's time		
Nogays	a branch of the Golden Horde, closely aligned with Moscow		
Nurhaci	founder of the Manchu state, Jurchen khan	1616–26	
Ögedei Khan	2nd supreme khan of the Mongols	1229–41	
Oirats	the westernmost Mongols	17th–18th centuries	Jungars, Zhungars, Dzungars, Eleuths

Name	Definition	Dates	Also known as
Ossetes	modern-day descendants of the Scythians and the Alans, living in the northern Caucasus		
Pashtuns	the dominant ethnic group of Afghanistan and Pakistan's Khyber Pakhtunkhwa province		
Pathans	Hindi and Urdu exonym for the Pashtuns		
Peter the Great	1st Russian emperor	1682–1725	
Polo, Marco	Venetian merchant, traveler	1254–1324	
Pratihara	early Indian dynasty		
Pugachev, Yemelyan	Cossack leader of a rebellion against Catherine the Great	1742–1775	
Qajars	a Turkmen clan whose khans became the last steppe rulers of Iran	1799–1923	
Qianlong	5th and greatest Qing emperor	1735–96	
Qing	dynastic name of the Manchu emperors of China	1636–1912	Ch'ing
Raghu	legendary Indian king		
Rajput	a warlike horse-breeding people of Central India		
Rakhsh	legendary steed of Rustam, hero of the *Shahnameh*		
Ranjit Singh	Sikh emperor, ruled Punjab, Kashmir, and what is now Khyber Pakhtunkhwa Province of Pakistan	1801–39	

Name	Definition	Dates	Also known as
Rashiduddin	author of a major history of Genghis Khan, *Compendium of Chronicles*	1247–1318	
Razin, Stenka	Cossack leader of a rebellion against the Romanovs	1630–71	
Romanus IV Diogenes	Roman emperor	1068–72	
Rong	a Chinese exonym for horse-breeding peoples of the western region		
Rubruck, William de	Franciscan emissary to the Mongols	fl. 1248–55	
Rus	a combination of Slavs and Scandinavians who established a state in today's Belarus, Ukraine, and Moldova	9th–13th centuries CE	
Rustam	Legendary Iranian hero of the *Shahnameh*		
Safavid	dynasty that reunited Iran after the collapse of the Timürid empire	1501–1736	
Saka	Iranian and Indian exonym for the Scythians		
Sanjar	9th sultan of the Seljuks of Iran	1097–1118	Ahmad Sanjar
Scindia	Maratha maharajas of Gwalior, in modern Madhya Pradesh	1731–1948	Shinde
Scudra	endonym for the Scythians		
Scythian	Greek exonym for the horse-breeding people who dominated the western steppe until the coming of the Huns		

Name	Definition	Dates	Also known as
Sei	Chinese exonym for the Scythians		
Seljuks	a Turkish clan that ruled Iran, Iraq, and Anatolia	1037–1194	
Sengge Rinchen	bannerman general in the Second Opium War	1811–1865	
Sennacherib	king of Assyria	705–681 BCE	
Shah Abbas	5th Safavid shah of Iran	1588–1629	
Shah Jahan	5th Mughal emperor	1628–58	
Shah Tahmasp	2nd Safavid shah of Iran	1524–76	
Shahin Giray	last Tatar khan of the Crimea	1777–83	
Shang	1st historical Chinese dynasty	1600–1045 BCE	
Shcherbatov, Nikolai Borisovich	Russian prince, political figure, and horse breeder	1868–1943	
Shi Huangdi	1st emperor of China, of the short-lived Qin dynasty	221–10 BCE	Zhao Zheng
Shivaji Bhonsle	founder of the Maratha Empire	1674–80	
Sigynnae	ancient Scythian people established in Bulgaria, mentioned by Herodotus		
Sima Qian	Han dynasty historian, author of the *Shiji* ("Historical Records")	145–86 BCE	Seema Chien
Siyavosh	legendary Iranian hero		
Skobelev, Mikhail	Russian general, conqueror of Turkmenistan	1843–82	
Strabo	1st-century Greek geographer	64 BCE–24 CE	

Name	Definition	Dates	Also known as
Suldus	a people living in Mongolia in Genghis Khan's time		
Taizong	2nd Tang emperor	626–49 CE	T'ai tsung
Tajiks	historically refers to settled Persian speakers of Transoxiana		
Tatars	see footnote on p. 183; originally a Turkish-speaking people of Mongolia		
Teke	a branch of the Turkmen people		
Tianzuo	last Khitan emperor	1101–25	Tien tsuo
Tipu Sultan	sultan of Mysore in southern India; foe of the British	1782–91	Tipoo
Tokharians	an enigmatic, sedentary nation of ancient Central Asia		
Tomyris	Scythian queen, mentioned by Herodotus	6th century BCE	
Tughlugh	Asia, either Turkish or Tokharian	1320–25	
Turanians	the *Shahnameh*'s name for the peoples of inner Asia, either Turkish or Tokharian		
Turkmen	a Turkish people; settled in Transoxiana, Iran, Iraq, and Anatolia in the 10th and 11th centuries		
Uyghurs	an ancient settled Turkish people of the Tarim Basin; the modern name for Turkish speakers of China's Xinjiang Province		

Name	Definition	Dates	Also known as
Uzbeks	a branch of the Golden Horde that conquered Transoxiana in the 16th century		
Vámbéry, Arminius	Hungarian explorer and linguist	1832–1913	
Vorontsov-Dashkov, Illarion Ivanovich	Russian imperial cavalry general, head of the imperial stud farm	1837–1916	
Wuling of Zhao	a ruler of the Zhao state, nominal vassals of the Zhou	325–299 BCE	
Xenophon	Athenian general	430–354 BCE	
Xuanzong	7th Tang emperor	713–56 CE	Hsuen tsu
Yakub Beg	leader of a Turkish revolt against the Qing dynasty	1865–77	
Yama	a deity of the Rig Veda corresponding to Jamshid in the Avesta		
Yomut	a branch of the Turkmen people		
Yongle	greatest emperor of the Ming dynasty	1402–24	Yung Lo
Yuezhi	Scythian people who emigrated from the Chinese frontier into Afghanistan; *see* Kushans		
Zaher Shah	last king of Afghanistan	1933–73	
Zimri-Lin	king of Mari, an ancient Mesopotamian state	1775–61 BCE	

Foreign Terms Used in the Text

Term	Source language	Explanation
arghamak	Turkish	superior horse
Arthashastra	Sanskrit	3rd-century BCE manual for rulers, attributed to Chanakya
asp	Persian	horse
assa	Hittite	horse, from Indo-Aryan *aspa*
assussani	Hittite	"master of the horse"
aśva	Sanskrit	horse
Aśvaka	Sanskrit	"master of the horse"; possible origin of the ethnonym Afghan
Avesta		oldest part of the Zoroastrian scriptures
ayraq, kumis	Mongol, Turkish	fermented mare's milk
Baburnama	Persian	the memoirs of the emperor Babur
battue	French	encirclement hunt
bottines	French	small boots
buzkashi	Persian	"goat dragging," the national game of Afghanistan
chabuk suwar	Turkish/Persian	rough rider
chanyu	Hunnic	title of the chief of the first Hunnic empire
chapandaz	Persian	buzkashi competitor
dagh	Turkish	mountain
Dasara	Sanskrit	an autumn festival in India
dasht	Persian	a desert
durbar	Persian	the (royal) court and its rituals
Equus	Latin	horse
Equus gallicus	Latin	a small equid living in Pleistocene western Europe
fei	Chinese	flying steed
fidalgos	Portuguese	Portuguese *hidalgos*, "gentlemen"
guilloché	French	a technique for engraving metals

Term	Source language	Explanation
Iranic		includes languages like Scythian, Ossetian, and Pashtu
Jin	Chinese	golden; the name of the Jurchen dynasty
Kamboja	Sanskrit	originally referred to Iran, later to Cambodia
Karabair	Turkish	a breed of Uzbek horses from Bukhara
kazakhlik	Turkish	"turning Cossack," brigandage
kazakhs	Turkish	originally "brigands," Cossacks
khaghan	Turkish	supreme khan; also spelled qa'an, qaghan
khané be-dûsh	Persian	"house on one's back," a nomad
kokboru, kokpar	Turkish	a steppe sport, similar to buzkashi
Kuchi	Persian	"one who travels about," a nomad
kumis, ayraq	Turkish, Mongol	fermented mare's milk
li	Chinese	a measure of distance; about one-third of a mile
Lipizzaner	German	a breed of horses originally from Iberia, favored by the Hapsburgs
mörin	Mongol	gelding
nawab	Persian, Arabic	a princely title used in India
nerge	Mongol	encirclement hunt, battue
nishan	Persian	animal brand; *see* tamgha
noker	Mongol	member of a khan's entourage
onager	English	wild donkey
ordu	Mongol	horde, army, camp, court
ovoo	Mongol	cairn; often a shrine with horse skulls and prayer flags
Powindahs	Persian-Pashto	long-distance traders
Przewalski	Polish	breed of wild or feral horses named for a 19th-century Polish officer in Russian service
qurchis	Mongol	the personal guard of the khan
ratha	Sanskrit	wheel, chariot, the rook in Indian chess
riyasat	Arabic	horsemanship, government

Term	Source language	Explanation
saxaul		a thorny shrub or small tree, beloved of camels
shabrack	Turkish	large saddle blanket
Shiji	Chinese	"Historical Records," the work of Sima Qian
siyasat	Arabic	horsemanship, politics
synšy	Turkish	horse expert
szlachta	Polish	the Polish nobility
tamgha	Turkish	a brand for horses; by extension, a heraldic symbol for a clan or a khan
tianma	Chinese	heavenly horses
töy	Turkish, Mongol	horse race, festival
Turki	Turkish, Persian	refers to the language as well as the horses of Central Asia
vizier	Arabic, Persian	a chief minister
xiangma	Chinese	equine physiognomy
yabgu	Scythian	a princely title in use among the Yuezhi and the Celestial Turks
yabusame	Japanese	horse archery
zuid	Mongol	frost, famine; also spelled *zud* and *dzud*

NOTES

Prologue

xvii **in London alone in the 1870s**: Jürgen Osterhammel, *The Transformation of the World: A Global History of the Nineteenth Century* (Princeton, NJ: Princeton University Press, 2014), 303.

xvii **in just a few generations**: Andrew Curry, "Horse Nations," *Science* 379, no. 6639 (2023): 1288–93.

xviii **"the state will totter to a fall"**: Tang Shu, 36 3718d, quoted in Edward H. Schafer, *The Golden Peaches of Samarkand: A Study of T'ang Exotics* (Berkeley: University of California Press, 1985), 58.

xviii **"nor no mighty monarch reign"**: quoted in R. B. Azad Choudhary, "Mughal and Late Mughal Equine Veterinary Literature: *Tarjamah-i-Saloter-i-Asban* and *Faras-Nama-i-Rangin*," *Social Scientist* 45, nos. 7–8 (July–August 2017): 60.

xix **"to the stars in the sky"**: Commandant Émile Bouillane de Lacoste, *Au pays sacré des anciens Turcs et Mongols* (Paris: Émile Paul, 1911), excerpted in *Le Voyage en Asie Central et au Tibet*, ed. Michel Jan (Paris: Robert Laffont, 1992), 1048.

Chapter 1: Domesticated for Milk

1 **Climates of North Africa and peninsular Arabia**: Good summaries of equine prehistory include Jean-Pierre Digard, *Une histoire du cheval: Art, techniques, société* (Arles: Actes Sud, 2004), and Susanna Forrest, *The Age of the Horse: An Equine Journey Through Human History* (New York: Atlantic, 2017).

2 **fascination with their beauty and speed**: Digard, *Une histoire du cheval*, 15, 18.

3 **a solid basis in nutrition, too**: Marsha A. Levine, "Eating Horses: The Evolutionary Significance of Hippophagy," *Antiquity* (March 1998). See also Carole Ferret, "Les avatars du cheval iakoute," *Études mongoles et sibériennes, centrasiatiques et tibétaines* (2010): 42.

3   **as part of their old pagan rituals**: Thomas Rowsell, "Riding to the Afterlife: The Role of Horses in Early Medieval North-Western Europe" (master's diss., University College London, 2012), 7.

3   **the skeletons of ten thousand slaughtered horses**: Digard, *Une histoire du cheval*, 25.

3   **than today's horses**: Véra Eisenmann, "L'évolution des équidés," *Études centrasiatiques et tibétaines*, 41 (2010): 11.

3   **emerged from either location**: Ludovic Orlando, "Ancient Genomes Reveal Unexpected Horse Domestication and Management Dynamics," *Bioessays-journal.com* (2019): 3.

3   **the permafrost line there moved north**: Pablo Librado et al., "The Evolutionary Origin and Genetic Makeup of Domestic Horses," *Genetics* 20, no. 4 (October 2, 2016): 423–34.

3   **multiplied in their new, natural sanctuary**: Vera Warmuth et al. "Reconstructing the Origin and Spread of Horse Domestication in the Eurasian Steppe," *Proceedings of the National Academy of Sciences of the United States of America* 109, no. 2 (May 22, 2012): 8202–06.

4   **which sites reflect hunting and which corralling**: Marsha A. Levine, "Botai and the Origins of Horse Domestication," *Journal of Anthropological Archaeology* 18 (1999): 29–78. David Anthony et al. challenge Levine's conclusions in their "Early Horseback Riding and Warfare, the Importance of the Magpie Around the Neck," in *Horses and Humans: The Origins of Human-Equine Relationships* (Oxford: Archaeopress, 2006). Scholars continue to debate evidence for domestication circa 3000 BCE.

4   **initially superficial and easily reversible**: Digard, *Une histoire du cheval*, 13.

4   **in the absence of wild adults**: Anatoly M. Khazanov, *Nomads and the Outside World* (Madison: University of Wisconsin Press, 1994), 28.

5   **half-dragon creatures emerged from the water**: This is how the magical foal of the Turco-Iranian epic *Kuroğlu* is sired. See Alexander Chodzko, *Specimens of the Popular Poetry of Persia* (London: W. H. Allen, 1842), 14.

5   **speed equaled that of birds**: "The Horse in Turkic Art," *Central Asiatic Journal* 10, nos. 3–4 (1965): 92.

5   **recruitment of wild mares into the domesticated herds**: Martha Levine, George Bailey, K. E. Whitwell, Leo B. Jeffcott, "Palaeopathology and Horse Domestication: The Case of Some Iron Age Horses from the Altai Mountains, Siberia," in *Human Ecodynamics: Symposia of the Association for Environmental Archaeology*, ed. George Bailey (Barnsley: Oxbow, 2000), 123–33, and Fiona B. Marshall, Keith Dobney, Tim Denham, and José M. Capriles, "Evaluating the Roles of Directed Breeding and Gene Flow in Animal Domestication," *Proceedings of the National Academy of Sciences* 111, no. 17 (April 29, 2014): 6153–58. More recent research by Ludovic Orlando suggests that modern horses are descended from a small set of wild ancestors. In this case the stallions outside the herd may not have been wild but feral.

5   **original habitat in Mongolia**: A. Turk: "A Scientific and Historical Investigation on Mongolian Horses," История: факты и символы [History: Facts and symbols] 2, no. 11 (2017): 24. Turk mistakenly claims the Przewalski horses are the ancestors of Mongolian ones.

5   **wild or a feral cousin of the modern horse**: Charleen Gaunitz et al., "Ancient Genomes Revisit the Ancestry of Domestic and Przewalski's Horses," *Science* 360. no. 6384 (2018):

111–14, and Orlando, "Ancient Genomes," 2. Orlando's most recent research argues that the Przewalski horse is a feral descendant of an earlier attempt to domesticate horses, associated with the Botai site mentioned in endnote to p. 4, "which sites reflect hunting and which corralling." See his *La conquête du cheval* (Paris: Odile Jacob, 2023), 30.

5 **willingness to socialize with humans**: Piet Witt and Inge Bouman, *The Tale of Przewalski's Horse: Coming Home to Mongolia* (Utrecht: KNNV, 2006).

6 **exploit mares for their milk**: William Timothy Treal Taylor et al., "Early Pastoral Economies and Herding Transitions in Eastern Eurasia," *Scientific Reports* 10, no. 1001 (2022); Shevan Wilkin et al., "Dairying Enabled Early Bronze Age Yamnaya Steppe Expansions," *Nature* 598 (September 15, 2021): 629–33. For a broader discussion of human-horse interdependency, see Gala Argent and Jeannette Vaught, eds., "Introduction: Humans and Horses in the Relational Arena," in *The Relational Horse* (Leiden: Brill 2022).

6 **for that matter, mother's milk**: Ewa Jastrzębska et al., "Nutritional Value and Health-Promoting Properties of Mare's Milk: A Review," *Czech Journal of Animal Science* 62, no. 12 (2017): 512, and Massimo Malacarne, "Protein and Fat Composition of Mare's Milk: Some Nutritional Remarks with Reference to Human and Cow's Milk," *International Dairy Journal* 12 (2002): 875–875.

7 **one stallion for six to ten mares**: On the development of the gelding, see William Taylor, "Horse Demography and Use in Bronze Age Mongolia," *Quaternary International* (2016): 10, and Marsha Levine, "The Origins of Horse Husbandry on the Eurasian Steppe," in *Prehistoric Steppe Adaptation and the Horse*, ed. Marsha Levine, Colin Renfrew, and Katherine V. Boyle (Cambridge: McDonald Institute for Archaeological Research, 2003), 22.

7 **produced more oxytocin**: Orlando, "Ancient Genomes," 6.

7 **from our sharing the hunt with them**: For more on the intensity of the horse-human relationship, see Laerke Recht, *The Spirited Horse: Equid–Human Relations in the Bronze Age Middle East* (London: Bloomsbury, 2022). For dogs, see p. 27.

7 **forming such attachments with humans**: Recht, *The Spirited Horse*, 32–33.

7 **the bond between the two became essential for the well-being of both**: Gala Argent, "Watching the Horses: The Impact of Horses on Early Pastoralists' Sociality and Political Ethos in Inner Asia," in *Hybrid Communities Biosocial Approaches to Domestication and Other Trans-species Relationship*, ed. Charles Stépanoff and Jean-Denis Vigne (Milton Park, Abingdon: Routledge, 2018), 145.

8 **the horse's digestive system**: Paul Sharpe and Laura B. Kenny, "Grazing Behavior, Feed Intake, and Feed Choices," in Paul Sharpe's *Horse Pasture Management* (New York: Academic Press, 2019), 126.

9 **to the grass beneath**: Khazanov, *Nomads and the Outside World*, 46.

9 **the leader of the flocks**: Taylor, "Early Pastoral Economies."

9 **which persists into modern times**: Nikolai Kradin, "Nomadic Empires in Inner Asia," in *Complexity of Interaction Along the Eurasian Steppe Zone in the First Millennium AD*, ed. Jan Bemmann and Michael Schmauder (Bonn: Rheinische Friedrich-Wilhelms-Universität, 2015), 17.

10 **desertification of much grassland**: Joel Berger, Bayarbaatar Buuveibaatar, and Charudutt Mishra, "Globalization of the Cashmere Market and the Decline of Large Mammals in Central Asia," *Conservation Biology* 27, no. 4 (August 2013): 684.

10 **coexisted with farming communities**: Natalia M. Vinogradova and Giovanna Lombardo, "Farming Sites of the Late Bronze and Early Iron Ages in Southern Tajikistan," *East and West* 52, nos. 1–4 (December 2002): 100.

10 **deeper into the steppe**: Philip L. Kohl, "The Early Integration of the Eurasian Steppes with the Ancient Near East: Movements and Transformations in the Caucasus and Central Asia," in *Beyond the Steppe and the Sown*, ed. David Peterson, Laura Popova, and Adam T. Smith (Leiden: Brill, 2006), 15.

10 **desirable or even feasible**: Khazanov, *Nomads and the Outside World*, 38.

11 **without riding them is extremely difficult**: Levine, "The Origins of Horse Husbandry."

11 **they were probably children**: Harold B. Barclay, "Another Look at the Origins of Horse Riding," *Anthropos* 77 (1982): 245.

12 **superficially domesticated horses of 3000 to 2500 BCE**: Martin Trautmann, Alin Frînculeasa, Bianca Preda-Bălănică, Marta Petruneac, Marin Focşăneanu, Stefan Alexandrov, Nadezhda Atanassova, et al. "First Bioanthropological Evidence for Yamnaya Horsemanship," *Science Advances* 9, no. 9 (2023). This recent article seeks to connect the expansion of the horse-herding cultures of the steppes with early riding. The authors state, "It is difficult to envision how this expansion could have taken place without improved forms of transportation." The improved transportation was not the horse. These early herders moved by wagons, in which they carried their household goods. Horses were not then used as beasts of burden. Moreover, as the paper allows, of the sampled skeletons only a few individuals showed signs of riding. This means riding was not ubiquitous, as it was in later pastoralist groups. The riders were probably the people in charge of the horse herds, since it is hard to herd horses without riding one. Horse domestication did result in the great expansion of the herding people across the steppe, but not because of riding. Rather the horses' environmental requirements— they need much more space to graze than ruminants—forced the humans to follow after them. Eventually this led to widespread and extensive riding but not for another one thousand years. For a good discussion of this paper, see Victor Mair, "The Earliest Horse Riders" in *The Language Log* (March 5, 2023 @ 10:40 am).

12 **intensive milking of horses in the period 3000 to 2500 BCE**: Wilkin et al., "Dairying." Ludovic Orlando points out that the dating of milk fats in ancient cooking vessels might be erroneous, and argues that breeding, not milking per se, could explain horses' growing docility. See his *Conquête*, 60, 75.

12 **much attention to this new phenomenon**: E. T. Shev, "The Introduction of the Domesticated Horse in Southwest Asia," *Archaeology, Ethnology & Anthropology of Eurasia* 44, no. 1 (2016): 133. Ianir Milevski and Liora Kolska Horwitz, "Domestication of the Donkey (*Equus asinus*) in the Southern Levant: Archaeozoology, Iconography and Economy," in *Animals and Human Society in Asia*, ed. R. Kowner et al. (New York: Springer, 2019).

12 **different written languages of the time**: Joachim Marzahn, "Training Instructions for Horses from Cuneiform Texts," in *Furusiyya*, ed. David Alexander (Riyadh: King Abdulaziz Public Library, 1996), 1:22.

12 **how best to date the emergence of riding**: As noted above, Anthony argues for early domestication and riding, Levine to a later development. For me the main point is that extensive riding did not come about until after charioting. This is the view of Robert

Drews in *Early Riders: The Beginnings of Mounted Warfare in Asia and Europe* (New York: Routledge, 2004).

13   **the animals and the riders**: Marsha Levine, G. Bailey, K. E. Whitwell, et al., "Palaeopathology and Horse Domestication: The Case of Some Iron Age Horses Horn the Altai Mountains, Siberia," in *Human Ecodynamics: Symposia of the Association for Environmental Archaeology*, ed. G. Bailey, R. Charles, and N. Winder (Barnsley: Oxbow, 2000), 125.

13   **a matter of life and death**: Diana K. Davis, "Power, Knowledge, and Environmental History in the Middle East and North Africa," *International Journal of Middle East Studies* 42, no. 4 (November 2010): 657–59, and Mehdi Ghorbani et al., "The Role of Indigenous Ecological Knowledge in Managing Rangelands Sustainably in Northern Iran," *Ecology and Society* 18, no. 2 (June 2013): 1.

14   **or water to be drunk**: Sharpe and Kenny, "Grazing Behavior," 130.

15   **original homeland north of the Black Sea and the Caspian**: Wilkin et al. "Dairying," 632; P. Librado, N. Khan, A. Fages, et al., "The Origins and Spread of Domestic Horses from the Western Eurasian Steppes," *Nature* 21 (October 2021). Orlando (*Conquête*, 55) estimates that the herders reached central Europe within two hundred years and China within five hundred of the initial domestication, making this a very fast transition indeed.

15   **the snow and ice of the Altai Mountains and Mongolia**: Philip L. Kohl, *The Making of Bronze Age Eurasia* (Cambridge: Cambridge University Press 2007), 159; Wilkin et al., "Dairying," 629; Philip L. Kohl, "Culture History on a Grand Scale: Connecting the Eurasian Steppes with the Ancient Near East ca. 3600–1900 BC," in *Beyond the Steppe and the Sown*, ed. David Peterson, Laura Popova, and Adam T. Smith (Leiden: Brill 2006), 27.

15   **the land of the horse breeders**: E. N. Chernykh, "Formation of the Eurasian 'Steppe Belt' of Stockbreeding Cultures: Viewed Through the Prism of Archaeometallurgy and Radiocarbon Dating," *Archaeology, Ethnology and Anthropology of Eurasia* 35, no. 3 (2008): 49–50.

16   **according to the season**: Laurent Touchart, "La steppe russe," in *Les milieux naturels de la Russie: Une biogéographie de l'immensité* (Paris: L'Harmattan, 2010), 306.

16   **in the feedbags of stabled horses**: See Recht, *The Spirited Horse*, 137.

16   **help oxygenate their blood for speed**: Alexandra Bröhm, "The World Map of a Trace Element," *Horizons: The Swiss Research Magazine*, March 4, 2017.

17   **varied flora and fauna in Asia**: D. M. Olson et al., "Terrestrial Ecoregions of the World: A New Map of Life on Earth," *Bioscience* 51, no. 11 (2001): 934.

20   **miles in every direction**: Robert N. Taaffe, "The Geographic Setting," in *The Cambridge History of Early Inner Asia*, ed. Denis Sinor (Cambridge: Cambridge University Press 1990), 20.

20   **for each grain planted**: Strabo, *The Geography*, trans. Horace Leonard Jones (Cambridge, MA: Harvard University Press, 1924), vol. 3, book 7, chapter 4, paragraph 6. Also available at https://penelope.uchicago.edu/Thayer/E/Roman/Texts/Strabo/7D*.html.

20   **flowing into the Black Sea**: J. M. Suttie, S. G. Reynolds, C. Batello, *Grasslands of the World* (Rome: FAO, 2005), 1111.

20   **steppe in Europe, the Hungarian plains**: Hortobágy National Park Directorate, "Grazing Animal Husbandry on the Puszta," https://www.hnp.hu/en/szervezeti -egyseg/CONSERVATION/oldal/grazing-animal-husbandry-on-the-puszta-i.

20 **wreaked havoc on the horse population**: Emily Kwong, "The Deadly Winters That Have Transformed Life for Herders in Mongolia," *Morning Edition*, National Public Radio, July 29, 2019.

21 **full of familiar landmarks**: Seïtkassym Aouelbekov and Carole Ferret, "Quand une institution en cache une autre . . . Abigéat et mise à sac chez les Kazakhs," *Études mongoles et sibériennes, centrasiatiques et tibétaines* 41 (2010): 13.

21 **the cairns respectfully as *ovoo***: Charlotte Marchina, "The Skull on the Hill: Anthropological and Osteological Investigation of Contemporary Horse Skull Ritual Practices in Central Mongolia," *Anthropozoologica* 52, no. 2 (December 2017): 174.

21 **The practice is ancient**: László Bartosiewicz, "Ex Oriente Equus: A Brief History of Horses Between the Early Bronze Age and the Middle Ages," *Studia Archaeologica* 12 (2011): 2, 6.

21 **"famous for foals"**: Ryan Platt, "Hades' Famous Foals and the Prehistory of Homeric Horse Formulas," *Oral Tradition* 29, no. 1 (2014): 139.

21 **humans' veneration for horses**: William Taylor et al., "Horse Sacrifice and Butchery in Bronze Age Mongolia," *Journal of Archaeological Science: Reports* 31 (June 2020). Victoria Peemot's research among the Tuva people shows that one can both be attached to a particular horse and feel good about eating it. V. Peemot, "Emplacing Herder-Horse Bonds in Ak-Erik, South Tyva," in *Multispecies Households in the Saian Mountains: Ecology at the Russia-Mongolia Border*, ed. Alex Oehler and Anna Varfolomeeva (Cheltenham, UK: Rowman and Littlefield, 2019), 162. See also Argent, "Watching the Horses," 150.

22 **"between tamed and wild"**: Philippe Swennen, "L'aśvamedha de Rāma a-t-il échoué?," in *Équidés: Le cheval, l'âne et la mule dans les empires de l'Orient ancien*, ed. Delphine Poinsot and Margaux Spruyt (Paris: Routes d'Oriente Actes, 2022), 222.

22 **above the human burial**: Laura Battini, "Le cheval, 2e partie," *Sociétés humaines du Proche-Orient ancien* (November 12, 2018).

22 **the hero of one Mongolian epic**: Veronika Veit, "The Mongols and Their Magic Horses: Some Remarks on the Role of the Horse in Mongol Epic Tales," in *Pferde in Asien: Geschichte, Handel und Kultur / Horses in Asia: History, Trade and Culture*, ed. Bernd Fragner et al. (Wien: Österreiche Akademie der Wissenschaften, 2009), 101.

22 **as though the steppe had swallowed up the deceased**: John Andrew Boyle, "Form of Horse Sacrifice Amongst the 13th- and 14th-Century Mongols," *Central Asiatic Journal* 10, nos. 3–4 (December 1965): 46.

22 **the vastness of the steppe**: Thomas William Atkinson, *Travels in the Region of the Upper and Lower Amur* (London: Murray, 1860), loc. 1142, Kindle; Fridrik Thordarson, "Bäx Fäldiṣin," *Encyclopaedia Iranica Online*, http://dx.doi.org/10.1163/2330 -4804_EIRO_COM_6744.

Chapter 2: Horses for Heroes

24 **"My lord should not ride a horse"**: Recht, *The Spirited Horse*, 115.

24 **horse-donkey hybrid provided a stately and reliable seat**: Recht (*The Spirited Horse*, 109–10) has much to say about the steadiness and reliability of donkeys, mules, and

kungas (hybrids of donkeys and onagers). See also Cécile Michel, "The Perdum-Mule, a Mount for Distinguished Persons in Mesopotamia During the First Half of the Second Millennium BC," *Man and Animal in Antiquity: Proceedings of the Conference at the Swedish Institute in Rome* (September 9–12, 2002).

24 **the royal standard of Ur,** *dating to 2500 BCE*: British Museum, museum no. EA 121201.

25 **recruited for driving, without great success**: Drews, *Early Riders*, 36, and Recht, *The Spirited Horse*, 93.

25 **"and a drawbar attached with a hook"**: *Avesta*, Mithra Hymn XXXII, Vendidad, chapter 2, lines 1–20, trans. James Darmesteter (New York: Christian Literature Company, 1898).

25 **on the steppe frontier, dated to 2200 BCE**: Julio Bensezu-Sarmiento, "Funerary Rituals and Archaeothanatological Data from BMAC Graves at Ulug Depe (Turkmenistan) and Dzharkutan (Uzbekistan)," in *The World of the Oxus Civilization*, ed. Bertille Lyonnet and Nadezhda A. Dubova (London: Routledge, 2021), 405.

26 **eight or ten per wheel**: The Louvre has such a rim it its collections, from 2000 BCE Sukkalmah in Iran, inventory no. SB 6829.

26 **horses along the central pole**: David W. Anthony and Nikolai B. Vinogradov, "Birth of the Chariot," *Archaeology* 48, no. 2 (March–April 1995): 36–41.

26 **twenty times lighter than its predecessor**: Gian Luca Bonora, "The Oxus Civilisation and the Northern Steppe," in *The World of the Oxus Civilisation* (New York: Routledge, 2020), 752.

26 **steadied the chariot's trajectory**: For hunting from chariots, see Recht, *The Spirited Horse*, 92, and Esther Jacobson-Tepfer, "The Image of the Wheeled Vehicle in the Mongolian Altai: Instability and Ambiguity," *Silk Road* 10 (2012): 3.

27 **they did not fight on horseback**: I am indebted for this insight to private communications from Kate Kanne and Igor V. Chechuskov. Kanne's research on early mounted herders in Hungary has found no evidence of warfare.

27 **sensitive means for directing or slowing down the horses**: Gail Brownrigg, "Harnessing the Chariot Horse," in *Equids and Wheeled Vehicles in the Ancient World*, ed. Peter Raulwing, Katheryn M. Linduff, and Joost H. Crouwel (Oxford: BAR, 2019), 85.

27 **required for mounted combat**: see Recht, *The Spirited Horse*, 77, 119, 137. Recht points out that tack is not necessary for long-distance riding but is crucial for wheeling about in combat.

28 **ancient chariot horses were no higher than eleven to twelve hands**: Jean Spruytte, *Attelages antiques libyens* (Paris: Éditions de la Maison des Sciences de l'Homme 1996), http://books.openedition.org/editionsmsh/6368.

28 **"used in sacrifice and upon field service"**: Edward L. Shaughnessy, "Historical Perspectives on the Introduction of the Chariot into China," *Harvard Journal of Asiatic Studies* 48, no. 1 (June 1988): 189–237.

28 **"subjugate the barbarian regions"**: Xiang Wan, "The Horse in Pre-Imperial China" (doctoral diss., University of Pennsylvania, 2013), 80, http://repository.upenn.edu/edissertations/720.

29 **that pace emerged much later**: horses naturally walk (one hoof off the ground) or gallop (four hooves off the ground). The trot and the amble (two hooves off the ground) are more comfortable for the riders. Not all horses can amble. On chariot

horses galloping, see Igor V. Chechushkov and Andrei V. Epimakhov, "Eurasian Steppe Chariots and Social Complexity During the Bronze Age," *Journal of World Prehistory* 31 (2018): 473.

30 **"let their approval encourage us"**: Rig Veda 1.163.1, 5, 6, 8–13; see also Wendy Doniger O'Flaherty, *The Rig Veda* (London: Penguin, 1981), 26, and David Anthony and Nikolai Vinogradov, "Birth of the Chariot," *Archaeology* 48, no. 2 (March–April 1995): 36–41.

30 **under the walls of Troy**: V. A. Dergachev, О скипетрах,о лошадях, о войне: Этюды в защиту миграционной концепции М.Гимбутас [On scepters, on horses, on war: Studies in the defense of the migration concepts of M. Gimbutas] (St. Petersburg: Institute of Cultural Heritage of the Moldavian Republic, 2007), 143. This attribution of scepters to the chariot-riding aristocracy of prehistoric Europe is challenged by other scholars, notably Robert Drews.

31 **He calls horses assa**: Our word "ass" comes from the Latin *asinus*, derived from a non-Indo-European source, perhaps Sumerian *anšu*, whereas many words for horse in European languages, including *equus*, *hippos*, and the archaic English *eh*, are related to the Avestan *aspa* and Rig Vedic *aśva*.

31 **Sanskrit phrase aśva-sana**: Daniel Potts advises that the whole question of loanwords and so-called Indic deities in Hurrian and Hittite is a minefield.

31 **procedures for either races or warfare**: Modern horse trainers have experimented with Kikkuli's advice to judge its practicality. They found his recommendations for interval training and peak loading surprisingly sensible. He recommended beer, for example, to supply electrolytes after a race. Recht, *The Spirited Horse*, 124.

31 **this recruitment was indeed a widespread phenomenon**: Recht, *The Spirited Horse*, 98.

34 **contemptuously characterized them**: Benjamin S. Arbuckle and Emily L. Hammer, "The Rise of Pastoralism," *Ancient Near East Journal of Archaeological Research* 27, no. 3 (2019): 391–449.

34 **and even the Fertile Crescent**: Xiang Wan, "The Horse in Pre-Imperial China," 33.

35 **with a bang, fully formed**: Shaughnessy, "Historical Perspectives," 190.

35 **dynasties with steppe origins**: Christopher I. Beckwith, *The Scythian Empire* (Princeton, NJ: Princeton University Press, 2023), 254; for petroglyphs see Shaughnessy, "Historical Perspectives," 202.

36 **the equivalent of modern tanks**: Shaughnessy, "Historical Perspectives," 211.

37 **or tip over their vehicles**: as did Darius III at Gaugamela. See Lloyd Llewellyn-Jones, *The Persians* (New York: Basic Books, 2022), 364.

37 **Prince Yang had to be carried off the field**: Tsung-Tung Chang, "A New View of King Wuding," *Monumenta Serica* 37 (1986–87): 1–12; see also Shaughnessy, "Historical Perspectives," 189–237.

37 **a model chariot of that era**: Now in the British Museum, part of the Oxus Treasure collection, a trove acquired in murky circumstances in the 1880s. Inventory no. 123908.

38 **replace him as the leader of the clan**: John Colarusso and Tamirlan Salbiev, eds., *Tales of the Narts: Ancient Myths and Legends of the Ossetians*, trans. Walter May (Princeton, NJ: Princeton University Press, 2016), 48.

39 **stronger leg bones than earlier horses**: Markku Niskanen, "The Prehistoric Origins

of the Domestic Horse and Horseback Riding," *Bulletins et mémoires de la Société d'Anthropologie de Paris* 35, no. 1 (2023): paragraph 42; https://doi.org/10.4000/bmsap.11881.

39   **gelding is an unavoidable practice**: American and British horse owners often complain that it is hard to find a stable that will accept a stallion nowadays. The danger to other horses and to stable employees is so great that they find it challenging to buy insurance against this or retain staff willing to run the risk.

40   **genetically very diverse**: Thomas Jansen, "Mitochondrial DNA and the Origins of the Domestic Horse," *Proceedings of the National Academy of Sciences of the United States of America* 99, no. 16 (Aug. 6, 2002): 10905–10.

40   **based on a few foundational stallions was unknown**: Orlando, "Ancient Genomes," 4.

40   **with closely related individuals**: Gaunitz et al., "Ancient Genomes Revisit the Ancestry."

40   **fearfulness of their hunted ancestors**: Julio Bendezu-Sarmiento, "Horse Domestication History in Turkmenistan and Other Regions of Asia," *Miras* 1 (2021): 22.

40   **the horse-human relationship unique**: Gala Argent, "Do the Clothes Make the Horse? Relationality, Roles and Statuses in Iron Age Inner Asia," *World Archaeology* 42, no. 2 (2010): 157–74.

41   **carry on when wounded**: Argent, "Do the Clothes Make the Horse?," 18. For the number of episodes where a horse rides through fire or water to save its rider, see also Samra Azarnouche, "Miracles, oracles et augures: Essai sur la symbolique du cheval dans l'Iran ancien et médiéval," in *Équidés: Le cheval, l'âne et la mule dans les empire de l'Orient ancien*, ed. Margaux Spruyt and Delphine Poinsot (Paris: Route de l'Orient Actes, 2022).

41   **loud noises, and water obstacle**: James F. Downs, "The Origin and Spread of Riding in the Near East and Central Asia," *American Anthropologist*, n.s., 63, no. 6 (December 1961): 1194.

41   **gradually emerged from these practices**: Digard, *Une histoire du cheval* (173–74), emphasizes that equestrianism developed over a long period of time, attaining its current form only in the later part of the nineteenth century.

41   **eating the horses they have used for riding**: Natasha Fijn, "In the Land of the Horse," in *Living with Herds* (Cambridge: Cambridge University Press, 2011).

41   **"like members of an affectionate family"**: Atkinson, *Travels*, loc. 4698.

41   **in their own right**: Argent, "Do the Clothes Make the Horse?," 168.

42   **will send a horse fleeing**: Argent, "Do the Clothes Make the Horse?," 157–74.

42   **the rider's thighs and coccyx**: Digard, *Une histoire de cheval*, 74.

43   **improved their horse tack with the snaffle bit**: Robert Drews, *Early Riders*, 139–42.

43   **riding would have been tiring and dangerous for horses**: Argent, "Watching the Horses," 153.

44   **who specializes in archery**: Mike Loades, "Scythian Archery," in *Masters of the Steppe: The Impact of the Scythians and Later Nomad Societies of Eurasia*, ed. Svetlana Pankova and St. John Simpson (Oxford: Archaeopress, 2021), 258–60.

44   **slowly into taut readiness**: This myth is illustrated on a golden wine decanter from the fourth century BCE found in the Crimea, now in the State Hermitage Museum, St. Petersburg, (inventory no. KO 11), with a humorous take on the wounded and howling older brothers.

45 **at a distance, with arrows**: *Marco Polo: Le devisement du monde*, ed. René Kappler (Paris: Imprimerie Nationale, 2004), section LXX, p. 81.

45 **human remains in steppe burials**: Marina Daragan, "Scythian Archers of the 4th Century BC," *Masters of the Steppe*, 122.

45 **Ashkenaz**: The term Ashkenaz became the Hebrew word for Europe and then, by extension, the ethnonym for European Jews themselves.

45 **Gansu Province in the east**: Beckwith argues otherwise in his provocative book *The Scythian Empire* (xi).

46 **an arrow from his quiver**: Natasha Fijn, "Human-Horse Sensory Engagement Through Horse Archery," *Australian Journal of Anthropology* 32 (2021): 67.

46 **one of our major sources for early steppe history**: Sima Qian [formerly romanized as Ssu-Ma Ch'ien, with his *Shiji* romanized as *Shih Chi*], *Records of the Grand Historian of China*, trans. Burton Watson (New York: Columbia University Press, 1961), vol. II, part 2, section 110, p. 155. Sima Qian summarized the history of China up to his own time, around 94 BCE. He is the Chinese equivalent to Herodotus or Strabo for our understanding of the early horse breeders.

46 **a herd of 824,925 mares within those twenty years**: Here is the calculation:

generation	female offspring	age of gen 1	brooding years in gen 1 lifetime
1	850	3	20
2	5,950	6	14
3	32,725	9	11
4	130,900	12	8
5	327,250	15	5
6	327,250	18	2
Total	824,925		

Note, of course the number of descendants in each generation will continue to expand but this table shows only the offspring of generations 5 and 6 born within the lifespan of the original mares. Generation 6 will have more fillies, but only when the first mares have died.

47 **quieter on the march**: Strabo, *The Geography*, vol. 3, book 7, chapter 4, paragraph 8.

47 **native-born riders**: Robin Archer, "Chariotry to Cavalry: Developments in the Early First Millennium," in *New Perspectives on Ancient Warfare*, ed. Garrett Fagan and Matthew Trundle (Leiden: Brill, 2010), 78. Archer argues that the settled states developed their cavalry independently, but this ignores the role of the Medes in the Assyrian Empire.

48 **and trained a cavalry arm**: Sima Qian, *Records of the Grand Historian of China*, vol. II, part 2, section 110, p. 159.

48 **adoption of riding breeches**: See such loops in the British Museum, inventory no. 1945,1017.201.

49 **ten thousand cavalry troopers in battle**: Zhi Dao, *History of Military System in China* (DeepLogic, n.d.), unpaginated.

49 **non-Chinese identity even in death**: Sophia-Karin Psarras, "Han and Xiongnu: A Re-examination of Cultural and Political Relations," *Monumenta Serica* 51 (2003): 70. Christopher Beckwith goes even further to argue that Zhao Wuling was a Scythian. See his *The Scythian Empire*, 210.

Chapter 3: Engines of Empire

50 **"like a man to the battle, against thee"**: Jeremiah 50:42.

51 **multinational states with ever-expanding territorial ambitions**: Kees van der Pijl, "Imperial Universalism and the Nomad Counterpoint," in *Nomads, Empires, States* (London: Pluto, 2007), 64. Dominic Lieven, *In the Shadow of the Gods: The Emperor in World History* (London: Penguin, 2022), 20–29. The connection between the char- ioteers and empires is also the subject of Peter Turchin, "A Theory for Formation of Large Empires," *Journal of Global History* 4, no. 2 (2009): 191–217.

51 **closely related to the Scythians of the steppe**: Daniel Potts, "Horse and Pasture in Pre-Islamic Iran" (Jean and Denis Sinor Faculty Fellowship Lecture, Indiana Univer- sity, Bloomington, April 9, 2019). Christopher Beckwith, again, goes one step further to claim that the Medes were themselves Scythians.

52 **the Assyrians had had no cavalry**: Robin Archer, "Chariotry to Cavalry," 70.

52 **Median horses would power their unprecedented expansion**: Potts, "Horse and Pasture in Pre-Islamic Iran," and Karen Radner, "An Assyrian View on the Medes," in *Continuity of Empire (?): Assyria, Media, Persia*, ed. G. B. Lanfranchi, M. Road, R. Rollinger (Padova: Sargon, 2003).

52 **bringing magnificent horses to the Assyrian king**: Ashurbanipal is viewable in the British Museum, inventory no. BM 124876. The Medes are on display in the Louvre Museum, inventory no. AO 19887.

52 **croupiers secured the saddlecloths**: Note the Luristani joined snaffle bits in the Louvre Museum, inventory no. AO 25002.

52 **established their own empire**: Herodotus, *Histories*, trans. A. D. Godley (London: Heinemann, 1920), 1.103.

53 **"every Persian child learns"**: Herodotus, *Histories*, 1.136.

53 **"the land of good horses"**: See the Achaemenid Royal Inscriptions at Livius: https:// www.livius.org/sources/content/achaemenid-royal-inscriptions/dpd/.   Christopher Tuplin, "All the Kings Horses," in Fagan and Trundle, *New Perspectives on Ancient Warfare*, 101–82, and Beckwith, *The Scythian Empire*, 176, argue that the Persians were less horse-mad than the Medes, but as they acquired the empire their attachment to horsemanship grew. See also Pierre Briant, "L'eau du grand roi," in *Drinking in Ancient Societies: History and Culture of Drinks in the Ancient Near East*, ed. Lucio Milano; papers of a symposium held in Rome, May 17–19, 1990, History of the Ancient Near East Studies 6 (Padua: Sargon, 1994). I am indebted to Dan Potts for these references.

53 **mounted on black chargers**: Azarnouche, "Miracles, oracles et augures," in Spruyt and Poinsot, *Équidés*, 241.

54 **grooms and harvested forage—at great expense**: Tuplin, "All the King's Horses," 117.

54 **solidly built and weighing some one thousand pounds**: Ahmad Afshar and Judith Lerner, "The Horses of the Ancient Persian Empire at Persepolis," *Antiquity* 53, no. 207 (March 1979): 44–47. These sizes and weights have been corroborated by Sandor Bökönyi, "Analysis of Ancient Horse Burials in Western Iran," quoted by David Stronach, "Riding in Achaemenid Iran, New Perspectives," *Archaeological, Historical and Geographical Studies* (2009): 216–37. See also Marcel Gabrielli, *Le cheval dans l'Empire achéménide*, vol. 1 of *Studia ad Orientem Antiquum Pertinentia* (Istanbul: Ege Yayınları 2006).

54 **to the weight of the rider**: Shing Müller, "Horse of the Xianbei 300–600 AD: A Brief History," in Fragner et al., *Pferde in Asien*, 187.

55 **requiring ninety days on foot**: Herodotus, *Histories*, 5.50–5.5. Archaeological corroboration is provided in the Persepolis fortification archive; see Richard T. Hallock, *Persepolis Fortification Tablets* (Chicago: University of Chicago Press, 1969), 6, and Daniel T. Potts, "Medes in the Desert: Some Thoughts on the Mounted Archers of Tayna," in *Klänge der Archaeologie: Festschrift für Ricardo Eichmann*, ed. Claudia Bührig et al. (Wiesbaden: Hassarowitz, 2021), 339.

55 **proved essential for the Persian and later empires**: Erin Almagor, "The Horse and the Lion in Achaemenid Persia: Representations of a Duality" *Arts* 10, no. 3 (2021): 41.

55 **required a whole bureaucracy to manage**: Hallock *Persepolis Fortification Tablets*, 47–48. For alfalfa, see R. Heyer, "Pû, Spreu als Pferdefutter," *Baghdader Mitteilungen* 12 (1981): 82–83. Recht (*The Spirited Horse*, 12) discusses the bureaucratic effort of earlier Middle Eastern states.

55 **just 650 horses in its cavalry**: J.A.S. Evans, "Cavalry About the Time of the Persian Wars: A Speculative Essay," *Classical Journal* 82, no. 2 (December 1986–January 1987): 101.

58 **worthy as a divine offering**: Stronach, "Riding in Achaemenid Iran," 216–37.

58 **the independent Scythian auxiliaries**: Xenophon, *Life of Cyrus the Great*, trans. Walter Miller (London: Heinemann 1914), VIII:3.

58 **pocket-sized cavalry forces**: Xenophon, *Cyropaedia*, trans. Walter Miller (London: Heinemann, 1914) VIII:3.

59 **performed in dressage events**: Evans, "Cavalry About the Time of the Persian Wars," 100.

59 **is the epitome of the superior warhorse**: Abolqasem Ferdowsi, *Shahnameh: The Persian Book of Kings*, trans. Dick Davis (New York: Viking, 2006), 132; see the Key Kavosh episode in Mazanderan Section 16.

60 **"more intelligence than his master"**: Atkinson, *Travels*, loc. 4707. In one of the Ossetian folktales, the horse warns the attackers, "Leave us alone. If my master wakes you'll be sorry" (Colarusso and Salbiev, *Tales of the Narts*, 49).

60 **breeding and feeding of some one hundred thousand animals**: When Artaxerxes III invaded Egypt, he brought thirty thousand cavalry, which probably included two or three remounts per trooper (Tuplin, "All the Kings Horses," 150). See also Jérémy Clément, "L'élevage des chevaux de guerre dans le royaume séleucide," in Spruyt and Poinsot, *Équidés*, 127–29.

61 **acrobatics on horseback**: Marina Vialloni, "Un rare mors de cheval sassanide et son caveçon conservés au Metropolitan Museum of Art," in Spruyt and Poinsot, *Équidés*, chapter 6.

61 **relied upon during a long campaign**: Evans, "Cavalry About the Time of the Persian Wars," 103.

62 **carries off racing prize after racing prize**: Carole Ferret and Ahmet Toqtabaev, "Le choix et l'entraînement du cheval de course chez les Kazakhs," *Études mongoles et sibériennes, centrasiatiques et tibétaines* 41 (2010): 4.

62 **associating them with celestial symbolism**: Azarnouche, "Miracles, oracles et augures," in Spruyt and Poinsot, *Équidés*, 245.

62 **harder to steal during the night**: Orlando, "Ancient Genomes," 6.

62 **reserved for ordinary geldings**: Carole Ferret, "Des chevaux pour l'empire," in *Le Turkestan russe: Une colonie comme les autres?*, special issue of *Cahiers d'Asie centrale* 17–18 (2009): 220. Ferret identifies in the Pazyryk burials both ordinary and elite horses.

63 **"doesn't touch the ground" and "gazelle-fast"**: Today's Kyrgyz horse names mostly reflect the physical qualities of the horses, but these names are very ancient. Zh. A. Tokosheva, "Application of Horse Names in Modern Kyrgyz Language from the Works of Mahmud Kashgari, 'Divan-i-Lugat At-Turk,'" Наука, Новые Технологии и Инновации Кыргызстана [Science, new technologies and innovation in Kyrgyzstan] 7 (2020) [in Kyrghyz].

63 **either a historical or an aspirational one**: Lâtife Summerer, "Picturing Persian Victory: The Painted Battle Scene on the Munich Wood," *Ancient Civilizations from Scythia to Siberia* 13 (2005): 3–30. The plundered tomb decoration is now in Munich.

64 **far from their base**: Herodotus, *Histories*, 1.202. The text mentions the river Araxes, which may be confused with the Arax river in the Caucasus. The content makes it clear that the river is in Central Asia, but it could be either the Oxus (modern Amu Darya) or the Jaxartes (Syr Darya).

64 **against the steppe peoples and awaiting their attacks**: Frantz Grenet, "Types of Town Planning in Ancient Iranian Cities, New Considerations," in *The History and Culture of Iran and Central Asia from the Pre-Islamic to the Islamic Period*, ed. D. G. Tor and Minoru Inaba (South Bend, IN: University of Notre Dame, 2022), 15.

65 **charioteers, and foot soldiers**: Ferdowsi, *Shahnameh*, 699.

66 **the monsoon cycle in India**: Irfan Habib, "The Geographical Background" in *The Cambridge Economic History of India*, ed. T. Raychaudhuri and I. Habib (Cambridge: Cambridge University Press, 1982), 1–13.

66 **horses are picky eaters**: Sharpe and Kenny, "Grazing Behavior," 126

66 **vital minerals, especially selenium**: See Bröhm, "The World Map of a Trace Element."

66 **horses are scarce on the ground**: Wendy Doniger, *Winged Stallions and Wicked Mares* (Charlottesville: University of Virginia Press, 2021), 13.

66 **as a region of dense forests**: Lawrence S. Leshnik, "Pastoral Nomadism in the Archaeology of India and Pakistan," *World Archaeology* 4, no. 2 (Oct 1972): 14.

67 **which requires only 20 pounds**: Thomas Trautman, *Elephants and Kings: An Environmental History* (Chicago: University of Chicago Press, 2015), 56.

66 **nor large cavalry forces maneuver**: Trautman, *Elephants*, 290.

66 **elephants all died of starvation**: This anecdote is told of Genghis Khan's conquest of Bukhara; see chapter 8.

68 **the overconfidence of their elephant-mounted adversaries**: Simon Digby.

"Warhorse and Elephant in the Delhi Sultanate: A Study of Military Supplies," *Oxford Monographs* (1971): 51.

68   **they do not reproduce well in captivity**: Trautman, *Elephants*, 86.

69   **hardy races of ponies flourish**: Yashaswini Chandra, *The Tale of the Horse: A History of India on Horseback* (Delhi: Picador, 2021), 71. These geographic differences came to the fore in 1947 when India and Pakistan gained their independence from Britain. Pakistan inherited most of the good horse country, as well as the best fodder for horses. Wealthy turf enthusiasts in Bombay and Calcutta worried about the future of horse races in a world where they could no longer visit their stud farms in Sindh or in Punjab. Progressively the government of India made it easier for the racing set to import horses and feed. Globalization, unimaginable in 1950s India, means that a posh stable in Mumbai today is equipped and provided with any requirement a top trainer from England or Dubai could require. Geography is no longer destiny, but that was very much the case in the preceding millennia.

69   **in the middle of the first millennium**: Jos J. L. Gommans, *Mughal Warfare: Indian Frontiers and High Roads to Empire, 1500–1700* (London: Routledge, 2002), 114.

69   **would spark India's cavalry revolution**: Jayarava Attwood, "Possible Iranian Origins for the śākyas and Aspects of Buddhism," *Journal of the Oxford Centre for Buddhist Studies* 3 (2012): 58. Beckwith also claims the Buddha was a Scythian. See his book *The Scythian Empire*, 242. It is not necessary to accept these arguments to see the influence of steppe horsemen in the beginning of Indian empires.

69   **in addition to three thousand war elephants**: Ranabir Chakravarti, "Equestrian Demand and Dealers: The Early Indian Scenario: Trade and Traders in Early Indian Society," in Fragner et al., *Pferde in Asien*, 150.

70   **the northern plains of Punjab**: Kautilya, *Arthashastra*, trans. R. Shamasastry (Mysore: 1915), 191.

70   **lonely, antisocial, and hard to manage**: Kautilya, *Arthashastra*, 188.

70   **mutton meat with clarified butter, was provided**: Kautilya, *Arthashastra*, 191. Earlier, the Persian kings had fed their horses wine.

70   **Indian equestrian and author Yashaswini Chandra**: Chandra, *Tale of the Horse*, 104.

71   **"turns a man into a racehorse"**: Doniger, *Winged Stallions*, 46.

71   **blinded by passion**: Vatsyayana, *Kamasutra*, trans. Richard Burton (London: Sacred Books of the East, 1883), chapter 7.

71   **the greater scale of horse power versus elephant power**: Plutarch, *Life of Alexander*, book III, chapter 62, section 2.

73   **a bulwark against steppe invasion**: Ranabir Chakravarti, "Equestrian Demand and Dealers," 151. See also Romila Thapar, *A History of India* (Harmondsworth, UK: Penguin, 1966), 1:138.

73   **resumed their raids into the subcontinent**: Bimal Kanti Majumdar, "Military Pursuits and National Defence Under the Second Magadhan Empire," *Proceedings of the Indian History Congress* 12 (1949): 108.

Chapter 4: Desperately Seeking Heavenly Horses

74 **no urgency to ride back to the steppe**: Feng Menglong, *Kingdoms in Peril: A Novel of the Ancient Chinese World at War*, trans. Olivia Milburn (Oakland: University of California Press, 2021), 69. Although Feng's is a seventeenth-century, fictionalized account of the fall of the Zhou dynasty, it has long been admired for its realistic evocation of ancient China.

75 **specific, identifiable ethnicity**: Beckwith, *The Scythian Empire*, 128.

75 **"those who draw the bow," *the same meaning as of the ethnonym Scythian***: Nicola Di Cosmo, *Ancient China and Its Enemies: The Rise of Nomadic Power in East Asian History* (Cambridge: Cambridge University Press, 2002), 171.

75 **Clamorous Barbarians, or Xiongnu**: In ancient Chinese pronunciation this name probably sounded more like "Khona." Some scholars see in the Xiongnu the ancestors of the Mongols or the Turks. Beckwith (*The Scythian Empire*, 180) identifies them as Scythians, albeit with some "creolization" (his term). Recent DNA analysis of their burials suggests that they were a mix of both westerners and easterners, or European and Mongolian types. See Christine Lee and Zhang Linhu, "Xiongnu Population History in Relation to China, Manchuria, and the Western Regions," in *Xiongnu Archaeology: Multidisciplinary Perspectives of the First Steppe Empire in Inner Asia*, ed. Ursula Brosseder and Bryan K. Miller (Freiburg: Vor und Frühgeschichte Archäologe Press, Universität Bonn, 2011), 48.

75 **for the sake of familiarity**: Étienne de la Vaissière, "Central Asia and the Silk Road" in *The Oxford Handbook of Late Antiquity*, ed. Scott Fitzgerald Johnson (Oxford: Oxford University Press, 2012), 147. La Vaissière states categorically that the ancient enemies of China were the same as the Huns of later Iranian and Roman history.

75 **placed petroglyphs of reindeer across their grasslands**: Christine Lee, "Who Were the Mongols (1100–1400 CE)? An Examination of Their Population History," *Current Archaeological Research in Mongolia* (Bonn: Rheinische Friedrich-Wilhelms-Universität, 2009), 583.

78 **received in return for horses**: Nicola Di Cosmo, "Aristocratic Elites in the Xiongnu Empire as Seen from Historical and Archaeological Evidence," in *Nomad Aristocrats in a World of Empires*, ed. Jürgen Paul (Wiesbaden: Dr. Ludwig Reichert Verlag, 2013), 39.

78 **in their dealings with steppe peoples**: Di Cosmo, *Ancient China*, 148.

78 **"customs differed little from those of the steppe peoples"**: Feng, *Kingdoms in Peril*, 76.

78 **for whom he procured horses**: Sima Qian, *Records of the Grand Historian of China*, vol. I, section 5, pp. 3–4.

80 **uniform brown of terra-cotta**: Ladislav Kesner. "Likeness of No One: (Re)presenting the First Emperor's Army," *Art Bulletin* 77, no. 1 (Mar 1995): 115–32.

80 **distinctive S-shaped cheek piece**: Pamela Kyle Crossley, "Flank Contact, Social Contexts, and Riding Patterns in Eurasia, 500–1500," in *How Mongolia Matters: War, Law, and Society*, ed. Morris Rossabi (Leiden: Brill, 2017), 14. For cheek pieces, see Annette L. Juliano, "The Warring States Period—the State of Qin, Yan, Chu, and Pazyryk: A Historical Footnote," *Notes in the History of Art* 10, no. 4 (1991): 28.

80 **funeral practices of the Shang and Zhou dynasties**: Xiang Wan, "The Horse in

Pre-Imperial China," 62. See also Sima Qian, *Records of the Grand Historian of China*, vol. II, section 28, p. 30.

80 **horse and human victims**: Sima Qian, *Records of the Grand Historian of China*, vol. I, section 6, p. 63.

80 **no longer life-sized but of great liveliness**: The practices are described by Sima Qian, *Records of the Grand Historian of China*, vol. II, section 28, p. 67.

81 **carefully monitored grooms**: Xiang Wan, "The Horse in Pre-Imperial China," 119.

81 **several directorates of pasturage**: Ruth I. Meserve, "Chinese Hippology and Hippiatry: Government Bureaucracy and Inner Asian Influence," *Zeitschrift der Deutschen Morgenländischen Gesellschaft* 148, no. 2 (1998): 283.

81 **recruited from the steppe peoples**: H. G. Creel, "The Role of the Horse in Chinese History," *American Historical Review* 70, no. 3 (April 1965): 670.

81 **"were reduced to riding about in ox carts"**: Sima Qian, *Records of the Grand Historian of China*, vol. II, section 30, p. 79.

83 **"will kill women"**: Yu Xin, "Étude sur la physiognomonie du cheval sous les dynasties des Han et des Tang (IIIe siècle av. è. c.–Xe siècle) à partir de documents archéologiques," *Cahiers d'Extrême-Asie* 25 (2016): 270.

84 **can cause accidents**: Jack Murphy and Sean Arkins, "Facial Hair Whorls (Trichoglyphs) and the Incidence of Motor Laterality in the Horse," *Behavioural Processes* 79, no. 1 (2008): 7–12; several papers in the *Journal of Equine Veterinary Science* also confirm the correlations between color, whorls, behavior, and laterality.

84 **practically useless in battle**: Morris Rossabi, *From Yuan to Modern China and Mongolia* (Leiden: Brill 2015), 61. Denis Sinor, "Horse and Pasture in Inner Asian History," *Oriens Extremus* 19, nos. 1–2 (December 1972): 172.

84 **"horses that look like this one"**: Ban Gu [formerly romanized as Pan Ku], *The History of the Former Han Dynasty* [漢書, Han Shu], translated by Homer H. Dubs, et al. (Baltimore: Waverly, 1938), 290. Also available online: https://xtf.lib.virginia.edu/xtf/view?docId=2003_Q4/uvaGenText/tei/z000000037.xml;query=;brand=default.

84 **"prince who tames horses"**: Wolfgang Kubin, "Vom Roß zum Schindmäre," in Fragner et al., *Pferde in Asien*, 196.

85 **but could not easily obtain**: The Flying Horse of Gansu, known as "Wu Wei," 武威, was excavated in 1969 and is now in the Gansu Provincial Museum. Chinese scholars believe this horse was directly inspired by Ma Yuan. See Yu Xin, "Étude sur la physiognomonie du cheval," 292.

86 **and, thus, the grass**: Guo-Xin Sun et al., "Distribution of Soil Selenium in China Is Potentially Controlled by Deposition and Volatilization?," *Scientific Reports* 6, no. 20953 (2016): 2.

86 **a thousand pieces of gold**: Madeline K. Spring, "Fabulous Horses and Worthy Scholars in Ninth-Century China," *T'oung Pao*, 2nd ser., 74, nos. 4–5 (1988): 189.

86 **"compare with those of the Huns"**: Creel, "The Role of the Horse," 657.

86 **fewer fears than stabled horses**: Sid Gustavson, "Equine Behavior Through Time," *Horseman's News* (December 1, 2022).

87 **"not knowing he was trying to spout jade"**: Spring, "Fabulous Horses," 190.

87 **often proved disappointing**: Ban Gu, *Food and Money in Ancient China: The Earliest*

Economic History of China to A.D. 25, trans. Nancy Lee Swann (Eastford, CT: Martino Publishing, 2013), 24B:26a/1–2.

87   **to turn the land over for cultivation**: Ban Gu, *Han Shu,* trans. Burton Watson (New York: Columbia University Press, 1974), 177–78.

87   **never managed to resupply their cavalry with adequate horses**: Di Cosmo, *Ancient China,* 132–35.

88   **"I cast your bones, my friend, into the dragon's spring"**: Spring, "Fabulous Horses," 29. The Chinese text reads: 傷我馬詞: 風雨孤征，簡書之威。俾予弗顛，我馬焉依。屑屑其勞也，非德而何？予至武陵，居沅水傍。或逾月未嘗跨焉，以故莫得伸其所長。踏顧望兮，頓其鎖繮。飲齕日削兮，精耗神傷。寒檻騷騷兮，瘁毛蒼涼。路聞蹢躞兮，逸氣騰驤。朔雲深分邊草遠，意欲往兮聲不揚。　然自不得其所而死，故其嗟也兼常。初，元宗屬大宛而盡有其名馬，命典牧以時起居。洎西幸蜀，往往民間得其種而蕃焉。故良毛色者率非中土類也。稽是毛物，豈祖於宛歟。漢之歌曰：龍爲友。武陵有水曰龍泉，遂歸骨於是川。且吊之曰：生於磧礫善馳走，萬里南來困邱阜。青菰寒菽非適口，病聞北風猶舉首。金台已平骨空朽，投之龍淵從爾友。

89   **more distant but more productive breeders**: Di Cosmo, *Ancient China,* 133.

89   **family with opportunely offered, well-born brides**: Di Cosmo, *Ancient China,* 195.

89   **frequently occasioned violence and disorder**: David Christian, *A History of Russia, Central Asia and Mongolia,* vol. 2, *Inner Eurasia from the Mongol Empire to Today, 1260–2000* (Hoboken: Wiley Blackwell, 2017), 2:65.

89   **"under the pretext of offering gifts"**: Armin Selbitschka, "Early Chinese Diplomacy: Realpolitik Versus the So-Called Tributary System," *Academia Sinica,* 3rd ser., 28, no. 1 (2015): 99, quoting the *Han Shu,* 94A, 3886. 今悔過來，而無親屬 貴人，奉獻者皆什賈賤人，欲通貨市買，獻爲名。

90   **Chinese products, like mirrors of silver, lacquer, and silk fabric**: Di Cosmo, *Ancient China,* 94. Yuri Pines, "Beasts or Humans: Pre-Imperial Origins of the Sino-Barbarian Dichotomy," in *Mongols, Turks, and Others, Eurasian Nomads and the Sedentary World,* ed. Reuven Amitai and Michael Biran (Brill: Leiden 2005), 80.

90   **these valuable and easily transportable objects**: Thomas Barfield, "The Hsiung-nu Imperial Confederacy: Organization and Foreign Policy," *Journal of Asian Studies* 41, no. 1 (November 1981): 56.

90   **to buy their political loyalty**: William Honeychurch, "Alternative Complexities: The Archaeology of Pastoral Nomadic States," *Journal of Archaeological Research* 22, no. 4 (December 2014): 308.

90   **could be, and had to be, used for war**: Sinor, "Horse and Pasture," 177.

91   **the horse breeders embargoed China**: Sinor, "Horse and Pasture," 173.

90   **many thousands of miles away**: Beckwith (*The Scythian Empire,* 128) claims that Modun himself was a Scythian named Bagatwan.

90   **and, finally, his father**: Y Yü, "The Hsiung-nu," in *The Cambridge History of Early Inner Asia,* ed. Denis Sinor (Cambridge: Cambridge University Press, 1990), 120.

92   **as much power and awe as the emperor himself**: William Honeychurch, "Alternative Complexities: The Archaeology of Pastoral Nomadic States," *Journal of Archaeological Research* 22, no. 4 (December 2014): 287. Psarras, "Han and Xiongnu: A Re-examination," likewise considers that the chanyu and the emperor of China were equals.

92 **equivalent to the later term khaghan**: Beckwith (*The Scythian Empire*, 193) draws a comparison with Genghis and suggest it means "Oceanic" or "Universal" ruler.

92 **what is today Mongolia**: Barfield, "The Hsiung-nu," 48.

92 **combined population of only one million souls**: Barfield, "The Hsiung-nu," 54.

92 **concentrate their forces locally**: Christian, *A History of Russia, Central Asia and Mongolia*, 2:12.

93 **augured world dominion for such an army**: Helmut Nickel, "Steppe Nomad Warriors, Their Horses and Their Weapons," in Alexander, *Furusiyya*, 1:45. Coat colors corresponding to the cardinal directions have been found in permafrost excavations in Mongolia. See also Sima Qian, *Records of the Grand Historian of China*, vol. II, section 110, pp. 165–66.

93 **"in order to make up the deficiency"**: Sima Qian, *Records of the Grand Historian of China*, vol. II, section 30, p. 87.

93 **"it would be no great addition to the empire"**: Ban Gu, *Han Shu* (trans. Watson), 179.

94 **were four times greater than those of the Huns**: Psarras, "Han and Xiongnu: A Re-examination," 132.

94 **transfer of so many costly gifts**: Sima Qian, *Records of the Grand Historian of China*, vol. II, section 110, pp. 170–72.

94 **extracting wealth from Han China**: The Metropolitan Museum in New York has some beautiful, representative pieces that came into its collection as a gift of John Pierpont Morgan.

95 **"due to appear from the northwest"**: Sima Qian, *Records of the Grand Historian of China*, vol. II, section 123, p. 240.

95 **A court poet accordingly rhapsodized**: 太一貺，天馬下，沾赤汗，沫流赭，志俶儻，精權奇，籋浮雲，晻上馳，體容與，迣萬里, from 藝文類聚 [A categorized collection of literary writing]. I am obliged to Jamie Greenbaum for this reference and for help with the translation, as well as with the other Chinese poems in this chapter.

96 **the wonderful properties of these unusual horses**: Sima Qian, *Records of the Grand Historian of China*, vol. II, section 123, p. 240.

96 **"ill with the wind"**: quoted in Liu Xiang, *Traditions of Exemplary Women*, chapter 6, appendix 5. Available online at http://www2.iath.virginia.edu/exist/cocoon/xwomen/texts/hanshu/d2.29/1/0/bilingual.

97 **sent back empty-handed**: Sima Qian, *Records of the Grand Historian of China*, vol. II, section 123, p. 232.

97 **improbable event of their success**: Sima Qian, *Records of the Grand Historian of China*, vol. II, section 123, p. 242.

97 **and vowed revenge**: Sima Qian, *Records of the Grand Historian of China*, vol. II, section 123, p. 246.

97 **and many smaller pack animals**: Sima Qian, *Records of the Grand Historian of China*, vol. II, section 123, p. 247.

98 **of their adventurous lives**: See Paul Pelliot, *Carnets de Route, 1906–1908* (Paris: Guimet Museum, 2008), 416.

98 **"plenty of water and grass"**: E. Bretschneider, *Mediaeval Researches from Eastern Asiatic Sources: Fragments Towards the Knowledge of the Geography and History of Central and Western Asia from the 13th to the 17th Century* (Strassburg: Trübner, 1888), 63.

100 **"a stew made from just one pheasant"**: Muhammad Zahiruddin Babur, *The Babur-nama: Memoirs of Babur, Prince and Emperor*, trans. Wheeler M. Thackston (New York: Modern Library, 2002), 85.

100 **and still does**: Zhu Yanshi and Liu Tao, "Looking for the City of the Horse: Mingtepa During the Time of Dayuan Kingdom," in *The World of the Ancient Silk Road*, ed. Xinru Liu (London: Routledge, 2023), 204. When these two scholars excavated the site of Mingtepa, which they identified as the citadel besieged by General Li, they noted that it was still rich in alfalfa. Sima Qian reported this fact: *Records of the Grand Historian of China*, vol. II, section 123, p. 245.

100 **three thousand superior horses**: Sima Qian, *Records of the Grand Historian of China*, vol. II, section 123, p. 250.

100 **with celebratory verses**: 天馬徠，從西極，涉流沙，九夷服。天馬徠，出泉水，虎脊兩，化若鬼。天馬徠，歷無草，徑千里，循東道。天馬徠，執徐時，將搖舉，誰與期?天馬徠，開遠門，竦予身，逝昆侖。天馬徠，龍之媒，游閶闔，觀玉臺. This poem is quoted in Sima Qian, *Shiji*, vol. 1, part 4, section 56; author's translation from the Chinese text on the Chinese Text Project website: https://ctext.org/shiji.

102 **the Hun monopoly over horses**: Sima Qian, *Records of the Grand Historian of China*, vol. II, section 110, p. 168.

102 **not to sack her city**: The identification of the Huns of China with those of Europe has riled scholars since the eighteenth century. A recent summary can be found in Alexander Savelyev and Choongwon Jeong, "Early Nomads of the Eastern Steppe and Their Tentative Connections in the West," *Evolutionary Human Sciences* 2, E20 (2020): 1–17.

Chapter 5: Silk Road or Horse Road

104 **went one saying**: Liu Xinru, "Migration and Settlement of the Yuezhi-Kushan: Interaction and Interdependence of Nomadic and Sedentary Societies," *Journal of World History* 12, no. 2 (Fall 2001): 273.

104 **"subdued and vanquished them"**: Ban Gu, *Han Shu* (trans. Watson), book 94A, line 3757. See also Sima Qian, *Records of the Grand Historian of China*, vol. II, section 110, p.168.

106 **force to be reckoned with**: Henry Falk, "Five Yabgu of the Yuezhi," *Bulletin of the Asia Institute*, new ser., 28 (2014): 36.

106 **"their bones are dragon wings"**: quoted in Schafer, *Golden Peaches*, 137.

106 **for the enterprising horse breeders**: Chakravarti, "Equestrian Demand and Dealers," 7.

107 **this fifteen-hundred-foot-high pass**: Jason Neelis, "Passages to India: Saka and Kushan Migrations in Historical Contexts," in *On the Cusp of an Era: Art in the Pre-Kuṣāna World*, ed. Doris Meth Srinivasan (Leiden: Brill, 2007), 62. Karl Jettmar, "Exploration in Baltistan," *South Asian Archaeology* 9, no. 2 (1990): 808.

107 **out of the market**: Müller, "Horses," in Fragner et al., *Pferde in Asien*, 189.

110 **"whispers to horses"**: Liu Xinru, "Migration and Settlement," 290; Trautman, *Elephants*, 126. Aśvaghosa was once teaching and singing the principles of dharma to a crowd in the royal city when the king deliberately offered food to seven hungry horses to test their reaction to Aśvaghosa's teaching. The horses were distressed due to hunger, but they did not touch the food. Instead, they listened to Aśvaghosa's sermon.

110   **China for the first time**: Liu Xinru, "Migration and Settlement," 290.

110   **cherkeskas, and big boots**: see Paris's Guimet Museum collection of Kushan art, inventories AO, 29071 and D-1790; a better-known version of Kanishka's statue is in the Government Museum, Mathura. For Khalchayan, see Galina A. Pugachenkova, *Skul'ptura Khalchaiana* [The sculpture of Khalchayan] (Moscow: Iskusstvo, 1971).

111   **for sale in Indian and Chinese markets**: Ulf Jaeger, "Some Remarks on the Silk Road," in Fragner et al., *Pferde in Asien*, 78. See also Orlando, *Conquête*, 122.

111   **horse armor in combat**: Müller, "Horses" in Fragner et al., *Pferde in Asien*, 187.

111   **carefully choreographed displays**: Thomas Druml, "Functional Traits in Early Horse Breeders of Mongolia, India and China from the Perspective of Animal Breeding," in Fragner et al., *Pferde in Asien*, 11.

111   **water consumption for the deserts**: The three-fold division of horses into "representational" (later called arghamak), "plateau sprinters," and durable ponies comes from Druml, "Functional Traits," in Fragner et al., *Pferde in Asien*, 10–11.

111   **create the first distinct breeds**: Orlando, "Ancient Genomes," 4–5. Naveed Khan, "The Genomic Origins of Modern Horses Revealed by Ancient DNA: From Early Domestication to Modern Breeding" (PhD thesis, Natural History Museum of Denmark, 2019), 59.

111   **was an important criterion for buyers**: Arne Ludwig et al., "Coat Color Variation at the Beginning of Horse Domestication," *Science* 324, no. 24 (April 2009): 485.

111   **in creating breeds**: Indeed, a higher degree of breeding tends to create monocolored coats. D. Bennet and R. S. Hoffman, "*Equus caballus* Linnaeus," *Mammalian Species* 628 (1999): 2–3.

111   **like their wild cousins**: Mongolian horses are not highly bred: almost every known color variant can be found within the Mongolian breed. However, 56.7 percent of the horse population in Mongolia remains dark-colored because of historical preferences; A. Turk, "A Scientific and Historical Investigation."

112   **a single, random mutation**: Orlando, *Conquête*, 146.

112   **began to acquire its modern characteristics**: Orlando, "Ancient Genomes," 3–4.

113   **centuries after their disappearance**: Emel Esin, "The Horse in Turkic Art," *Central Asiatic Journal* 10, no. 3–4 (1965): 170.

113   **descendants of the Kushans**: Johnny Cheung, "On the Origin of the Name Afghan and Pashtun (Again)," in *Studia Philologica Iranica Gherardo Gnoli Memorial Volume*, ed. Enrico Morano et al. (Rome: Scienze e Lettere, 2017). Cheung believes this is a folk etymology, though Michael Barry (personal communication) vigorously asserts the contrary.

113   **adding a year to their journey into China**: Dilnoza Duturaeva, *Qarakhanid Roads to China: A History of Sino-Turkic Relations* (Leiden: Brill, 2022), 67.

113   **were not professional merchants**: Khazanov, "Steppe Nomads in the Eurasian Trade," *Chungara Revista de Antropología Chilena* 51, no. 1 (2019): 88.

114   **"sea of beasts"**: Joseph Kessel, *Le jeu du roi: Reportage en Afghanistan* (Paris: Arthaud, 2022), 150. Author's translation.

114   **traders crossing the passes**: This situation is mentioned in the sixth century, again in sixteenth-century documents, and was witnessed by the English in the nineteenth

century. Frantz Grenet, "The Nomadic Element in the Kushan Empire (1st–3rd century AD)," *Journal of Central Eurasian Studies* 3 (2012): 9.

114 **"those who travel"**: Jos J. L. Gommans, *The Rise of the Indo-Afghan Empire c. 1710–1780* (New Delhi: Manohar, 2019), 21.

115 **these troublesome fairs**: Hilda Ecsedy, "Trade-and-War Relations Between the Turks and China in the Second Half of the 6th Century," *Acta Orientalia Academiae Scientiarum Hungaricae* 21, no. 2 (1968): 141.

116 **for centuries, a big business**: Chakravarti, "Equestrian Demand and Dealers," 12–15.

116 **spaces all across the subcontinent**: Gommans, "Warhorse and Post-Nomadic Empire in Asia, c. 1000–1800," *Journal of Global History* (2007): 10.

116 **you could probably not afford it**: The description is based on my own experience and corroborated by C.J.C. Davidson, *Diary of Travels and Adventures in Upper India* (London: Henry Colburn, 1843), I:94.

117 **silver a year to live**: Bas van Leeuwen et al., "The Standard of Living in Ancient Societies: A Comparison Between the Han Empire, the Roman Empire and Babylonia," *Centre for Global Economic History*, Working Paper 45 (University of Utrecht 2013): 8–11.

117 **skinny horses and fattening them up**: I discovered this for myself when I needed to resell horses in Afghanistan. We had been caught by surprise in heavy snow and could no longer find forage for our horses, which became too weak to ride, turning literally into wasting assets. The longer we rode them, the less they were worth, and in the end we had to sell them at a huge loss. The Powindahs who bought them reckoned they would survive the winter if no one rode them. Then, after fattening them up with spring grasses, they would sell them for a handsome profit.

118 **in and around Haridwar**: Few horses are offered for sale in the market now, though the livestock market is lively. Godmen have replaced Powindahs. In 2021, despite COVID-19, nine million pilgrims attended the festival.

118 **the spiritual map of India**: Jos J. L. Gommans, *The Indian Frontier: Horse and Warband in the Making of Empire* (London: Routledge, 2017), chapter 3.

118 **money around 1000 CE**: Syed Ejaz Hussain, "Silver Flow and Horse Supply to Sultanate Bengal with Special Reference to Trans-Himalayan Trade (13th–16th Centuries)," *Journal of the Economic and Social History of the Orient* 56, no. 2 (2013): 265.

119 **diplomatic or commercial exchange**: To this day in northern Afghanistan, men like to wear these stiff silk robes off their shoulders, resplendent in silver, green, red, and other iridescent colors. Former Afghan president Hamid Karzai always wore one, along with his signature lambswool cap.

119 **wards off biting insects, especially bedbugs**: Saglar Bougdaeva, trans., *Jangar: The Epic of the Kalmyk Nomads* (Oakland: University of California Press, 2022), 12.

119 **heart of Asian trade**: Khodadad Rezakhani, "The Road That Never Was: The Silk Road and Trans-Eurasian Exchange," *Comparative Studies of South Asia, Africa and the Middle East* 30, no. 3 (2010): 429.

119 **to those distant markets**: Tim Williams, "Mapping the Silk Roads," in *The Silk Road: Interwoven History* (Paris: UNESCO, 2015), 7.

120 **the capital at Chang'an**: Étienne de la Vaissière, "Trans-Asian Trade, or the Silk Road Deconstructed (Antiquity, Middle Ages)," in *The Cambridge History of Capitalism*

(Cambridge: Cambridge University Press, 2014), I:114–15; also Di Cosimo, *Ancient China*, 183.

120 **but the Horse Road**: Ulf Jaeger, "Some Remarks," in Fragner et al., *Pferde in Asien*, 82.

120 **for local consumption**: David Christian, "Silk Roads or Steppe Roads? The Silk Roads in World History," *Journal of World History* 11, no. 1 (Spring 2000): 7.

120 **Luxury simply piggybacked on the vital trade**: Duturaeva, *Qarakhanid Roads*, 196; La Vaissière, "Trans-Asian Trade," 113.

120 **budget on imported horses**: Christopher I. Beckwith, "The Impact of the Horse and Silk Trade on the Economies of T'ang China and the Uighur Empire," *Journal of the Economic and Social History of the Orient* 34, no. 2 (1991): 194.

121 **and from there to China**: Suchandra Ghosh, "The Route of Horse Trade Early in India (up to c. 500 AD)," *Proceedings of the Indian History Congress*, vol. 61, part 1 (2000–2001), 128.

121 **diplomats, not merchants**: Khazanov, "Steppe Nomads in the Eurasian Trade," 96.

122 **modern-day Afghanistan or Tajikistan**: Khazanov, "Steppe Nomads in the Eurasian Trade," 88; Ursula Brosseder, "A Study on the Complexity and Dynamics of Interaction and Exchange in Late Iron Age Eurasia," in Bemmann and Schmauder, *Complexity of Interaction Along the Eurasian Steppe Zone*, 208.

122 **a standardized amount**: Helen Wang, "Textiles as Money on the Silk Road?" *Journal of the Royal Asiatic Society* 23, no. 2 (2013): 167.

122 **silk for one horse**: Tan Mei Ah, "Exonerating the Horse Trade for the Shortage of Silk: Yuan Zhen's 'Yin Mountain Route,'" *Journal of Chinese Studies* 57, no. 47 (2013): 64.

122 **was ten to one**: Tan, "Exonerating the Horse Trade," 64.

122 **ceased to be a Chinese monopoly**: Berit Hildebrandt, "Roman Silk Trade and Markets," in Liu Xinru, *The World of the Ancient Silk Road*, 499.

122 **from Iran to China**: Liu Xinru, "Regional Study," in *A World with States, Empires and Networks, 1200 BCE–900 CE*, ed. Craig Benjamin (Cambridge: Cambridge University Press, 2015), 4:466.

122 **to buy the product on offer**: Hildebrandt, "Roman Silk," in Liu, *The World of the Ancient Silk Road*, 499.

123 **female fingers to weave the silk**: Tan, "Exonerating the Horse Trade," 54.

123 **mulberry trees and silkworms**: Chen Zhonghai (陈忠海), "The Southern Song's Tea and Horse Agency," trans. Peter Micic, Tea Horse Road Project, https://teahorseroadproject.wordpress.com/tag/tea-and-horse-agency/.

123 **hardy Himalayan ponies**: Jeff Fuchs, "The Tea Horse Road," *Silk Road* 6, no. 1 (Summer 2008): 63. Tibetans were quite different from their steppe neighbors. They neither drank horse milk nor ate horse meat. Rather, like the Bedouins, they raised horses for prestige and raiding, in addition to transport. See Suttie, Reynolds, and Batello, *Grasslands*, 956. A well-off herding family kept 4 horses for 380 ruminants and 18 yaks.

Chapter 6: Equine Mania

125 **training elite horses to dance**: Paul W. Kroll, "The Dancing Horses of T'ang," *T'oung Pao*, 2nd ser., 67, nos. 3–5 (1981): 243.

125 **before the spectators**: Thomas O. Höllmann, "On the Road Again: Diplomacy and Trade from a Chinese Perspective," in Bemmann and Schmauder, *Complexity of Interaction Along the Eurasian Steppe Zone*, 562.

126 **preeminent branch of the military**: Jonathan Karam Skaff, "Straddling Steppe and Sown: Tang China's Relations with the Nomads of Inner Asia (640–756)" (PhD thesis, University of Michigan, 1998), 36; Höllmann, "On the Road Again," 561.

126 **"the state will be in danger of perishing"**: see Curry, "Horse Nations," 1288–93.

127 **"cannot be ignored"**: *Zizhi Tongjian*, chapters 195 and 192, quoted in Jack W. Chen, *The Poetics of Sovereignty: On Emperor Taizong of the Tang Dynasty* (Leiden: Brill, 2020), 35.

127 **forcing him reluctantly to accede**: Li Jinxiu, "The Square Matrix, Elite Cavalry and the Modao: On the Military Tactics for Combat with the Türks Adopted by the Sui and Tang Empires," *Eurasian Studies* 2 (2014): 69.

130 **forty thousand to fifty thousand remounts a year**: Jonathan Karam Skaff, *Sui-Tang China and Its Turko-Mongol Neighbors: Culture, Power, and Connections, 580–800* (New York: Oxford University Press, 2012), 259.

130 **clan of origin**: Peter B. Golden, "The Türk Imperial Tradition in the Pre-Chinggisid Era," in *Imperial Statecraft*, ed. David Sneath (Bellingham: Western Washington University Press, 2006), 31.

130 **either as grooms or as cavalrymen**: Schafer, *Golden Peaches*, 148, and Skaff, "Straddling Steppe and Sown," 183–84.

131 **certify their state of readiness**: Jonathan Karam Skaff, "Tang China's Horse Power: The Borderland Breeding Ranch System," in *Eurasian Empires in Antiquity and the Early Middle Ages: Contact and Exchange Between the Graeco-Roman World, Inner Asia and China*, ed. H. Kim, F. Vervaet, and S. Adali (Cambridge: Cambridge University Press, 2017), 38.

131 **ready for the emperor's commands**: Kroll, "The Dancing Horses of T'ang," 182.

131 **five "thousand-li" foals**: Xiuqin Zhou, "Zhaoling: The Mausoleum of Emperor Tang Taizong," *Sino-Platonic Papers* 187 (April 2009): 174.

132 **of actual horses**: Schafer, *Golden Peaches*, 155.

133 **magically come back to life**: Zhou, "Zhaoling," 137.

133 **in equestrian competitions**: Indeed, it appears to have been easier to secure honors in a foreign court than at home. An adviser to the Roman emperor warned, "Don't promote foreigners, who are not of royal birth in their own land, to great honours, nor entrust great offices to them; for you will certainly injure yourself by doing so, as well as the Romans who are your officials"; quoted by Charlotte Mary Roueche, "Defining the Foreign in Kekaumenos," *Strangers to Themselves: The Byzantine Outsider* (Farnham: Ashgate Variorum, 2000), 209.

133 **invented the saddle tree**: Irina Dmitrievna Tkačenko, "Riding Horse Tack Among the Cattle-Breeders of Central Asia and Southern Siberia in the First and Second Millennia CE," *Études mongoles et sibériennes, centrasiatiques et tibétaines* 41 (2010): 210.

134 **the characteristic bucket shape of the Turco-Mongol saddle**: Digard, *Une histoire du cheval*, 74.

135 **recruited as mercenaries and auxiliaries**: Thomas Salman, "Combattre à cheval pendant les guerres byzantino-perses," in Spruyt and Poinsot, *Équidés*, 164.

135 **prevailed across eastern Europe, as in China**: Bartosiewicz, "Ex Oriente Equus," 3.

135   **deployed by the enemy**: Daniel T. Potts, "The Antiquity and Nature of Horseshoe-
      ing in Iran" (unpublished manuscript), 5.

136   **Siyavosh's Shabrang**: Yves Porter, "Rakhsh et Shabdiz, chevaux héroïques de la lit-
      térature persane," in *Chevaux et cavaliers arabes dans les arts d'Orient et d'Occident*, ed.
      Jean-Pierre Digard (Paris: Gallimard, 2002), 205.

136   **adventure and exploits**: Johannes Preiser-Kapeller, "Heroes, Traitors and Horses:
      Mobile Elite Warriors in Byzantium and Beyond, 500–1100 CE" (lecture given at
      Columbia University, November 25, 2013). Also: Skaff, *Sui-Tang China and Its Turko-
      Mongol Neighbors*, 75 and 104, and Vitomir Mitevski, "The Akritic Hero in Byzantine
      and Macedonian Epic Poetry," *Colloquia Humanistica* 7 (2018).

136   **courtly manners in polo games**: Thomas Allsen, *The Royal Hunt in Eurasian History*
      (Philadelphia: University of Pennsylvania Press, 2006), 223–26; Matthew P. Canepa,
      The Two Eyes of the Earth (Oakland: University of California Press, 2017), 174–82; V. L.
      Bower and C. MacKenzie, "Polo: The Emperor of Games," *Asian Games: The Art of Con-
      test* (New York: Asia Society, 2004), 223–303; V. L. Bower, "Polo in Tang China: Sport
      and Art," *Asian Art* 4, no. 3 (1991): 23–45; James T. C. Liu, "Polo and Cultural Change:
      From T'ang to Sung China," *Harvard Journal of Asiatic Studies* 45, no. 1 (1985): 203–24.

136   **rank of provincial governor**: Joel Thomas Walker, *The Legend of Mar Qardagh: Nar-
      rative and Christian Heroism in Late Antique Iraq* (Berkeley: University of California
      Press, 2006), 128.

137   **"the Turks get possession"**: Ferdowsi, *Shahnameh*, 248. This text is my translation.

137   **Sirkeci train station**: Matthew P. Canepa, "Distant Displays of Power: Understand-
      ing the Cross-Cultural Interactions Among the Elites of Rome, Sasanian Iran and
      Sui-Tang China," *Ars Orientalis* 38 (2010): 137.

138   **as if they were in flight**: Höllmann, "On the Road Again," 561.

138   **to reduce the risk of serious injuries**: Hu Songmei, Yaowu Hu, Junkai Yang, Miaomiao
      Yang, Pianpian Wei, Yemao Hou, and Fiona B. Marshall, "From Pack Animals to Polo:
      Donkeys from the Ninth-Century Tang Tomb of an Elite Lady in Xi'an, China," *Antiq-
      uity* 94, no. 374 (2020): 455–72. See also Yin Hung Young, *The Horses of China* (Paramus,
      NJ: Homa & Sekey, 2021), 87. Young recounts how China's sole female sovereign, the
      empress Wu Zetian, had her own all-woman team, dressed in red satin and gold livery.

138   **his political enemies killed**: Liu, "Polo and Cultural Change," 203–24.

139   **lateral movement to their mounts**: Crossley, "Flank Contact," in Rossabi, *How Mon-
      golia Matters*, 139.

139   **ball on a string**: John Masson Smith Jr., "From Pasture to Manger: The Evolution
      of Mongol Cavalry Logistics in Yuan China and Its Consequences," in Fragner et al.,
      Pferde in Asien, 68.

140   **"horse and the spear"**: al-Mutanabbi, *Poems of al-Mutanabbi*, trans. and ed. A. J.
      Arberry (Cambridge: Cambridge University Press, 1967), 73 (poem 12, line 22).

140   **speed for raiding**: see Comte Waclaw Seweryn Rzewuski, *Impressions d'Orient et
      d'Arabie* (Paris: José Corti, 2002), 455–80, for a complete description of Bedouin eques-
      trian practices.

141   **different horse breeds**: For a description of these see Digard, *Une histoire du cheval*,
      101. See also Digard, "Les cultures équestre à l'origine de l'équitation arabe," in *Che-
      vaux et cavaliers arabes*, 25.

141 **princely dilettante and horse lover** *Mubarak Qasim Zangi*: Esin, "The Horse in Turkic Art," 180.

141 **a present for the caliph of Baghdad**: Records of the Caliph Hisham tell of his organizing horse races involving four thousand riders at a time. Alastair Northedge, "Horse Racing at Samarra," in Alexander, *Furusiyya*, 1:106.

142 **the Arabic-speaking world**: Abû Abdallah Ibn Akhî Hizâm al-Khuttalîl, *Chevaux et Hippiatrie*, trans. Abdelkrim El Kasri et Jamal Hossaini-Hilali (Rabat: Association du Salon du Cheval d'El Jadida, 2018).

142 **evoked this cult of speed**: Emel Esin, "At Mitleri," https://www.zdergisi.istanbul/makale/at-mitleri-304.

143 **to Genghis Khan himself**: Walther Heissig, "A Note on the Custom of Seterlekü," *Harvard Ukrainian Studies* 3–4, part 1 (1979–80): 394–98.

143 **dragons and horses continued for centuries**: Azarnouche, "Miracles, oracles et augures," in Spruyt and Poinsot, *Équidés*, 241.

144 **"the highest illumination"**: Tsangnyön Heruka, *The Life of Milarepa*, trans. Andrew Quintman (London: Penguin, 2010), 151–52.

144 **the persistence and power of this metaphor**: Azarnouche, "Miracles, oracles et augures," in Spruyt and Poinsot, *Équidés*, 240.

144 **their capital, Konya**: Esin, "The Horse in Turkish Art," 172.

144 **south, north, east, west, and center**: Fijn, "In the Land of the Horse," 151.

145 **"The army knows its royal horseman"**: quoted in Esin, "The Horse in Turkish Art," 172.

145 **foraging on roots and scrub**: M. N. Mouraviev, *Voyage en Turcomanie et à Khiva, Fait en 1819 et 1820* (Paris: Louis Tenré, 1823), 246.

145 **be stubborn and bad-tempered**: Esin, "The Horse in Turkish Art," 169.

146 **"thus impaled upon the hill"**: Ibn Battuta, *The Travels*, trans. Samuel Lee (London: Oriental Translation Committee, 1828), 238.

146 **American presidents Lincoln and Kennedy**: See Robert Hillenbrand, *The Great Mongol Shahname* (London: Hali, 2023), 205.

147 **into a prize racer**: Ferret and Toqtabaev, "Le choix et l'entraînement du cheval de course chez les Kazakhs," 4–6.

147 **for just so many days**: Berdali Ospan, Почему казахи так хорошо знают коней? [Why do Kazakhs know horses so well?], https://365info.kz/2020/02/pochemu-kazahi -tak-horosho-znayut-. In the famous Iranian bandit ballad cycle *Kuroğlu*, the hero's father, a synšy, picks a foal for the king. The foal is so ugly, the king has the unlucky horse expert executed. The bereaved son runs off with the foal, who turns into a formidable warhorse. Later they make short work of the king and his entourage. See Alexander Chodzko, *Specimens of the Popular Poetry of Persia, as Found in the Adventures and Improvisations of Kurroglou, The Bandit-Minstrel of Northern Persia; and in the Songs of the People Inhabiting the Shores of the Caspian Sea. Orally Collected and Translated, with Philological and Historical Notes* (London: W. H. Allen, 1842).

147 **"on a potter's wheel"**: Robert E. Harrist Jr. "The Legacy of Bole: Physiognomy and Horses in Chinese Painting," *Artibus Asiae* 57, no. 1–2 (1997): 151.

147 **with ink on silk or paper**: Kubin, "Vom Roß zum Schindmäre," in Fragner et al., *Pferde in Asien*, 199.

148   **"hooves, and joints"**: Harrist, "The Legacy," 152.

149   **"Your art reflects genius"**: Du Fu, "A Painting Song for General Cao Ba," *300 Tang Poems: A New Translation*, ed. Yuan-zhong Xu et al. (Hong Kong: Commercial Press, 1987), poem no. 61. The Chinese text, 丹青引, 贈曹將軍霸, is available here: http://wengu.tartarie.com/wg/wengu.php?l=Tangshi&no=61.

150   **viewed Chinese collections**: This seems to be the case of the anonymous artist known as Siyah Qalam (Black Brush), whose Chinese-inspired sketchbook includes horses; it now belongs to Istanbul's Topkapi Palace Museum Library.

151   **pleasures offered by China**: E. Denison Ross, "The Orkhon Inscriptions: Being a Translation of Professor Vilhelm Thomsen's Final Danish Rendering," *Bulletin of the School of Oriental and African Studies* 5, no. 4 (1930): 862.

151   **started a fatal revolt**: This is the starting point for the classic Chinese opera *The Palace of Eternal Youth*, by Hong Sheng.

151   **from distant steppe horse breeders**: Schafer, *Golden Peaches*, 145.

152   **at the sound of military music**: Schafer, *Golden Peaches*, 152.

Chapter 7: Hunting for Supremacy

153   **"shoot birds with arrows and chase deer"**: Geoffrey Lewis, trans., *The Book of Dede Korkut* (London: Penguin, 2011), 43.

154   **"they would be gone for months"**: Allsen, *The Royal Hunt*, 21.

154   **milking the mares six times a day**: Suttie, Reynolds, and Batello, *Grasslands*, 852.

154   **in the thirteenth century**: Marco Polo, *Devisement*, section CXXI, p. 130.

154   **back to the campsite**: Lewis, *The Book of Dede Korkut*, 152.

155   **thieves falling on a caravan**: Asadi Tusi, *Garshaspname*, sections 26–29.

155   **"may eat the hunter"**: Sa'di Shirazi, *Gulistan*, trans. Wheeler M. Thackston (Bethesda, MD: Ibex, 2008), 96. The text reads: "صياد نه هر بار شگالی بَرد * افتد که يکی روز پلنگش بدرد" ("Hunters do not bag a jackal every time; but many a day it happens that a leopard tears one of them to bits.")

156   **"the skill is in the horse"**: Faruk Sümer, Ahmet Uysal, and Warren Walker, trans., *The Book of Dede Korkut* (Austin: University of Texas Press, 1991), 136.

156   **attacks by wild beasts**: Allsen, *The Royal Hunt*, 131. See also Lewis, *The Book of Dede Korkut*, 35.

156   **could constitute a larger following**: Allsen, *The Royal Hunt*, 219.

156   **three thousand or even five thousand horsemen**: Wang Bo and Zhang Renjiang, "Brief Analysis on Hunting Procedures and Culture of Liao Dynasty Through *Zhuoxie Figures*," *International Journal of Literature and Arts* 9, no. 4 (2021): 168–72.

156   **ties with the local people**: Allsen, *The Royal Hunt*, 192–93.

157   **Unlike the courtiers of the Tang, who criticized hunting**: Patricia Ebrey, "Remonstrating Against Royal Extravagance in Imperial China," in *The Dynastic Centre and the Provinces: Agents and Interactions*, ed. Jeroen Duindam and Sabine Dabringhaus (Leiden: Brill, 2014), 132.

157   **the apogee of its power in the eighth century**: Cai Meibiao, "Khitan Tribal Organization and the Birth of the Khitan State," in *Chinese Scholars on Inner Asia*, ed. Luo

Xin and Roger Covey (Bloomington: University of Indiana Press, 2012), 256–59, and
Shiba Yoshinobu, "Sung Foreign Trade: Its Scope and Organization," in *China Among
Equals: The Middle Kingdom and Its Neighbors, 10th–14th Centuries*, ed. Morris Rossabi
(Berkeley: University of California Press, 1983), 267.

157 **the growing chaos**: Denis C. Twitchett and Klaus-Peter Tietze, "The Liao," in *The
Cambridge History of China*, vol. 6, *Alien Regimes and Border States, 907–1368*, ed. Herbert
Franke and Denis Twitchett (Cambridge: Cambridge University Press, 1994), 6:53.

158 **lost to history**: "In 920 AD, What Was the 'Dragon' Shot by Yelu Abaoji, the Founder
of the Liao Dynasty?," iNEWS, October 17, 2023, https://inf.news/en/history/27471d
968e41ebc9dbdfe8bc5f7ee395.html.

158 **and blue for the east and grass**: Alfred Schinz, *The Magic Square: Cities in Ancient
China* (Stuttgart: Edition Axel Menges, 1996), 272.

159 **The trap was complete**: Thomas William Atkinson, *Travels*, loc. 5065.

159 **than required by hunting with beaters**: see Kohchahar E. Chuluu, "The Encircling
Hunt of Mongolia" (conference paper, New Directions in Central and Inner Asian
History, Harvard University, 2015).

160 **shooting them down from behind**: Allsen, *The Royal Hunt*, 216.

160 **before their horses had fat on them**: Maurice, *Strategikon*, trans. George T. Dennis
(Philadelphia: University of Pennsylvania Press, 1984), 95.

160 **war is a continuation of politics with different means**: Dan Mureşan, "Un empire
à cheval," in *Histoire monde, jeux d'échelles et espaces connecté* (Paris: Sorbonne, 2016), 62.

161 **"It is a means of practicing for warfare"**: *Liao Shih* [The annals of the Liao dynasty],
line 565, quoted by Timothy May, "The Training of an Inner Asian Nomad Army in
the Pre-Modern Period," *Journal of Military History* 70, no. 3 (July 2006): 662; see also
Karl A. Wittfogel and Fêng Chia-Shêng, "History of Chinese Society: The Liao (907–
1125)," *Transactions of the American Philosophical Society* 36 (1946): 56.

161 **"your thoughts turn to hunting"**: https://ganjoor.net/farrokhi/divanf/ghasidefk/sh36

چونکه لختی جنگراماند شکار، از حرص جنگ

چون بیاسایی ز جنگ، آید ترا رای شکار

تا شکار شیر بینی کم گرایی سوی رنگ

آن شکار اختیارست این شکار اضطرار

161 **warm-up for the troops**: Allsen, *The Royal Hunt*, 222–23.

161 **one hundred miles to the east**: Twitchett and Tietze, "The Liao," 74.

161 **the Khitans as China itself**: Giovanni da Pian del Carpini may have been the first
European to use this name. See Henry Yule, *Cathay and the Way Thither* (London:
Hakluyt Society, 1866), 1:23.

161 **several western languages as Cathay**: Duturaeva, *Qarakhanid Roads*, 17.

162 **inside the ring**: Wittfogel and Chia-Shêng, "History of Chinese Society: The Liao,"
267; see also Christopher P. Atwood, "Imperial Itinerance and Mobile Pastoralism:
The State and Mobility in Medieval Inner Asia," *Inner Asia* 17, no. 2 (2015): 293–349.

163 **to see that those laws were properly executed**: Wittfogel and Chia-Shêng, "History
of Chinese Society: The Liao," 119.

163 **"I set foot in the Middle Kingdom I never feel happy"**: Sergey A. Vasyutin, "The

Model of the Political Transformation of the Da Liao as an Alternative to the Evolution of the Structures of Authority in the Early Medieval Pastoral Empires of Mongolia," in Bemmann and Schmauder, *Complexity of Interaction Along the Eurasian Steppe Zone*, 419.

166 **supplying fine horses to the Khitans**: In fact, the Jurchens were already known to the Tang as breeders of fine horses. James K. Chin, "Negotiation and Bartering on the Frontier: Horse Trade in Song China," in Fragner et al., *Pferde in Asien*, 206.

167 **Roman Limes in Germania**: Jebrael Nokandeh, Eberhard W. Sauer, Hamid Omrani Rekavandi, Tony Wilkinson, Ghorban Ali Abbasi, Jean-Luc Schweninger, Majid Mahmoudi, et al., "Linear Barriers of Northern Iran: The Great Wall of Gorgan and the Wall of Tammishe," *Iran* 44, no. 1 (2006): 121.

168 **the dominant form of land use**: Xavier de Planhol, "Geography ii: Human geography," *Encyclopaedia Iranica Online* (New York: Columbia University, 2020).

168 **Georgia, and Iraq**: Keith Edward Abbott, *Cities and Trade: Consul Abbott on the Economy and Society of Iran, 1847–1866* (London: Ithaca, 1983). The British consul in Tabriz wrote,

> Persia is differently circumstanced to most other countries and the nature of its climate, its natural features and the general habits of the people require that it should possess a population which can adapt itself to variations of mountain and plain and draw from that condition of life resources which are in a great measure denied the fixed inhabitants. It is on these great pastoral communities that the population of the cities and plains nearly depend for their supplies of animal food for the flocks, for the butter, cheese and other preparations from Milk which are so largely consumed in Persia and for many coarse but useful articles of woollen and other manufacture for which the produce of the fields and cities is exchanged. The Tribes are a further advantage to the country in consequence of their wealth in camels which afford a cheap means of conveyance for merchandize to the most distant parts; but these advantages are in great measure lost to the country when the tribes are compelled to renounce their nomadic condition. I think it impolitic in the Persian Government to seek to render its great nomad Tribes a stationary people.

See also Suttie, Reynolds, and Batello, *Grasslands*, 1263.

169 **while the wealth of Iran attracted those fleeing**: Jürgen Paul, "Nomads and Bukhara: A Study in Nomad Migrations, Pasture, and Climate Change (11th Century CE)," *Der Islam* 93, no. 2 (2016): 506.

169 **as slave soldiers**: Marshall G. S. Hodgson, *The Venture of Islam: Conscience and History in a World Civilization* (Chicago: University of Chicago Press, 2009) 2:33.

170 **"manpower for his army"**: The eleventh-century Iranian historian Abu Sa'id Gardizi, quoted in A. Sevim and C. E. Bosworth, "The Seljuqs and the Khwarazm Shahs," *History of Central Asia* (Paris: UNESCO, 1992), 4:154.

170 **in close proximity with settled peoples**: Hodgson, *Venture*, 2:43.

170 **"devastated by the pasturing of [the Turkmen's] flocks"**: The fifteenth-century historian Mirkhwand, quoted by Richard Nelson Frye, *The Cambridge History of Iran* (Cambridge: Cambridge University Press, 1975), 4:193.

171 **any excuse to return to plundering**: Hodgson, *Venture*, 2:43.

172 **an escape valve to clear Iran of their troublemaking**: Hodgson, *Venture*, 2:44.

172 **and he soon slipped away**: Erdogan Merçil, "Selçuklularda Av" [Hunting practices of the Seljuks], *Selçuk Üniversitesi Selçuklu Araştırmaları Dergisi* (2018): 138.

172 **including horses, camels, sheep, and goats**: Speros Vryonis, *The Decline of Medieval Hellenism in Asia Minor and the Process of Islamization from the Eleventh Through the Fifteenth Century* (Berkeley: University of California Press, 1971), 258.

173 **mercenary warriors and suppliers of cavalry horses**: Aleksander Paroń, *The Pechenegs: Nomads in the Political and Cultural Landscape of Medieval Europe* (Leiden: Brill, 2021), 380. Kipchaks also served as mercenaries in Hungary, Egypt, and even the kingdom of Georgia. See Christopher Baumer, *History of the Caucasus* (London: Bloomsbury, 2023), 2:16.

175 **"All of Afghanistan and India fear him"**: Duturaeva, *Qarakhanid Roads*, 130.

175 **co-opt these horsemen and recruit them into his armies**: Duturaeva, *Qarakhanid Roads*, 21.

176 **killing too many animals**: For Mahmud's lion hunting, see Abul-Fazl Bayhaqi, *Tarikh-e Bayhaqi* [The histories of Bayhaqi], ed. Ali Akbar Qiyaz (Tehran: Iranshahr, 1350/1972), 134–35; the story of the deer is also told of his father, Sebuktegin (225–26).

176 **rode to the hunt every third or fourth day**: Duturaeva, *Qarakhanid Roads*, 127.

176 **"Aśvakas," for masters of horses**: Audrey Trushke, *The Language of History: Sanskrit Narratives of Indo-Muslim Rule* (New York: Columbia University Press, 2021), 11.

176 **as well as Turks and Afghans**: see Bayhaqi, *Tarikh-e Bayhaqi*, 681.

177 **the basis of the mamluks' power**: Jos Gommans, "The Warband in the Making of Eurasian Empires," *Prince, Pen, and Sword: Eurasian Perspectives*, ed. Maaike van Berkel and Jeroen Duindam (Leiden: Brill, 2018), 10.

177 **drawing devotees away from more ancient temple sites**: Jos J. L. Gommans, "The Silent Frontier of South Asia, c. A.D. 1100–1800," *Journal of World History* 9, no. 1 (Spring 1998): 9–10; and Thapar, *A History of India*, 260.

178 **rajas in their own right**: Gommans, "Warhorse and Post-Nomadic Empire," 10.

178 **cut him off from Central Asian horses**: Chakravarti, "Equestrian Demand and Dealers," 16.

179 **"2,000 horses at a time"**: Marco Polo, *Devisement*, section CLXXV, p. 178.

179 **this estimate to thirteen thousand horses annually**: Iftikhar Ahmad Khan, "The Import of Persian Horses in India 13–17th Centuries," *Proceedings of the Indian History Congress* 45 (1984): 346–51.

179 **one for 100 rupees**: Ali Bahrami Pour, "The Trade in Horses Between Khorasan and India in the 13th–17th Centuries," *Silk Road* 11 (2013): 130.

180 **"No virtuous ruler would do this!"**: Sima Xiangru, 天子遊獵賦 [Fu on the emperor's hunts]. The Chinese text of this long poem appears in Cai Zong Qi, ed., *How to Read Chinese Poetry* (New York: Columbia University Press, 2008), 61.

Chapter 8: As Far as Our Horses' Hooves Run

182 **imperiously in front of the city's main gate**: Rashiduddin, *Jami'u't-tawarikh*, in the Bibliothèque Nationale de France, Supplément persan 1113, folio 65v.

182 **a thousand miles to the north**: Igor de Rachelwiltz, trans., *The Secret History of the Mongols* (Leiden: Brill, 2015), 169.

184 **a reputation as daring and capable**: A colorful description of Genghis Khan's youth is provided by Rachelwiltz, *The Secret History of the Mongols*, 13–21. For the Golden Khan's tyranny over the Mongols, see Rashiduddin, *Jami'u't-tawarikh: Compendium of Chronicles: A History of the Mongols*, trans. Wheeler M. Thackston, tome 1, part 1, chapter 2 (Cambridge, MA: Harvard University, 1998), 33.

184 **in order to raise animals for the lucrative horse trade**: Robert T. Turley, "Climatic and Economic Conditions of Northern Manchuria," *Geographical Journal* 40, no. 1 (1912): 57–59.

184 **separated them from the Song**: Chin, "Negotiation and Bartering on the Frontier," in Fragner et al., *Pferde in Asien*, 206.

186 **into the valleys in the winter**: Suttie, Reynolds, and Batello, *Grasslands*, 856; the authors actually identify five zones, but I have simplified this.

186 **gullies and ravines**: P. Nick Kardulias, ed. *The Ecology of Pastoralism* (Denver: University Press of Colorado, 2015), 54. See also Suttie, Reynolds, and Batello, *Grasslands*, 866.

186 **sodium-rich grass**: Knut Schmidt-Nielsen and Bodil Schmidt-Nielsen, "Water Metabolism of Desert Mammals," *Physiological Reviews* 32, no. 2 (1952): 158.

186 **"each distinguish their own"**: S. Jagchid and C. R. Bawden, "Some Notes on the Horse-Policy of the Yüan Dynasty," *Central Asian Journal* 10, nos. 3–4 (December 1965): 250.

187 **30 percent of Mongolian livestock**: Mureşan, "Un empire," 56.

187 **"Even the poor have to have one or two"**: Jagchid and Bawden, "Some Notes," 250.

187 **important center for the horse and livestock trade**: Marie Favereau, *The Horde: How the Mongols Changed the World* (Cambridge, MA: Harvard University Press, 2021), 35.

187 **the case in the first decades of the thirteenth century**: Neil Pederson, Amy E. Hessl, Nachin Baatarbileg, Kevin J. Anchukaitis, and Nicola Di Cosmo, "Pluvials, Droughts, the Mongol Empire, and Modern Mongolia," *Proceedings of the National Academy of Sciences of the United States of America* 111, no. 12 (2014): 4375–79.

187 **could not sell the excess to the Golden Khan**: Denis Sinor, "Horse and Pasture," was the first to point out that horse breeders either had to sell their excess horses or use them for war.

187 **What do we do with them?**: Rachelwiltz, *The Secret History of the Mongols*, 106.

187 **his conquests are impossible to understand without them**: see Argent, "Watching the Horses," 145. While arguing that horses had mostly a pacific influence on humans, she acknowledges "influence between the species was bi-directional and . . . horses influenced only human structures, but also political ethos— . . . humans mimicked horses' ways of being." So in this case both humans and horses needed *lebensraum*, with all the fateful consequences that implied.

188 **successful Mongol generals**: Rashiduddin, *Jami'u't-tawarikh*, tome 1, part 1, chapter 4, section 2, p. 77.

188 **fulfillment of his vow**: Ata-Malik Juwayni, *The History of the World-Conqueror* [*Tarikh-i Jahangusha*], trans. John Andrew Boyle (Manchester, UK: Manchester University Press, 1958), 1:141.

188 **"the whip handle"**: Rashiduddin, *Jami'u't-tawarikh*, part 2, chapter 2, section 2, p. 127.

188 **"for thousands of years"**: Mureşan, "Un empire," 57.

188 **time itself, in steppe tradition**: Juwayni, *History of the World-Conqueror*, I:68.

189 **world dominion**: Fijn, "In the Land of the Horse," 157.

191 **"Feed them"**: Murşan, "Un empire," 66. The tale is told by Rashiduddin, *Jami'u't-tawarikh*, part 2, chapter 2, section 2, p. 173.

193 **warriors would not be a fable**: John Masson Smith Jr., "Mongol Manpower and Persian Population," *Journal of the Economic and Social History of the Orient* 18, no. 3 (Oct 1975): 271–99.

193 **to move to survive**: Smith, "From Pasture to Manger," 65.

193 **a would-be conqueror**: Khazanov, *Nomads and the Outside World*, 73.

194 **and discussed military and political strategies with them**: Favereau, *The Horde*, 121–25.

194 **sons of traditional chiefs**: May, "The Training of an Inner Asian Nomad Army," 635.

194 **"seized and beaten"**: Rachelwiltz, *The Secret History of the Mongols*, 120.

195 **all became Mongols**: Rashiduddin, *Jami'u't-tawarikh*, tome 1, part 1, chapter 2, p. 32.

195 **western steppe and of Egypt**: Favereau, *The Horde*, 47.

196 **conquering an empire of grass**: Peter Jackson, *The Mongols in the West, 1221–1410* (London: Routledge, 2005), 125; for Bayan, see Mureşan, "Un empire," 65.

197 **was also forbidden**: Sinor, "Horse and Pasture," 177.

197 **"neither watered nor fed"**: Rashiduddin, *Jami'u't-tawarikh*, part 2, chapter 2, section 17, p. 511.

197 **a rendezvous date and place set in advance**: Denis Sinor, "The Mongols in the West," *Journal of Asian History* 33, no. 1 (1999): 6.

197 **trains of camels and elephants**: Ibn Athir, *Al-Kamil fi al-Tarikh* [The complete history], ed. Samir Shams (Beirut: Dar Sader, 2009), 12:177.

197 **Mongols' logistical planning was meticulous**: Favereau, *The Horde*, 86.

197 **general assigned the Mughan to his most loyal troops**: Bayarsaikhan Dashdondog, *The Mongols and the Armenians* (Leiden: Brill, 2011), 61. It is interesting to note that the Armenians referred to the Mongols as "a nation of archers," recalling both the Huns and the Scythians.

198 **"in the borderlands of Mongolia"**: Juwayni, *History of the World-Conqueror*, 2:257.

198 **died of starvation**: Christian, *A History of Russia, Central Asia and Mongolia*, 2:27.

198 **"in summer and winter, in spring and autumn"**: Willem van Ruysbroeck, *The Journey of William of Rubruck to the Eastern Parts of the World, 1253–55, as Narrated by Himself*, ed. William Woodville Rockhill (London: Hakluyt Society, 1900), 53

199 **feed all the animals**: Juwayni, *History of the World-Conqueror*, 2:248–51.

200 **one every sixteen miles**: Rashiduddin, *Jami'u't-tawarikh*, tome 1, part 2, chapter 2, section 4, p. 233. Marco Polo, *Devisement*, section XCIX, pp. 111–13.

200 **they were going to enjoy wealth**: Juwayni, *History of the World-Conqueror*, 2:194.

201 **Mongol paper currency**: See https://www.mongolbank.mn/en/p/1390. On forced conversion to paper, see J. W. Dardess, "Shun-ti and the End of Yuan Rule in China," in Franke and Twitchett, *The Cambridge History of China*, 6:585.

201 **as they fancied**: Juwayni, *History of the World-Conqueror*, 2:159–60.

202 **ruled in Cairo and Damascus as mamluk sultans**: Favereau, *The Horde*, 144.

204 **against the annual requirement of one hundred thousand**: Jagchid and Bawden, "Some Notes," 262.

204 **shelved the proposal**: Morris Rossabi, "The Reign of Kublai Khan," in Franke and Twitchett, *The Cambridge History of China*, 6:416.

205 **barges along the Yellow River**: Jagchid and Bawden, "Some Notes," 257.

206 **draining the treasury**: Sinor, "Horse and Pasture," 176.

206 **richly arrayed with silk robes and jewelry**: Juwayni, *History of the World-Conqueror*, 2:241. Boyle, the translator, argues that his burial site is hard to discover because the earth would have been tamped down to make it completely indistinguishable from the surrounding steppe—see Boyle, "Form of Horse Sacrifice," 46.

207 **"area affords very fine grazing lands"**: Ruysbroeck, *The Journey of William of Rubruck*, 140.

207 **simply pushed the old inhabitants aside**: Rashiduddin, *Jami'u't-tawarikh*, part 2, chapter 2, section 17, p. 511.

207 **immigrated into Iran under the Mongols**: That would be 17 tumans, 170,000 warriors, and 1 million in all. Estimates are from Smith, "Mongol Manpower," 278.

208 **in the late thirteenth century**: Christian, *A History of Russia, Central Asia and Mongolia*, 2:35.

208 **the politics of Shiraz**: Reuven Amitai, "Did the Mongols in the Middle East Remain Pastoral Nomads?" (seminar, Max Planck Institute, Halle, Germany, 2019), 16.

208 **highly dependent on irrigation**: Gommans, "Warhorse and Post-Nomadic Empire," 6; Xavier de Planhol, *Fondements géographiques de l'histoire de l'Islam* (Paris: Flammarion 1968), 210–12; Peter Christensen, *The Decline of Iranshahr: Irrigation and Environment in the Middle East, 500 B.C.–A.D. 1500* (London: Bloomsbury, 2015), 324.

208 **death of Möngke in 1259**: Christian, *A History of Russia, Central Asia and Mongolia*, 2:31–32,

208 **"or extort the farmers"**: Christian, *A History of Russia, Central Asia and Mongolia*, 2:31.

209 **"return for necessary provisions"**: Marco Polo, *Devisement*, section LXXVIII, p. 89.

209 **Hungary, Poland, and Bulgaria**: Favereau, *The Horde*, 74.

209 **were sent to fight in China**: Smith, "Mongol Manpower," 289.

209 **enforce tax collection and engage in trade**: Carlos Quiles, "The Genetic and Cultural Barrier of the Pontic-Caspian Steppe–Forest-Steppe Ecotone," *Indo-European.eu* (February 4, 2019).

210 **a tiny minority of these Turkish-speaking herders**: René Grousset, *L'empire des steppes* (Paris: Payot, 1980), 468.

210 **gave rise to the name *Golden Horde***: Favereau, *The Horde*, 100.

210 **larger population of settled peoples, four to five million**: Christian, *A History of Russia, Central Asia and Mongolia*, 2:36.

Chapter 9: Riding the Whirlwind

211 **performing for the troops**: Maulana Sharafuddin Ali Yazdi, *Zafarnameh* [in Persian], ed. Muhammad Abbasi (Tehran: Amir Kabir, 1336/1957), 2:419.

212 **some of the animal's vigor**: This occurs in the modern Mongolian horse race, the Naadam. See Fijn, "Human-Horse Sensory Engagement Through Horse Archery," 68.

212 **the winner was never determined**: On Turkish traditional races, see Abdullah Özen et al., "Equestrian Games in Turkish History," *Fırat Üniversitesi Sağlık Bilimleri Dergisi* 26, no. 3 (2012): 197–202; see also Yaprak Pelin Uluışık and Kara Mehmet, "Türk destanlarındaki töy geleneğinde at yarişi: Hakas destani altin tayci örneği" [Horse

racing in the wedding tradition of Turkish epics: The example of Altın Taycı in the Khakas epic], *Sanat ve Dil Araştırmaları Enstitüsü* 42, no. 7 (2018): 99–105.

212 **embossed with silver**: Yazdi, *Zafarnameh*, 2:442.

212 **king of Castille and the mamluk sultans of Egypt and India**: González de Clavijo, *Narrative of the Embassy of Ruy Gonzalez de Clavijo to the Court of Timour, at Samarcand, A.D. 1403–6*, trans. Clements R. Markham (London: Hakluyt Society, 1859), 135; Yazdi, *Zafarnameh*, 2:449.

212 **accept the primacy of the Ming** *emperor, Yongle*: Morris Rossabi, "Chengho and Timür: Any Relation?," *Oriens Extremus* 20, no. 2 (December 1973): 131–32.

213 **which included eight hundred camels**: Clavijo, *Narrative of the Embassy*, 291.

213 **a springboard for the conquests of Timür**: Like Genghis Khan, Timür also turned agricultural land over to pastures. See Baumer, *History of the Caucasus*, 2:76.

213 **their own stables and stud farms**: See Marco Polo, *Devisement*, section XXXIII, p. 55; Jean Chardin, *Voyages du Chevalier Chardin en Perse et autres lieux d'orient* (Paris: Langlès, 1811), 263.

213 **one hundred horses in his tall ships**: Ralph Kautz, "Horse Exports from the Persian Gulf," in Fragner et al., *Pferde in Asien*, 130.

213 **Iran had become a horse superpower**: Bahrami Pour, "The Trade in Horses," 128; also Adam Olearius, Thomas Dring, Johann Albrecht von Mandelson, and John Davies, *The Voyages & Travels of the Ambassadors from the Duke of Holstein, to the Great Duke of Muscovy, and the King of Persia* (London: Thomas Dring and John Starkey, 1662), 309.

213 **which are modern concepts**: A. Solṭānī Gordfarāmarzī, "ASB iii: In Islamic Times," *Encyclopædia Iranica* 2, no. 7 (December 30, 2012): 731–36.

213 **no thought of purity or race**: "Timourlane introduced, from his conquests in China and India, Persia, and Turkey, the finest horses of those distant countries to his capital of Samarcand and his native and adjacent city of Shuhr Subz. In this very neighbourhood, we now find, in the hands of the Uzbek tribe of Karabeer, the most matchless horses of the East." Alexander Burnes, *Travels into Bokhara; Being the Account of a Journey from India to Cabool, Tartary, and Persia; also, Narrative of a Voyage on the Indus, from the Sea to Lahore, with Presents from the King of Great Britain; Performed Under the Orders of the Supreme Government of India, in the Years 1831, 1832, and 1833* (London: John Murray, 1834), 3:235.

214 **the clan that raised them**: French scholar Carole Ferret points out that horses tend to mirror the peoples that raise them; see her study "À chacun son cheval! Identités nationales et races équines en ex-URSS (à partir des exemples turkmène, kirghize et iakoute)," *Cahiers d'Asie centrale* 19–20 (2011): 405–58.

214 **on his return to Samarkand**: see folio from a *Zafarnameh* (recto: "Samarqand receives the prince and his troops"; verso: "Timur's entry into Samarqand"), National Museum of Asian Art, Smithsonian Institute, inventory no. F1948.18

214 **realism of Mughal horse paintings**: Sheila Canby. "Persian Horse Portraits and Their Cousins," in Alexander, *Furusiyya*, 1:190–95.

214 **near the Oxus River in Genghis Khan's time**: His rank was nokar, a boon companion to a khan. Marie E. Subtelny, *Timurids in Transition* (Leiden: Brill, 2007), 23.

215 **base in Transoxiana and Khorasan**: Beatrice Forbes Manz, *The Rise and Rule of Tamerlane* (Cambridge: Cambridge University Press, 1989), 45.

215 **as high as the horses' bellies**: Yazdi, *Zafarnameh*, 1:332.

215 **for the remaining two-thirds**: Yazdi, *Zafarnameh*, 1:360.

215 **to feed the hungry army**: Yazdi, *Zafarnameh*, 1:331.

216 **Timür's historian Sharafuddin Yazdi**: Yazdi, *Zafarnameh*, 1:360.

216 **Some who fought on foot**: Russian officer and historian Mikhail Ignatiev Ivanin points out that Timür's foot soldiers traveled to the battlefield by horse. Mikhail Ignatiev Ivanin, О военном искусстве и завоеваниях монголо-татар и средне-азиатских народов при Чингис-Хане и Тамерлане [On the art of war and the conquests of the Tatar-Mongols and Central Asian peoples under Genghis Khan and Tamerlane] (St. Petersburg: Obshchestvennaya Pol'za, 1875), 147.

217 **to collect taxes from Timür**: Clavijo *Narrative of the Embassy*, 133.

218 **"their soldiers and horses"**: Rashiduddin, *Introduction à l'histoire des Mongols*, ed. Edgard Blochet (Leiden: Brill, 1910), 139.

218 **in the era of Timür**: S.A.M. Adshead, *Central Asia in World History* (London: Palgrave Macmillan, 1993), 88.

219 **another horse to transport a tent**: Gergely Csiky, "The *Tuzūkāt-i Tīmūrī* as a Source for Military History," *Acta Orientalia Academiae Scientiarum Hungaricae* 59, no. 4 (2006): 478. The *Tuzukat* is now generally agreed to be a forgery from the sixteenth century, full of anachronisms, but some of the practices described may date back to Timür's time. See Ahat Andican, *"Tuzukat-i Timüri*: Sham or Authentic," chapter 2 of *Amir Timür: History, Politics, Legacy* (Istanbul: Selenge Yayınları 2019) [in Turkish].

219 **from the word for alfafa**: Csiky, "The *Tuzūkāt-i Tīmūrī*," 472.

219 **the irreplaceable conqueror**: Manz, *Rise and Rule of Tamerlane*, 84.

220 **stopped giving milk, they could be eaten**: Muhammad Haydar Dughlât, *Tarikh-i Rashidi*, trans. Wheeler M. Thackston (translator), vol. 33 of *Sources of Oriental Languages and Literatures, Central Asian Sources* (Cambridge, MA: Harvard University, 2012).

220 **one thousand mounted retainers**: Clavijo, *Narrative of the Embassy*, 174.

221 **as Timür's historians described it**: Yazdi, *Zafarnameh*, 2:452.

221 **retainers dispatched in his pursuit**: Dughlât, *Tarikh-i Rashidi*, 19.

221 **in his newly built Forbidden City**: Morris Rossabi, "From Chen Cheng 陳誠 to Ma Wensheng 馬文升: Changing Chinese Visions of Central Asia," *Crossroads* 1–2 (September 2010): 25; Ghiyathuddin Naqqash, "Report to Mirza Baysunghur on the Timürid Legation to the Ming Court at Peking," trans. Wheeler M. Thackston, in *A Century of Princes: Sources on Timürid History and Art* (Cambridge, MA: Aga Khan Program for Islamic Architecture at Harvard University and the Massachusetts Institute of Technology, 1989).

221 **with his faithful retainers, into exile**: Babur, *The Baburnama*, 138.

222 **of pasture but of plunder**: Joo-Yup Lee, *Qazaqlïq, or Ambitious Brigandage, and the Formation of the Qazaqs' State and Identity in Post-Mongol Central Eurasia* (Leiden: Brill, 2023), 18–19.

222 **his raids as kazakh expeditions**: Babur, *The Baburnama*, 108.

222 **they needed to eat**: Babur, *The Baburnama*, 123.

223 **and plentiful game**: Babur, *The Baburnama*, 143.

223 **precisely why he was able to conquer it**: Babur, *The Baburnama*, 244.

223 **most professional artillery service in Asia**: Kaushik Roy, *Military Transition in Early*

Modern Asia, 1400–1750: Cavalry, Guns, Governments and Ships (London: Bloomsbury, 2014), 45.

223 **he earned the nickname "the beggar"**: Gulbadan Begum, *The History of Humāyūn*, trans. Annette S. Beveridge (Calcutta: Royal Asiatic Society, 1902), 6.

225 **one hundred thousand horses annually**: Bahrami Pour, "The Trade in Horses," 130.

225 **in the foothills of the Himalayas**: Richard M. Eaton, *India in the Persianate Age* (London: Penguin, 2020), 72.

225 **to pass in review**: Niccolao Manucci, *Storia do Mogor*, trans. William Irvine (London: John Murray, 1907), 1:30.

226 **"attainment of personal greatness"**: Abul Fazl Allami, *Ain-i Akbari*, trans. H. Blochmann (Calcutta: Asiatic Society of Bengal, 1873), 1:133.

227 **banditry and horse rustling**: Chandra, *Tale of the Horse*, 128.

227 **a huge proportion of India's total herd**: Chandra, *Tale of the Horse*, 148.

227 **riding into battle but fighting on foot**: As reported by the Jesuit priest Monserrate, quoted in Chandra, *Tale of the Horse*, 143.

228 **lowest category of horse**: Abul Fazl, *Ain-i Akbari*, 1:137–40.

228 **accordingly promoted or demoted**: Abul Fazl, *Ain-i Akbari*, 1:137–40.

229 **"from Iraq to Hindustan"**: Jahangir, *Tuzuk-i Jahangiri*, trans. Alexander Rodgers (London: Royal Asiatic Society, 1909), 151.

229 **ranged between 10 and 30**: Trautman, *Elephants*, 179.

229 **with bureaucratic efficiency**: Jagjeet Lally, "Empires and Equines: The Horse in Art and Exchange in South Asia, ca. 1600–ca. 1850," *Comparative Studies of South Asia, Africa and the Middle East* 35, no. 1 (May 2015): 99.

229 **would have been given away**: The system is described in Abul Fazl, *Ain-i Akbari*: "The horses are always coming in, so there are others daily going out as gifts" (1:149).

229 **equestrian practice and statecraft**: Gommans, "Warhorse and Post-Nomadic Empire," 3.

230 **50 percent of the state budget, or 51 million rupees**: Chandra, *Tale of the Horse*, 18.

230 **to grow these crops**: Gommans, *Mughal Warfare*, 133.

230 **imported horses from Central Asia**: Abu Fazl reported proudly that "drove after drove arrives from Central Asia and Iran": *Ain-i Akbari*, 1:132.

230 **one hundred thousand such horses each year**: Manucci, *Storia do Mogor*, 2:390.

230 **"Khan of Merchants"**: Jahangir, *Tuzuk-i Jahangir*, 444.

230 **for the caravanners, dancing girls or boys**: Chandra, *Tale of the Horse*, 35.

231 **confidence in the merchandise**: Abul Fazl, *Ain-i Akbari*, 1:133.

231 **local horses in their cavalry**: Chandra, *Tale of the Horse* page, 33.

231 **"are said to be the finest"**: Abul Fazl, *Ain-i Akbari*, 1:133.

231 **the language of the court and the army**: Choudhary, "Mughal and Late Mughal Equine Veterinary Literature," 59.

232 **burned off through exercise**: Chandra, *Tale of the Horse*, 104.

232 **a risk factor for esophageal cancer in humans**: M. Nagabhushan and S. V. Bhide, "Nonmutagenicity of Curcumin and Its Antimutagenic Action Versus Chili and Capsaicin," *Nutrition and Cancer* 8, no. 3 (1986): 201–10.

232 **"victorious against the enemy"**: Monica Meadows, "The Horse: Conspicuous Consumption of Embodied Masculinity in South Asia, 1600–1850" (PhD diss., University

of Washington, 2014), 36. Interestingly, there were also medieval Persian texts on horse colors, including a treatise attributed to the eleventh-century polymath Omar Khayyám. See Azarnouche, "Miracles, oracles et augures," in Spruyt and Poinsot, *Équidés*, 247.

232 **as well as behavior**: Jack Murphy and Sean Arkins, "Facial Hair Whorls (Trichoglyphs) and the Incidence of Motor Laterality in the Horse," *Behavioural Processes* 79, no. 1 (2008): 7–12.

233 **for an archer or a musketeer to hit**: Meadows, "The Horse: Conspicuous Consumption," 35.

233 **equestrian portraits of the builder of the Taj Mahal**: Chandra, *Tale of the Horse*, 127.

233 **muscular horse flesh**: This painting is in the Windsor Castle collection, RCIN 1005025.

234 **enjoyed mounted sports**: Lally, "Empires and Equines," 98.

234 **in addition to playing polo**: Gulbadan Begum, *History of Humāyūn*, 120.

234 **they rode draped head to toe in gauzy veils**: See the Akbarnama, Chester Beatty Library, object 03.25.

237 **lost by his ancestor Babur to the Uzbeks**: Gommans, *Mughal Warfare*, 179.

237 **the seventeenth-century Mughal army**: Lieven, *In the Shadow of Gods*, 268.

237 **nostalgia for the era of Timür**: Eaton, *India in the Persianate Age*, 185.

237 **importing Turki horses**: Abul Fazl noted, "The wise of ancient times considered Kābul and Kandahar as the twin gates of Hindustan, the one leading to Turkestan and the other to Persia. The custody of these highways secured India from foreign invaders, and they are likewise the appropriate portals to foreign travel." Abul Fazl, *Ain-i Akbari*, trans. H. S. Jarrett (Calcutta: Royal Asiatic Society, 1891), 2:404.

238 **"from Hormuz [on the Persian Gulf] to Goa"**: Rui Manuel Loureiro, "Portuguese Involvement in the Sixteenth Century Horse Trade Through the Arabia Sea," in Fragner et al., *Pferde in Asien*, 137–43. The viceroy of India, Afonso de Albuquerque, admitted that it was too easy to make money in this trade: *"O trato dos cavalos é um ganho desordenado, porque se ganha trezentos por cento, e quatrocentos por cento, e quinhentos por cento d'Ormuz e da costa d'Arábia a Goa afora os direitos que pagam os cavalos na Índia"* ("The horse business is one of crazy profits, for one gets 300 percent, 400 percent, 500 percent between Ormuz and the Arabian Coast, and Goa, after paying the taxes on horses in India"). Henrique Lopes de Mendonça e Raimundo António Bulhão Pato, eds., *Cartas de Afonso de Albuquerque e documentos que as elucidam* [Correspondence of Afonso de Albuquerque and explanatory documents] (Lisbon: Academia das Ciências de Lisboa, 1884–1935), 1:410.

238 **"throughout the Deccan [southern India]"**: Loureriro, "Portuguese Involvement," 139.

238 **Arab dhows could carry only seventy**: Al-Salimi, Abdul Rahman, and Eric Staples, "Reflections of a Muslim-Portuguese Maritime World in a Sixteenth-Century Portuguese Source," in *Proceedings of the Seminar for Arabian Studies* (Archaeopress, 2015), 322.

239 **just like the Rajputs**: See Chandra, *Tale of the Horse*, 85, and Eaton, *India in the Persianate Age*, 198.

240 **to plunder the Mughals**: Chandra, *Tale of the Horse*, 86.

240 **"is my country"**: Oral Marathi tradition.

240 **from this traditional source of political troubles**: Gommans, "Warhorse and Post-Nomadic Empire," 10.

240 **policy against internal rebellion**: Eaton, *India in the Persianate Age*, 203.

241 **mobilizing the tardy Iranian resistance to the invaders**: Giorgio Rota, "In a League of Its Own? Nader Shah and His Empire," in *Short-Term Empire*, ed. Robert Rollinger, Julian Degen, and Michael Gehler (Wiesbaden: Springer, 2020), 215–18.

242 **supplying his soldiers with horses**: Michael Axworthy, "The Army of Nader Shah," *Iranian Studies* 40, no. 5 (Dec 2007): 644.

242 **into further, endless campaigns**: Rota, "In a League of Its Own," in Rollinger, Degen, and Gehler, *Short-Term Empire*, 220.

243 **ambassador to Beijing**: Angela Schottenhammer, "Horses in Late Imperial China and Maritime East Asia: An Introduction into Trade, Distribution, and Other Aspects (c. Sixteenth to Eighteenth Centuries)," in Fragner et al., *Pferde in Asien*, 12.

Chapter 10: The Empires Strike Back

244 **the emperor's favorite horses**: Schottenhammer, "Horses in Late Imperial China," in Fragner et al., *Pferde in Asien*, 4 and 16.

244 **chewed his food with appalling manners**: Lin Shih Hsuan, 玉質純素。隱 有青文 [Pure jade, hidden purity], *National Palace Museum Monthly of Chinese Art* 391 (October 2015).

245 **supreme ruler of the steppe**: see also Hou Ching-Lang and Michèle Pirazzoli, "Les chasses d'automne de l'empereur Qianlong à Mulan," *T'oung Pao*, 2nd ser., 65 nos. 1–3 (1979): 40.

245 **Son of Heaven and the supreme khan**: Schottenhammer, "Horses in Late Imperial China," in Fragner et al., *Pferde in Asien*, 5.

245 **priceless antiquities in the imperial collection**: See his annotations on items in the National Palace Museum in Taipei. "Tien-lu-lin-lang Library: The Ch'ien-Lung Emperor's Treasures of Rare Books, Exhibition" (December 1, 2007, to May 30, 2008).

247 **a day for their survival**: David A. Bello, "Relieving Mongols of Their Pastoral Identity: Disaster Management on the Eighteenth-Century Qing China Steppe," *Environmental History* 19, no. 3 (July 2014): 489–90.

247 **mobilizing the resources of China to pay for this largesse**: Bello, "Relieving Mongols," 481.

247 **received honorary Chinese titles**: Seonmin Kim, *Ginseng and Borderlands* (Oakland: University of California Press, 2017), 26–27.

248 **and the Manchu people**: Mark C. Elliott, *The Manchu Way* (Stanford, CA: Stanford University Press, 2001), 47.

248 **equality between the two peoples**: Pamela Kyle Crossley, "The Conquest Elite of the Ch'ing Empire," in *The Cambridge History of China*, vol. 9, part 1, *The Ch'ing Dynasty to 1800*, ed. Willard J. Peterson (Cambridge: Cambridge University Press, 2002) 9:318.

248 **nine white animals each year in perpetuity**: Evariste Régis Huc, *Travels in Tartary, Thibet, and China: During the Years 1844–5–6*, trans. William Hazlitt (London: Office of the National Illustrated Library, 1852), 241; Veronika Veit points out that the Mongols considered white horses to be magic; see "The Mongols and Their Magic Horses" in Fragner et al., *Pferde in Asien*, 102.

249 **largest army in the world**: Yingcong Dai, "Qing Military Institutions and Their

Effects on Government, Economy, and Society, 1640–1800," *Journal of Chinese History* 1, no. 2 (2017): 329–30.

249 **to manage the imperial herds**: Schottenhammer, "Horses in Late Imperial China," in Fragner et al., *Pferde in Asien*, 25.

249 **twelve thousand mares**: Schottenhammer, "Horses in Late Imperial China," in Fragner et al., *Pferde in Asien*, 6. Jesuit explorer Evariste Huc reported the numbers slightly differently: 360 herds of 1,200 horses each. Huc, *Travels in Tartary*, 46.

249 **during the state horse purchases**: Schottenhammer, "Horses in Late Imperial China," in Fragner et al., *Pferde in Asien*, 12.

250 **modern artillery from them**: Nicola Di Cosmo, "The Extension of Ch'ing Rule over Mongolia, Sinkiang, and Tibet, 1636–1800," in *The Cambridge History of China*, vol. 9, part 2, *The Ch'ing Dynasty to 1800*, ed. Willard J. Peterson (Cambridge: Cambridge University Press, 2016), 9:126.

250 **as an existential one**: Schottenhammer, "Horses in Late Imperial China," in Fragner et al., *Pferde in Asien*, 7.

253 **its troops and most of its horses**: Thomas Barfield, *The Perilous Frontier: Nomadic Empires and China, 221 B.C. to A.D. 1757* (Cambridge: Blackwell, 1989), 56.

254 **Hami, in the Tarim Basin**: Peter C. Perdue, "Military Mobilization in Seventeenth and Eighteenth-Century China, Russia, and Mongolia," *Modern Asian Studies* 30, no. 4 (1996): 777–78.

254 **as they carried no strategic stores**: Perdue, "Military Mobilization," 779.

254 **By the time he captured Moscow, he had no more cavalry**: Dominic Lieven, "Mobilizing Russian Horsepower in 1812," *History* 96, no. 322 (2011): 152; see also Dominic Lieven, *Russia Against Napoleon* (London: Allen Lane, 2009), 252.

255 **"to serve me as grooms"**: Fourteenth poem by Qianlong, 平定回部獻俘. [Suppressing rebellion, the army returns, presenting their captives] See Paul Pelliot, "Les conquêtes de l'empereur de la Chine," *T'oung Pao*, 2nd ser., 20 nos. 3–4 (August 1920–August 1921): 261.

255 **thought to have perished**: Christian, *A History of Russia, Central Asia and Mongolia*, 2:191.

255 **seemed to defy description**: Europe took a great interest in these combats; see "Monument de la conquête des Eleuths [Oirats]," *Mémoires concernant l'histoire, les sciences, les arts, les moeurs, les usages, &c. des chinois* (Paris: Nyon 1776–91).

256 **now in the Louvre**: Pascal Torres-Guardiola, "À la gloire de l'Empire de Chine," *Grande Galerie: Le journal du Louvre* 7 (March–May 2009): 24–25.

258 **in the wars with Timür**: Yazdi, *Zafarnameh*, 1:331.

259 **and other steppe produce**: Mikhail Khodarkovsky, *Russia's Steppe Frontier* (Bloomington: Indiana University Press, 2002), 27.

259 **"50, 60, up to 100 rubles"**: Capitaine [Jacques] Margeret, *Estat de l'empire de Russie et grand duché de moscovie* (Paris: Poitier, 1855), 56–57.

259 **estimated the trade to be twice as big**: Giles Fletcher, *Of the Rus Commonwealth* (Ithaca, NY: Cornell University Press, 1966), 97; see also Margeret, *Estat de l'empire*, 36.

259 **on the sale and branding of horses**: Christian, *A History of Russia, Central Asia and Mongolia*, 2:87.

260 **twenty thousand or more allied Tatar cavalry**: Margeret, *Estat de l'empire*, 50.

260 **four horses from each corral**: Khodarkovsky, *Russia's Steppe Frontier*, 26.

260 **for his own private income**: Fletcher, *Of the Rus Commonwealth*, 41.

260 **"my people will be ruined"**: Khodarkovsky, *Russia's Steppe Frontier*, 26.

261 **never moving on foot, just like the Tatars**: Sigismund von Herberstein, *Notes upon Russia*, trans. R. H. Major (London: Hakluyt Society 1852), 108.

261 **divided into the left and right wings**: Margeret, *Estat de l'empire*, 43; see also Diane L. Smith, "Muscovite Logistics, 1462–1598," *Slavonic and East European Review* (1993): 37.

261 **to the rhythm of kettledrums**: Fletcher, *Of the Rus Commonwealth*, 77.

261 **fighting each other on the steppe**: Smith, "Muscovite Logistics," 38.

261 **look and feel of their Tatar rivals**: "They have small gelded horses, unshod, and with very light bridles, and their saddles are so adapted that they may turn round in any direction without impediment, and draw the bow. They sit on horseback with the feet so drawn up, that they cannot sustain any more than commonly severe shock from a spear or javelin. Very few use spurs, but most use the whip, which always hangs from the little finger of the right hand, so that they may lay hold of it and use it as often as they need" (Herberstein, *Notes upon Russia*, 96).

261 **set with pearls and emeralds**: João Carvalho Dias, ed., *Os czares e o Oriente*, catalog for the exhibition, February 28–May 18, 2014 (Lisbon: Museu Calouste Gulbenkian, 2014).

261 **his victories over the steppe horsemen**: For the visit of Jerome Horsey, see the 1875 painting by Alexander Litvochenko, *Ivan the Terrible Shows His Treasures to the English Ambassador Horsey*, in the Mikhailovsky Palace, St. Petersburg. Margeret also describes the Kremlin treasures in *Estat de l'empire*, 37.

262 **from his Genghisid lineage**: Donald Ostrowski, "Simeon Bekbulatovich's Remarkable Career as Tatar Khan, Grand Prince of Rus', and Monastic Elder," *Russian History* 39, no. 3 (2012): 272.

263 **he had acquired the empire to go with this title**: Charles J. Halperin, "Ivan IV and Chinggis Khan," *Jahrbücher für Geschichte Osteuropas* 4 (2003): 497.

263 **and instilling terror among the Russians**: Smith, "Muscovite Logistics," 42.

263 **could not match Tatar horse power**: Margeret, *Estat de l'empire*, 47.

264 **bandits of any ethnicity**: Christian, *A History of Russia, Central Asia and Mongolia*, 2:63. See also Lee, *Qazaqlïq*, 23 and 59: "Chroniclers also began using the Ukrainian word *kozak* in a variety of senses, which probably reflected the contemporary Tatar usage of the term. Jan Dlugosz, writing about the Tatar raid into Poland in 1469, remarked that the Tatar army had been 'collected from fugitives, expellees, and robbers, whom they call in their language *kozaks*' (*exercitus ex fugitivis, predonibus et exulibus, quos sua lingua Kozakos appellant*)" (43).

264 **and tie them to their saddles**: Lee, *Qazaqlïq*, 84. On the cultural influence of the Turkic nomads on the Ukrainian Cossacks, see J. Kočubej, "Les éléments orientaux dans la culture et dans la vie quotidienne des cosaques ukrainiens," in *Les Cosaques de l'Ukraine: Rôle historique, représentations littéraires et artistiques*, ed. Michel Cadot and Emile Kruba (Paris: Presses de la Sorbonne Nouvelle, 1995), 117–24, and Omeljan Pritsak, "Das erste türkisch-ukrainische Bündniss (1648)," *Oriens* 6 (1953): 266–98.

264 **another fifty thousand horses**: Halil Inalçik, "The Khan and the Tribal Aristocracy: The Crimean Khanate Under Sahib Giray I," *Harvard Ukrainian Studies*, vols. 3–4, part 1 (1979–80): 463.

264 **command the respect of their neighbors**: Roy, *Military Transition in Early Modern*

Asia, 46–47. As far as exporting their horses, see Christian, *A History of Russia, Central Asia and Mongolia*, 2:278.

264 **rustling raids against them**: Inalçik, "The Khan and the Tribal Aristocracy," 463.

265 **resented the control of their own khans**: Inalçik, "The Khan and the Tribal Aristocracy," 449.

265 **bribes to dissident clansmen**: Christian Noack, "The Western Steppe: The Volga-Ural Region, Siberia and the Crimea Under Russian Rule," in *The Cambridge History of Inner Asia*, ed. Nicola Di Cosmo, Allen J. Frank, and Peter B. Golden (Cambridge: Cambridge University Press, 2009), 2:318.

265 **in today's Ukraine**: Austéja Braisünaité, "Stud Farm of the Grand Duke of Lithuania: Traditions and the Importance of the Horse in Warfare and Messenger Service 14–16 Century," in *Las caballerizas reales y el mundo del caballo*, ed. Juan Aranda Doncel and José Martínez Millán (Cordoba: Instituto Universitario "La Corte en Europa" y Córdoba Ecuestre, 2016), 167.

265 **as the return of native sons**: Janusz Maciejewski, "Sarmatyzm jako formacja kulturowa: Geneza i główne cechy wyodrębniające" [Sarmatism as a cultural phenomenon: Genesis and distinctive features], in *Teksty: Teoria literatury, krytyka, interpretacja* 4 [Texts: Literary theory, critique, and interpretation] 4, no. 16 (1974): 13–42. These Poles sought affinities between themselves and the ancient Sarmatians, a western branch of the Scythian nation.

265 **control of the steppe**: Noack, "The Western Steppe," in Di Cosmo, Frank, and Golden, *The Cambridge History of Inner Asia*, 2:318.

266 **never exceeded half a million**: Our World Data. "Крымское ханство" [The Crimean khanate], Большая Российская Энциклопедия [The great Russian encyclopedia]; https://old.bigenc.ru. For Russia's population growth, see Christian, *A History of Russia, Central Asia and Mongolia*, 2:217.

266 **land-hungry farmers**: Christian, *A History of Russia, Central Asia and Mongolia*, 2:163.

267 **Opposing her designs were the Kazakh hordes**: Gulbanu Bolatovna Izbassarova, "On the Character of Mutual Relations of the Kazakhs and Bashkirs in 18th Century," *Oriente Moderno*, new ser., 96, no. 1 (2016): 158.

267 **both Moscow and Beijing**: Gommans, *The Rise of the Indo-Afghan Empire*, 30.

267 **pastures of the Kalmyks**: Michael Khodarkovsky, "Russian Peasant and Kalmyk Nomad: A Tragic Encounter in the Middle of the Eighteenth Century," *Russian History* 15, no. 1 (1988): 46.

268 **threat to Russia's steppe hegemony disappeared**: This episode received a lot of attention in Europe. Thomas De Quincey dedicated a pamphlet to the subject: "The Revolt of the Tartars," *Blackwood's Edinburgh Magazine* 42 (July–December 1837): 89.

268 **the aridity of their ancestral steppe**: Christian, *A History of Russia, Central Asia and Mongolia*, 2:274.

Chapter 11: The Great Game

270 **which ultimately numbered two hundred thousand**: Jagjeet Lally, "Beyond 'Tribal Breakout': Afghans in the History of Empire, ca. 1747–1818," *Journal of World History* 29, no. 3 (September 2018): 378 .

270 **as a source of power**: Chandra, *Tale of the Horse*, 88.

270 **"rendered more so by continued exercise"**: James Baillie Fraser, *Military Memoirs of Lt. Colonel James Skinner* (London: Edler & Smith, 1851), 1:10.

271 **alive but permanently lame**: Fraser, *Military Memoirs of Lt. Colonel James Skinner*, 1:17. This anecdote is also recounted in Phillott's translation of Rangin's *Faras-nama-e, or The Book of the Horse* (London: Bernard Quaritch, 1911), 11. It also appears in the poem "With Scindia to Delhi" in Rudyard Kipling, *Poems: Inclusive Edition* (Garden City, NY: Doubleday, 1921), 28.

271 **"are always singing the songs of their gurus"**: Ratan Singh Bhangu, *Pracheen Panth Prakash*, trans. Kulwant Singh (Chandigarh: Institute of Sikh Studies, 2010) 2:xxv.

272 **simply fought for subsistence**: Fraser, *Military Memoirs of Lt. Colonel James Skinner*, 1:85.

272 **he plundered everyone indiscriminately**: Fraser, *Military Memoirs of Lt. Colonel James Skinner* 2:69.

273 **dyed in blood-red henna**: Victoria and Albert Museum, inventory no. IS.143–1952.

273 **the endless wars of this era**: Robert Greville, *The Provincial and Revenue Establishments of Tipoo Sultaun and of Mohamedan and British Conquerors in Hindustan* (London: Faulder, 1795), I:56.

273 **new Indian horse powers**: Shahamat Ali, *The Sikhs and Afghans* (London: Murray, 1847), 24.

274 **"the artillery to be of any service"**: William Moorcroft and George Trebeck, *Travels in the Himalayan Provinces of Hindustan and the Panjab* (London: John Murray, 1841), 1:98.

274 **its lineage of sires, and its strengths and weaknesses**: Burnes, *Travels into Bokhara*, 1:108.

274 **spent on their cavalry**: Gommans, *The Rise of the Indo-Afghan Empire*, 87.

274 **warring cavalry armies**: Gommans, "Warhorse and Post-Nomadic Empire," 5.

274 **influence of horsey people**: A. T. Yarwood, *Walers: Australian Horses Abroad* (Melbourne: Melbourne University Press, 1989), 26.

276 **used against the Mughals**: G. J. Bryant, "The Cavalry Problem in the Early British Indian Army, 1750–1785," *War in History* 2, no. 1 (1995): 2.

276 **failed to make a common front against their shared enemy**: William Dalrymple, *The Anarchy* (London: Bloomsbury, 2019), 257.

276 **They recruited mercenary cavalry forces**: Bryant, "Cavalry Problem," 3.

276 **taking his last name for the Persian "Sikander," or Alexander**: Fraser, *Military Memoirs of Lt. Colonel James Skinner*, 2:258.

276 **"the conquering Moguls of Timour"**: Edward Archer, *Tours in Upper India and in Parts of the Himalaya Mountains*, 1:375.

277 **had the better of its enemies**: Lepel Griffin, *Ranjit Singh* (Oxford: Clarendon,1905), 14. This high imperial administrator observed that the British Empire was won by fraud or force.

277 **to thirty thousand by 1819**: Gommans, *The Rise of the Indo-Afghan Empire*, 85.

277 **enjoy a peace dividend**: Bryant, "Cavalry Problem," 4. For the impact of these wars on the British, see Dalrymple, *The Anarchy*, 389.

277 **Ranjit Singh's thirty-thousand-strong cavalry threatened**: Lally, "Empires and Equines," 97. Lally points out that, contrary to the school of thought that says the eighteenth century brought about an infantry revolution in the subcontinent, cavalry

remained the main source of political power. The decline of Indian cavalry reflected tight supply in Central Asia, rather than lower demand in India.

277 **"what it shall derive from cavalry"**: quoted in G. J. Alder, "The Origins of 'the Pusa Experiment': The East India Company and Horse-Breeding in Bengal, 1793–1808," *Bengal Past and Present: The Journal of the Calcutta Historical Society* 98 (1979): 28.

278 **"barbaric inroad upon British India"**: G. J. Alder, "Standing Alone: William Moorcroft Plays the Great Game, 1808–1825," *International History Review* 2, no. 2 (1980): 193.

278 **on the wealthy subcontinent**: Fernand Hue, *Les Russes et les Anglais dans l'Afghanistan* (Paris: E. Dentu, 1885). See also H. Sutherland Edwards, *Russian Projects Against India from the Czar Peter to General Skobeleff* (London: Remington, 1885), 285.

278 **took these threats seriously**: See Burnes, *Travels into Bokhara*, 2:26: "History tells us, that many armies have fought in and crossed this desert; but they consisted of hordes of light cavalry, that could move with rapidity. Light horse might pass such a desert, by divisions, and separate routes; for besides the high road to Merve, there is a road both to the east and the west. Where water lies within thirty feet of the surface, an energetic commander may remedy his wants, since we have an instance of it in the advance of the Orgunje Khan to the banks of the Moorghab."

278 **expedition to the Oxus in 1839**: Alexander Morrison, "The Russian Conquest of Central Asia and the Myth of the 'Great Game'" (webinar, Royal Society for Asian Affairs, July 1, 2020). Note that Russian senior officials of the early nineteenth century frequently expressed themselves in French, as not all their colleagues could read and write Russian properly.

278 **than the English animals**: Transport from the Persian Gulf worked out to 588 rupees per horse. Gommans, *The Rise of the Indo-Afghan Empire*, 85.

279 **"well adapted to its operations"**: Champagné quoted in Alder, "Standing Alone," 178.

279 **"they almost entirely subsisted"**: Based on National Archives of India, New Delhi, Military Department Proceedings, June 14, 1814, no. 76, "Report E. Wyatt," fols. 75rr-83r. Quoted in Gommans, *The Rise of the Indo-Afghan Empire*, 92. Wyatt also procured horses from Persia, as attested by his neatly penned letter to the British resident in Bushire, on the Persian Gulf: https://www.qdl.qa/en/archive/81055/vdc_100040046184.0x000064.

279 **"positive scarcity shall arrive"**: Moorcroft quoted in Alder, "Standing Alone," 178.

279 **buy a good warhorse from traders**: Garry Alder, *Beyond Bokhara: The Life of William Moorcroft, Asian Explorer and Pioneer Veterinary Surgeon, 1767–1825* (London: Century, 1985), 103–05; see also Saurabh Mishra, "The Economics of Reproduction: Horse-Breeding in Early Colonial India, 1790–1840," *Modern Asian Studies* 46, no. 5 (2012). For 400 rupees, see Lally, introduction to Gommans, *The Rise of the Indo-Afghan Empire*, xxix.

280 **Bukhara flourished throughout the nineteenth century**: Jagjeet Lally, "Beyond 'Tribal Breakout,'" 393, and Lally, introduction to Gommans, *The Rise of the Indo-Afghan Empire*, xxvii. In the mid-nineteenth century, when Iran's and Afghanistan's populations were 7 million and 4 million, respectively, Bukhara had 3 million inhabitants. See https://www.statista.com/statistics/1066934/population-iran-historical/ and https://www.statista.com/statistics/1066644/total-population-afghanistan-1813-2020/ . See also Scott Levi, "India, Russia and the Eighteenth-Century Transformation of the Central Asian Caravan Trade," *Journal of the Economic and Social History of the Orient* 42, no. 4 (1999): 522. According to Levi, there was *urban* decline in Central Asia but not

economic decline. Balkh in Afghanistan, for example, fell into ruins, while agricultural land around this ancient city was given over to more profitable horse raising.

280 **business away from India**: Lally, introduction to Gommans, *The Rise of the Indo-Afghan Empire*, xxvii.

281 **spend 1,000 to 3,000 rupees**: [Mir Izzatullah Khan], *Travels in Central Asia by Meer Izzut-oollah in the Years 1812–1813*, trans. Captain Henderson (Calcutta: Foreign Department Press, 1872), 58.

281 **Balkh (today's Mazar-e Sharif)**: Mir Izzatullah, *Travels in Central Asia*, 62.

282 **the finest of these as gifts**: Moorcroft and Trebeck, *Travels*, 1:100.

283 **the Afghan Waziri clan**: G. T. Vigne, *A Personal Narrative of Ghuzni Kabul and Afghanistan* (London: Routledge, 1843), 82.

283 **"for 1,000 rupees"**: Moorcroft and Trebeck, *Travels*, 1:343.

283 **Afghan cavalry, twenty thousand strong**: Mishra, "Economics of Reproduction," 1122.

283 **"in the spring in the most excellent condition"**: Moorcroft and Trebeck, *Travels*, 2:383.

284 **the flow of horses to the market**: "Mr. Moorcroft," *Asiatic Journal*, 714. Moorcroft would have preferred this explanation as only a temporary reduction in supply, versus the more structural impact of Chinese and Russian buyers.

284 **"to the point from which he started"**: Moorcroft archive in the British Library where his diary entries are listed under the heading "MSS.Eur.D. 254–Bukhara and Return from Bukhara," digitized by Janet Rizvi and Dan Jantzen.

284 **Russia's move toward the Indus**: Devendra Kaushik, "British Designs in Central Asia in the Nineteenth Century," *Proceedings of the Indian History Congress*, vol. 29, part II (1967): 242.

284 **the opening round of the Great Game**: Peter Hopkirk, *The Great Game* (London: John Murray, 1990). Hopkirk devotes two chapters to Moorcroft's expedition.

285 **no deep-water naval forces to mention**: Chung Yam Po, "Conceptualizing the Blue Frontier: The Great Qing and the Maritime World in the Long Eighteenth Century" (PhD diss., Heidelberg Universität, 2015). Po points out that mid-nineteenth-century China had a navy one hundred thousand strong, but it was a river navy, not a blue-water navy, and so of little defensive value against the armored gunboats of the Europeans.

285 **In fact, they numbered thirty thousand**: *Expédition des armées françaises en Chine, 1857–1860* (Paris: Librairie des Villes et des Campagnes, 1874), xx.

286 **Cossack incursions into Xinjiang**: Peter Waldron, "Przheval'skii, Asia and Empire," *Slavonic and East European Review* 88, nos. 1–2 (January–April 2010): 321–22; this article details the imperialist ambitions of Nikolai Przevalski, the explorer after whom the wild horse was named.

286 **discouraged the Russians from recognizing Yakub Beg's regime**: Demetrius Charles Boulger, *The Life of Yakub Bey* (London: W. H. Allen, 1878), 247.

286 **outcome against the bannermen**: S.C.M. Paine, *Imperial Rivals* (Armonk, NY: M. E. Sharpe, 1996), 119–20.

286 **fifteen hundred in some years**: Lally, introduction to Gommans, *The Rise of the Indo-Afghan Empire*, xxix.

287 **"taking on new grooms; swearing"**: Rudyard Kipling, *Kim* (Project Gutenberg e-book, 2000), 36.

287 **"Back of Beyond"**: Kipling, *Kim*, 46.

288 **"as an old coat of lice"**: Kipling, *Kim*, 50.

288 **and conclude the transaction**: Davidson, *Diary of Travels*, 94.

288 **"what a merchant can readily obtain from the opulent native"**: John Pelling Pigott, *A Treatise on the Horses of India* (Calcutta: James White, 1794), x.

288 **their wares to British customers**: Mishra, "Economics of Reproduction," 1119.

288 **follow the market prices**: Phillott, *Farasnama*, 43–44.

288 **a trusted dealer like Mahbub Ali**: It's not incidental that Kipling assigns Mahbub Ali to the Suleiman Khel clan, then as now a powerful people living on the eastern Afghanistan frontier. Both the president of Afghanistan in 2014–21 and the leadership of the Taliban hailed from the Suleiman Khel. Kipling had in fact modeled his character on a real Afghan horse dealer, a man who had befriended the young writer when he was a cub reporter working in Lahore in 1886 and 1887. Whenever the real Mahbub Ali would return from one of his caravan expeditions, he would call on Kipling and regale him with tales of intrigue from beyond the Khyber Pass. Mahbub Ali's father had been a horse dealer in Kabul but had supported the British side during First Anglo-Afghan War, and so had had to flee the country with his family following the British defeat. They established themselves in Lahore. See Omar S. K. Tarin, "My Quest for Mahbub Ali," *Kipling Society Journal* 82, no. 3 (April 26, 2008), and Peter Hopkirk, *The Quest for Kim* (London: John Murray, 1996).

288 **perceived as relics of ancient times**: Mishra, "Economics of Reproduction," 1127.

288 **and sometimes tried to repress them**: Lally, introduction to Gommans, *The Rise of the Indo-Afghan Empire*, xlviii.

289 **even an empire in India**: Jagjeet Lally, "Beyond 'Tribal Breakout,'" 376.

289 **a Central Asian army could conquer India**: Ivanin, О военном искусстве [On the art of war], 237.

289 **"terminate in the presence of the Russian banners at Benares"**: published in the *Russian Monthly Historical Review* (December 1883), quoted in Edwards, *Russian Projects Against India*, 281.

290 **largely on enslaved workers**: N. M. Mouraviev, *Voyage en Turcomanie*, 115.

290 **blood-sweating horses of Ferghana**: Ferret, *Des chevaux*, 224.

290 **"a particularly fine and glossy coat"**: Arminius Vámbéry, *Travels in Central Asia* (London: John Murray, 1864), 422.

290 **"do good work under the saddle"**: *"sont de purs produits du désert. Les chevaux tékés se distinguent par leur noblesse, la beauté de leurs lignes, une constitution bien proportionnée et d'excellentes extrémités; ils sont secs, assez grands (jusqu'à deux archines et trois-quatre verchoks) et travaillent très bien sous la selle. Ils ont pour défaut un poitrail peu profond et une croupe un peu plate, dus à la mauvaise alimentation des jeunes et à leur débourrage dès un an. Avec un nourrissage et un dressage corrects, ces défauts disparaissent"*; quoted in Ferret, "Des chevaux," 225.

290 **bring down opposing riders**: Araz Imamov, personal communication. Araz Bey is head of the Akhal-Teke Association of Azerbaijan.

291 **remounts for India's cavalry**: Ferret, "Des chevaux," 226. Also see British intentions to procure Turkmen horses: Valentine Baker, *Clouds in the East* (London: Clowes, 1876), 366.

291 **on the Oxus ever more likely**: In fact, there were many British missions, some of which, like *Mission Impossible* assignments, were disavowed by the Indian Office when they were uncovered. Kaushik, "British Designs," 241.

292 **the Russian military establishment to justify them**: Income from the territories amounted to 32 million rubles between 1868 and 1878, while the cost of running the new territories was 99 million; see Paine, *Imperial Rivals*, 115.

292 **"abundance with the infinite steppes"**: quoted in Ferret, "Des chevaux," 219.

Chapter 12: March, Trot, Gallop, Charge

293 **wrote one Russian animal husbandry expert**: G. Krivcov, "Туркестанская выставка плодов и овощей, коневодство в Кульдже / Exposition de fruits et de légumes du Turkestan, l'élevage du cheval à Kouldja" [Exposition of fruit and vegetables of Turkistan, horse breeding in Kul'ja], Всемирная иллюстрация, Туркестанский сборник [International illustrated, Turkestan collection] 43 (1873): 241–42, quoted in Ferret, "Des chevaux," 235.

294 **Central Asia to Europe**: Ferret, "Des chevaux," 214.

294 **were sent west every year**: Ferret, "Des chevaux," 244.

294 **as Vámbéry put it**: Vámbéry, *Travels*, 422.

294 **less resistant to disease**: Ferret, "Des chevaux," 215.

295 **compared to 50 percent in the open steppe**: Ferret, "Des chevaux," 215.

295 **traditional way of managing the herds**: Ferret, "Des chevaux," 215.

295 **"low level of civilization" of the Tatars**: Ferret, "Des chevaux," 216.

295 **where they live to this day**: Ferret, "Des chevaux," 234.

295 **"source of remounts for our cavalry"**: Ferret, "Des chevaux," 213.

296 **a feather under the belly unlucky**: Sa'adat Yar Khan Rangin, *The Faras-nama-e Rangin, or The Book of the Horse*, trans. D. C. Phillott (London: Bernard Quaritch, 1911), 2–4 and 8–9. For a discussion of Rangin, see Monica Meadows's dissertation: "The Horse: Conspicuous Consumption of Embodied Masculinity in South Asia, 1600–1850," 93.

296 **and with short forelimbs**: Lally, "Empires and Equines," 111.

296 **to come and admire them**: Burnes, *Travels into Bokhara*, 1:108. I have taken some liberties with the chronology here since the gift of carriage horses took place several years earlier.

296 **in a scholarly publication**: The letter from "Major Gwatkin, Superintendent of the Hon. East India Company's Stud in Northern India," was published as a supplement to C. H. Smith's *Natural History of Horses* (Calcutta: Asiatic Society, 1842).

297 **versus 200 pounds for the later**: Yarwood, *Walers*, 69.

297 **the size of the horse mattered less**: Yarwood, *Walers*, 70.

297 **brought their own mounts**: Yarwood, *Walers*, 65.

298 **nature always wins**: Hallen's paper is included in Walter Gibley, *Horse Breeding in England and India, and Army Horses Abroad* (London: Vinton, 1906), 62.

298 **go for long periods without water**: Yarwood, *Walers*, 17.

298 **competitively priced resource**: Amit Sarwal, "Australian Waler Horses in India," SBS Hindi, March 5, 2016; https://www.sbs.com.au/language/hindi/en/podcast -episode/australian-waler-horses-in-india/84esyglc0.

298   **close to 3,000 rupees per head**: Yarwood, *Walers*, 86.

299   **the success of Genghis Khan on such horses**: Yarwood, *Walers*, 74–77.

299   **invincible force of nature**: Ferret, "Des chevaux," 222.

299   **there was always the matter of size**: Ferret, "Des chevaux," 227.

299   **"each has merit in its own country"**: Kipling, *Kim*, 309.

300   **turned into a major war**: Christopher M. Wyatt, "Change and Discontinuity: War and Afghanistan, 1904–1924," *Asian Affairs* 47, no. 3 (2016): 371.

300   **resist Russian invasion**: Wyatt, "Change and Discontinuity," 372.

301   **asserting their claim to the legacy of the Mughal Empire**: Charles Tupper, *Our Indian Protectorate* (London: Longman, 1893), quoted in Thomas R Metcalf, "Ideologies of the Raj," *Cambridge History of India* (Cambridge: Cambridge University Press, 1997), 4:196.

301   **missed his entry entirely**: Yarwood, *Walers*, 7.

302   **ridden by British units**: Phillott, introduction to Rangin, *Faras-nama-e*, p. xvii.

302   **sympathized with the maharaja**: Charles W, Nuckolls, "The Durbar Incident," *Modern Asian Studies* 24, no. 3 (1990): 536–37.

302   **"the poorest people in the world"**: "Military Expenditure of the Indian Empire," *Hansard Commons Debate* (February 26, 1903), vol. 118, cols. 977–96.

302   **"to the last degree improbable"**: Arthur Balfour's intervention during the King's Speech, February 4, 1903, *Hansard Parliamentary Debates*, vol. 118.

303   **to use their weapons**: Gervase Phillips, "Scapegoat Arm: Twentieth-Century Cavalry in Anglophone Historiography," *Journal of Military History* 71, no. 1 (January 2007): 37–74.

303   **and former steppe lands**: Ferret, "Des chevaux," 217.

304   **entered triumphantly into Damascus**: Jean Bou, "Cavalry, Firepower, and Swords: The Australian Light Horse and the Tactical Lessons of Cavalry Operations in Palestine, 1916–1918," *Journal of Military History* 71, no. 1 (Jan 2007): 121. For the success of the Indian lancers, see p. 118.

305   **"in every fold of the vast hills"**: T. E. Lawrence, *Revolt in the Desert* (London: Cape, 1927), 392.

305   **look like unrealistic visionaries**: Gregory A. Daddis, *Armageddon's Lost Lessons* (Maxwell Air Force Base, AL: Air University Press, 2005).

306   **had in the eighteenth-century wars**: General Staff Branch, Army Headquarters, India, *The Third Afghan War 1919: Official Account* (Calcutta: Government of India, 1926), 132.

306   **horse trade, had dwindled**: Gommans, *The Rise of the Indo-Afghan Empire*, 180.

307   **one last combat charge**: General Staff Branch, *Third Afghan War*, 134.

307   **the hills around the Khyber**: General Staff Branch, *Third Afghan War*, 133.

308   **all influence over Afghan affairs**: In recognition of Afghanistan's full independence, George V invited Amanullah for a state visit in 1927. The Afghan king gave his host Firuz Jang's Persian treatise on hippology. See Lally, introduction to Gommans, *The Rise of the Indo-Afghan Empire*, xlvii.

308   **made famous by Kipling**: "Some Kipling Originals," *Argus* (Melbourne), September 17, 1927.

Epilogue

311 **his voluminously folded turban**: This description draws largely on French journalist
Joseph Kessel's reporting of the game, *Le jeu du roi* (Paris: Gallimard, 1956). He reused
it for his popular novel *Les cavaliers* (Paris: Gallimard, 1967), which was made into a
film, *The Horsemen*, with Omar Sharif and Jack Palance (1971).

312 **a more sophisticated public**: Kessel, *Le jeu du roi*, 271.

313 **the Uzbeks in the north**: G. Whitney Azoy, *Buzkashi: Game and Power in Afghanistan*
(Long Grove, IL: Waveland, 2003), 64.

314 **"the herd belonged to the horseman"**: Khazanov, *Nomads and the Outside World*, iii.

315 **three million in 1932**: Martha Brill Olcott, "The Collectivization Drive in Kazakhstan," *Russian Review* 40, no. 2 (April 1981): 122.

315 **fled from the Soviet Union and China**: Amantur Žaparov, "L'élevage du cheval au
Kirghizstan," *Études mongoles et sibériennes, centrasiatiques et tibétaines* 41 (2010): 7.

315 **who could raise the finest horses**: Azoy, *Buzkashi*, 12.

315 **fetched up to $100,000**: Agence France-Presse, "Afghanistan's Buzkashi Horses Pre-
pare for a Game of Courage," January 17, 2018.

316 **the return of the Taliban in 2022**: On the future of such games, see a thought-
provoking analysis by Simone de Boer, "Dynamics of Perpetuity: Traditional Horse
Games in Kyrgyzstan," *Memory and Commemoration Across Central Asia* (Leiden: Brill,
2023), 177–97.

SELECTED BIBLIOGRAPHY

Abul Fazl Allami. *Ain-i Akbari*. Translated by H. Blochman et al. Calcutta: Asiatic Society of Bengal, 1873–1907.

Alder, Garry. *Beyond Bokhara: The Life of William Moorcroft, Asian Explorer and Pioneer Veterinary Surgeon, 1767–1825*. London: Century, 1985.

Alexander, David, ed. *Furusiyya*. 2 vols. Riyadh: King Abdulaziz Public Library, 1996.

Allsen, Thomas. *The Royal Hunt in Eurasian History*. Philadelphia: University of Pennsylvania Press, 2006.

Amitai, Reuven, and Michal Biran. *Mongols, Turks, and Others: Eurasian Nomads and the Sedentary World*. Leiden: Brill, 2005.

Anthony, David. *The Horse, the Wheel and Language*. Princeton: Princeton University Press, 2007.

Atkinson, Thomas William. *Travels in the Region of the Upper and Lower Amur*. London: Murray, 1860.

Atwood, Christopher Pratt. *Encyclopedia of Mongolian and the Mongol Empire*. New York: Facts on File, 2004.

Azoy, G. Whitney. *Buzkashi: Game and Power in Afghanistan*. Long Grove, IL: Waveland, 2003.

Babur, Muhammad Zahiruddin. *The Baburnama: Memoirs of Babur, Prince and Emperor*. Translated and edited by Wheeler M. Thackston. New York: Modern Library, 2002.

Barfield, Thomas J., and Nikolai N. Kradin. *Nomadic Pathways in Social Evolution*. Lac Beauport, QC: Russian Academy of Sciences, 2003.

Beckwith, Christopher I. *Empires of the Silk Road: A History of Central Eurasia from the Bronze Age to the Present*. Princeton, NJ: Princeton University Press, 2009.

———. *The Scythian Empire*. Princeton, NJ: Princeton University Press, 2023.

Burnes, Alexander. *Travels into Bokhara; Being the Account of a Journey from India to Cabool, Tartary, and Persia; also, Narrative of a Voyage on the Indus, from the Sea to Lahore, with Presents from the King of Great Britain; Performed Under the Orders of the Supreme Government of India, in the Years 1831, 1832, and 1833*. London: John Murray, 1834.

Chandra, Yashaswini. *The Tale of the Horse: A History of India on Horseback*. Delhi: Picador, 2021.

Christian, David. *A History of Russia, Central Asia and Mongolia*. Vol. 2, *Inner Eurasia from the Mongol Empire to Today, 1260–2000*. Hoboken: Wiley Blackwell, 2017.

Clavijo, González de. *Narrative of the Embassy of Ruy Gonzalez de Clavijo to the Court of Timour, at Samarcand, A.D. 1403–6*. Translated by Clements R. Markham. London: Hakluyt Society, 1859.

Colarusso, John, and Tamirlan Salbiev, eds. *Tales of the Narts: Ancient Myths and Legends of the Ossetians*. Princeton, NJ: Princeton University Press, 2016.

De Quincey, Thomas. "The Revolt of the Tartars." *Blackwood's Edinburgh Magazine* 42 (July–December 1837).

Di Cosmo, Nicola. *Ancient China and Its Enemies: The Rise of Nomadic Power in East Asian History*. Cambridge: Cambridge University Press, 2002.

Digard, Jean-Pierre, ed. *Chevaux et cavaliers arabes dans les arts d'orient et d'occident*. Paris: Gallimard, 2002.

Digard, Jean-Pierre. *Une histoire du cheval: Art, techniques, société*. Arles: Actes Sud, 2004.

Doniger, Wendy. *Winged Stallions and Wicked Mares: Horses in Indian Myth and History*. Charlottesville: University of Virginia Press, 2021.

Drews, Robert. *Early Riders: The Beginnings of Mounted Warfare in Asia and Europe*. New York: Routledge, 2004.

Dughlât, Muhammad Haydar. *Tarikh-i Rashidi*. Translated by Wheeler M. Thackston. Vol. 33, *Sources of Oriental Languages and Literatures, Central Asian Sources*. Cambridge, MA: Harvard University, 2012.

Duturaeva, Dilnoza. *Qarakhanid Roads to China*. Leiden: Brill, 2022.

Eaton, Richard M. *India in the Persianate Age*. London: Penguin, 2020.

Elliot, Mark C. *The Manchu Way*. Stanford, CA: Stanford University Press, 2001.

Favereau, Marie. *The Horde: How the Mongols Changed the World*. Cambridge, MA: Harvard University Press, 2021.

Feng Menglong. *Kingdoms in Peril: A Novel of the Ancient Chinese World at War*. Translated by Olivia Milburn. Oakland: University of California Press, 2022.

Ferret, Carole, ed. *Le cheval: Monture, nourriture et figure*. Special issue of *Centre d'Études Mongoles & Sibériennes*. Paris: École Pratique des Hautes Études, 2010.

Ferret, Carole. *Une civilisation du cheval: Les usages de l'équidé de la steppe à la taïga*. Leipzig: Belin, 2009.

Ferdowsi, Abolqasem. *Shahnameh: The Persian Book of Kings*. Translated by Dick Davis. New York: Viking, 2006.

Fletcher, Giles, and Jerome Horsey. *Russia at the Close of the Sixteenth Century, Comprising the Treatise of the Russe Common Wealth and the Travels of Sir Jerome Horsey*. Edited by Edward A. Bond. London: Hakluyt Society, 1856.

Forrest, Susanna. *The Age of the Horse: An Equine Journey Through Human History*. New York: Atlantic, 2017.

Fragner, Bert G., and Ralph Kauz, Roderich Ptak, Angela Schottenhammer, eds. *Pferde in Asien: Geschichte, Handel und Kultur / Horses in Asia: History, Trade and Culture*. Wien: Österreiche Akademie der Wissenschaften, 2009.

Fraser, James Baillie. *Military Memoirs of Lt. Colonel James Skinner*. London: Edler & Smith, 1851.

General Staff Branch, Army Headquarters, India. *The Third Afghan War 1919: Official Account*. Calcutta, 1926.

Gommans, Jos J. L. *The Indian Frontier: Horse and Warband in the Making of Empire*. London: Routledge, 2017.

———. *Mughal Warfare: Indian Frontiers and Highroads to Empire 1500–1700*. New York: Routledge, 2002.

———. *The Rise of the Indo-Afghan Empire c. 1710–1780*. New Delhi: Manohar, 2019.

Gorshenina, Svetlana, and Sergeij Abašin, eds. *Le Turkestan russe: Une colonie comme les autres?* Vols. 17–18 of *Cahiers de l'Asie centrale*. Paris: Petra, 2009.

Gulbadan Begum. *The History of Humāyūn (Humāyūn-Nāma)*. Translated by Annette S. Beveridge. Calcutta: Royal Asiatic Society, 1902.

Halperin, Charles. *Russia and the Golden Horde: The Mongol Impact on Medieval Russian History*. Bloomington: Indiana University Press, 1987.

Herberstain, Sigmund Freyherr zu. *Moscovia, der Hauptstat in Reissen*. Wien, 1557.

Herodotus. *The Persian Wars*. Translated by A. D. Godley. 8 vols. Cambridge, MA: Harvard University Press, 1982.

Hodgson, Marshall. *The Venture of Islam*. Vol 2. Chicago: University of Chicago Press, 1974.

Hopkirk, Peter. *The Great Game*. London: John Murray, 1990.

Ibn Battuta. *Travels in Asia and Africa, 1325–1354*. Translated by H.A.R. Gibb. London: Routledge, 1953.

Jackson, Peter. *The Mongols in the West, 1221–1410*. London: Routledge, 2005.

Juwayni, Ata-Malik. *The History of the World-Conqueror [Tarikh-i Jahangusha]*. Translated by John Andrew Boyle. Manchester, UK: Manchester University Press, 1958.

Kautilya [attributed]. *Arthashastra*. Translated by R. Shamasastry. Mysore, 1915.

Kessel, Joseph. *Le jeu du roi: Reportage en Afghanistan*. 1956. Reprint: Paris: Arthaud, 2022.

Khazanov, Anatoly M. *Nomads and the Outside World*. Madison: University of Wisconsin Press, 1994.

Khodarkovsky, Mikhail. *Russia's Steppe Frontier*. Bloomington: Indiana University Press, 2002.

Kipling, Rudyard. *Kim*. London: Penguin, 2011.

Lee, Joo-Yup. *Qazaqlïq, or Ambitious Brigandage, and the Formation of the Qazaqs State and Identity in Post-Mongol Central Eurasia*. Leiden: Brill, 2023.

Lewis, Geoffrey, trans. *The Book of Dede Korkut*. London: Penguin, 2011.

Liu, Xinru, ed. *The World of the Ancient Silk Road*. New York: Routledge, 2023.

Margeret, Capitaine Jacques. *Estat de l'empire de Russie et du grand duché de moscovie*. Paris: Poitier, 1855.

Moorcroft, William, and George Trebeck. *Travels in the Himalayan Provinces of Hindustan and the Panjab; in Ladakh and Kashmir; in Peshawar, Kabul, Kunduz, and Bokhara*. London: John Murray, 1841.

Morrison, Alexander. *The Russian Conquest of Central Asia: A Study in Imperial Expansion, 1814–1914*. Cambridge: Cambridge University Press, 2021.

Mouraviev, M[onsieur]. N. [Nikolai Nikolaevich Muraviev-Karsky]. *Voyage en Turcomanie et à Khiva, fait en 1819 et 1820*. Paris: Louis Tenré, 1823.

Orlando, Ludovic. *La conquête du cheval*. Paris: Odile Jacob, 2023.

Pankova, Svetlana, and St. John Simpson, eds. *Masters of the Steppe: The Impact of the Scythians and Later Nomad Societies of Eurasia.* Oxford: Archaeopress, 2021.

Paroń, Aleksander. *The Pechenegs: Nomads in the Political and Cultural Landscape of Medieval Europe.* Leiden: Brill, 2021.

Perdue, Peter. *China Marches West.* Cambridge, MA: Harvard University Press, 2005.

Poinsot, Delphine, and Margaux Spruyt, eds. *Équidés: Le cheval, l'âne et la mule, dans les empires de l'orient ancien.* Paris: Routes de l'Orient, 2022.

Polo, Marco. *The Description of the World.* Translated and annotated by A. C. Moule and Paul Pelliot. London: Routledge, 1938.

———. *Marco Polo: Le devisement du monde.* Edited by René Kappler. Paris: Imprimerie Nationale, 2004.

Potts, Daniel. *Nomadism in Iran: From Antiquity to the Modern Era.* Oxford: University of Oxford Press, 2014.

Psarras, Sophia-Karin. *Chinois et Xiongnu à l'époque Han: Rapports culturels, rapports politiques.* Paris: Université de Paris 7, 1989.

Qazwini, Muhammad Amin. *Padshahnamah.* Translated by John Dowson. London: Trubner, 1867–77.

Rachelwiltz, Igor de, trans. *The Secret History of the Mongols.* Leiden: Brill, 2015.

Rangin, Sa'adat Yar Khan. *The Faras-nama-e Rangin, or The Book of the Horse.* Translated by D. C. Phillott. London: Bernard Quaritch, 1911.

Rashiduddin, Fazlullah. *Jami'u't-tawarikh: Compendium of Chronicles: A History of the Mongols.* Translated by Wheeler M. Thackston. Vol. 45, *Sources of Oriental Languages and Literatures.* Cambridge, MA: Harvard University, 1998.

Recht, Laerke. *The Spirited Horse: Equid–Human Relations in the Bronze Age Middle East.* London: Bloomsbury, 2022.

Rossabi, Morris, ed. *How Mongolia Matters: War, Law, and Society.* Leiden: Brill, 2022.

Ruysbroeck, Willem van. *The Journey of William of Rubruck to the Eastern Parts of the World, 1253–55, as Narrated by Himself.* Edited by William Woodville Rockhill. London: Hakluyt Society, 1900.

Schafer, Edward H. *The Golden Peaches of Samarkand: A Study of T'ang Exotics.* Berkeley: University of California Press, 1985.

[Sima Qian.] *Records of the Grand Historian of China* [the *Shiji*]. Translated by Burton Watson. 2 vols. New York: Columbia University Press, 1961.

Skaff, Jonathan Karam. *Sui-Tang China and Its Turko-Mongol Neighbors: Culture, Power, and Connections, 580–800.* New York: Oxford University Press, 2012.

Strabo. *The Geography.* Vol. 3. Translated by Horace Leonard Jones. Cambridge, MA: Harvard University Press, 1924.

Suttie, J. M., S. G. Reynolds, and C. Batello, eds. *Grasslands.* Rome: Food and Agriculture Organization of the United Nations, 2005.

Tapper, Richard. *Frontier Nomads of Iran: A Political and Social History of the Shahsevan.* Cambridge: Cambridge University Press, 1997.

Trautman, Thomas. *Elephants and Kings: An Environmental History.* Chicago: University of Chicago Press, 2015.

Wittfogel, Karl A., and Fêng Chia-Shêng. *History of Chinese Society: The Liao (907–1125).* Philadelphia: American Philosophical Society, 1946.

Xenophon. *Cyropaedia*. Translated by Walter Miller. London: Heinemann, 1914.

Yarwood, A. T. *Walers: Australian Horses Abroad*. Melbourne: Melbourne University Press, 1989.

Yazdi, Maulana Sharafuddin Ali. *Zafarnameh*. [In Persian.] Edited by Muhammad Abbasi. Tehran: Amir Kabir, 1336/1957.

ILLUSTRATION CREDITS

183   Genghis Khan besieges Beijing. Bibliothèque Nationale de France (Supplement oriental 1113 fol. 65v).

205   Empress Chaabi participating in a hunt. Wikimedia.

216   Amir Timür pursuing the Golden Horde. The John Work Garrett Library, Sheridan Libraries, Johns Hopkins University.

233   A page from the *Salihotra*. Nasser D. Khalili Collection of Islamic Art (MSS 475).

234   An equestrian portrait of Mughal emperor Shah Jahan. Metropolitan Museum of Art.

235   A Mughal couple enjoy a ride together. Metropolitan Museum of Art.

236   The young Aurangzeb battles an elephant in front of the whole court. Royal Collection Trust / © His Majesty King Charles III 2023.

245   A portrait of Emperor Qianlong by Giuseppe Castiglione. Beijing Palace Museum.

246   Emperor Qianlong receives tribute horses from steppe emissaries. Photo © RMN-Grand Palais (MNAAG, Paris) / image RMN.

256   The Qing armies defeat the Oirats, engraving from "The Conquests of the Emperor of China." Photo © Musée du Louvre, Dist. RMN-Grand Palais / Michel Urtado.

262   Tsar Ivan IV showing Ambassador Horsey the Kremlin treasure rooms. Mikhailovski Palace.

272   Warlord Amir Khan. Victoria and Albert Museum, London.

282   Ranjit Singh, founder of the Sikh empire. Victoria and Albert Museum, London.

291   Akhal-Teke. Irina Kazaridi.

301   Lancers on parade during the 1911 durbar. Royal Collection Trust / © His Majesty King Charles III 2023.

312   Zaher Shah on horseback. Universal Images Group North America, LLC / Alamy.

316   Buzkashi competitors. Kevin Kelly.

INDEX

Page numbers in *italics* refer to illustrations or maps.